Volkswagen in the Amazon

From 1973 to 1987, Volkswagen's 140,000-hectare "pioneer" cattle ranch on the Amazon frontier laid bare the limits of capitalist development. These limits were not only economic, with the core management of a multinational company engaged in the "integration" of an extreme world periphery, but they were also legal and ethical, with the involvement of indentured labor and massive forest burning. Capitalist development's physical limits were exposed by an unpredictable ecosystem refusing to submit to VW's technological arsenal. Antoine Acker reveals how the VW ranch, a major project supported by the Brazilian military dictatorship, was planned, negotiated, and eventually undone by the intervention of internationally connected actors and events.

Antoine Acker earned his PhD at the European University Institute and has extensively researched and taught in seven different countries on a broad range of topics, including environmental and Brazilian history and German culture and language, as well as political sciences. He was a lecturer at the Sorbonne Nouvelle in Paris (2013–2014) and at the University of La Rochelle (2014–2015), and a guest scholar in the universities of Bielefeld, Maastricht, and Bern (2015–2016). He is currently a postdoctoral researcher at the University of Turin in affiliation with the Marie Skłodowska-Curie excellence fellowships program co-funded by the European Commission.

D0912246

Global and International History

Series Editors:

Erez Manela, *Harvard University*
John McNeill, *Georgetown University*
Aviel Roshwald, *Georgetown University*

The Global and International History series seeks to highlight and explore the convergences between the new International History and the new World History. Its editors are interested in approaches that mix traditional units of analysis such as civilizations, nations, and states with other concepts such as transnationalism, diasporas, and international institutions.

Titles in the Series

Christopher R. W. Dietrich, *Oil Revolution: Anti-Colonial Elites, Sovereign Rights, and the Economic Culture of Decolonization*
Stefan Rinke, *Latin America and the First World War*
Nathan Citino, *Envisioning the Arab Future: Modernization in U.S.–Arab Relations, 1945–1967*
Timothy Nunan, *Humanitarian Invasion: Global Development in Cold War Afghanistan*
Michael Goebel, *Anti-imperial Metropolis: Interwar Paris and the Seeds of Third World Nationalism*
Stephen J. Macekura, Of *Limits and Growth: International Environmentalism and the Rise of "Sustainable Development" in the Twentieth Century*

Volkswagen in the Amazon

*The Tragedy of Global Development
in Modern Brazil*

ANTOINE ACKER

University of Turin

CAMBRIDGE
UNIVERSITY PRESS

CAMBRIDGE
UNIVERSITY PRESS

University Printing House, Cambridge CB2 8BS, United Kingdom

One Liberty Plaza, 20th Floor, New York, NY 10006, USA

477 Williamstown Road, Port Melbourne, VIC 3207, Australia

4843/24, 2nd Floor, Ansari Road, Daryaganj, Delhi – 110002, India

79 Anson Road, #06-04/06, Singapore 079906

Cambridge University Press is part of the University of Cambridge.

It furthers the University's mission by disseminating knowledge in the pursuit of education, learning, and research at the highest international levels of excellence.

www.cambridge.org
Information on this title: www.cambridge.org/9781316647776
DOI: 10.1017/9781108178464

First published 2017

Printed in the United States of America by Sheridan Books, Inc.

A catalogue record for this publication is available from the British Library.

ISBN 978-1-107-19742-8 Hardback
ISBN 978-1-316-64777-6 Paperback

Contents

Figures

Preface and Acknowledgments

I do not exactly remember where I first saw it mentioned that VW had run a farm in the Amazon, but it was probably no more than a footnote. This case caught my attention because it appeared to me, at first sight, to be a paradigm of the exploitation of the South by the North. Yet, as I started to trace the connections involved in that story, I realized it was something else, more than just another example of unequal exchange. It was about the irony of modern capitalism, which was feeding a context of global political connections at the same time as an expansion of global trade, a context of circulation of imaginaries at the same time as an exchange of commodities, a context of growing risk awareness at the same time as an increasing impact of technological progress on humans and the environment.

The trope of the earth's lungs burning, which has emerged as an internationalized definition of the Amazon, is thus an outgrowth of capitalist globalization in both the material and imaginary sense. The tremendous influx of exogenous capital into the region from the late 1960s, combined with misguided beliefs in development as a global doctrine, did concretely give impulsion to uncontrollable forest burning, and revitalized old networks of social exploitation. But it is precisely the acceleration of global connections in and about the Amazon that constructed transforming rainforest ecologies into a mirror of the modern world's excesses, reflecting the latter's astonishing destructive capacities. Embedded in the postmodernist wave of the 1970s, which saw the rise of transnationally networked initiatives to question the ins and outs of our insatiable economic model, the history of VW in the Amazon incarnates that tragedy of global development. It gives a picture of the extraordinary capacity of the modern, globalized capitalist system to permanently hit back at itself.

Kiran Klaus Patel is the one person who challenged me to think about my project in terms of its meaning for global history. He has accompanied this research from the beginning, and I cannot say enough how remarkable an advisor and a support he has been. Several other scholars have, very generously, read and extensively commented on my drafts, and I feel indebted to all of them: Sebastian Conrad, Dirk Moses, Claudia Damasceno Fonseca, Christof Mauch, João Klug, Kevin Niebauer, Corinna Unger, Leila Hadj-Abdou, Julia Tischler, and Stella Krepp. Among the many colleagues who kindly received me to discuss the design of my research or who attended presentations of my work in progress in Europe, Brazil, and the United States, José Augusto Pádua, Olivier Compagnon, François-Michel Le Tourneau, Georg Fischer, Jana Otto and Sidney Chalhoub gave particularly precious advice. In 2014, an article related to this research resulted in unexpected and extremely interesting feedback from inside and outside the academic sphere, and I owe this opportunity to Alexandre Fortes, who encouraged me submitting it to the *Revista Brasileira de História*. Two anonymous reviewers at Cambridge University Press, with their rich and knowledgeable reading and warm encouragement, gave the ultimate impulse to improve this book's content. James Naylor Green, who contacted me thereafter, was one of them: I cannot thank him enough for the fineness and precision of his feedback.

This work would not have been possible without the PhD grants I received from the Gulbenkian Foundation and the French Ministry of Superior Education and Research. The unique staff, infrastructure, library, and traveling grants of the EUI, Florence, enabled me to develop this project in the best possible conditions. The kind support of Antonella Romano was particularly meaningful in this context. I have to mention the help of the EUI language center (particularly Nicki Hargreaves and Nicky Owtram), thanks to whom I also met Ann-Marie Kilgallon, who gave a precious contribution to making the English in this book read more smoothly. Later, my fellowships at the Center for InterAmerican Studies in Bielefeld and at the Walter Benjamin Kolleg in Bern were wonderful opportunities to re-conceptualize my research as a book, thanks to the generous working conditions offered by these institutions and the stimulating exchange I had with their researchers. In Bielefeld, I am especially grateful for the trust placed in me by Olaf Kaltmeier and Anne Tittor, with whom I had wonderful conversations about the intersection between power and environment in history. Finally, I brought the last corrections to this book in Turin, boosted by the dynamism of Serenella Iovino, who welcomed me so warmly in the environmental humanities research group she created. In this final phase, I received funding from the European Union's Seventh Framework program for research and innovation under the Marie Skłodowska-Curie grant agreement No 609402 – 2020 researchers: Train to Move (T2M).

This work benefited from the engagement of many archivists and librarians. In Germany, I would like to address particular thanks to Joaquim Peito in Göttingen, and to the staff of the historical office of the VW company in Wolfsburg. Manfred Grieger, who was VW's chief historian at the time of my research, was particularly open to my project and always available for interesting discussions. In the Amazon, my greatest gratitude goes to Jane Silva at the CPT in Belém and Odila Tavares de Andrade at the FINAM archive. I had a very fruitful journey collecting archival material, factual knowledge, and stimulating ideas in Rio de Janeiro thanks to the members of GPTEC, especially Adônia Antunes Prado and Ricardo Rezende Figueira. The latter helped me not only with his enlightening analysis on forced labor, but also in the way he welcomed me in Rio and with the memories he shared about his time in the Araguaia. Several other close witnesses and actors of the history analyzed in this book deserve immense thanks for sharing their personal memories and/or documents with me: Thomas Hax, Lúcio Flávio Pinto, Frei Henri de Roziers, and Julio Rodriguez. Finally, in September 2016, I met the NDR journalist Stefanie Dodt, who has shot a documentary movie about the traces left by VW in the Amazon, and we had discussions about the credibility, value and interpretation of some historical sources, for which I would like to thank her. For the preparation of her film, she gathered new material which I did not have the chance to integrate to my research. I am certain that the final product of her work will bring interesting insights, to put in perspective with the findings exposed in this book.

There are so many names I would like to add to this list, persons who helped with useful advice, a text revision, or some friendly support, who accompanied me on parts of my research trips, offered me a place to stay on these occasions, shared pleasant breaks with me during writing times, or helped me find my way through academic life. Space limits make it impossible to mention them all here and I will make sure to thank them personally for it. There is no doubt that my parents and my brothers deserve warm thanks, because the attraction for the Portuguese-speaking world that inspired this book surely has to do with the tasty Portuguese meals, funny car trips to Algarve and heady Cape Verdean music that accompanied my childhood. Last, but truly, not least, I am grateful to Antonio, for having helped me with almost everything, and at any time. I hope he enjoys this book.

Acronyms

This list represents only the acronyms used in at least two sections of the text.

AEA   Associação dos Empresários da Amazônia
AK3W   Freiburger Aktion Dritte Welt AND Aktionskreis Dritte Welt Recklinghausen
ARENA   Aliança Renovadora Nacional
BASA   Banco da Amazônia
CDU   Christlich Demokratische Union
CONDEL   Conselho Deliberativo da SUDAM
CONTAG   Confederação Nacional dos Trabalhadores da Agricultura
CPT   Comissão Pastoral da Terra
CVRC   Companhia Vale do Rio Cristalino
DIEESE   Departamento Intersindical de Estatística e Estudos Sócioeconômicos
FAO   Food and Agriculture Organization of the United Nations
FAZ   Frankfurter Allgemeine Zeitung
FBCN   Fundação Brasileira para a Conservação da Natureza
FETAGRI   Federação dos Trabalhadores Rurais
FRG   Federal Republic of Germany
GPTEC   Grupo de Pesquisa Trabalho Escravo Contemporâneo
IFC   International Finance Corporation
ILA   Informationsstelle Lateinamerika
INCRA   Instituto Nacional de Colonização e Reforma Agrária
INPA   Instituto Nacional de Pesquisas da Amazônia
ISI   import-substituting industrialization
MDB   Movimento Democrático Brasileiro

MIRAD	Ministério da Reforma Agrária
MST	Movimento dos Trabalhadores Rurais Sem-Terra
NASA	National Aeronautics and Space Administration
PMDB	Partido do Movimento Democrático Brasileiro
PT	Partido dos Trabalhadores
SBPC	Sociedade Brasileira pelo Progresso da Ciência
SPD	Sozialdemokratische Partei Deutschlands
STR	Sindicato de Trabalhadores Rurais
SUDAM	Superintendência do Desenvolvimento da Amazônia
VW(B)	Volkswagen (do Brasil)

Introduction

In September 2015, after the United States Environmental Protection Agency (EPA) found that Volkswagen (VW) had equipped vehicles with a "defeat device" capable of outwitting diesel emission tests, a global storm followed. The multinational company fell into a spiral of executive resignations, governmental investigations, lawsuits, falls in stock values, and massive drops in sales worldwide.[1] In Brazil, the modest fine imposed on VW by the country's main environmental agency had a particularly bitter taste as it coincided with stunning revelations about the company's past.[2] In the midst of the diesel scandal, twelve retired automobile workers filed a lawsuit accusing VW of having helped the military dictatorship, in power between 1964 and 1984, to spy on, arrest, and torture them. The workers' action was a foreseeable consequence of the investigations by the Comissão Nacional da Verdade (CNV), mandated by the federal government to elucidate crimes committed under military rule. In 2014 and 2015, these investigations resulted in two reports based on damning evidence that at various moments VW had used its logistical, financial, and security resources to participate in state repression against workers it deemed "subversive."[3]

---

[1] "Abgas-Skandal: VW hat Ärger an allen Fronten," *Automobilwoche*, October 2, 2015.

[2] "Ibama multa Volkswagem do Brasil em R$ 50 milhões por fraude," *Ascom Ibama*, November 12, 2015.

[3] CNV, *Relatório da CNV: Volume II. Textos temáticos* (Brasília: CNV, 2014), 66–72, 85, 321, 330; final report of the Fórum de Trabalhadores por Verdade, Justiça e Reparação (2015), downloaded from: http://cspconlutas.org.br/2015/09/forum-de-trabalhadores-entrega-o-mpf-denuncia-da-participacao-da-volks-na-ditadura-civil-militar-do-brasil/; access date December 15, 2015.

The military era corresponded to a form of golden age for VW do Brasil (VWB), which remained Latin America's largest private corporation during the entire period, under the lead of its charismatic chief executive officer (CEO), Wolfgang Sauer.[4] In his autobiography published in 2012, Sauer spoke of his nostalgia for the osmosis between the multinational company and the military government.[5] He paid tribute to the "Brazilian miracle" of the 1970s, when historic growth figures, driven by policies that favored capital concentration, led the automobile industry to blossom. Sauer's memories reflected the "developmentalist" mentality of the elites in the period, that is, the belief that production growth, based on technical progress rather than social reform was the sole key to the improvement of society and the nation's self-realization. Of these bright years, Sauer wrote that only one thing still "pained" him when he "remembered or talked about it."[6] He did not refer thereby to any harm done to the workers, but to the "splendid disaster" of a "state of-the-art farm in the midst of the Amazon jungle," run by VW from 1973 to 1986, under the name Companhia Vale do Rio Cristalino (CVRC).[7] The history of this 140,000-hectare "pioneer" cattle ranch on the rain forest frontier, depicted by Sauer as "monumental," is an astounding example of the authoritarian development model, which the Brazilian state promoted in the early 1970s, in conjunction with private partners. At a moment when censorship covered the noise of torture throughout the country, the dictatorship invited domestic and foreign companies to participate in the "conquest of the Amazon," under the admiring eye of political, business, and media actors in Europe, the United States, and Brazil. Yet, in his book, Sauer underlined how, for him, this dream of conquest "transformed into a nightmare." As it awakened transnational protest, condemnation, and interventions in defense of rain forest populations and nature, the farming project gave rise to "grave difficulties," "criticisms," and "threats" for Sauer, preventing his "ascension towards head of global VW."

What Sauer experienced, to his cost, was a global shift in perceptions of tropical forests, from a developmentalist consensus based on the

---

[4] Antoine Acker, "The Brand that Knows Our Land: Volkswagen's 'Brazilianization' in the 'Economic Miracle,' 1968–1973." *Monde(s). Histoire, Espaces, Relations* 5, no. 6 (2015).

[5] Maria Lúcia Doretto, *Wolfgang Sauer. O homem Volkswagen. 50 anos de Brasil* (São Paulo: Geração, 2012).

[6] Note on translations: All translations from Portuguese or German to English are mine, except for a small number, which were already translated in the sources or literature that I have used.

[7] For this and the following: ibid., 342–50.

intensive exploitation of resources to a risk-centered approach marked by controversies over socioenvironmental disruption. This book tells the history of this global shift. Its main argument is that developmentalist policies in the Amazon, which were intended to integrate the region into the global economy, unwittingly made it an arena of global politics, which generated energetic debates about the future of humanity and its relation to nature. The modern colonization of the Amazon took the form of a joint venture combining Brazilian and foreign interests to construct a development model for what was considered an extreme world periphery. It rapidly became a globally watched experiment. The expectations it raised became doubts as the complex ecology of the region, home to the world's richest but also most fragile biodiversity, proved an insurmountable challenge even to farming projects with the most up-to-date technological arsenal. At the same time, the policies of farming modernization encouraged massive changes in land use, whose effects on the tropical ecological balance rose to being one of the central questions of a global environmental agenda in the making. The road to "Amazon development" also revealed itself to be full of ethical obstacles regarding the attitude to adopt toward native rural populations, as well as landless newcomers in search of work, in a – as the world suddenly discovered – not so virgin forest. In this highly inflammatory context, VW became enmeshed in successive scandals that revealed to the world the interconnection between capital influx, deforestation, and the reemergence of forced labor in the Amazon region.

VW arrived in the Amazon together with hundreds of other private companies, which embarked on extractive or farming projects to take advantage of the government's fiscal incentives or to pursue speculative goals. But the German carmaker had a different, politically more ambitious, approach. As Sauer underlines, "We were not just cattle producers, we were bringing civilization." Celebrated in Brazil, Germany, and elsewhere as a technological revolution in tropical farming, the "VW ranch" was supposed to pave the way for the conversion of the Amazon into a modern export economy and to function as a laboratory of solutions to help overcome hunger in the "Third World." However, this consensual image vanished after Cristalino became the subject of a multitude of controversies, leading to the mobilization of transnational networks of protest against the project. This pressure left no other possibility for VW than to sell the ranch off after only thirteen years of business. There were three main reasons for the demise of the CVRC: the conflicting interests behind a constructed, apparent consensus of development, a growing awareness of the scarcity of resources, and the project's disappointing results in the areas of labor conditions and human welfare. Above all, the misfortune of Cristalino's "pioneers," and the protests they unleashed around the world, were the first manifestation of a radical shift in thinking about the Amazon, from the world's supposed granary to its burning lungs.

This historical example invites questions about the loss of authority of the politics of development in Brazil from the second half of the 1970s. How did the idea of development lose its framing role in politics? Why, in particular, did the project of developing the tropical forest fade a few years after it had been put into practice? These questions can be posed in the light of the Brazilian national imaginary, which traditionally saw the Amazon as a horizon for completing the territorial integration of the country. They must also be considered against the recent emergence of the rain forest agenda as a global issue. The intervention of a multinational company in Brazil's internal colonization project must draw attention to the international context of deforestation. Such a process was not only linked to a global demand for tropical commodities, but also gave rise to transnational chains of protest in the name of biodiversity and human rights. In this sense, Cristalino illustrates the start of a self-critical era of globalization, characterized by an increasing number of counter-systemic actors and trends along with the process of capitalist modernization and the multiple transnational connections the latter produced.

Due to the exceptional visibility of the VW ranch, the controversies that accompanied the project played the role of a catalyst, which both captured and contributed to shaping global trends of politicization of the Amazon. Cristalino was thus an early case in the succession of alarms about "rain forest disappearance" that have made the Amazon a popular symbol of socioenvironmental destruction. By exploring this case, this book sheds light on the concrete interconnections, the multiple-scale controversies, and the actors involved in the late wave of globalization of the Amazon. It offers a microhistorical perspective on how a high-tech farming project was transnationally planned, negotiated, and eventually deconstructed in dialog with environmental factors. It analyzes both the projections made by exogenous actors on the rain forest, and the encounters and conflicts that took place in the Cristalino ranch and its surroundings. The tumultuous history of the VW ranch, I argue, reveals how much the construction of the Amazon as a global place was intertwined with the decline of a particular worldwide narrative. This narrative had held that, in economically disadvantaged nations, nature had to be exploited more and more for the sake of development.

Key Word Development

Global historians have never quite known in what box to classify development, for it has alternatively taken the form of a Western ideology or of non-Western nationalism. While this transfer of a biological term into the vocabulary of governance is said to have inspirers as diverse as Adam Smith, Karl Marx, or Sun-Yat Sen, it became systematically used by economic experts in the context of the later British and French empires.[8] It referred to the politics of socioeconomic improvement of colonies, according to measurable standards such as the degree of industrialization, per capita income, or literacy rate.[9] With the emergence of a new wave of international organizations at the end of the Second World War, with accelerating decolonization, and with competition between the United States and the Soviet Union to expand their influence in the southern hemisphere, development became a global reference for "good change."[10] Fixing the standards of political organization, economic production, and social welfare of industrialized societies as an ideal to achieve for every nation, it was intended to pull the so-called Third World countries out of poverty.

Drawing on the postcolonial call to decentralize knowledge, critical writings later deconstructed the development model as a discourse through which the "West" imposed its norms to expand its domination on the "rest" in the context of capitalist globalization.[11] However, historical examples of southern nationalist approaches of development, which

[8] Heinz Wolfgang Arndt, *Economic Development: The History of an Idea* (Chicago: University of Chicago Press, 1987); Gilbert Rist, *Le développement: histoire d'une croyance occidentale* (Paris: Presses de Sciences Po, 1996); David Ekbladh, *The Great American Mission: Modernization and the Construction of an American World Order* (Princeton, NJ: Princeton University Press, 2011), 32.

[9] Nick Cullather, *The Hungry World: America's Cold War Battle Against Poverty in Asia* (Cambridge, MA: Harvard University Press, 2010), 30–1; Frederick Cooper, "Modernizing Bureaucrats, Backward Africans and the Development Concept," in *International Development and the Social Sciences: Essays on the History and Politics of Knowledge*, ed. Frederick Cooper and Randall M. Packard (Berkeley: University of California Press, 1997); Christophe Bonneuil, "Development as Experiment: Science and State Building in Late Colonial and Postcolonial Africa, 1930–1970," *Osiris* 15 (2000).

[10] Marc Frey, Sönke Kunkel, and Corinna R. Unger, eds. *International Organizations and Development, 1945–1990* (Basingstoke: Palgrave Macmillan, 2014); Odd Arne Westad, *The Global Cold: Third World Interventions and the Making of Our Times* (New York: Cambridge University Press, 2005).

[11] For a reference that gathers the points of view of many major post-development thinkers: Wolfgang Sachs, ed. *The Development Dictionary. A Guide to Knowledge as Power* (Johannesburg: Zed Books, 1992).

were able to emancipate themselves from Western influence, abound. Much ink has been spilled to describe how actors from the Global South have adapted, transformed, and sometimes deliberately parodied Western patterns of modernization with the purpose of consolidating local identities.[12] Yet, most scholarly literature has depicted these processes as a one-way street, analyzing development as a ready-to-consume product from the "West," which left the "rest" with nothing other than to build on it, deform it, or reject it. This book looks at the opposite movement by examining actors with Western roots who sought to position themselves within the nationalist agenda of the "receiving" country in the Global South, as in VW's case in Brazil. The politics of "economic integration" of the Amazon opened the door to European and North American investors as the Brazilian government saw in them the carriers of a model of development. However, to be qualified to participate in the colonization of the rain forest, foreign firms had to prove their Brazilian patriotism. Cristalino was a step in VW's strategy of "Brazilianization," which consisted of constructing the firm's local image in harmony with nationalist symbols, in order not only for VW products to take root in the country, but also to create a political context favorable to the company.

In this sense, we should see development as something other than just a vehicle of power pushing from north to south. In the history of the VW ranch, development repeatedly appears as the dominant term used by government and company executives, in both Brazil and Germany, to legitimize large-scale projects, in which centralized technical expertise prevailed over local knowledge. Unlike parent terms, such as "civilization," which had an imperialist connotation, or modernization, too narrowly affiliated with theories of postwar U.S. intellectuals, development possessed the quality of being malleable.[13] Its universal appeal resided in its semantic ambivalence, reinforced by a multiplicity of historical origins

[12] Frederick Cooper, "Writing the History of Development," *Journal of Modern European History*, vol. 8, no. 1 (2010), 5–23; Dirk van Laak, *Weisse Elefanten. Anspruch und Scheitern technischer Grossprojekte im 20. Jahrhundert* (Stuttgart: Deutsche Verlags-Anstalt, 1999); Arjun Appadurai, *Modernity at Large: Cultural Dimensions of Globalization* (Minneapolis: University of Minnesota Press, 1996); Kathryn Sikkink, *Ideas and Institutions: Developmentalism in Brazil and Argentina* (Ithaca, NY: Cornell University Press, 1991); Daniel Klingensmith, *"One Valley and a Thousand': Dams, Nationalism, and Development* (New Delhi: Oxford University Press, 2007).

[13] Boris Barth and Jürgen Osterhammel, eds. *Zivilisierungsmissionen: imperiale Weltverbesserung seit dem 18. Jahrhundert* (Konstanz: UVK, 2005); Nils Gilman, *Mandarins of the Future: Modernization Theory in Cold War America* (Baltimore, MD: Johns Hopkins University Press), 2003.

and political influences.[14] Envisaged in a Westernized international context, development could refer to well-intentioned ideals stressing the right of poorer populations to address basic needs. But it also evoked a global extension of the market-centered growth strategies that had permitted industrial revolutions in advanced capitalist countries. Latin American economists, especially within the United Nations Economic Commission for Latin America and the Caribbean (CEPAL) in the 1950s, intended the term differently. They viewed development as a process through which their nation-states would free themselves from dependence on foreign capital and demand while placing industrialization at the service of reducing domestic inequalities.[15] Not only charismatic leaders of the Brazilian left, but also the nationalist components of the conservative dictatorship that took power in Brazil in 1964 made this anticolonial conception their own. By contrast, the authoritarian governments that ruled thereafter forgot the ideal of social redistribution. They situated development as a march toward economic welfare, which only made sense within a strategy of national security, shielding the country from a supposed temptation by communism.

In this book, the examination of the making and unmaking of a large private–public, domestic–foreign partnership in farming modernization permits an understanding of development as a discourse constantly in the making, a political consensus resulting from bargaining between competing authorities. I do not claim to elaborate a synthesis of all the possible meanings of development, but rather to highlight how actors in the colonization of the Amazon manipulated the concept to serve different purposes. According to the context, development served as a key word to attract private investment, but also as a horizon meant to gather Brazilian citizens behind patriotic claims, as a pretext for the dictatorship to deprive society of political participation, and as a tool for foreign actors to be accepted within the Brazilian nation.

The late 1960s in Brazil marked the climax of a discourse of development taking place under the lead of an authoritarian regime, which was at the same time demonstratively patriotic and widely open to foreign investment. A showcase of this ecumenical model of development, the

---

[14] About the polymorphous uses of development, see Corinna R. Unger, "Histories of Development and Modernization: Findings, Reflections, Future Research," *H-Soz-Kult*, December 9, 2010, www.hsozkult.de/literaturereview/id/forschungsberichte-1130; Julia Tischler, *Light and Power for a Multiracial Nation: The Kariba Dam Scheme in the Central African Federation* (Basingstoke: Palgrave Macmillan, 2013).

[15] Octavio Rodríguez, *La teoría del subdesarrollo de la CEPAL* (Madrid: Siglo XXI, 1988).

project of state-planned colonization of the Amazon emerged in 1966. It was a platform for transfer of capital and "know-how" from industrial countries and intended, simultaneously, to assert Brazil's national sovereignty over its northern territory. The widely shared belief that the Amazon was an endless reserve of natural resources convinced both the Brazilian government and multinational companies that it had to be "populated," "civilized," and "developed." With the support of international organizations such as the Food and Agriculture Organization (FAO) or the World Bank, they designed a development agenda based on a set of certitudes: human will would win the war against nature; soil and subsoil resources would be integrated into a process of production, making the Amazon a global exporter; technical progress would connect the region to the rest of the country. Big farming projects like Cristalino, where high-level technology associated with ambitious politics and considerable supposed economic benefits, were the main testing places for this integrative model of forest colonization.[16]

Yet, this euphoria did not survive the empirical experience of colonization. From the mid-1970s, deforestation reached previously unseen proportions and violent land conflicts proliferated, so that socioecological disturbance in the Amazon began to worry actors from the areas of science, journalism, activism, and politics around the world. It also awakened numerous voices within Brazilian nationalism, created opportunities for constructing a major topic of identification for Brazilian environmentalist movements and gave rise to local Amazonian protest initiatives. The CVRC is a fruitful case for exposing disruption in the politics of development in the Amazon as they were being implemented. Triumphant visions of development repeatedly encountered their limits in the course of the VW project taking shape. The process of taming nature through modern techniques and transforming the peasants of northern Brazil into obedient and sedentary workers did not unfold as planned. What is more, the CVRC attracted international attention to the region and unwittingly helped transform it into the subject of impassioned political debates, notably about ecological sustainability and human rights. The military regime and VW made Cristalino the flagship of the Amazon's integration into national and global trade. However, by claiming to bring modern, high-tech, and globalized capitalism to a peripheral region, they also exposed the ranch to the controversies that modernization programs were likely to generate. In this regard, the "model ranch" suffered from

[16] Laak, *Weisse Elefanten*, 10.

an unfavorable historical timing characterized by a conjunction of trends that challenged authoritarian modernism at various scales.

At the local scale, the early 1970s corresponded to the beginning of accelerated mechanization and territorial expansion of farming in the Amazon, sustained by a capital flux from industrialized foreign countries and richer states of southeastern Brazil.[17] This (re)integration of the region into the national and international economy created new social and ecological risks. Ecological risks needed only a few years to become perceptible even to farmers themselves through the impoverishment of the soils cleared for cultivation or breeding. By the late 1980s, most state-funded agricultural projects by big companies had proved unproductive and had been abandoned or sold off. Social risks became manifest in the exponential intensification of land conflicts, culminating between 1985 and 1987, when, according to the Brazilian Ministry of Land Reform, 458 rural workers and their exponents were murdered, the majority in the Amazon.[18] It was clear, at the time VW left the region, that agricultural colonization had been a factor of social disintegration rather than of stability through development.

At the national scale, the life of the CVRC started at the highest stage of authoritarian rule, when the military regime, besides generalizing repression, followed a hard-line developmentalist policy. Making economic growth the supreme goal of all political undertakings, state developmentalism was interwoven with aggressive nationalist rhetoric, illustrated by Brazil's obstructive attitude during the United Nations Conference for Environment and Development in 1972.[19] However, this historical context only accompanied the launching of the CVRC. The larger part of the project's lifespan actually corresponded to a long period of political transition in Brazil. The phases of *distensão* (easing of authoritarian control from 1974 to 1979), *abertura* (gradual opening to democratic standards from 1979 to 1984), and *democratização* (the period from the demise of military rule to the adoption of a new constitution in 1988) created

---

[17] José de Souza Martins, "The Reappearance of Slavery and the Reproduction of Capital on the Brazilian Frontier," in *Free and Unfree Labour. The Debate Continues*, ed. Tom Brass and Marcel van der Linden (Bern: Peter Lang, 1997), 281–302; Anna Luiza Ozorio de Almeida, *The Colonization of the Amazon* (Austin: University of Texas Press, 1992).

[18] By comparison, 646 such murders had been committed during the previous twenty years: Anthony Gross, "Amazonia in the Nineties: Sustainable Development or Another Decade of Destruction?" *Third World Quarterly* 12, no. 3–4 (1990), 22.

[19] Leila da Costa Ferreira and Sergio B. F. Tavolaro, Environmental Concerns in Contemporary Brazil: An Insight into Some Theoretical and Societal Backgrounds (1970s–1990s), Working Paper (University of Campinas, 2008).

a space for civil society to mobilize and for new actors to participate in politics. These transformations deeply affected the authority of top-down narratives such as development.

Over roughly the same period, development as grand narrative for worldwide history also saw itself contested by cross-border initiatives. In the early 1970s, the writings of Ivan Illich, embedded in the thought of liberation theology, laid the theoretical ground for other actors to reject the politics of development, which industrial nations promoted in the southern hemisphere.[20] The thinkers of the Club of Rome published an internationally discussed report dismissing the idea that economic growth was a synonym for good change.[21] In the 1980s, global NGOs set an agenda for protecting biodiversity and indigenous rights in the rain forests, and even international development organizations like the World Bank integrated ecological and humanitarian clauses into their funding programs.[22] By starting to speak of "human," "cooperative," or "sustainable" development, they rubber stamped the end of the concept's symbolic hegemony, signaling that the simple evocation of development no longer sufficed to legitimize policies.

Development projects that looked modern in the early 1970s appeared in the late 1980s as the products of old-fashioned intellectual software disconnected from any kind of long-term vision. As Sauer explains, VW was acclaimed as a pioneer hero when it arrived in the Amazon, but was then decried by Brazilians and foreigners as "criminal" after the Amazon had risen from the status of endless reserve of resources to that of "lungs of the earth" and the local population from "primitive tribes" to "endangered peoples." Sauer, the "Volkswagen man," as he called himself, realized that the key word "development" had progressively ceased to be an uncontested paradigm, as it had been when the CVRC project started: "Theories about environmental preservation and sustainability would be part of the future, but in early 1973, when the government called me, a representative of Volkswagen, and a group of entrepreneurs, to occupy areas close to the farming frontiers, to develop the region and to settle Brazilians in their habitat, the key word was development."[23]

---

[20] Ivan Illich, *Celebration of Awareness: A Call for Institutional Revolution* (New York: Doubleday & Company, 1970).

[21] Dennis Meadows et al., *The Limits to Growth: A Report for the Club of Rome's Project on the Predicament of Mankind* (New York: American Library, 1972).

[22] Philippe Le Prestre, *The World Bank and the Environmental Challenge* (Toronto: Susquehanna University Press, 1989).

[23] Doretto, *Wolfgang Sauer*, 342–3.

Studying the Global Amazon

The shared narrative about the Amazon has become one of progressive annihilation of the forest through its commodification. This narrative ascribes the responsibility for ongoing deforestation to central features of globalization: the regional division of the economy and global chains of production and consumption, along with multinational companies. Yet, this book is the first historical study of a concrete example of "globalization" of the Amazon since the 1970s, that is, the starting decade for major impulses in deforestation, capital investment, and farming expansion.[24] Most of the academic knowledge on the topic so far stems from historical sociology, which regards tropical destruction as a general process resulting from the abstract movement of capitalism. Cardoso's "dependent development" has been highly influential in this respect, pushing scholarship to envisage economic transformations in the Amazon as a mechanical consequence of Brazil's semi-peripheral role in global capitalism.[25] Cardoso himself analyzed the peripheral function imposed on the Amazon since the late 1960s with regard to the production of primary goods, which were intended to gain currency to finance in turn the importation of capital and machinery for Brazil's southeastern, industrializing core.[26] Apesteguy, Ianni, and Pompermayer described the authoritarian state's role in organizing this process through creating legislative, infrastructural, and fiscal conditions to advance private farming and extraction projects in the Amazon.[27] Martins examined the mechanisms of labor exploitation resulting from the increasing integration of the region into global cycles of exchange, which had the effect of accentuating pressure on local production.[28]

[24] Almeida, *The Colonization of the Amazon.*

[25] Fernando Henrique Cardoso and Enzo Faletto, *Dependencia y desarrollo en América Latina: ensayo de interpretación sociológica* (Santiago de Chile: Ed. limitada para circulación interna, 1967). See also Peter Evans, *Dependent Development: The Alliance of Multinational, State, and Local Capital in Brazil* (Princeton, NJ: Princeton University Press, 1979).

[26] Fernando Henrique Cardoso and Geraldo Müller, *Amazônia: expansão do capitalismo* (São Paulo: Brasiliense, 1977).

[27] Christine Apesteguy, "L'Intervention fédérale en Amazonie: éléments pour une définition de l'état militaire au Brésil" (EHESS, 1976); Octavio Ianni, *Ditadura e agricultura. O desenvolvimento do capitalismo na Amazônia: 1964–1978* (Rio de Janeiro: Civilização Brasileira, 1979); Malori José Pompermayer, "The State and the Fontier in Brazil: A Case Study of the Amazon" (Stanford University, 1979).

[28] Martins, José de Souza. *Expropriação e violência: a questão política no campo* (São Paulo: Hucitec 1980).

These works, which were published in the late 1970s and early 1980s, highlighted the political project of land concentration, capitalist accumulation, and authoritarian control that lay behind the claim of developing the Amazon.[29] However, their systemic vision of institutions and their disembodied view of capitalism, as well as their tendency to confine the local populations and ecologies to a passive role, led them to overestimate the homogeneity and rationality of colonization in the Amazon. The story told in this book, by contrast, is full of oddities, starting with a car company engaging with such unexpected enthusiasm in a clumsily planned ranching project. It is full of moves back and forth in a tiresome partnership between a paranoid military state and a divided company, of disagreements over agronomic and commercial planning, of misunderstandings between people expecting different things from development. It is full of acts of resistance as well. Shifting away from the cliché of capitalist development annihilating nature and native villages symbolized by the invincible, forest-destroying bulldozer, it shows how uncertain the path of that bulldozer actually was. Even in the case of a project involving powerful states, a multinational company, and world-class scientific institutions, the path of the clearing vehicle was not straightforward, its mechanisms far from well-oiled, and the people and objects it encountered not so readily flattened.

Top-down analyses have failed to see that the globalization of the Amazon in the last third of the twentieth century was a negotiated, uneven, and multidimensional process. Amerindian representatives learned how to use the mass media of industrialized societies to address the Brazilian state, environmentalists influenced the agenda of the World Bank, Amazonian subsistence communities sometimes made pacts with neighboring ranchers to earn a space within capitalist society.[30] This produced blurred networks of actors, coming into contact through fluctuating conflict or alliances. Since the 1990s, authors have rekindled Amazon studies against this dynamic background to identify factors of change

---

[29] The "dependency" approach was later refined in the light of the environmental question, especially by Stephen G. Bunker, *Underdeveloping the Amazon: Extraction, Unequal Exchange and the Failure of the Modern State* (Urbana: University of Illinois Press, 1985).

[30] Kathryn Sikkink and Margaret E. Keck, *Activists beyond Borders: Advocacy Networks in International Politics* (Ithaca, NY: Cornell University Press, 1998); Kathryn Hochstetler and Margaret E. Keck, *Greening Brazil, Environmental Activism in State and Society* (Durham, NC, and London: Duke University Press, 2007); Seth William Garfield, *A luta indígena no coração do Brasil: política indigenista, a marcha para o oeste e os índios xavante (1937–1988)* (São Paulo: UNESP, 2011).

beyond the sole framework of production relationships. Hecht, Pádua, and Escobar suggested that endangered tropical rain forests are places of confrontation between different perceptions of nature, whose encounter is decisive in producing socioenvironmental change.[31] Lipschutz explained how a context of rapidly altering nature, disputed resources, and growing needs for ecological sustainability affected the structure of social relations.[32] Foresta, a geographer who analyzed Amazonian policy in the 1970s and 1980s, also demonstrated how conservationist forces within Brazilian developmentalist institutions could ally with civil society actors in a struggle against deforestation.[33] Finally, recent anthropological works have shown that the Amazon's constantly changing landscape was not only due to massive capitalist projects, but also, and maybe even more so, to the everyday technologies and agrarian practices of rural populations.[34]

A few studies addressing earlier decades have come to strengthen this interpretation of the rain forest as a multiple, transformable, and negotiable space, rather than as a homogeneous and consensually defined object. Grandin's *Fordlândia*, which analyzed Henry Ford's attempts to grow rubber in the forest between the 1920s and 1940s, demonstrated that even the most powerful multinational companies could come unstuck when confronted with the complexity of the Amazon's ecology.[35] In a book on the mobilization of northeastern Brazilian workers to tap rubber in the Amazon for the United States during the Second World War, Garfield suggested that the encounters that took place during this episode

---

[31] Susanna B. Hecht and Alexander Cockburn, *The Fate of the Forest: Developers, Destroyers and Defenders of the Amazon* (Chicago: University of Chicago Press, 1990); José Augusto Pádua, "Biosphere, History and Conjuncture in the Analysis of the Amazon Problem," in *The International Handbook of Environmental Sociology*, ed. Michael Redclift and Graham Woodgate (Cheltenham, Northampton: Edward Elgar, 2000); Arturo Escobar, *Territories of Difference: Place, Movements, Life*, redes (Durham, NC, and London: Duke University Press, 2008).

[32] Ronnie D. Lipschutz and Judith Mayer, *Global Civil Society & Global Environmental Governance: The Politics of Nature from Place to Planet* (New York: State University of New York Press, 1996).

[33] Ronald A. Foresta, *Amazon Conservation in the Age of Development: The Limits of Providence* (Gainesville: University of Florida Press, 1991).

[34] Hugh Raffles, *In Amazônia: A Natural History* (Princeton, NJ: Princeton University Press, 2002); Jeremy M. Campbell, *Conjuring Property: Speculation and Environmental Futures in the Brazilian Amazon* (Seattle: University of Washington Press, 2015); Jeffrey Hoelle, *Rainforest Cowboys: The Rise of Ranching and Cattle Culture in Western Amazonia* (Austin: University of Texas Press, 2015).

[35] Greg Grandin, *Fordlândia: The Rise and Fall of Henry Ford's Forgotten Jungle City* (New York: Metropolitan Books, 2009).

constituted a prelude to the region's rise to the status of a global ecological symbol.[36] Grandin and Garfield made clear that the Amazon's history cannot be understood without considering global interactions. But like most other authors studying the topic, they mainly limited their understanding of the "global" to interventions coming from the United States. By analyzing a project that involved German actors and provoked reactions in other Western countries, this book makes a much needed move toward extending the narrow geographical focus, which has characterized studies of global exchange in the modern Amazon so far. Stressing the role of a German company is not just an exotic novelty in the literature, it also highlights the differentiated view Brazilians had of their foreign partners. The experience of a stunning "economic miracle" after the Second World War, its non-imperialist diplomacy, and a flexible approach to the concept of development made Germany an attractive model for emerging Third World countries in the 1970s.[37] U.S. companies also participated in agrarian colonization, but Brazilian leaders would never have appointed one of them as the bridgehead of their politics of Amazon development, such as they did with VW. Suspicions of imperialism made it impossible for U.S. actors to appropriate the *"integrar para não entregrar"* ("integrate so as not to surrender") slogan, which the Brazilian military had coined for the Amazon.[38]

The size of VW do Brasil, its political links with the dictatorship, and its ability to appropriate national symbols make it a crucial example for scholars wishing to study the strategies of European multinationals to secure emerging markets in the Global South. The history of VW in Brazil has been neglected so far, and I hope to stimulate new research on the topic.[39] At the same time, this book is not only about VW. It involves a

---

[36] Seth William Garfield, *In Search of the Amazon: Brazil, the United States, and the Nature of a Region* (Durham, NC: Duke University Press, 2014).

[37] This book addresses a period during which Germany was divided into two different states. However, the activities of VW in Brazil had no direct connection with the German Democratic Republic (GDR). For reasons of legibility, I will always refer to the Federal Republic of Germany (FRG), its society, state, and interests as "German." Therefore, "German" has to be understood in this text as a simplifying term for "West German."

[38] Benjamin Singer, *L'homme et les forêts tropicales: une relation durable* (Versailles: Quae, 2015), 59.

[39] A recent global history of the Beetle seemed to overlook that Brazil was VW's largest foreign market for more than half a century, while another study, addressing the history of the automobile industry in Brazil, focused on U.S. companies with more minor market shares than VW: Bernhard Rieger, *The People's Car: A Global History of the Volkswagen Beetle* (Cambridge, MA: Harvard University Press, 2013); Joel Wolfe, *Autos and Progress: The Brazilian Search for Modernity* (Oxford: Oxford University Press, 2010).

particularly broad array of actors (from seasonal workers to international managers, from grassroots church activists to high-ranking politicians), institutions (international NGOs, political parties, private companies, state agencies, trade unions), scales, and issues (from deforestation to forced labor, from import-export models to land distribution). It studies a process where state policies, international debates, protest or support coming from society and the agency of nonhuman objects all contribute to the politicization of the rain forest. Consequently, the following chapters feature a representative sample of the competing visions of nature, the diverging expectations from development and rival agro-economic models, which collectively negotiated the making of the modern Amazon on a transnational basis.

Organization of This Book

This book provides the first comprehensive account of the CVRC project, across its entire lifespan as well as a broad range of social, political, and environmental dimensions.[40] It is based on sources collected in Brazil and Germany, which document daily life and labor practices at the VW ranch, but also the actions of individuals who, in places such as São Paulo, Brasília, Belém, Bonn, or Wolfsburg, worked for the powerful institutions that supported the project. Further archival material used in this book sheds light on transnational connections as a means of protest for subaltern actors in the age of globalization, especially for Amazonian workers, who were victims of forced labor. As this study is driven by a concern to show how the interaction between humans and nature influenced the evolution of a big development project, it also draws on technical data regarding farming management, agro-technology, company accounts, and tropical ecology.

Three central questions succeeded each other over the thirteen years that witnessed the launch of the Cristalino ranch, its attempt to blossom without ever quite achieving it, and its fading: development (1973–5),

[40] A few short analyses on the topic already exist: Lúcio Flávio Pinto, "A internacionalização da Amazônia," *Revista USP* 13 (1992); Benjamin Buclet, "Entre tecnologia e escravidão: a aventura da Volkswagen na Amazônia," *Revista do programa de pós-graduação em serviço social da PUC* 13 (2005). Various specialists of modern slavery have evoked the VW ranch as a major example of the increase in forced labor occurrences in the Amazon during the 1970s and 1980s: Martins, *Expropriação e violência*; Binka Le Breton, *Trapped: Modern-Day Slavery in the Brazilian Amazon* (London: Kumarian Press, 2003); Ricardo Rezende Figueira, *Pisando fora da própria sombra: a escravidão por dívida no Brasil* (Rio de Janeiro: Civilização Brasileira, 2004).

nature (1975–83), and labor (1983–6). These notions, and the different interpretations underpinning them, dominated the agreements and disputes that concerned the project in these respective periods. They compose the three central chapters of this book, which are framed by two smaller chapters: the first addressing the historical background of the VW ranch, prior to 1973, and the last exposing the conditions and direct consequences of its fall, after 1986.

The first chapter, presenting "the Amazon as a Horizon," situates the object of this book in its deeper context, by addressing three major historical processes that shaped the conditions for a project like Cristalino to take place. The first process refers to the historical construction of the Amazon as a forest region, which I claim was both virtual, as an encounter between manifold imaginaries, and concrete, as it resulted from a multiplicity of human experiences of exchange with nature. The second process I describe is the construction of a developmentalist consensus by Brazilian elites from the 1930s onward, articulating rapid industrialization, centralized coordination of economic production, and territorial integration. The "conquest of the Amazon" imposed itself progressively as the ultimate objective of this national march toward development. The third process explored in this chapter is how VW took advantage of this developmentalist consensus to establish itself in Brazil. Although it was a German company, it managed to appear as a central actor in the territorial expansion of productive activities within the country. Cristalino stood in symbolic continuity to this contribution.

Chapter 2, on the "Making of a Model Ranch," explains how the CVRC was born out of a national-developmentalist compromise between the Brazilian state and a multinational firm between 1973 and 1975. Behind the obvious ambition of the project to showcase Brazilian modernization existed different expectations, often founded on the tension between nationalist feelings and openness to foreign capital. To demonstrate this, I examine the background negotiations that preceded the project. After revealing the reasons that led the military regime to invite private firms into the Amazon and that convinced VW to participate in the colonization, I observe the conditions of Cristalino's beginning and analyze the plans according to which the ranch was built. Subsequently, I discuss the internal tensions that the CVRC project caused both within VW and the Brazilian development institutions. In its final section, the chapter analyzes how a multifunctional model of technology and civilization was created against the background of this tension. Cristalino's multifunctional character was a strength, because it ensured broad international support for the operation. At the same time, it lay on fragile agreements, which exposed the project to a broad range of potential contestation.

The third chapter, "Development in the Age of Scarcity," shows how the project became enmeshed in the debate about diminishing resources from 1976 onward. The awareness of scarcity emerged out of entanglements between the ecological vicissitudes of colonization, the increasing disputes over land properties, and the emergence of a global environmental agenda. The chapter begins with the analysis of a deforestation scandal, which damaged the reputation of VW in the Amazon, and proved to be an early case for the Brazilian environmental movement, with strong repercussions in the industrialized world. Following this controversy, VW had difficulties in responding to the attacks of environmentalists, while in parallel it revealed itself unable to cope with major agro-ecological obstacles on its ranch. In consequence, VW and its Brazilian partners were forced to admit the growing influence of nature and of its defenders in the Amazonian context. The end of the chapter extends this reflection about the influence of diminishing resources in redefining Amazonian politics, as it discusses the issue of land. I argue that, as the progress of deforestation and soil erosion prepared the ground for rising land conflicts, actors from the left and rural workers' movements tended increasingly to include the VW estate in the representations of their political struggle for land. They transformed Cristalino discursively into a *latifundio*, a symbol of the inequalities that plagued rural Brazil.

Chapter 4, "Out-of-Date Modernity," details a forced labor scandal that became linked with the image of the CVRC from 1983 onward and was criticized by protesters as a case of "modern slavery." Ultimately, this scandal caused the end of the project because it created a gap between the promises of social improvement and the perceived enmeshment of VW with primitive forms of production. The actors protesting against Cristalino, from Amazonian clearing workers to German Third World solidarity groups, attacked what they saw as the incoherence of a dominant discourse of modernization, which produced the contrary of what it had announced it would do. The chapter starts with a section detailing the Amazonian networks of forced labor, which furnished a workforce for the CVRC, and analyzing the coalition of actors that mobilized against the case in Brazil. A further section examines the internationalization of the affair, mainly through the involvement of German groups in transnational networks of solidarity. This chapter demonstrates that the multinational dimension of VW became a crucial opportunity for activists in establishing the first impactful campaign against forced labor in the Amazon, as similar accusations against Brazilian firms had never achieved a comparable echo before.

The fifth chapter is about "Cristalino's Unhappy Ending" during and after the transition to democracy in Brazil. After an inglorious retreat from the Amazonian front in the "war of development," VW had to bear the financial and judiciary consequences of its unlucky agricultural experiment. As for Cristalino, it became a place emblematic of the failure of the Brazilian state's modernization plans, as thousands of landless peasants invaded the estate, where they had to fight a fierce battle against ranchers, land-grabbers, poachers, and gold miners. Hesitant and clumsy interventions by the government to solve the situation showed that alternatives to the model of dependent development once symbolized by the partnership between VW and the Brazilian state failed to emerge, leaving the future of the Amazon uncertain. This uncertainty, worsened by persisting concern over ecological stability, constitutes the biggest difference with the conquering spirit of the early 1970s, when new-coming ranchers could still proclaim themselves "pioneers" in a promising "virgin" forest.

The chapters included in this volume reveal the process of politicization of a place. With the dismantling of the developmentalist consensus, the management of the Amazon rain forest became an open issue, negotiated through the prism of multiple projections, viewpoints, actors, and scales of intervention. At the crossroads between global and Brazilian history, the present research brings a triple contribution to these fields. It analyzes the new patterns of interconnection, which promoters of developmentalist projects unwittingly helped to produce by making the Amazon a place of global entanglements. It presents the arrival of environmental topics into debates about the Amazon in a new light, by showing how concern with endangered natural resources contributed to reshaping the idea of development and interrogating the latter's coordinating role within forest politics. Finally, it provides a historical case study of the link between agricultural modernization, deforestation and the regeneration of forced labor networks. It highlights the process by which this link became a catalyst for social movements in Brazil and abroad, contributing to sensitizing public opinion and lobbying policy makers on rain forest protection issues. I pursue these analytical objectives by bringing institutional and protest politics into dialog. The result is to show the relationship between the multi-scaled dismantlement of a top-down development consensus and the construction of the Amazon into a transnational symbol of socio-environmental injustice.

I

Setting the Stage: The Amazon as a Horizon

At the end of a two-year river voyage, which had begun from the volcanoes of Ecuador in 1541, Spaniard Francisco de Orellana reported seeing female warriors next to the mouth of the river where he emerged.[1] He called them Amazons in reference to figures from Greek mythology, and Europeans associated this name with the hydrographic basin through which Orellana had traveled. Thus, the very name of the region is the result of a projection drawn by exogenous actors. The circulation of legends and the creation of fictive human and nonhuman characters have contributed to the construction of the Amazon as a regional unity ever since.[2] At the same time, the Amazon cannot be reduced to a web of myths. It is also a space bearing the socioecological traces of a long history of agricultural experiments, adaptation of human communities to their – changing – environment and even strategies of natural conservation.

This multiplicity of experiences tended to disappear from collective memory as, during the second third of the twentieth century, the Brazilian political elites made the conquest of the rain forest the horizon of Brazil's march toward modernity. Adroitly, VW framed its implantation in the country within this myth of national expansion, by highlighting the contribution of its automobile production to Brazil's economic and territorial growth. This strategy, in step with the "national-developmentalist" vision adopted by the successive federal governments, helped the German

---

[1] Juan de Onis, *The Green Cathedral: Sustainable Development of Amazonia* (New York: Oxford University Press, 1992), 37.
[2] Alain Gheerbrant, *The Amazon: Past, Present, and Future* (New York: Harry N. Abrams, 1992), 43–5.

company become the ideal partner in the colonization of the Amazon, reconceptualized as a virgin frontier. This chapter explores the different historical processes that set the stage for the arrival of VW in the Amazon. After introducing the many histories of the Amazon, both as an imagined and a concrete place, it describes the construction of a national-developmentalist consensus in Brazil and, finally, recounts VW's journey in time and space, from Nazi Germany to the Brazilian tropics.

The Untraceable Forest

One common definition of the Amazon is to consider it, as did Europeans in reference to Orellana's "discovery," "all the territory drained by rivers flowing into the Amazon system," encompassing an area of nearly 7 million square kilometers from the Atlantic to the Andes.[3] Nonetheless, some students of the region find it unsatisfactory to limit the Amazon to its watershed, and point at ecological characteristics that extend northward over the Guianas. For Betty Meggers, what makes the Amazon a distinctive ecosystem is "the dominant vegetation below 5,000 feet in elevation, where annual average temperature variation does not exceed 5°, where rain falls on 130 or more days of the year, and where relative humidity normally exceeds 80 percent."[4] There may be less complex ways of defining the Amazon, for example, by drawing singly on the climatic aspect, relief, or dominant vegetation types. To select one of these criteria of geographical delimitation would not bring one much further, as most evocations of the Amazon that will emerge in the history of the CVRC correspond to projected ideas on a territory. This territory's limits vary according to the cultural background, economic interest, social imaginary, or political position of the actors naming it. Just as Orellana named the river out of his own cultural experience, the Amazon's delimitation as a region is a varying product of manifold imaginaries.[5]

As relative as they might be if one considers them singly, these many visions of the Amazon sometimes converge into consensual representations: for example, that of a region dominated by exuberant vegetation, a high density of trees, a forest. Admittedly, even this idea of forest is no satisfying synthesis of all the potential definitions of the Amazon

---

[3] Onis, *The Green Cathedral*, 13.

[4] Betty Meggers, *Amazonia: Man and Culture in a Counterfeit Paradise* (Washington, DC: Smithsonian Institution Press, 1996), 7–8.

[5] Candace Slater, *Entangled Edens: Visions of the Amazon* (Berkeley: University of California Press, 2002).

(metropolises like Belém and Manaus are symbols of Amazonian identity in Brazil, although the cityscape they offer is far removed from the common conception of forest). However, there is a consensus among NGOs, the media, governmental organizations, and even indigenous organizations in the northwest region of Brazil to consider the Amazon the world's largest area of tropical forest. According to various estimations, it contains between 25 percent and 40 percent of the world's species and up to 30 percent of its freshwaters.[6] It extends throughout almost one-third of South America and covers more than half of Brazil's territory. It is viewed as one of the most puzzling ecological systems on the planet, especially insofar as it combines very nutrient-poor soils with rich and dense forests, displaying an astonishing level of biodiversity. It is estimated that the region is home to about 250,000 plant species, 300 mammal species, 2,000 fish species, and 2 million species of insects, as well as microscopic forms of life.[7]

As this biodiversity exists not only at the regional scale but even on tiny parcels of forest – in the area of Manaus, botanists have counted nearly 300 species of trees on one single hectare – single species are often geographically dispersed.[8] This dispersion has been a challenge to human beings in their extraction of forest resources. It was for this reason that rubber collection – the Amazon's main economic activity in the late nineteenth century – required an extremely high investment in labor. The distance between trees could be up to 100 meters, and a fungus peculiar to the region spread rapidly through closely planted rubber trees, making plantation cropping impossible.[9] The historical misfortune of Ford investing to grow rubber in the Tapajos, or of American multibillionaire Daniel Keith Ludwig, who failed to implement massive cellulose production in the late 1960s, illustrated the Amazon's tendency to resist large-scale cultivation.[10] The move by Brazilian authorities and private firms like Volkswagen toward cattle breeding in the last third of the twentieth century resulted partly from the hope that pasturing, as a very basic and

---

[6] José Augusto Pádua, "Um país e seis biomas: ferramenta conceitual para o desenvolvimento sustentável e a educação ambiental," in *Desenvolvimento, justiça e meio ambiente*, ed. José Augusto Pádua (Belo Horizonte: UFMG, 2009).

[7] Onis, *The Green Cathedral*, 34; Susanna Bettina Hecht, *Cattle Ranching in the Eastern Amazon: Evaluation of a Development Policy* (Berkelely: University of California, 1982), 182.

[8] Onis, *The Green Cathedral*, 5.

[9] Bunker, *Underdeveloping the Amazon*, 68–9.

[10] Grandin, *Fordlândia*; Lúcio Flávio Pinto, *Jari: toda a verdade sobre o Projeto de Ludwig. As relações entre estado e multinacional na Amazónia* (São Paulo: Marco Zero, 1986).

adaptable form of cropping, would survive in the forest ecology with less difficulty.

The region's diversity and its resistance to homogenization have led Hecht to underline that the Amazon constitutes "a mosaic of forests of similar structure (and seral states)," rather than "a heterogeneous but essentially uniform formation."[11] This mosaic is reflected in the many forest soil typologies, whose three main categories are the "*terra firme*," which never experiences flooding; the "*igapós*," where the water remains stagnant for a certain time after flooding; and the "*várzea*," which are inundated over the entire rainy season and remain dry the rest of the year. As they do not display a uniform landscape, there are potentially different critiques regarding their exploitation by humans. Agricultural techniques that are ecologically devastating in certain parts of the Amazon might prove suitable in other parts. Paradoxically, the region seems to rebel against concepts such as nature or forest, which could situate it as an "objectifiable" unity, even if various ecological parameters such as those advanced by Meggers can lead to the conclusion of its having certain homogeneous features. These features have influenced the widespread perception of such a vast territory as a distinct geographic ensemble. Needless to say, they are not pre-given, but result from a complex history over the *longue durée*, for example at the inorganic level, which led to the formation of this vast ecosystem. The rising of the Andes mountain chains between 40 million and 70 million years ago, which caused the formation of an extensive freshwater lake eastward, is, for example, an often-cited element of geological history that led to the formation of the Amazon.[12]

Humans in the Amazon Forest: Dynamics of Exchange and Disruptions

It is a widely known but a frequently oversimplified fact that nonhuman life in the Amazon has stood in a dynamic of exchange with various human groups. This history is more nuanced than the widespread dichotomous chronology dividing it between a pre-Colombian era of harmony between "primitive" peoples and nature on one side, and an ecologically devastating colonial era on the other side. Undeniably, some forms of economic exploitation of the forest proved to have greater effects than others on the ecological balance of the region. However, forest landscapes

[11] Hecht, *Cattle Ranching in the Eastern Amazon*, 182.
[12] Meggers, *Amazonia*, 9; Hecht and Cockburn, *The Fate of the Forest*, 19.

had been encountering the economic activities of human groups long before the arrival of, for example, Portuguese colonizers. Moreover, the Amazon's ecosystem did not undergo any major deregulation due to massive human exploitation until the last third of the twentieth century.

Humans have lived there for more than 10,000 years, most of them in communities distributed in the *várzea* floodplains. Early reports of European travelers as well as archeological evidence point at a dense native population at the arrival of the Portuguese colony in the sixteenth century. The total number of human inhabitants could have reached about 7 million for the entire Amazon watershed – a figure comparable to the region's population in the 1950s – and there were densities of at least thirty inhabitants per square kilometer in the *várzeas*.[13] By coordinating hunting, fishing, and agriculture with the seasonal fluctuation of river water levels, the Amerindians extracted resources in a relatively balanced and sustainable mode. This is not to say that their activities did not produce alterations – including in a destructive sense – on nonhuman life. Various animal species disappeared due to intensive hunting. The Cipó, a patchily occurring forest vine in the eastern Amazon, might be a consequence of the extraction by native populations of Babaçú and Brazil nuts, which required clearing and the formation of open forest gaps.[14] On other locations, large, ridged fields seem to point at prehistoric irrigation sites while throughout the Amazon basin there are also thousands of so-called *terra preta* ("black earth") deposits, which, according to Cleary, are "the product of long-term mulching and composting of agricultural fields."[15] However, these examples are limited in scale. While narratives of a perfect harmony of the natives with the forest belong to an idealization of history, it remains that indigenous interventions on the Amazonian environment had nothing of the dimensions that occurred under the impulsion of state-planned colonization from the 1970s.

No significant waves of deforestation resulted from Portuguese colonialism from the sixteenth to the nineteenth centuries either. The new crops – mainly cocoa and sugar – as well as the cattle-raising activities early settlers introduced into the region remained constrained to areas next to the riverbanks, which were in part already cultivated by natives.[16]

[13] Bunker, *Underdeveloping the Amazon*, 58–61.
[14] Hecht, *Cattle Ranching in the Eastern Amazon*, 189–92.
[15] David Cleary, "Towards an Environmental History of the Amazon: From Prehistory to the Nineteenth Century," *Latin American Research Review* 36, no. 2 (2001), 73–5.
[16] Pádua, "Biosphere, History and Conjuncture in the Analysis of the Amazon Problem," 408.

However, some serious ecological disruptions due to colonial production provided a bitter foretaste of the imbalances an enlarged colonial occupation might be able to engender. For example, the massive exploitation of turtle eggs for oil export nearly provoked the decimation of the species, broke the river's ecological chain, and deprived Indian communities of vital fishing resources.[17] Such disruption, together with the colonial enslavement of Indians and the introduction by the Europeans of infectious diseases, led to a drastic reduction in the indigenous population.

At the same time, colonialism led to the formation of the Caboclo culture, mixing native and Portuguese influences. This culture developed into a riverine population of poor settlers, many of whom moved further in the direction of forest areas by traveling on the tributaries in the Amazon basin. Some Caboclos practiced slash-and-burn agriculture on a reduced scale and thus provoked the transformation of portions of rain forest into areas of secondary vegetation.[18] Although there is no evidence of massive forest degradation by Caboclos, their farming practices, historically dismissed as primitive and unsustainable, served as justification for the Brazilian government for promoting technologically assisted forms of forest colonization in the twentieth century.[19] The Caboclo were constructed into a symbol of the irrational exploitation of nature, justifying the importation of foreign knowledge into the region. Ironically, large-scale cattle ranches such as the CVRC ended up recuperating the slash-and-burn method to limit their costs of production, this time with much more serious consequences for the environment due to the alliance of traditional slash-and-burn with the use of powerful defoliants.

Many other human groups have contributed to transforming the Amazon. The forest's thick vegetation proved an ally for the black, fugitive, *quilombolas* slaves who founded independent communities dispersed over various parts of the Amazon in the late eighteenth and nineteenth centuries, sometimes mixing with Indian or Caboclo populations.[20] Mestizo, mulatto, and native insurrectionists, after making war on the colonial elite in Belém in 1835–40, also sought refuge within the forest. On the contrary, many of the hundreds of thousands of northeastern

[17] Bunker, *Underdeveloping the Amazon*, 63–4.
[18] Warren Dean, *With Broadax and Firebrand: The Destruction of the Brazilian Atlantic Forest* (Berkeley: University of California Press, 1995), 258.
[19] Natascha Stefania Carvalho de Ostos, "O Brasil e suas naturezas possíveis (1930–1945)," *Revista de Indias* 72, no. 255 (2012), 588.
[20] Berta Gleizer Ribeiro, *Amazônia urgente: cinco séculos de história e ecologia* (Belo Horizonte: Itatiaia, 1990), 123.

peasants, who migrated to the Amazon to extract *hevea* during the first "rubber boom" of 1880–1920, lived in the forest as a place of captivity. Middle men contracted by rubber entrepreneurs maintained these workers in a state of financial indebtedness and physical dependence.[21] The first rubber boom ended in a drastic impoverishment of the region as the British, out of seeds originally collected – some have said, stolen – in the Amazon, managed to develop large rubber-cropping farms in Malaysia.[22] There, the local ecology allowed much cheaper modes of extraction of the *hevea*. Nevertheless, other actors enriched the Amazon with new species, one group being Japanese farmers, which settled there from the 1930s to start the production of jute and black pepper.[23]

A multitude of other human agents have played a role in fashioning the image of the Amazon. In the nineteenth century, Carl Friedrich Philipp von Martius noted how frightening Brazilian forests were for the local inhabitants, while Alexander von Humboldt saw the Amazon as the world's "future granary."[24] Religious missionaries, scientific explorers, and adventurers (the most famous of them being American president Theodore Roosevelt in 1913–14), made extended trips through the region and delivered reports, which followed the same patterns of representation.[25] During the new rubber boom, which took place during the Second World War, this "Amazonian imaginary" found a popular declination through the tales that spread within northeastern migrant networks. Young northeasterners enrolled as "rubber soldiers" under the influence of governmental propaganda that idealized the region as a place of many opportunities. But the migrants often underlined to their families and friends the inauspicious climate, diseases, and other natural plagues they faced in the forest.[26] This double image – on one side the myth of an opulent Eldorado, on the other side that of a place of submerging natural ferocity – have predominated in representations of the Amazon. Perceived

---

[21] Mary Helena Allegretti, "A construção social de políticas ambientais – Chico Mendes e o movimento dos seringueiros" (Universidade de Brasília, 2002), 154–71.

[22] John Merson, "Bio-prospecting and Bio-piracy: Intellectual Property Rights and Biodiversity in a Colonial and Postcolonial Context," *Osiris* 15 (2000), 286.

[23] Nigel J. H. Smith, *The Amazon River Forest: A Natural History of Plants, Animals, and People* (New York: Oxford University Press, 1999), 114.

[24] Onis, *The Green Cathedral*, 24; Shawn William Miller, *Fruitless Trees: Portuguese Conservation and Brazil's Colonial Timber* (Stanford, CA: Stanford University Press, 2000), 7.

[25] Candice Millard, *The River of Doubt: Theodore Roosevelt's Darkest Journey* (New York: Broadway Books, 2005).

[26] Garfield, *In Search of the Amazon*, 155–61.

abundant and untamed nature appeared as a challenge providing fuel for dreams of human conquest. Politics of colonization in the second half of the twentieth century proved strongly influenced by this vision of the forest as a virgin space, as if the obsession with the future contained in the concept of development had to go hand in hand with ignorance of the region's past.

The idea of forest as a space to be conquered is at the origin of what geographers call the pioneer frontier: a "free space" (or rather seen as such by incoming settlers) in the process of being economically appropriated.[27] In the late 1960s, southeastern Pará, where VW chose to locate its ranch, became Brazil's principal pioneer frontier, succeeding to the southward spread of coffee between the 1940s and 1960s in the state of Paraná, and the expansion of cattle farming into the plains of the center-west in the 1950s and 1960s.[28] Understanding themselves as pioneers gave to the actors in the colonization a historical legitimacy; being those who traced a new frontier made them masters of the land they claimed to civilize.

Governmental organizations and nationalist newspapers made of the "pioneer" advancement in the Amazon a chapter in the national epic. It is useful here to recall that although more than 60 percent of the Amazon forest is legally part of Brazil, it extends over six other countries. This territorial division is the result of centuries of diplomatic maneuvers and/or military confrontations, first in the colonial period between the Spanish and the Portuguese crowns – with French, English, and Dutch implications – then between diverse independent states in Latin America.[29] In this context, the progressive occupation of the region by farmers included a nationalist meaning. The pioneers were often compared in the late 1960s and early 1970s with the *bandeirantes* – patriotic figures glorified by the military regime in power, the *bandeirantes* were settlers from São Paulo who, notably in the seventeenth century, marched into Brazil's backlands in search of mineral riches and enslaved Indian groups on their way. Thus, *Manchete*, one of Brazil's main magazines at the time, published an article in 1969 dedicated to entrepreneurs and settlers in the tropical rain forest, under the title "The *Bandeirantes* of the Amazon."[30] A number of

[27] Martine Droulers and François-Michel Le Tourneau, "Amazonie: la fin d'une frontière?" *Caravelle*, no. 75 (2000).

[28] Joe Foweraker, *The Struggle for Land: A Political Economy of the Pioneer Frontier in Brazil from 1930 to the Present Day* (New York: Cambridge University Press, 1981).

[29] Onis, *The Green Cathedral*, 43–5.

[30] João Antônio, "Os bandeirantes da Amazônia," *Manchete*, August 23, 1969.

members of the team who first organized the Cristalino settlement for VW appropriated this image for themselves. One such person was an assistant of Sauer who declared: "We were the trailblazers, pioneers, we were *Bandeirantes* on Amazonian soil."[31]

The Setting of National-Developmentalism

The "pioneer frontier mentality" was in line with the predatory tendencies that had caused the progressive destruction of 93 percent of the Mata Atlântica. This tropical forest covering about 1 million square kilometers once extended along the major part of the Brazilian coastline, stretching into the interior for several hundred kilometers.[32] In only a few decades after the arrival of the Portuguese in 1500, dyewood cutting eliminated most of the woods located on the coast. Sugar planting, as the leading export activity in the seventeenth century, caused the deforestation of the northeastern coast of Brazil.[33] From the late seventeenth century the mining of gold in the southeast brought large waves of population into areas of the interior. It came at a high cost to the forest to supply these populations with food and fuel sources, besides the impact caused by miners burning off hillsides to access gold.[34] After independence in 1822, coffee progressively became the main export activity. It was planted in coastal southeastern regions around Rio de Janeiro and São Paulo, where it expanded dramatically westward, leading to the progressive burning of forest surfaces. Next to these export staples, food crops and the raising of livestock had been structural factors of deforestation. These activities grew in increasing dimensions along with demographic growth, which was boosted by strong immigration. Between 1872 and 1930, the Brazilian population increased from 9.9 million to 35 million people.[35]

In spite of this context, the Amazon forest did not undergo the same devastation as the Mata Atlântica. From the sixteenth to the twentieth century, the region even enjoyed a long period of vegetal regeneration.

---

[31] Doretto, *Wolfgang Sauer*, 344.

[32] Dean, *With Broadax and Firebrand*.

[33] Thomas D. Rogers, *The Deepest Wounds: A Labor and Environmental History of Sugar in Northeast Brazil* (Chapel Hill: University of North Carolina Press, 2010).

[34] John McNeill, "Agriculture, Forests, and Ecological History: Brazil, 1500–1983," *Environmental Review* 10 (1986).

[35] Sebastian Dorsch and Michael Wagner, "Gezähmter Dschungel–industrialisierte Agrarwirtschaft–romantisierter Landloser. Die Mystifizierung des Ländlichen in der deagrarisierten Gesellschaft Brasiliens," *Geschichte und Gesellschaft* 33 (2007), 548–9.

Due to the dramatic decrease of the Amerindian population after the arrival of the Portuguese, flood agriculture partly deserted the Amazon's riverbanks, which were quickly covered by new trees.[36] The patterns of colonial occupation, characterized by a concentration of non-native populations in coastal areas, where the main production and exchange activities took place, kept less accessible, far western regions beyond the scope of deforestation. Even during the imperial (1822–89) and so-called old republican (1889–1930) periods, agrarian colonization movements engendered by demographic pressure occurred primarily in the southern half of the country, mainly to serve the extension of coffee production. Planter oligarchies from the richest federal states, whose fluctuating alliances and rivalries constituted the power structure of the Old Republic, had no interest in favoring the emergence of production activities in the Amazon.

Centrally driven, integrative policies of territorial exploitation only emerged after 1930, when the army forcibly installed statesman Getúlio Vargas into power in a move intended to curb the political hegemony of São Paulo's coffee producers. Vargas seized power as a result of a conflict between different regional interests much more than of the intent to free Brazil from its dependency on coffee. But the context of the world depression, which engendered a dramatic crisis of liquidity through a brutal fall in coffee export prices, convinced the new government of the necessity to diversify the country's economic structure.[37] From then on, the state sought to put in place a national project of centrally controlled expansion of production activities. "Modernity" and then "development" became mottos distilled from the top to all sectors of society, which had mixed consequences for Brazil's relationship to its forests. On the one hand, the progressive transformation of Brazil from an agrarian into an industrial country led to an ever-growing pressure on natural wealth. On the other hand, the shift from a model of spontaneous exploitation of the soil and subsoil to a state-regulated strategy of agricultural and extractive production created a new space for conservationist approaches. Against the background of this complex articulation between exploitation and conservation, national-developmentalism reshaped the Amazon as the ultimate space for the Brazilian nation to appropriate in its path toward development.

---

[36] Shawn William Miller, *An Environmental History of Latin America* (New York: Cambridge University Press, 2007), 57.

[37] Stanley E. Hilton, "Vargas and Brazilian Economic Development, 1930–1945," *Journal of Economic History* 35, no. 4 (1975).

Putting the State at the Service of Development

Vargas governed at the head of a provisional government (1930–4) and subsequently a constitutional government (1934–7), then as a dictator (1937–45), and finally as a democratically elected president (1951–4). He claimed that Brazil should develop its own industry to reduce dependency on foreign economies. He endowed the country with new tools supposed to sustain this perspective, such as a substantial increase of state investment in education and health, the first brushstrokes of a policy of economic planning, and the creation of various credit institutions. He also launched a basic labor protection structure, as well as a system of labor control and organization. This structural shift in the governmental organization of production activities showed results, especially between 1933 and 1939, when the average annual growth of industrial production reached 11.2 percent.[38]

This success was equally due to the government's efforts to attract foreign capital and firms in order to finance the creation of basic infrastructure and a national industrial park.[39] Such efforts stood in apparent contradiction with Vargas's national populist discourse, put into practice through some decisions thought to increase Brazil's sovereignty over natural resources. For example, the government engaged in a process of nationalization of the soil and subsoil, which culminated in a law of 1953 establishing a state monopoly over the exploration and refining of petroleum. Vargas's approach, identified by historians as the emergence in Brazil of "national-developmentalism" was to combine economic development with national interest.[40] It did not take form immediately in the early 1930s, but rather in the long run, with the adoption of a policy of import-substituting industrialization (ISI). The ISI strategy resulted in measures such as the 1953 prohibition of the import of built-up motor vehicles, thought to favor the creation of a local auto industry.[41]

Industrial growth under Vargas partly profited from a new government philosophy, according to which the central state would oversee the economic modernization of the country. The creation, between 1930

---

[38] Ibid., 757.
[39] Pedro Paulo Zahluth Bastos, "A construção do nacional-desenvolvimentismo de Getúlio Vargas e a dinâmica de interação entre estado e mercado nos setores de base," *Revista economia* 7, no. 4 (2006), 257.
[40] Izabel Noll, "La construction du Varguisme. L'Ordre pour principe, le progrès comme fin" (EHESS, 2003).
[41] Helen Shapiro, *Engines of Growth: The State and Transnational Auto Companies in Brazil* (New York: Cambridge University Press, 1994), 76.

and 1945, of expert councils, planning institutes, state companies, and foundations orienting the legislative process, financing industrialization, and developing technological research served this goal.[42] The dedication of all government policies to the development of industry, prioritizing heavily polluting sectors such as steel, petrochemicals, or mining, left only little room for environmental concern. However, the consolidation of the administrative structure and the generalized promotion of technical expertise offered spaces for lobbying for those who, in Brazilian educated circles, had conservationist tendencies. The capacity for political articulation of a handful of scientists and technocrats concerned with nature, and well positioned in prestigious institutions such as the National Museum or the Geographical Society of Rio de Janeiro, proved legislatively efficient.[43]

In 1934, the government passed a "Forest Code," which constituted the first serious legislative basis for a federal policy of forest conservation. It created a public fund to finance initiatives of conservation, oriented by the Federal Forestry Council, whose representatives were recruited in institutions known for their conservationist concern, such as the National Museum, the Botanic Garden of Rio de Janeiro, and the Touring Club of Brazil.[44] The Code, which distinguished forests destined for economic exploitation from forests requiring measures of soil, water, and biodiversity protection, had limited effects. Although sixteen national parks were created on its basis from 1934 to 1965, their establishment did not receive serious infrastructural support. Thus, the appraisal of the conservationist laws from the Vargas era both highlights the potential role of the state as a space that can expand the advocacy of nature, and the difficulty for conservationist and industrialist goals to merge into a common politico-economic model.[45]

The national-developmentalist planners saw the interior, still widely forested parts of Brazil as spaces to be conquered, in order to make their soil and subsoil resources economically exploitable. From the late 1930s, the Varguist discourse started to link its vision of modernization more strongly

[42] Laurent Vidal, *De Nova Lisboa à Brasília. L'invention d'une capitale (19e–20e siècles)* (Paris: IHEAL, 2002), 158.
[43] Dean, *With Broadax and Firebrand*, 260.
[44] Roseli Senna Ganem and Titan de Lima, "Código florestal: revisão sim, mais desmatamento não," in *Os 30 anos da política nacional do meio ambiente conquistas e perspectivas*, ed. Suzi Huff Theodoro (Rio de Janeiro: Garamond, 2011), 253.
[45] José Luiz de Andrade Franco and José Augusto Drummond, "Wilderness and the Brazilian Mind (I): Nation and Nature in Brazil from the 1920s to the 1940s," *Environmental History* 13, no. 4 (2008), 737; Dean, *With Broadax and Firebrand*, 278–9.

with the idea of national unity, by promoting the economic integration of Brazil's less populated regions. The motto became the "interiorization of development," concretely applicable through the occupation of the countryside and the decongestion of the littoral.[46] In his traditional end-of-year speech on December 31, 1939, Vargas said it was "an urgent reality to climb the mountain, step on the central plain and stretch ourselves into the latitudes."[47] The government encouraged this "march to the West," through the establishment of "national farming colonies" absorbing waves of migration principally in the states of Goiás and Mato Grosso during the 1940s.[48]

At the end of the Vargas era, this expansionist view expressed itself in the idea of a national policy of colonization of the Amazon, illustrated by the creation in 1953 of the first federal agency in charge of the economic development of the region, the Superintendência do Plano de Valorização Econômica da Amazônia (SPVEA).[49] In practice, the colonization of the Amazon remained little more than patriotic poetry during Vargas's rule, apart from the short-lived, circumstantial revitalization of the rubber economy between 1940 and 1945.[50] In the absence of substantial state investment, the Amazon's gross regional product continued until 1956 to grow about two points below the national average, and SPVEA even defined itself as a mere "experimental" project.[51] Yet, Vargas marked minds through his famous "Speech of the Amazon River" in October 1940 in Manaus, exhorting the country to "resume the crusade of deforestation and overcome step by step the great enemy of Amazonian progress: immense and unpopulated space."[52] The speech, which would serve as historical shibboleth for colonization policies in the following decades, made the penetration of the Amazon a necessary

---

[46] Maurício Andrés Ribeiro, "Origens mineiras do desenvolvimento sustentável no Brasil: ideias e práticas," in *Desenvolvimento, justiça e meio ambiente*, ed. José Augusto Pádua (Belo Horizonte: UFMG, 2009), 82.

[47] Vidal, *Nova Lisboa à Brasília*, 163.

[48] The rhetoric of the "march to the West" quickly transformed into a dominant discourse promoting a "march to the Amazon," as is shown by Maria Veronica Secreto, "A ocupação dos 'espaços vazios' no Governo Vargas: do 'discurso do Rio Amazonas' à saga dos soldados da borracha," *Estudos Históricos*, no. 40 (2007).

[49] Mário de Barros Cavalcanti, *Da SPVEA à SUDAM: (1964–1967)* (Belém: SUDAM, 1967).

[50] Garfield, *In Search of the Amazon*.

[51] Marvin Katzman, "Paradoxes of Amazonian Development in a 'Resource Starved' World," *Journal of Developing Areas* 10 (1976), 454; SPVEA, *Política de desenvolvimento da Amazônia. Superintendência do Plano de Valorização Económica da Amazônia 1954–1960* (Rio de Janeiro: SPVEA, 1961), 28.

[52] Allegretti, "A construção social de políticas ambientais," 113.

step in the process of territorial unification underpinning the notion of national development.

That this notion had become the main governing principle in Brazil is illustrated by Vargas's" last official trip in 1954. Like many of his public appearances, this trip to the state of Minas Gerais was meant to celebrate the emerging heavy industry sector: it brought Vargas together with state governor Juscelino Kubitschek at the inauguration of a giant steelwork mill.[53] Although nobody could predict that Vargas would die in power two weeks later, seen from today's point of view, this moment might look like a symbolic transfer between the two men of the task of developing Brazil. Kubitschek was elected president in 1955 representing the Social Democratic Party. Although he had no direct political filiation to Vargas, he similarly articulated the processes of industrialization, state consolidation, and territorial integration, merging into a political project of modernization. His "targets program," a plan supposed to achieve "fifty years [of development] in five," contained thirty precise objectives distributed over five big sectors, namely, energy, transport, agro-food, basic industries, and "education to development." Kubitschek's objective of boosting industrialization through planning proved effective insofar as economic growth reached a yearly average of 7.8 percent during his time in office.[54]

Kubitschek's pompous conception of national-developmentalism implicitly fixed the integration of the rain forest as the horizon of Brazil's modernization. His main achievement, the building of the new capital, Brasília, from 1956 to 1960, on an unpopulated plateau of the Brazilian central steppes, gave a decisive impulsion to the territorial penetration of the country. Kubitschek expressed this goal in sentences such as "We must conquer our land, possess our soil, march toward the West, turn our back to the sea" (1957).[55] Brasília moved Brazil's center of gravity closer than ever to the forest areas of the north. This historical march of the nation took on a nearly mystical dimension, as it featured in the first mass celebrated in the new capital city, when the archbishop of São Paulo, Dom Carlos Carmelo de Vasconcelos, announced that "Brasília is the trampoline to the conquest of the Amazon."[56] As a next step, the

---

[53] Sikkink, *Ideas and Institutions*, 122.

[54] Dorsch and Wagner, *Gezähmter Dschungel–industrialisierte Agrarwirtschaft–romantisierter Landloser*, 554.

[55] Dieter Richter, *Die Fazenda am Cristalino: eine Rinderfarm im Gebiet des feuchten Passatwaldes Brasiliens; ein Film der Volkswagenwerk AG; Lehrerbegleitheft* (Wolfsburg: Volkswagen A.G., 1980), 4. In: VW Unternehmensarchiv.

[56] Maurício Vaitsman, *Brasília e Amazônia: reportagens* (Rio de Janeiro: SPVEA, 1959), 54.

federal government started the construction of the Belém–Brasília, the first highway to cross the Amazon. Many environmentalists would later see this highway as the founding step of a predatory colonization, leading to an accelerated deforestation in the last third of the twentieth century. Senator Evandro Carreira declared during a parliamentary debate in June 1976 that Kubitschek, by building the new capital and the highway linking it to Belém, "was one of the great criminals in relation to the Amazon" because "the opening of roads is an insult to its ecology."[57]

The "War of Development" of the Military Regime

Vargas and Kubitschek were not the only leaders to govern Brazil from the 1930s to the 1960s, but they gave life to a national imagery of development. They cultivated an esthetic association between central power and economic progress, not least by regularly posing in pictures together with "modern" objects symbolizing productive activities, such as motor vehicles, factories, or skyscrapers. Their personalities incarnated developmentalist willpower, for they physically irradiated energy, rapidity, and even territorial unity through their multiple, well-orchestrated, and media-reported travels throughout the country. In 1940, Vargas, the first president to ever visit Brazil's central regions, portrayed himself as a twentieth-century *bandeirante* as he flew to Mato Grosso and rode on horseback in a forested river island where he came to break the geographic "isolation" of a "fierce" Indian tribe.[58] Kubitschek displayed his determination to push through territorial unification as soon as in 1955, when he logged more than 205,000 kilometers in a record time, performing the first truly nationwide electoral campaign in Brazilian history.[59]

Besides, these two presidential figures incarnated a populist leadership, which fit with the national-developmentalist tune, as they sought the direct support of the working class and resorted to emotionalizing evocations of patriotism. At the same time, this unmediated relationship between a president and the people was intolerable to certain fractions of the Brazilian elites. Especially conservative sectors of the Brazilian army, organized around structures of corporatist reproduction such as the National School of War, which trained military officers, saw in populism a perverted form of government.[60] After they contributed to the

---

[57] Evandro Carreira, *Recado Amazônico*, vol. 4 (Brasília: Senado Federal, 1977), 295.

[58] Garfield, *A luta indígena no coração do Brasil*, 35–8.

[59] Wolfe, *Autos and Progress*, 113.

[60] Maud Chirio, "La politique des militaires. Mobilisations et révoltes d'officiers sous la dictature Brésilienne (1961–1978)" (Université Paris I – Panthéon Sorbonne, 2009), 37–8.

pressure leading Vargas to suicide in 1954, and unsuccessfully attempted to block Kubitschek's investiture as president, the military found an ideal target in laborist João Goulart. "Jango," as the latter was called, acceded to presidential office in 1961, although one year earlier he had only been elected as vice president. From the start of his mandate, his legitimacy was fiercely contested: he came to power due to the unexpected withdrawal of Kubitschek's successor, Jânio Quadros, and incarnated, for many conservative Brazilians, the far left of Varguism.

Despite a context of inflation (in part in consequence of Kubitschek's spending policies), Jango projected a substantial income redistribution in favor of the working class and was tempted by a radical reform of the land property system.[61] He also established restrictions on the circulation of foreign capital (for example, by firmly increasing the limits of profit remittances) and promoted a strict implementation of the ISI. As the Congress refused to follow the president in this path, Jango's term turned into a crisis of democratic institutions. A large coalition of interests (bankers, businessmen, rural landlords, conservative politicians), feeling threatened by Jango's political projects, organized an intensive propaganda campaign against him.[62] On the pretext of corruption and communist danger, the military overthrew him on April 1, 1964.

The conspiracy was connected with aspirations exogenous to the army: the coup had a popular base, at least within the middle class.[63] Especially a myriad of local women's leagues, close to the conservative segments of the Catholic Church, campaigned all over the country against the "bolshevization of Brazil." Several urban demonstrations in March 1964 gathered millions of participants and contributed to the social support of the putsch.[64] The popular fervor preceding the overthrow of Goulart has recently led historians to insist on denominating the political system created in 1964 a "civilian-military" regime.[65] However, as Carlos Fico underlines, even though the movement that politically

[61] Angela de Castro Gomes and Jorge Ferreira, *Jango: as múltiplas faces* (Rio de Janeiro: FGV, 2007), 142–4.
[62] Carlos Fico, "Versões e controvérsias sobre 1964 e a ditadura militar," *Revista Brasileira de História* 24, no. 47 (2004), 52.
[63] Carlos Fico, "La classe média Brésilienne face au régime militaire. Du soutien à la désaffection (1964–1985)," *Vingtieme siècle* 105, no. 1 (2010), 155–7.
[64] Solange de Deus Simões, *Deus, pátria e família. As mulheres no golpe de 1964* (Petrópolis: Vozes, 1985), 105–12.
[65] Maria Helena Moreira Alves, *Estado e oposição no Brasil. 1964–1984* (Bauru: Edusc, 2005); Daniel Aarão Reis Filho, *Ditadura militar, esquerdas e sociedade* (Rio de Janeiro: Zahar, 2000).

destabilized Goulart was civilian, the coup of 1964 was undoubtedly carried out by the army.[66] The governments instituted after this coup were all coordinated by and in a large majority composed of military officers. This makes the appellation "military regime" acceptable, as long as one recognizes the notable role civilian actors played in support of the coup.

The first military president, Humberto de Alencar Castelo Branco, felt mandated by the "revolution" of 1964 to restore the economic order. His government abandoned social concern for the working class, limited credit and purchase power in order to recover a "healthy economy," and stopped the restrictions for the participation of foreign capital in Brazil. This radical rupture between the economic line under Goulart and that under Castelo Branco only prevailed for a short historical moment. Looking at the long-term period from 1930 to 1980, economic historians have rather noted a remarkable continuity of the various federal governments on major features such as import substitution, focal points of economic growth, or the progressive intensification of foreign participation in the economy.[67]

Instead of pursuing Castelo Branco's monetarist line, the following military presidents returned to a policy of state-funded growth. Despite this major discontinuity, the politics of development during the military regimes featured a number of common characteristics. This common platform comprehended an almost unrestricted openness toward foreign capital and the financing of growth to a significant extent through foreign loans. It also included a policy favorable to industrial monopolistic expansion through the intervention of the state in the production process, notably via economic planning. Finally, it comprised a redistribution of the national income in favor of capitalist accumulation and at the expense of workers, and the increase of economic investment in regions categorized as underdeveloped, especially the Amazon.[68] In this perspective, the growth policy of the military regime was not disposed to restricting itself through preoccupations about the environment. Particularly the government of President Emílio Garrastazu Médici (1969–74), marked by pharaonic highway and dam projects, displayed an absence of awareness of pollution and its consequences for ecology and human health. For Viola,

[66] Fico, "Versões e controvérsias sobre 1964 e a ditadura militar."

[67] João Paulo dos Reis Velloso, *O último trem para Paris: de Getúlio a Sarney: "milagres," choques e crises do Brasil moderno* (Rio de Janeiro: Nova Fronteira, 1986); Werner Baer, *The Brazilian Economy: Growth and Development* (Boulder, CO: Lynne Rienner, 2008).

[68] Günter Schölermann, "Volkswagen do Brasil: Entwicklung und Wachstum unter den wirtschaftspolitischen Verhältnissen in Brasilien" (Universität Oldenburg, 1982), 12.

the Medici mandate was the paroxysm of an "ideology of accelerated and predatory growth." In the midst of the Médici years, the Brazilian government went so far as to publish advertisements in the media of industrial countries, inviting polluting industries to transfer to Brazil, where they would not undergo any ecological control or tax.[69]

More than ever, development under the military regime took the form of a top-down political project, underpinned by the repression of dissident initiatives. In 1965, the existing political parties were dissolved to be replaced by two formations. The Aliança Renovadora Nacional (ARENA) constituted the political base of the military governments. The Movimento Democrático Brasileiro (MDB), in fact the only authorized parliamentary opposition, was an aggregation of politicians covering a large spectrum that went from Marxism to moderate conservatism. From 1965 to 1968, a series of laws and "institutional acts" set the basis of authoritarian rule, limiting civil rights, creating a "crime against national security" that would serve to eliminate political opponents, and transferring a large part of the legislative competencies to the executive power.[70] The media started to be systematically subjected to censorship. In this climate of inhibition, many newssheets or magazines became vehicles to praise the grandiosity of the government's infrastructural projects and "educate" Brazilians about the virtues of industrial growth. In fact, a law of 1970 explicitly defined the role of the Special Committee of Public Relations, an agency in charge of the circulation of governmental propaganda in the mass media, as that of "motivating and stimulating the collective will to the national effort of development."[71]

In order for dissident voices not to disturb the idyllic image of a country marching toward material wealth, an intelligence agency was created to track down subversive individuals and started to resort frequently to the use of torture. This system of persecution primarily targeted leftist groups and trade union activists. The escalation toward dictatorial rule culminated in 1968 with "institutional act number 5" (AI-5), which suppressed the fundamental right of the accused to habeas corpus in case of

---

[69] Eduardo Viola, "O movimento ecológico no Brasil (1974–1986), Do ambientalismo à ecopolítica," in *Ecologia e política no Brasil*, ed. José Augusto Pádua (Rio de Janeiro: Espaço e Tempo, 1987), 83–4.

[70] For this and the following information about the formation of the military regime: Alves, *Estado e oposição no Brasil*; Thomas E. Skidmore, *The Politics of Military Rule in Brazil, 1964–1985* (New York: Oxford University Press, 1989).

[71] Luisa Maria N. de Moura e Silva, "'Segurança e esenvolvimento': a comunicação do Governo Medici," *Intercom* 9, no. 55 (1986), 44.

"crime against national security." Interestingly, the governmental concept of "national security" was intimately linked with the much-proclaimed development imperative, as the military considered economic growth a necessity to deviate a fantasized communist threat.[72]

As the authoritarian logic of the regime implied that no part of Brazil should escape state control, the interest in regions perceived as desert was even greater than in the previous governments. In particular, the occupation of the Amazon was a central preoccupation. This attention to the rain forest area corresponded to the geographic continuity of the Varguist march to the West and the building of Brasília, but it also lay in the lineage of the successful prospecting effected in the region in the years preceding the military coup. Many major and potentially lucrative discoveries had been made in the Amazon from the mid-1950s to the early 1960s. The oil-refining company Petrobrás found salgema, oil, and gas ores, notably around 1955 in Nova Olinda, in the state of Amazonas.[73] In the late 1950s and the early 1960s, gold-seekers found new gold and cassiterite ores in the Tapajos (Pará), where some private companies discovered reserves of manganese and bauxite. The ever-enlarging inventory of mineral riches excited the appetite of politicians for the exploitation of the forest.

Besides, the objective of full economic exploitation of the Amazon integrated itself perfectly into the doctrine of development as a condition of national security, as expressed in the writings of General Golbery, the army's most influential ideologue. His book *Geopolitics of Brazil*, published in 1966, exerted much influence on the government's economic and military strategy. One of the points of his doctrine was to see the occupation of the Amazon as a necessity for preventing foreign penetration of the region. Golbery defined the integration of the "empty spaces" of Brazil (made "passive," "devitalized," and "deprived of creative energy" because of their "lack of people") as a national priority.[74] Therefore, it was urgent to "overflow with civilization" the Amazon watershed.

Before Golbery, other intellectuals had warned that if Brazil "did not fully occupy the Amazon, someone else would."[75] Historian Artur Cesar

[72] Gilvan Veiga Dockhorn, *Quando a ordem é segurança e o progresso é desenvolvimento* (Porto Alegre: EDIPUCRS, 2002), 56–8.

[73] Breno Augusto dos Santos, *Amazônia: potencial mineral e perspectivas de desenvolvimento* (São Paulo: EdUSP, 1981), 12–3.

[74] Golbery do Couto e Silva, *Geopolítica do Brasil* (Rio de Janeiro: José Olympio, 1966), 44.

[75] Robert F. Shillings, "Economic Development of the Brazilian Amazon," *The Geographical Journal* 151, no. 1 (1984), 50.

Ferreira Reis published a successful book in 1960 called *Amazonia and the International Greed*, raising the specter of a foreign invasion.[76] After the military coup, Reis was appointed governor of the state of Amazonas by Castelo Branco. In the middle of the 1960s, a project of the U.S.-based research center Hudson Institute speculated about the possibility of building a huge artificial lake situated on the border of various Amazonian countries.[77] Although it was nothing but a scientific study, the Hudson initiative spread panic among Brazilian nationalists, who saw behind it the imperialistic hand of the United States. Journalists and intellectuals started to write that the Hudson plan heralded the perspective of an international protectorate dispossessing Brazil from its control over the rain forest. Eudes Prado Lopes, chief engineer at Petrobrás, saw as a great danger the simple fact that foreign scientists might be researching on the Amazon.[78] The investigations pushed through by the Hudson Institute, he said, "put considerable information about the country's politico-economic structure into their hands, chiefly regarding its natural wealth infrastructure and conditions of soil exploitation." "This," he added, "evidently is a threat to the equilibrium of national security."

In this xenophobic context, essentially fomented by the regime's own ideologues, Castelo Branco and his henchmen were prompt to make of the Amazon a showcase of their politics of development. In the logic of the military regime, the Amazon was to Brazil what developing countries were to the world: an area where economic modernization should intervene as a priority. Thus, in a speech in front of an audience that included Castelo Branco, Reis depicted Brazil as a country divided into three areas.[79] The first was the area of prosperity. It corresponded to the south and southeast of the country and was characterized by strong indicators of progress. The second was an area "marching to development," the northeast, a region of poverty moved by its determination to go forward. Finally, the Amazon was "the Third World" of Brazil, a listless area that needed to be developed urgently.

A consensus existed in considering the Amazonian question a priority, but not everybody within the regime agreed with the same conception of national development. The oil shocks of 1973 and 1978–1979, as well as a debt crisis, which grew in the early 1980s, brought about lively debates

---

[76] Artur Cezar Ferreira Reis, *A Amazônia e a cobiça internacional* (Rio de Janeiro Edinova, 1960).

[77] Genival Rabelo, *Ocupação da Amazônia* (Rio de Janeiro: Gernasa, 1968), 23.

[78] "Albuquerque aceita dolares na Amazônia," *A folha de São Paulo*, January 8, 1968.

[79] SUDAM, ed. *Operação Amazônia*, 55–6.

within the political arenas of the regime about sticking points such as the participation of foreign capital and firms in Brazilian development. To be sure, the civilian-military regime was never completely unified. In twenty years of military rule, there were five different presidents, each governing between three and five years. The ideology and practices of their administrations were by no means linear.[80] Although historical studies have pointed out the diversity between the different phases of the regime, only little has been said about the political division occurring at given moments – if not constantly – within its institutional structure.[81] In reality, there was a broad spectrum of shades within the political expression of the military regime's actors. Questions like the role left to free enterprise, the distribution of the social benefits of growth, or the place of oil-consuming activities in the economy were often the subject of diverging views. Divisions did not necessarily occur at the top of the government, but certainly within the ministries, the federal administration, and the ARENA party.

A large study of this multilayered politico-economic spectrum is missing. The following chapters, which do not have the divisions within the military regime as a central theme, will not fill such a gap, but they will provide an insight into the very complex, often concealed war that took place within the regime between different conceptions of development. Unexpectedly, the question of the management of natural resources offers a window through which the vast spectrum of opinions within the regime becomes visible.

Volkswagen as Traveling Model

The military regime was at least unanimous in its support of the automobile industry as a symbol of modernity. In this aspect, the regime did not differ from its predecessors, for VW always benefited from good relations with governments in Brazil. The German firm successfully took root in the country in 1953 because its strategy of making a car for the middle class fit into the national-developmentalist intentions of Vargas. In the following decades, VW managed to appear not as a representative of European imperialism, but as a truly "Brazilianized" institution. This

---

[80] Rubens Penha Cysne, "A economia brasileira no período militar," *Estudos econômicos* 23, no. 2 (1993).

[81] Saulo de Castro Lima, "Da substituição de importações ao Brasil potência: concepções do desenvolvimento 1964–1979," *Aurora V*, no. 7 (2011); Velloso, *O último trem para Paris*; Maud Chirio, "La politique des militaires."

certainly helped the Brazilian government to encourage the company to participate in the colonization of the Amazon.

From Germany to Brazil

It is useful to briefly recall the origin of the company, born out of Hitler's wish of making a people's car, as this idea actually remained VW's raison d'être for the postwar decades. The people's car was supposed to break with the German tradition of luxurious cars and reach a scale of mass production capable of offering the middle class an affordable vehicle for everyday use.[82] The project emerged in 1937 under the name "Society for the Preparation of the German Volkswagen," but the people's car idea did not concretize under Nazi rule, as in wartime the Volkswagen factory served as an armament production plant. It was in the first place the British occupier, which, after Germany was defeated by the Allies decided to continue the processing of the people's car project.[83] At the same time, Volkswagen's Nazi origins left indelible traces, especially in view of the massive exploitation of slave labor during the war period. More than 11,000 forced laborers, especially from Russia and Poland, often pulled from concentration camps, were held in the VW factory in dehumanizing conditions.[84]

Even decades later, this troubled past has occasionally incited external critics to demand of the company a strong ethic of responsibility toward workers, especially in economically marginalized countries. This exigency appears in an allusion made by sociologist Reinhard Doleschal, who said in 1982 that, "especially in view of Volkswagen history, we have to ask whether everything has been undertaken to remove as fast as possible the unbearable conditions reigning in the Brazilian and South-African VW factories."[85] Such historical awareness did not particularly animate VW leadership during the company's international expansion in the 1950s/1960s. Neither in Germany nor in the countries where VW opened foreign branches did the firm organize the conditions to reflect on its own history of slave labor – at least until 1986, when the company

---

[82] David Kiley, *Getting the Bugs Out: The Rise, Fall and Comeback of Volkswagen in America* (New York: John Wiley & Sons, 2002), 36–48.

[83] Volker Wellhöner, *"Wirtschaftswunder" – Weltmarkt – westdeutscher Fordismus. Der Fall Volkswagen* (Münster: Westfälisches Dampfbot, 1996), 99.

[84] Kiley, *Getting the Bugs Out*, 55–6.

[85] Reinhard Doleschal, "Zur geschichtlichen Entwicklung des Volkswagenkonzerns," in *Wohin läuft VW? Die Automobilproduktion in der Wirtschaftskrise*, ed. R. Doleschal et al. (Reinbek: Rowohlt, 1982), 18–54, 53.

asked a team of historians to research the topic.[86] That the case had been little researched until this date explains why, when a forced labor scandal appeared at Cristalino in the mid-1980s, nobody thought about drawing a comparison with forced labor in the Volkswagen factory during the war.

The company's Nazi past proved an almost absent topic as the German economy, from 1948 on, reemerged out of its ashes to become one of the world's main industrial powers, with VW being a foreground actor of this "economic miracle."[87] In the context of an impressively expanding German market of durable goods, VW became by far Germany's main motor vehicle company and exporter. It also symbolized the economic miracle because it built the image of its plants as social enclaves, offering the best salaries of the sector, workers' profit-sharing and social services at reduced tariffs.[88] The social-friendly image of VW, the first German company to introduce the forty-hour workweek in 1958, was in part due to its model of democratic governance, which included an above-average influence of the trade unions. For these reasons, VW was seen as the archetype of an economic growth that favored both the elites and the working class.[89] The middle class also participated in this project, and not only as consumers. As a result of the "VW law," adopted in 1960 in the aftermath of a compromise made between the main German political parties, VW became a joint stock company held at 60 percent by small shareholders. The remaining 40 percent was divided equally between the West German federal state and the state of Lower Saxony, where the main VW plant was located. By virtue of a specific system of governance, the exponents of public authorities in the company board had a veto right over all important decisions. The VW law also foresaw the creation of a "Volkswagen Foundation" to promote higher education and research, financed out of part of VW dividends.

As it started in the early 1950s to expand abroad, VW also stood as an ambassador for Germany's international renaissance. As *Der Spiegel* magazine wrote in 1968 in the obituary of VW's first postwar CEO, Heinrich Nordhoff, "the humpy vehicles coming out of his factories signified in 140 countries the rebirth of the defeated people. The Beetle showed the

---

[86] Hans Mommsen and Manfred Grieger, *Das Volkswagenwerk und seine Arbeiter im Dritten Reich* (Düsseldorf: Econ, 1996).

[87] Rieger, *The People's Car*, 123–87.

[88] Reinhard Doleschal et al., "... zum Beispiel Volkswagen," in *Wohin läuft VW?* Ed. Reinhard Doleschal et al. (Reinbek: Rowohlt, 1982), 7–14.

[89] Doleschal, *"Zur geschichtlichen Entwicklung des Volkswagenkonzerns,"* 46–9.

whole world that the Germans were starting to move again."[90] In light of this international reputation, VW advertised throughout the world the export of a German model of capitalism with a human face. A subsidiary was founded in Canada in 1952, Brazil in 1953, the United States in 1955, South Africa in 1956, and France in 1960. Others opened in the 1960s, including in several Latin American countries. Volkswagen was present as an export company on the international market even before the creation of these foreign branches, as the export strategy was the condition for pushing through the logic of mass production.[91] Yet, in some of the export countries, local conditions made it unsustainable in the long run not to install a local company branch with its own plants. This was the case in Western countries like the United States or France, where the well-established domestic competition made local establishment a condition for being able to compete with equal weapons.[92] This was also the case in countries finding themselves in the opposed situation, namely the lack of an existing automobile industry, for example, Brazil, Australia, or South Africa. There, governments set measures to hinder the access of vehicle importers to the national market, in order to favor the emergence of a local industry.

Together with the strengthening of the national economy, a growing part of the German population became concerned with the problems of poverty in the "Third World." Volkswagen started to portray its activities within countries of the Global South as humanitarian. "More than cars": "a partner of the world" became in the 1970s the motto of VW's expansion.[93] This meant that Volkswagen identified in its transmission to Brazil, Mexico, or South Africa of economic, social, and technological instruments for development one of its missions. In communication campaigns, VW boasted about bringing "development aid in the best sense" and putting the human being at the center of its action. Brazil was the main showcase of this strategy of establishment in emerging countries. As Carl Horst Hahn, a former VW chairman, remembers in his memoirs, "Brazil was our flagship object number one: exemplary social services spoke for our entrepreneurial philosophy there."[94] In Brazil, where a president had

---

[90] "Mister Volkswagen," *Der Spiegel*, April 22, 1968.

[91] Wellhöner, "Wirtschaftswunder," 211.

[92] Ibid., 107.

[93] Öffentlichkeitsarbeit Volkswagenwerk A. G., *Volkswagen – ein transnationales Unternehmen, Partner der Welt* (Wolfsburg: Volkswagenwerk A. G., 1980). In: VW Unternehmensarchiv.

[94] Carl H. Hahn, *Meine Jahre mit Volkswagen* (München: Signum, 2005), 164.

convinced voters by claiming to achieve fifty years of development in five, VW's intimate link with the German economic miracle was an asset. The recovery achieved in a few years by a German industry that everybody thought destroyed by the war was a suitable symbol for emerging countries hoping for accelerated growth. It could not but raise the enthusiasm of the Brazilian developmentalists. That VW's social-humanist propaganda was particularly focused on Brazil also had to do with the growing importance taken by the country in the company's global strategy. In the 1950s, Volkswagen do Brasil (VWB) became – by far – VW's most important financial engagement outside Germany.[95] The importance of the Brazilian subsidiary grew even more during the 1970s, when Brazil had its own "economic miracle." From 1971 to 1975 VW's volume of production in Brazil in comparison to that of VW in Germany grew from 17 percent to 48 percent. The growth of VW do Brasil processed at a speed that VW senior management in Germany did not expect as it hesitatingly started a business in the country in the early 1950s.[96]

VW's "Brazilianization"

The fact that in 1953 Vargas assured his support for the project of building a VW plant in São Paulo confirmed the existence of a favorable political climate in Brazil for the expansion of the auto industry.[97] The same year, VW made its first step into the local market by opening a small assembly plant, whose few hundred workers mounted 3,000 passenger cars until 1957. While Ford or General Motors (GM) had been offering large-size quality cars for the happy few, the Beetle immediately found its public in the emerging Brazilian middle class thanks to its comparatively low price, good resistance, simple mechanics, small size, and low fuel consumption.[98] As early as 1962, VW became market leader with 53,342 vehicles produced that year. While in the late 1950s a majority of vehicle parts was imported from Germany, in 1962, 98 percent of the components were manufactured in Brazil.[99] This figure was reached under pressure from Kubitschek, who believed that the access of a growing number of Brazilians to personal vehicles would contribute to opening up the

---

[95] Ibid., 222.

[96] Schölermann, "Volkswagen do Brasil," 41.

[97] Luiz Alberto Moniz Bandeira, *Das deutsche Wirtschaftswunder und die Entwicklung Brasiliens – Die Beziehungen Deutschlands zu Brasilien und Lateinamerika* (Frankfurt am Main: Vervuert, 1995), 86.

[98] Shapiro, *Engines of Growth*, 110.

[99] Wellhöner, "Wirtschaftswunder."

country's interior. By facilitating individual travel within the national territory, passenger cars should also strengthen Brazilians' patriotic feeling. Hence Kubitschek launched a historically unprecedented highway-building program, and ordered that the new capital city, Brasília, be designed and built according to technical criteria facilitating car travel.

Kubitschek almost built the Brazilian automotive industry from zero, intervening personally to convince reluctant car brands to develop their production in the country. In 1956, he created the Executive Group for the Automobile Industry, a commission organizing the expansion of the automotive industrial park, which was responsible for fixing production targets, validating single investment projects, and monitoring their progress.[100] For Kubitschek, the automotive industry was purely and simply a synonym of development. He counted on this industry to correct the unfavorable position of Brazil in the international division of labor. In this respect, Kubitschek's strategy of industrial growth did not substantially differ from the choices later made by the military regime: the dynamic of growth was entirely based on the production of durable goods, collective transport was neglected, and the railway networks left abandoned in favor of road transport.[101] This meant that multinational car companies became the central actors in Brazilian economic growth. With his outspoken demands addressed to VW senior management ("The Volkswagen is the ideal vehicle for our roads. I need your car"), Kubitschek contributed to VWB's development into a mass producer.[102] As on March 1, 1959 the first Beetle entirely produced in Brazil came off the assembly line, the president was sitting in the vehicle, smiling to photographers side by side with São Paulo's governor and VWB's general director.[103] When a couple of months later VW's international head Heinz Nordhoff inaugurated the first VW factory in the industrial outskirts of São Paulo, it was again in the presence of Kubitschek.

VW's ability to develop good contacts with the top Brazilian political elites was largely thanks to its partnership with the local firm Monteiro Aranha (MA), which held 20 percent of VWB's shares.[104] Originally a glass producer founded in 1917, MA had a long experience of negotiation with political decision makers because of its participation in a wide

[100] Shapiro, *Engines of Growth*, 48–9.
[101] Philippe Faucher, *Le Brésil des militaires* (Montréal: Presses de l'Université de Montréal 1981), 131–2.
[102] Wellhöner, "Wirtschaftswunder," 274–5.
[103] Alexander Gromow, *Eu amo Fusca* (São Paulo: Ripress, 2003).
[104] Evans, *Dependent Development*, 156.

array of businesses, many of them linked with public contracts. MA's help proved crucial for VW to obtain import licenses – a delicate task, due to the strategy of ISI practiced by Brazil. However, VW knew convincing ways to overcome the restrictions implied by the import-substitution policy, as was proved in 1961 by delivering free personal vehicles to Brazilian senators and congressmen before the vote of a law on duty-free imports.[105]

Only in 1962 did the understanding between VW and the political class start to be in serious jeopardy, as Goulart came out with a decidedly protectionist platform. The government set a series of obstacles in the way of multinational companies. It introduced higher restrictions on import licenses, increased from 100 percent to 150 percent the obligatory deposit for multinational firms to leave at the Banco do Brasil for every dollar spent in import purchase, and pressed VW to completely stop importing vehicle components from Germany.[106] The galloping inflation under Goulart was another problem that preoccupied VW and threatened the cost-effectiveness of its Brazilian branch.[107] In reality, most of Brazil's business circles and foreign partners, particularly the United States, were preoccupied by Goulart's leftist measures. The Federação das Indústrias do Estado de São Paulo (FIESP), of which VW was an important member, supported in various ways the military coup that toppled the government.[108]

VWB itself did not necessarily lean toward dictatorship, as the company's rise had largely begun through its collaboration with democratic governments. Still, the putschists offered to solve most of the issues that preoccupied multinational companies under Goulart: the political instability, a still underdeveloped infrastructural network, the high inflation, and the growing influence of workers' unionism. At VWB, the favorable economic climate created by the governing junta mattered more than the state violence established to maintain this new economic order. As VWB's chief, Werner P. Schmidt, synthesized in an interview of 1971 about economic progress in Brazil, "of course the police and the military torture prisoners to obtain important information; of course political dissidents are often not fairly judged but simply shot. But an objective report

---

[105] Wellhöner, "Wirtschaftswunder," 286.
[106] Ibid., 287.
[107] Inflation reached 51.3 percent in 1962, 81.3 percent in 1963, and 91.9 percent in 1964. Werner Baer, Dan Biller, and Curtis T. Mc Donald, "Austeridade sob diversos regimes politicos: o caso do Brasil," *Cadernos de estudos sociais* 3, no. 1 (1987), 6, 17.
[108] CNV, *Relatório da CNV*, 62, 322.

should always add that things just do not go forward without severity. And things are going forward."[109]

Things were going forward above all for foreign investors thanks to a revised approach of national-developmentalism. Multinational firms ceased to be the scapegoats of politicians in periods when governments sought to restore their popularity, and the regime's political leaders did not balk at saying publicly that Brazil needed foreign capital if it wanted to become a great industrial power. In the absence of fair electoral competition, the military governments were not concerned to the same degree as their predecessors with losing popular support. They could dedicate a greater part of their public discourse to gaining market confidence. This approach encouraged VW to appropriate the official nationalist rhetoric. The firm's advertisement strategy changed after the arrival of the military into power, when VW started to refer intensively to the link between automobile production and national development.[110] VW commercials sought harmony with key elements of government propaganda, which had the advantage of appealing directly to the patriotic vein of middle-class consumers. A significant part of this middle-class agreed with the regime's discourse of national progress and restoration of a stable economic order.[111] In this context, VW was both helping national feelings to develop and using these feelings to build itself a Brazilianized image, on the basis of a liberal version of the national-developmentalist discourse, close to the government's rhetoric.

Even in Germany, VW executives made no secret of their sympathy for certain orientations of the regime, especially the economic ones. A senior management member in Wolfsburg declared in 1970 that VWB needed "an economic policy, which recognizes that private entrepreneurial initiative is indispensable for success." He added: "During my talk with President Médici in Rio, I again received confirmation that this policy will continue."[112] Concretely, "this policy" consisted of various labor policy measures that contributed to reducing VWB's production costs. Under the official motive of containing inflation, the military acted to maintain

[109] Manfred von Conta, "Ein Volk bleibt im Schatten," *Süddeutsche Zeitung*, February 16, 1973.
[110] Deborah Caramel Marques, "O progresso sob quatro rodas: propagandas do Fusca, aspirações da classe média, consumo e transformações políticas (Brasil 1964–1968)," *História e-História* (2011).
[111] Fico, "La classe média Brésilienne face au régime militaire."
[112] Schölermann, "Volkswagen do Brasil," 38–9.

low wages.[113] It also passed a law in 1966 to facilitate dismissals, thus provoking an augmentation of worker turnover at VWB.[114] The company could also take advantage of the repression of protest unionism.[115]

Needless to say, the high growth over a long period of military rule was not the least factor to favor VW. Castelo Branco, who took power in a context of exploding deficit, governed until 1967 under the motto of recovering stability through credit restriction. Instead of prolonging this policy, the successive military governments used the readjusted economy left by Castelo Branco as an opportunity to finance growth. Through massive state intervention in infrastructural sectors such as communications, energy, or heavy (not least transport) industry, and a large opening to foreign credit, they oriented Brazil on a path of double-digit annual growth that did not slow down between 1968 and 1973. Volkswagen knew its take-off during these "miraculous" years, with a clear hegemony among passenger car brands (stable over 50 percent of the market share).[116] By 1975, 3 million vehicles had rolled out of the VWB plant. This success brought juicy gains, especially in 1971, when VWB made the highest profits of all private companies in Brazil with dividends of about US$103 million.[117] Not only did the military boost VWB's profits, it also simplified the transfer of an increasing part of these to Germany. The government enlarged the possibilities for sending profit remittances abroad, and showed a limitless tolerance toward the diverse maneuvers of VW to circumvent the remaining maximal remittances limit.[118] For example, VWB paid unusually high consulting fees to, and bought machinery equipment for overvalued prices from, the German parent company. Besides cautioning such practices through a public discourse systematically glorifying European know-how and technological expertise, the Brazilian government even made the consulting fees tax-free.[119]

---

[113] Real wages shrank by between 20 percent and 25 percent over the period 1964 to 1967. Baer, Biller, and Donald, "Austeridade sob diversos regimes politicos," 11.

[114] Werner Würtele and Harald Lobgesang, *Volkswagen in Brasilien – Entwicklungshilfe im besten Sinne?* (Bonn: Arbeitsgemeinschaft Kath. Hochsch.- und Studentengemeinden, 1979), 77.

[115] According to the CNV, VW even provided help to the political police in this matter: CNV, *Relatório da CNV*, 66–72.

[116] Reinhard Doleschal, *Automobilproduktion in Brasilien und 'neue internationale Arbeitsteilung': eine Fallstudie über Volkswagen do Brasil* (Universität Hannover, 1986), 114.

[117] *Conjuntura Econômica*, July 1972.

[118] Schölermann, "Volkswagen do Brasil," 19–21.

[119] Doleschal, "Automobilproduktion in Brasilien und 'neue internationale Arbeitsteilung,'" 112.

There is no doubt that VW benefited from the Brazilian economic miracle. Remarkably, the firm also managed to feature as a decisive contributor to this miracle. Brazilians appropriated the Beetle to the point of giving it a proper local name, *Fusca* (derived from the Brazilian pronunciation of *Volks*). The Fusca became part of daily life and gained a kind of cultural hegemony in the car sector. In São Paulo – by 1967 the city with the biggest quantity of VW vehicles in the world, the entire police force was equipped with VW vehicles, as were nearly all taxis.[120] The company also owed its fame to a clever communication strategy. When it started producing the Beetles, VWB inaugurated a historically unseen relationship between a firm and the media in Brazil, by opening the doors of its factory to reporters and photographers. In the 1960s, VW published commercials in almost every single issue of the country's main magazines. In 1961, VWB senior management invited Alaor Gomes, a reputable TV journalist and political advisor, to build a media relations section within the company. This initiative, the first press office in Brazil's business history, enabled VW not only to reinforce its advertising, but also to become an actor in shaping Brazilian public opinion, as is underlined by Chaparro: "The press sector [of VW] became a compulsory source of query for publishers, assignment editors and economic reporters of the big printed media, it took the role of an agenda-setter."[121]

This rigorous public relations work became the brand's main instrument for spreading the message that VW was a symbol of socioeconomic improvement in Brazil. Volkswagen even portrayed itself as an actor financing economic growth and producing national cohesion, for example, by publishing commercials that recalled its own contribution to national tax revenues.[122] Commercials also suggested to consumers that they imagine the price of "progress infrastructure" (electricity, factories, hospitals, schools, and roads) in numbers of Beetles, thus creating a mathematical association between VW and the concrete benefits Brazilians earned from economic growth. This kind of advertisement made of the VW vehicle a typical national-developmentalist product, driving Brazilians toward a glorious, prosperous future on the path of growth – not only economic growth, but also growth of the nation's size in all senses of the term. For example, a 1971 commercial celebrated the building of highways in the

---

[120] Acker, "The Brand that Knows Our Land," 208.
[121] Manuel Carlos Chaparro, "Cem anos de assessoria de imprensa," in *Assessoria de imprensa e relacionamento com a mídia: teoria e técnica*, ed. Jorge Duarte (São Paulo: Atlas, 2002), 45.
[122] Marques, "O progresso sob quatro rodas."

country's western regions as a way of expanding human occupation in the national territory. Another commercial expressed pride in seeing the Brazilian population rapidly increasing, underlining how VW was apt to meet this challenge and accompany demographic growth with an even more rapid increase in Beetle production.[123]

From a corporate point of view, this advertising was not unjustified, as VW believed to have participated in the economic development of the country, in the first place by creating nearly 40,000 jobs.[124] According to company figures, by 1974, VW was indirectly contributing to the maintenance of 330,000 jobs (enabling a living for 1.5 million individuals). It had helped its suppliers to develop with loans, bridge financing, and advance payments. The increase in production at VW had enabled 803 VW resale companies to open. Besides, VW's sales credits – an innovation in the Brazilian car sector – had helped the middle class to equip itself with vehicles. By 1974 allegedly, even one-third of VW employees themselves had a VW. Unfortunately, there is no alternative statistics to corroborate or invalidate these figures. Volkswagen also claimed to distribute to its workers the highest wages in the sector as well as health care, pension insurance, financial aid for public transport and canteens, and a wide range of entertainment offers. A 1973 company brochure said that VWB was "one of the most progressive and social enterprises of the country" and, more importantly, "a successful symbiosis between industrialization and the protection of the national interest."[125]

How far this eulogistic self-portrait differentiated from reality has been discussed by authors like Doleschal, Schölermann, and Würtele.[126] They have pointed to the negative weight of VW in the Brazilian trade balance, revealed that wages at VW were actually lower than in other multinational firms, and denounced the firm's repressive attitude toward workers. Although these criticisms are often backed up by serious statistics, they fail to address the impact of VW within the Brazilian industry and the chain of demand possibly created by the company's investments. However, it remains that behind VW's alleged progressiveness, the main tendency was to maximize profits at the expense of human aspects. In these conditions, VWB needed more than good corporate responsibility marketing to conquer the sympathy of the nation. From 1973–4, as the

---

[123] Ibid.

[124] Toni Schmücker, "Soziale und wirtschaftliche Auswirkungen der VW do Brasil," *Deutsch-Brasilianische Hefte*, May 1975, 298–305.

[125] Volkswagenwerk A. G., *VW in Brasilien: mehr als Autos* (Wolfsburg: Volkswagen, 1973). In: VW Unternehmensarchiv.

[126] Doleschal, "*Zur geschichtlichen Entwicklung des Volkswagenkonzerns*"; Schölermann, "Volkswagen do Brasil"; Würtele, "VW do Brasil."

Brazilian economic miracle faced the beginning of its end, due to the uncertainty brought by the first global oil shock, it became clear that VW had to invest its self-promotion efforts in other fields than its sole identification with economic growth: it had to demonstrate even more clearly its Brazilian patriotism. The Cristalino farming project would be a contribution to this, making VW looking toward the same horizon as the Brazilian nation: the Amazon.

The Making of a Model Ranch (1973–1976)

In the 1970s, most of the information written in the mainstream news-papers about the Cristalino farm was furnished by VW, through printed documentation, press conferences with VW officials, or guided tours of the ranch, which were offered to reporters. Although VW published information in both Brazil and Germany, there were some slight but significant differences in the communication strategy between the two countries. These differences reveal much about the image that VW wanted to convey of its ranch depending on the audience it addressed. Brazilian publications tended to depict the CVRC as the invention of Wolfgang Sauer, the CEO of VW do Brasil. It was said that Sauer's bravery led him to take up the "challenge" of Amazonian colonization, which the Brazilian government had posed to all entrepreneurs.[1] The German media were more likely to state that VW had been directly "invited" by the Brazilian government to start an Amazonian adventure.[2]

Why were different versions offered of Cristalino's origins? Most probably, the Brazilian version represented VW's pledge of commitment to the national "march to the interior." Once again, VW wanted to assert its avant-garde position on the Brazilian path to development. In Germany, the company attempted to handle the topic more carefully, since it was

---

[1] "Pecuária. Projeto VW," *Veja*, June 19, 1974; "Jovem executivo. Amazônia, o desafio para o administrator," *A folha de São Paulo*, December 12, 1976; Sérgio Buarque, "A capitania da Volkswagen," *Movimento*, June 26, 1978.

[2] "Volkswagen züchtet Rinder," *Deutsch-Brasilianische Hefte*, January 1975; "Wie dem Urwald eine Hazienda abgerungen wird," *Süddeutsche Zeitung*, December 24–6, 1979; Martin Gester, "Gefrierfleisch aus der 'Grünen Hölle' Brasiliens," *Frankfurter Allgemeine Zeitung*, September 25, 1981.

clearly difficult for a major car company to "sell" a tropical ranching project to a Bundesrepublik (Federal Republic of Germany) depressingly affected by the oil shock of 1973. Given that Wolfsburg announced a drastic redundancy plan for its German factories in 1974, how was it to justify the spending of profits in such an alien economic sector as tropical farming?

Moreover, concern over the lack of equality and freedom in the Third World was growing in Germany, especially since the Chilean military coup of 1973, widely reported in the Western European media and by social movements. In 1974, the Federal Parliamentary Commission for Economic Cooperation in Bonn invited VW executive Horst Backsmann, as a representative of the company, for a hearing.[3] In the event, German Members of Parliament posed aggressive questions about supposed unethical practices by VW in Brazil: low wages, a restrictive credit policy, the outsourcing of German production combined with insufficient adaptation to the needs of Brazilian consumers. These questions reflected how concerned a segment of German society was about the behavior of its "multis" in the Third World.[4] In this context, VW could not raise any suspicion that its activities were encroaching upon Brazilian sovereignty. This is probably why Wolfsburg informed the German press that VW was creating a ranch in the Amazon not as a result of its own will, but because the Brazilian government insisted on finding private partners to "develop" the country.

There are two reasons why it makes sense to stress that the creators of the project spread two different stories about its origins. First, the existence of these two distinct narratives, constructed for two separate audiences, points toward the multifunctional dimension that marked the CVRC for the entire duration of its existence. Not only was the CVRC both "German" and "Brazilian"; it was also both a private and a state project, a personal and collective creation, a nationalist and global idea, among other seemingly irreconcilable polarities. As such, its planning and implementation turned out to be the result of a negotiated conception of development, rather than the product of a unified developmentalist ideology. The CVRC was praised as a model ranch because it was a project of reconciliation between different visions of development.

---

[3] Ausschuss für wirtschaftliche Zusammenarbeit des Deutschen Bundestages, 31. *und* 32. *Sitzung. Öffentliche Anhörung von Sachverständigen über das Thema, Tätigkeit und entwicklungspolitischer Einfluss deutscher multinationaler Unternehmen in Entwicklungsländern*, November 11–12, 1974.
[4] "Multi" is a rather pejorative German designation for "multinational firms."

Second, the fact that VW told two versions of the CVRC's genesis in two different countries demonstrates the complex situation in which the project had its beginnings. The CVRC was squeezed between different cultures, public opinions, and contexts of pressure – because of its genuine multifunctionality. The use of different strategies of communication in Germany and Brazil demonstrates that the CVRC, which aimed at being a model in at least two different contexts, had to satisfy different expectations of the development promise. In Germany and in Brazil, the social, political, and economic representations of what development should bring to the people were not the same. Obviously, the fact that VW was able to publicize different explanations about the same thing, according to the country, illustrates the considerable resources in terms of communication and power that are available to a multinational company. However, it also highlights the limits of this power, because it shows that VW had to deal with a multitude of actors who might project their own ideas of development onto the CVRC project.

The CVRC was a VW project, but it was also integrated into a Brazilian national plan: it had multiple purposes. This multifunctionality turned out to be a source of contention from the very inception of the project. Multifunctionality does not only mean that the CVRC was inspired by two main backgrounds – Brazilian national developmentalism and German multinational business. Multifunctionality also means that Brazilian developmentalists on the one hand and VW businessmen on the other saw the CVRC as both their own and an alien project. In other words, neither the Brazilians, nor the Germans participating in developing the project – except for a few directly involved individuals – succeeded in identifying themselves completely with the CVRC. At VW, the ranch gave rise to polemic because it was alien to the company's traditional activities. In Brazilian governing circles, the CVRC encountered criticism because it meant that Brazil, in order to achieve the nationalist goal of colonizing the Amazon, allied itself with a powerful foreign institution, which might erode Brazilian sovereignty.

Only by considering the CVRC as a response to a plurality of expectations is it possible to envisage the model of development that VW and its allies attempted to construct. This chapter depicts the making of a model ranch as a paradox, resulting from complex and sometimes conflicting negotiation between two poles. One pole was the Brazilian military regime and the other was Volkswagen as a multinational company. Both poles were themselves heterogeneous structures combining the expectations of multiple actors. As will be seen, this made the model ranch both powerful (as the result of an alliance between powerful institutions) and fragile (as a project squeezed between various contexts of pressure).

The "Invitation": How VW Came to the Amazon

VW spokespeople continued to inform their German interlocutors that the company entered the farming sector because the Brazilians wanted it to. Even the company's president, Rudolf Leiding, introduced the CVRC project as the direct consequence of an "invitation."[5] He asserted that the Brazilian minister of the interior had solicited him in a personal letter to start an agribusiness in the Amazon. In the VW corporate journal, *Autogramm*, film director Wolfgang Büblitz went beyond the "invitation" thesis, alleging that the Brazilian government had "forced" VW to undertake a colonization project.[6] A leading conservative newspaper in Germany depicted the proposal made to VW as the kind of "invitation" a company does not really have the choice to refuse, a sort of duty that VW owed to the Brazilian state if it wanted to maintain its privileged position in the country.[7] Given the fiscal advantages offered to VW and the enthusiasm of certain high-ranking company leaders in opening the Amazonian ranch, that thesis distinctly lacks credibility. The present study will show, however, that the Brazilian government made substantial efforts to make a cattle-ranching project in the southeastern Amazon attractive in the eyes of a large, multinational company of VW's profile.

Operação Amazônia

Everything started two years after the coup of 1964, under pressure from nationalist intellectuals, who exhorted Castelo Branco to finally assert Brazilian control over the northern territory of the country. This time the government was determined to show that it was serious about the Amazon. The modernization of the region, "Brazil's Third World," would provide flamboyant evidence of development, akin to the *Brasilia* of the 1964 "Revolution." In October 1966, a law package christened Operação Amazônia created the political and financial conditions for a strategy of massive Amazonian development based on public planning. According to an official document, "*Operação Amazônia* is a complex

---

[5] VW Unternehmensarchiv 174/533/2, November 14, 1973, "65. Sitzung des Aufsichtsrats der VW-AG."

[6] "Der Urwald überwuchert Alles," *Autogramm*, September 1985.

[7] Gester, "Gefrierfleisch aus der 'Grünen Hölle' Brasiliens."

of laws and measures that aims to promote definitive integration of that region into the national socioeconomic context. The way to achieve this result is to exploit the region's natural potentialities, to enhance the level of income and well-being of its populations, and to enable consequent settlement and amplification of these populations in the area."[8] The Operação Amazônia laws defined a planning territory of 5 million square meters: about 60 percent of Brazil's total territory, including nine Brazilian states grouped together under the concept of Amazônia Legal.[9] SUDAM (Superintendência do desenvolvimento da Amazônia), a powerful institution that would plan and manage the development of this administrative super-region, was set up. The old Rubber Bank of Amazonia was transformed into a large public development bank, BASA (Banco da Amazônia), with a widely expanded banking network. One of the bank's missions was to distribute public funding for the development projects selected by SUDAM.

Hardly had Parliament adopted Operação Amazônia than a propaganda campaign began, constructing and publicizing the "new attitude" toward the forest.[10] To sensitize the nation, a yearly "Amazonia Day" was instituted in 1968. Operação Amazônia asked Brazilians to reject the two images that had cohabited until then in representations of the rain forest: the "picturesque region worthy of a literature topic" on the one hand, and the "green hell" on the other.[11] These pictures symbolized passive attitudes. They were to be replaced by the "new philosophy of development" marked by willpower and action.[12] In this context, nature had to be redefined. The frightening, wild, and untouchable landscapes, which used to be feared or admired for their abundance, diversity, and exuberance, were discursively transformed into "empty spaces" of "green desert" needing to be conquered and dominated.[13] After a SUDAM meeting in December 1966, a group of Amazonian governors, federal ministers, and national businessmen issued the *Declaration of the Amazon*, which promoted a confident and dominating attitude toward the rain forest: "Today the Amazon, seen as a whole, still constitutes one of the largest empty spaces

[8] SUDAM, *Investimentos privilegiados na Amazônia* (Belém: SUDAM, 1966), 226.
[9] Three of these nine states had only parts of their territory integrated into Amazonia Legal.
[10] CNDDA, *A Amazônia en foco*, ed. Comissão nacional de defesa e pelo desenvolvimento da Amazonia, vol. 1 (1967), 5.
[11] Cavalcanti, *Da SPVEA à SUDAM*, 676.
[12] SUDAM, ed. *Operação Amazônia*, 70.
[13] Extracts of the *Revista manchete*, November 1968, April 1972, January 1973, February 1973 (unorganized) in: "Brasile," at: Archive of the Biblioteca Amilcar Cabral, Bologna.

of the world, and a challenge to our capacity for realization. The rational occupation of this empty space is the main necessity for our own national security."[14] As proclaimed in a special edition of the pro-regime magazine *Manchete* in 1968, the "immense area of 5 million square kilometers" of Brazilian rainforest constituted the "scenario" that Operação Amazônia had to rewrite, thus "awakening" the region and reshaping its identity in the "battle of Amazonian development."[15] Modernity was thus to write the story of the forest, as if the Amazon had no history yet and no possibility for creating its own future. Only modernity gave sense to things; developmentalism saw no meaning but emptiness in forest spaces if these were not massively exploited.

There lay, according to SUDAM, the difference between development and sub-development. In development, "man overcomes nature," whereas in sub-development, the dialectic of domination is reversed: it is nature that imposes its rule.[16] Therefore, the war against nature that Operação Amazônia instituted was also a war against the sub-developed mentalities that, according to the official discourse, still reigned in the Amazon: that "beggar region" characterized by "parasitism," with an "entrepreneurial mentality in a primitive state, hesitant, coward," a "culture deprived of creative expression" and "technical skill in a state of inferiority."[17] Operação Amazônia would "overcome the terrible sore of misery and sub-development," thanks to the "Brazilian economy," "marching to the interior" as an army would do, to quote the words of President Castelo Branco in 1966.[18]

The regime wanted to make of Amazonian colonization a project that would unify the different social classes within the nation. The Amazon contained the promise of fruitful resources to be capitalized on by the economic elites as well as new land to be distributed among the poor. Under the horizon of Amazonian development, the military, which was at the same time pushing through socioeconomic policies that aggravated the gulf between rich and poor, had found a way to unify the diverse parts of Brazilian society into one single national project.

In 1970, President Médici infused Amazonian development programs with a social color. The official story recounts that, in June, the president

---

[14] "Encerrada reuniao da Amazonia," *O estado de São Paulo*, December 13, 1966.
[15] Extracts of the *Revista manchete*, Archive of the Biblioteca Amilcar Cabral, Bologna.
[16] João Walter de Andrade, *A problemática amazônica e a atuação da SUDAM* (Belém: SUDAM, 1968), 5.
[17] Cavalcanti, *Da SPVEA à SUDAM*, 672; SUDAM, *Operação Amazônia*, 56.
[18] Ibid., 16–17.

remained shocked after a visit to the northeastern town of Recife and its hinterland, where he was faced with the dramatic social consequences of a devastating drought.[19] Having in view both the chronic precarity of the northeastern peasant classes and the "problem" of "Amazonian emptiness," Médici idealized the project of a massive stream of human migration proceeding from the northeast to the Amazon. In a sentence that remained etched in the national imaginary, he described this new objective of interregional planning as "the solution to two problems: men without land and land without men." Médici's dream was written into law via the Plano de Integração Nacional (PIN), adopted and completed between 1970 and 1971. One of PIN's main measures was the construction of the Transamazonian, a highway of nearly 5,000 kilometers that would cross the rain forest from east to west. Another highway, the Cuiabá-Santarém, would traverse the Amazon from south to north. A margin of 100 kilometers on either side of these roads was reserved for agricultural colonization. The federal agency Instituto Nacional de Colonização e Reforma Agrária (INCRA), created for the occasion, would distribute small plots of land to about 100,000 migrant families until 1975 (so, at least, was the plan), and launch a series of small centers of urbanization along the two highway axes.[20]

As enlarged territorial integration meant a greater necessity for motor vehicles, VW openly supported the official Amazon policy. In 1970, the company, which was used to articulating its own communications in the governmental discourse of modernization, launched a TV commercial for the "Beetle" car, praising the building of the Transamazonian. The advertisement, which staged bulldozers clearing a path within the immensity of the forest, contained a message that extended Médici's triumphal declarations of conquest over nature as a condition for national development. Preceded by a pompous, aggressive musical introduction, a narrator's voice proclaimed: "This is the Transamazonian, the work of definitive conquest of one of the world's richest regions. Men and machines are fighting restlessly against the forest, against the climate, to give Brazil its masterpiece highway; but the effort and victory will be rewarded; within a short time, any vehicle will be comfortably driving here."[21] The end of

---

[19] Sue Branford, *The Last Frontier: Fighting over Land in the Amazon* (London: Zed Books, 1985), 60.

[20] Gerd Kohlepp, "Planung und heutige Situation staatlicher kleinbäuerlicher Kolonisationsprojekte an der Transamazônica," *Geographische Zeitschrift* 64, no. 3 (1976), 174, 79–80.

[21] David A. Castro Netto, "Legitimação e ditadura: a propaganda comercial em foco," paper presented at *ANPUH: XXV Simpósio Nacional de História*, Fortaleza, 2009.

the commercial displayed the future arrival of the Beetle on this road, as a symbol of taming the "green hell" and making it accessible to Brazilians. With this commercial, VW was not only helping the government to push through its highway-building policy, which could only favor the growth of the auto industry; the company was also underlining its contribution to the national effort the president had demanded for conquering the Amazon region. In sum, VW was carrying out both advertising for itself and propaganda for PIN.

Designed on the basis of efficiency and rapidity, and sustained by a heavy propaganda apparatus, PIN was a typical national-developmentalist plan. Nevertheless, its results proved highly disappointing. By 1975, only 6,500 of the planned 100,000 families were farming land within the INCRA colonization program. The building of new roads and state propaganda presenting the Amazon as an Eldorado did attract hundreds of thousands of northeastern migrants. However, most of them came on a spontaneous basis, outside the supervision of INCRA, and settled elsewhere than in the state-planned colonization villages. The failure of the INCRA colonization program was not so much due to a low number of incoming migrants, but rather to the high rate of families leaving the zones of colonization after a few months of residency.[22] Bad harvests, the geographic isolation of the plots INCRA offered (often too distant from water or badly connected to secondary road networks), the lack of access to consumer markets, and the spread of tropical infectious diseases were the main causes of these departures. The responsibility of public powers for this failure has been unanimously pointed out by academic observers.[23] Most of the infrastructural investment announced by the government did not come, and INCRA often supervised the planning of crops in an improvised way. Undermined by recurrent affairs of corruption, the agency proved unable to use its financial resources efficiently and to distribute the land to the advantage of small peasants.

When Médici left power in 1974, most governmental voices were already saying that PIN had not produced the expected results.[24] INCRA's shortcomings served as an argument for SUDAM to disqualify the small colonization strategy and to make more intensive use of the political

---

[22] Kohlepp, "Planung und heutige Situation staatlicher kleinbäuerlicher Kolonisationsprojekte an der Transamazônica," 194.

[23] Ibid.; Branford, *The Last Frontier*; Hochstetler and Keck, *Greening Brazil*.

[24] Susanna B. Hecht, "Environment, Development and Politics: Capital Accumulation and the Livestock Sector in Eastern Amazonia," *World Development* 13, no. 6 (1985), 673.

competence it was given in 1966, regarding the distribution of tax incentives to private companies. In a public document, the organization stated that small settlers "carry out the only and most dangerous activity they can undertake: deforestation and the exhaustion of soil for subsistence agriculture."[25] The German embassy in Brasília shared this opinion. In a communication in 1974 to the German Ministry of Foreign Affairs, partly written to legitimize the VW ranch project, the institution stated that the small settlers implanted by INCRA were not able to make a rational use of the land placed at their disposal.[26]

With the socially distributive colonization falling into disgrace, the idea that large-scale and capital-intensive development projects were more efficient invaded the institutional discourse. It is no accident that in 1974 the VW development project was definitely accepted by SUDAM, after a year of complicated talks between the German company and the Brazilian authorities. The climate was again becoming much more favorable for big investors. In May 1974, the government's national radio program, *Voz do Brasil*, stated that "it is imperative that entrepreneurial agriculture be brought to the Amazon as it is the only type of farming which can produce an agile response to the need to increase national production of foodstuffs."[27] In addition, on November 10, 1974, Raymundo Nonato de Castro, a minister of the federal government, made clear that "the government's aim is the economic occupation of the region, not its settlement. And this will be achieved more through capital and technology than through labor."[28] The Operação Amazônia laws comprised a series of fiscal measures, which became the main legislative tool to favor the shift from small peasant colonization to the implementation of big projects.

Calling Big Business

The incentive system proposed to potential investors was generous and particularly adapted for companies like Volkswagen do Brasil (VWB). Three kinds of incentives created in the perspective of Amazonian development were relevant for agribusiness: reinvestment tax credits, income tax exemptions, and fiscal breaks on import/export activities. Reinvestment tax credits were the most spectacular possibility. According to the rules

[25] Ibid.
[26] BArch B102/8643, Botschaft der BRD to Auswärtiges Amt, November 4, 1974.
[27] Branford, *The Last Frontier*, 73.
[28] Ibid., 67.

established by Operação Amazônia, a corporation could invest up to 50 percent of its tax liability in a development project of its own, if it was located in Amazônia Legal and declared of national interest by SUDAM. Up to 75 percent of the shares in a development project could be financed with credit funds coming from the tax liabilities of the investing company.[29] Distributed to the individual companies by BASA, these monies made up the Fundo de Investimento da Amazonia (FINAM) fund, whose sovereign manager was the SUDAM high council (Conselho de Deliberacão, CONDEL). This made SUDAM virtually the largest shareholder of the projects it funded, except that it had no voting rights on the boards of management of individual projects, and no right in connection with the projects' profits.[30] Nonetheless, since CONDEL decided which project could benefit from the tax incentive mechanism and for what amount, SUDAM was clearly in a position to negotiate the content of the projects with its private investors.

VWB had the best possible profile to take advantage of the tax reinvestment system. First, as Hecht notes, it was the first time in history that state legislation stipulated the eligibility of foreign firms for incentives in the Amazon.[31] Until then, the traditional paranoia of the Brazilian elites toward foreigners interested in the rain forest had made such a provision taboo. Second, it was not "just anybody" who sat on CONDEL – besides the heads of the various Brazilian agencies and lenders involved in Amazonian development, it included major political figures such as ministers and state governors (or, in case these could not attend a CONDEL meeting, their direct representatives). The prestigious composition of the high council could be said to favor investors who enjoyed either excellent relations in governing circles or strong institutional support. Volkswagen enjoyed both. Third, as stressed by World Bank expert Hans Biswanger, "reinvestment tax credits would only be relevant for nonagricultural enterprises which have positive taxable profits."[32] As Brazil's biggest taxpayer, VW might be interested by this fiscal offer in the first place.

Besides the reinvestment tax credits, agribusinesses selected by SUDAM could benefit from two other kinds of incentives. There was an

---

[29] Hans P. Binswanger, "Fiscal and Legal Incentives with Environmental Effects on the Brazilian Amazon" (World Bank, 1987), 12.
[30] VW Unternehmensarchiv 373/190/2, August 18, 1976, "Brasilien-Schlachtprojekt."
[31] Hecht, "Environment, Development and Politics," 671.
[32] Binswanger, "Fiscal and Legal Incentives with Environmental Effects on the Brazilian Amazon," 12.

exceptionally generous income tax exemption. The financial results of a project validated by SUDAM remained up to 100 percent tax-free for a period of ten to twelve years after the starting date of the business.[33] Finally, the import of foreign machinery and equipment were completely free of charge, as long as no material of the same technological level was available in Brazil. This point would prove particularly interesting for VW, which would partly build the reputation of its ranch on technical superiority and a mechanization structure on par with the standards of industrial countries. Companies approved by SUDAM were also exempted from export duties for a series of products classified as regional, such as timber – a product that the VW ranch would export. Needless to say, all the tax incentives previously cited were cumulative. As a result of this combination of credits and fiscal advantages, the risk of financial losses in an Amazonian project was considerably reduced for private investors.

These uncommonly generous public funding mechanisms show that the Brazilian authorities were ready to seek the support of private companies at any price. Indeed, the advertising campaign accompanying the incentives was massive and all the arguments were honed to attract private firms, especially foreign ones. Brochures, conferences, seminars, and public ceremonies addressed to a business audience emphasized the works effectuated throughout the Amazon by state-owned companies to build roads, expand electricity networks, and develop telecommunications.[34] This new infrastructure should facilitate the implantation and reduce the costs of large agro-industrial projects in the region as well as optimize their connection with the rest of the Brazilian territory. The message that the rain forest was finally about to be connected with the world economy was also publicized abroad. The Brazilian Trade Bureau in New York was particularly active in generating advertisements about the new investment conditions in the Amazon.[35] While SUDAM published its "manuals for businessmen in the Amazon" in several foreign languages, Brazilian embassies in developed countries circulated promotion documents produced by BASA.[36]

[33] VW Unternehmensarchiv 373/190/2, August 18, 1976, "Brasilien-Schlachtprojekt"; Hecht, "Environment, Development and Politics," 670.
[34] SUDAM, *Operação Amazônia; Discursos*, 49; SUDAM, ed. *Sudam 40 ano* (Belém: SUDAM, 1970), 11.
[35] Frances M. Foland, "A Profile of Amazonia: Its Possibilities for Development" *Journal of InterAmerican Studies and World Affairs* 13, no. 1 (1971), 70.
[36] Extracts of the *Revista manchete*, at: Archive of the Biblioteca Amilcar Cabral, Bologna.

Cattle ranching was a particular subject in advertising. Media and officials, drawing on the studies of scientists working for the regime (but whose credibility was controversial among environmental specialists), speculated about the future benefits of this activity.[37] The Ministry for Agriculture estimated that within a couple of decades, 20 million head of cattle would graze in the Amazon – a very optimistic objective in view of the fact that the region was home to hardly 2 million cattle in 1970.[38] The massive transformation of forest into pastures, implied by the development of tropical cattle ranching, was presented as an excellent technique for adding value to soils. This belief, spread by Brazilian development agencies such as SUDAM, was widespread around 1974, as shown by Fearnside, who explains how cattle ranching was considered as an activity that would improve the ecological stability of the land.[39] Agronomist Henrique Pimenta Veloso offered the main scientific caution to this point of view. His research sought to demonstrate that the Amazon was "senile and gradually suffocated by creepers" and therefore needed to be urgently cleared.[40] He participated as a specialist in various governmental programs.

Why did VW and other foreign companies believe this propaganda campaign by the Brazilian government about the promising future of Amazonian agribusiness? Maybe because the media and experts in developed countries did. In December 1974, for example, *Die Welt* seemed convinced that, thanks to the development of the Amazon, within a few years, Brazil would become as big an exporter of meat as Argentina.[41] Internationally renowned professors shared this thesis. In a widely commented article of 1970, German geographer Wolfgang Brücher had already sought to demonstrate that livestock farming was an economic form with a great future for rain forests in South America.[42] A few years later, his Dutch colleague Jan Kleinpenning wrote that cattle production in the Brazilian Amazon could be increased many times if the Brazilians

---

[37] Branford, *The Last Frontier*, 74–6.
[38] *Deutsch-Brasilianische Hefte*, January 1975; Hecht, "Cattle Ranching in the Eastern Amazon," 74.
[39] Philip M. Fearnside, "The Effects of Cattle Pasture on Soil Fertility in the Brazilian Amazon: Consequences for Beef Production Sustainability," *Tropical Ecology* 21, no. 1 (1980).
[40] Branford, *The Last Frontier*, 75.
[41] Antonio Nogueira, "Neuer Aufbruch in den Westen," *Die Welt (Supplement)*, December 4, 1974.
[42] Wolfgang Brücher, "Rinderhaltung im Amazonischen Regenwald. Beiträge zur Geographie der Tropen und Subtropen," *Tübinger geographische Studien* 34 (1970).

"were to change to a more intensive form of farming, with regular applications of fertilizers and the growing of special fodder crops, if they were to build an extensive network of cold-stores and to use refrigerated lorries for meat transports."[43]

Since the mid-1960s, United Nations FAO experts had also encouraged countries of the Global South to explore and expand the reserves of resources found in their rain forests, and in which worldwide demand was increasing, such as timber or meat.[44] Even the World Bank was helping to increase cattle production in the Amazon through granting significant loans for building highways in the region, and through offering funds to modernize Brazilian livestock agriculture. If international organizations acted as patrons of Brazilian agricultural policy, why should a foreign company not trust the perspectives painted by the Brazilian government? Far from being reduced to a merely Brazilian mania, the enthusiasm for cattle production was a global trend. In the early 1970s, the global exchange volume of beef enjoyed an annual increase of 12 percent.[45] Brazil had already succeeded in conquering a promising position in this expanding market. The country's contribution to global beef sales increased from 1 percent to 5 percent between 1965 and 1975. In these conditions, Brazil appeared as an interesting place for foreign companies to invest in cattle production, be it in a still ecologically unknown region such as the Amazon.

Introducing the Amazon to VW

In the last half of Médici's mandate (1973 and 1974), the climate of growing sympathy toward private investment in the tropical forest led important company directors to consider joining the colonization movement. As for Wolfgang Sauer, it is impossible to say if the idea originally came from his own initiative, or was directly suggested to him by a representative of the government – some voices said it might have been whispered to Sauer by former president Castelo Branco himself.[46] Since his arrival at the head of VWB, Sauer had discussions about this topic with important politicians in the regime. He asked his friend agronomist Oscar Thompson Filho for advice. Thompson was the minister of agriculture under the Castelo Branco government, and would later become VW's

---

[43] J. M. G Nijmegen Kleinpenning, *The Integration and Colonisation of the Brazilian Portion of the Amazon Basin* (Nijmegen: Katholieke Universiteit, 1975), 20.
[44] Hecht, "Environment, Development and Politics," 669–70.
[45] Hecht, "Cattle Ranching in the Eastern Amazon," 52.
[46] Buarque, "A capitania da Volkswagen."

special farming advisor, helping to set up the CVRC.[47] In his position as a former minister of agriculture, he could be the interface between VW and the regime's political circles. In 1973, Thompson introduced Sauer to his son Mário.[48] Mário Thompson Filho had failed the university selection exams to the Faculty of Agronomy, but thanks to his passion for hunting partridge in varying places throughout the countryside, he had knowledge of Brazilian rural territories, which impressed Sauer. The political connections that Mário could bring to the Cristalino project were probably even more impressive, and so the company chief immediately enrolled him to supervise the installation of the future ranch. After Mário dissuaded Sauer from starting a project in Mato Grosso, the most southerly state of Amazônia Legal ("too dry"), they both agreed that southern Pará could be an interesting option.

Located along the axis formed by the newly built Belém–Brasília roadway, the southeastern part of Pará state had been deemed by SUDAM experts as "the most prosperous cattle-raising area in Brazil, maybe in the world."[49] The government wanted to make this region a pole of technical excellence and intensive capital investment. In August 1973, it selected twenty major businessmen, mostly based in São Paulo, and invited them to visit southern Pará, in a tour organized by BASA.[50] Four federal ministers (including the ministers of planning, the interior, and farming) accompanied the entrepreneurs. Wolfgang Sauer, the best-paid executive in Brazil, was probably the most important of the guests.[51] The BASA visit to the Amazon had a highly symbolic meaning: it sealed the alliance between public powers and private capital for the colonization of the forest. Even if some of them rapidly forgot this engagement, all the invited entrepreneurs swore to the government, during a somewhat orotund

---

[47] This role would not bring luck to Thompson Filho. While he was on a business trip for the CVRC in the Amazon, he died in an airplane crash on March 13, 1975, together with German business executive Ernest Otto Klinger, who had traveled to the Amazon to discuss a slaughterhouse project with VWB. As the two men had met with Sauer in Belém the day before, the accident caused much emotion in São Paulo. For a few hours, most VW executives and journalists believed that Sauer had traveled in the same airplane (which was flying from Belém to São Paulo) and perished in the crash. In reality, Sauer had taken another flight to Rio de Janeiro: "Jatinho cai no Pará e provoca 4 mortes," *O estado de São Paulo*, March 14, 1975; *A folha de São Paulo*, March 18, 1975.

[48] "Jovem executivo. Amazônia, o desafio para o administrator."

[49] SUDAM, ed. *SUDAM 40 ano*, 5.

[50] BArch B116/61917, Georg Trefftz, February 14, 1975, "Landwirtschaftliches Großprojekt der Volkswagen do Brasil."

[51] *O estado de São Paulo*, August 18; September 4, 1973; "O mercador de Volkswagens," *Quatro rodas*, November 1983.

ceremony, that they would invest considerable sums in a monumental farming project.[52] The minister of planning announced that a new phase was beginning for the Amazonian economy and provided ecological reasons for this strategy, which was sympathetic to big business groups. "Until now," he said, "the Transamazonian has emphasized colonization, but the necessity for us to avoid predatory occupation, with the deforestation process going with it, and to promote maintenance of the ecological equilibrium, leads us to invite the big companies to assume the task of developing the region."[53]

To legitimize this discourse, the businessmen even received a master class in ecology during their trip, delivered by Henrique Pimenta himself. The military regime's favorite natural scientist told the company chiefs why they were the most appropriate actors to colonize southeastern Pará:

This is an area for big properties. The climatic characteristics and the *cipós* are leading on the one hand to the death of the trees, and on the other hand they are impeding the growth of new trees. Therefore, never will small landholders be able to establish investment criteria, which could simultaneously achieve an optimal utilization of the forest and preserve it through conservation and reforestation.[54]

Pimenta summed up the core of his message in one sentence: "Either the businessmen conquer the forest now, or it will disappear by the force of its own nature." The minister of the interior, who was in charge of the colonization, added that "the future of the Amazon lies in the hands of businessmen, whether Brazilian or foreign, for Brazil has lost its fear of foreign capital."[55] This reference to foreign capital was undoubtedly an allusion to Sauer's participation in the visit. Thus, the BASA mission was a public demonstration of common interests, in which the investment policy of big companies such as VW and the nationalist goals of the regime (to secure the Amazon area, to populate it, and to find powerful actors for showing the way toward a massive exploitation of forest resources) converged.

The Birth of the CVRC

Only a few weeks after Sauer's visit to the Amazon, VW had already selected the ideal location for its ranch. At that point, Leiding traveled for seven days to Brazil with the head of VW's supervisory board,

---

[52] *Veja*, June 19, 1974.
[53] "A Volks no Rio Cristalino," *Opinião*, January 1974.
[54] Lúcio Flávio Pinto, "Grandes planos para a Amazônia," *Opinião*, August 1973.
[55] Branford, *The Last Frontier*, 71.

Franz-Josef Rust (Christian-Democratic Union, CDU), the state secretary at the German Finance Ministry, Hans Hermsdorf (Social-Democratic Party of Germany, SPD), also a member of the supervisory board, and their respective spouses.[56] They were only peripherally interested in VW's biggest foreign factory at São Bernardo do Campo. The entire object of the trip was more about land purchase and cattle raising. Without informing the rest of the VW board of directors, they acquired a portion of land of 58,000 hectares, which was traversed by the Cristalino River, a sub-affluent of the Araguaia. The terrain, situated on a hillside and sup-posedly endowed with great aquatic potential, was located in the county of Santana do Araguaia, southeastern Pará. The closest town, Barreira do Campo, lay at a distance of ninety kilometers from the ranch.[57]

Above all, the southeastern border of the estate brushed the future layout of the BR-158. The BR-158 was a highway that the federal gov-ernment planned to expand during the following years, in order to link the northern Amazonian city of Altamira with the very south of Brazil, up to the Uruguayan border.[58] The road would cross most of Pará from north to south and pass by the state of São Paulo – this of course, meant a lot for the future supply of the VW ranch, for connection with the national headquarters of VW do Brasil and commercial outlets for cat-tle production. The sellers of the estate were the Lunardellis, an influen-tial Italian family from São Paulo.[59] The Lunardellis had bought nearly 700,000 hectares of rain forest land in the mid-1960s as they sensed that state initiatives to develop the Amazon were becoming the trend. They were at the head of the Associação dos Empresários da Amazônia (AEA), a powerful lobby group of entrepreneurs, mostly from São Paulo, with interests in the Amazon.

The property purchased from the Lunardellis was still completely covered by vegetation, and virtually unreachable by any vehicle. In September 1973, a pioneer staff enrolled by VWB, and headquartered

---

[56] *Die Zeit*, December 14, 1973; *Der Spiegel*, November 19, 1973. In Germany, the *Aufsichtsrat* (supervisory board) is a committee in a stock corporation that oversees the decisions of management. It is distinct from the managing board, which forms the executive management of the company. I express thanks to Corinna Ludwig for this clarification.

[57] VW Unternehmensarchiv 174/533/2, November 14, 1973, "65. Sitzung des Aufsichtsrats der VW-AG"; Max Scheifele, "Erschliessung des Amazonasgebietes," *Deutsch-Brasilianische Hefte*, June 1979.

[58] *Brasilien Nachrichten* (81), 1983.

[59] BArch B102/172779, Altenhofen to Moller-Racke, October 17, 1974; Branford, *The Last Frontier*, 40–1.

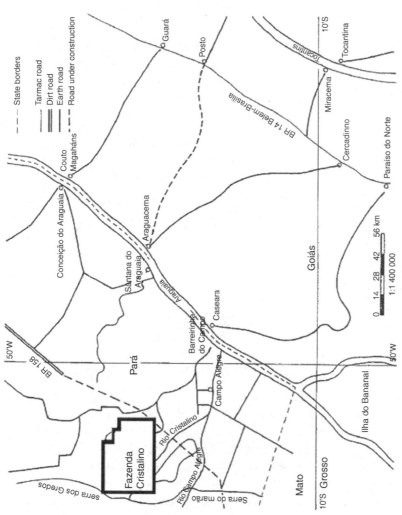

FIGURE 2.1 Final territory and region of the Cristalino ranch. Image courtesy of Volkswagen Aktiengesellschaft.

Source: Dieter Richter, Die Fazenda am Cristalino: eine Rinderfarm im Gebiet des feuchten Passatwaldes Brasiliens: ein Film der Volkswagenwerk AG; Lehrerbegleitheft (Wolfsburg: Volkswagen A. G., 1980).

FIGURE 2.2 Geographic position in the Brazilian territory.
Source: Image courtesy of Bernd Lobgesang. *Brasilien Nachrichten* (81), 1983.

in the Santa Cristina ranch, fifty kilometers from Cristalino, cleared a first path providing access to the edge of the future CVRC site.[60] By mid-November, Leiding revealed to a surprised and somewhat incredulous managing board in Wolfsburg that the land transaction had taken place with the sole preliminary agreement of Rust.[61] He further required the board to vote on the extension of the land to 183,000 hectares and on the start of a ranching project designed to accommodate up to 200,000 head of cattle. In December, VWB bought 81,000 hectares of land adjacent

---

[60] Volkswagen do Brasil, *Cristalino* (Volkswagen: São Bernardo do Campo, 1980). In: VW Unternehmensarchiv.
[61] VW Unternehmensarchiv 174/533/2, November 14, 1973, "65. Sitzung des Aufsichtsrats der VW-AG."

to the already acquired terrain, thus amounting to an estate of "only" 139,000 hectares, with an objective of up to 100,000 head of cattle by the mid-1980s.[62] Although the support of SUDAM (and above all its financial resources) was still uncertain (at least officially), the Sociedade Civil Agropecuária Companhia Vale do Rio Cristalino Ltda was founded as a limited liability company at the end of 1973.[63] Eighty-two percent of the company's capital was owned by VWB and 18 percent by VW's Brazilian partner (and "Brazilian guarantee") Monteiro Aranha.[64] VW was officially becoming a rancher.

Examining the Company's Motivations

There was no ambiguity that the ranching project was above all an operation of fiscal optimization. VW representative Backsmann did not hesitate to confess in his hearing before the Commission for Economic Cooperation in Bonn in 1974: "You know that, in the framework of the regional development plans of the Brazilian government for the north of the country, we invest in the agricultural sector. We obviously do not do it just out of mere ethical duty; in fact we do it in the first place because it gives us a series of advantages regarding profit taxation."[65] In order to recycle profits that otherwise would have flowed into the Brazilian tax department, VWB had already been investing in the most unexpected sectors.[66] It had shares in hundreds of businesses, from fisheries to cement factories or breweries, mostly registered in the poor northeastern regions that were the target of federal development programs and tax incentives. This strategy was not only due to the attractiveness of tax cuts: since VWB profits largely exceeded the amount allowed to be transferred to the holding company in Germany, it was virtually obliged to invest the surplus in the most varied branches.[67] But these were mere financial participations, and VWB had no influence on the development of the corresponding industries. Considerable amounts of money were lost in these operations.[68]

---

[62] Richter, *Die Fazenda am Cristalino*, 14.
[63] Ibid., 9.
[64] Arquivo do FINAM, SUDAM, Parecer 037/74, November 29, 1974.
[65] Ausschuss für wirtschaftliche Zusammenarbeit, *31. und 32. Sitzung.*
[66] VW Unternehmensarchiv 174/533/2, November 14, 1973, "65. Sitzung des Aufsichtsrats der VW-AG"; BArch B116/61917, Vanselow to Hoffman, February 14, 1978.
[67] NLA-HStAH NS V.V.P. 70 (187/97) Nr111, 1978.
[68] BArch B116/61917, Vanselow to Hoffman, February 14, 1978.

Meanwhile, the car company had been looking for years for a possibility to acquire a business on its own, where it could invest a certain amount of tax credits every year, and have a better overview and control over their use. Leiding argued (probably rightly, given the very favorable fiscal regulations on opening Amazonian businesses) that no better possibility existed of doing this than starting a ranching project in the tropical forest.[69] He knew that given the financial configuration of the project, the likelihood that VW would register gross losses was low, even in the case of disappointing business results. He believed that it would be a mistake not to avail of such an advantageous opportunity, since it was offered to VW by the Brazilian government.[70] One might object to Leiding's argument that tax exemptions, especially when they serve as tools for attracting investment in a targeted "pole of development," are most likely transitional instruments. Hence, for the long term, getting involved in the ranching modernization sector remained a risky bet for a car company. Still, Leiding and Sauer had true economic ambitions for the project, which they believed could be a source of long-term profit. The cattle-raising activities, after a first consolidation phase of fifteen years, were expected to generate a profit margin of 9 percent per year that could be used either for new investments or poured back to Wolfsburg.[71]

It was not just about cattle raising, however: the two VW leaders had a comprehensive project in mind, which encompassed the entire chain of beef production and marketing. In a press conference in May 1974, Leiding stated that the *fazenda* would be equipped with its own slaughterhouse, cold storage buildings, and even a meat factory.[72] After a few months, preparatory works were already under way to build a slaughterhouse. By mid-1974, company sources announced to the international press that VW planned to export its future tropical beef to Europe, Japan, and the United States.[73] Most probably, the FAO's assumption that tropical ranching was a promising response to exploding beef consumption in developing countries contributed to convincing VW that the operation would prove fruitful. In addition, the forecasts of the Brazilian authorities, which foresaw that all investments in the CVRC would have

[69] VW Unternehmensarchiv 373/169/1, October 5, 1973, "Sitzung des Vorstands der Volkswagenswerk AG."
[70] VW Unternehmensarchiv 174/533/2, November 14, 1973, "65. Sitzung des Aufsichtsrats der VW-AG."
[71] Ibid.; Laurette Coen, "Les multinationales rêvent aussi," *L'Hebdo*, February 16, 1983.
[72] "VW Auf vier Beinen," *Handelsblatt*, May 18, 1974.
[73] Marvine Howe, "VW Adding Cattle to Beetle in Brazil," *New York Times*, July 25, 1974.

recouped their value within six years, seem to have been taken for granted by Sauer.[74] This was maybe due to the confident relationship he had with several members of the federal government.

Of course, one thing was to sail on the enthusiasm of the Brazilian developmentalist government; another was to convince VW executives in Germany that the project would be viable eventually. In front of the company's board of management in November 1973, Leiding contended that the acquired estate was profitable *per se*, for it contained exploitable wood at a value of 15 million Deutschmarks (DM).[75] Moreover, the scramble for land was still at its beginnings in the Amazon and the government encouraged landlords to sell their properties to large-scale modern companies. As Hecht noted, "the influx of incentives that permitted acquisition of land as part of the development cost created a situation where the value of Amazonian land was increased by 100 percent per year in real terms" in the 1960s and 1970s.[76] In these favorable circumstances, the land purchase made by VW, which in the end amounted to only 7.3 million DM for 139,392 hectares (52.37 DM/hectare), was at least an excellent operation in speculation.[77]

This shows that the project could be of potential economic interest for the VW Company. However, a further aspect is the economic interest for Germany as a nation, which was not necessarily the main, but certainly a noteworthy factor in VW's action. It should not be forgotten that, by virtue of its juridical status and management structure, VW was interwoven with the highest sectors of German politics. This plays a role even regarding issues taking place thousands of kilometers away from Wolfsburg and Bonn. It is no casual coincidence that a visit to the "VW ranch," though not exactly a suitably reachable destination for such very short trips, rapidly became a usual part of the travel programs of German officials coming to Brazil.[78] In September 1974, important German interests underlay the visit to Germany of the just-nominated governor of Pará, Aloyso da

---

[74] Arquivo da SUDAM, CONDEL, "Reunião ordinária, 22/11/1974," in *Reuniões do Condel. Atas ordinárias. Jul./Dez.* 1974; "VW Konzern. Durchgewirbelt," *Der Spiegel*, March 12, 1973.

[75] VW Unternehmensarchiv 174/533/2, November 14, 1973, "65. Sitzung des Aufsichtsrats der VW-AG."

[76] Hecht, "Environment, Development and Politics," 671.

[77] BArch B116/61917, Georg Trefftz, February 14, 1975, "Landwirtschaftliches Großprojekt der Volkswagen do Brasil"; Arquivo do FINAM, SUDAM, Parecer n°037/74, November 29, 1974.

[78] PA AA, Zwischenarchiv, Bd. 116.031; VW Unternehmensarchiv 373/49/2; "Deutsche Parlamentarier machten Station in São Paulo," *Deutsche Zeitung*, March 15, 1980.

Costa Chaves, as appears from the communication between the German embassy in Brasília and the German Ministry of Foreign Affairs. It was not only "the building of an exceptional export oriented cattle business (the VW-project)" which interested the German authorities in Pará, but also the launching of two large mining projects and an electric plant.[79] Indeed, the VW ranch was only the most visible of several large-scale operations, including German participation in the Amazon region. In the scramble for the exploitation of primary resources in the Amazon, Germany had every reason to secure a good position for itself. For its access to crucial natural resources like timber, uranium, or valuable minerals, Germany could not resort to the same neocolonial networks as other world industrial powers such as the United States, Great Britain, or France. Volkswagen's status as a pioneer and major ally of the Brazilian government in the Amazonian colonization might serve as a springboard for the implantation of German investors in the crucial extractive projects being planned in the region.

Moreover, a very specific economic concern, quite distinct from Sauer and Leiding's beef production fantasies, triggered Bonn to push for the expansion of the VW ranch: Germany needed timber. Its cellulose and paper industry was in crisis. The countries exporting timber to Germany were developing their own cellulose factories, thus threatening the very existence of the German ones. The Scandinavian countries continued to export unprocessed timber, but exportable wood production in Finland and Sweden was showing signs that this resource might become scarce. The German paper industry faced the risk of running out of its most vital resource.[80] In addition, the Scandinavians had been running a cartel-like export price policy, placing the German paper producers in a position of constant fragility. Federal Minister of the Economy Hans Friderichs (SPD) hoped that Amazonian wood would save the German paper industry. He imagined that the 1.5 million-hectare pole of farming development (the Xingu-Araguaia pole), in which the VW ranch was the leading unit, could become Germany's timber reserve. Volkswagen and its potential partner farms should cover the needs of the paper industry and guarantee Germany's independence from the Scandinavian countries. As early as 1974, the Ministry of the Economy was playing the role of intermediary between Wolfgang Sauer and timber production businessman Karl Richtberg, encouraging them to design a

---

[79] PA AA, Zwischenarchiv, Bd. 100.480, Deutsche Botschaft to Auswärtiges Amt, September 24, 1974.

[80] BArch B102/172779.

common project of massive timber extraction. As the vice president of the German Society of Timber Research, Richtberg was truly interested in the undertaking, and was ready to mobilize a team of experts to evaluate the timber potential of the VW estate.

At the symbolic level, the project of a VW ranch could be envisaged in Wolfsburg or even the German capital city of Bonn as a further illustration of Germany's technical excellence and economic success. As Unger notes in a study on German investment in the 1960s in India, the German government saw the reinforcement of connections between German companies and developing countries as a precious tool for improving the "international prestige" of the Bundesrepublik.[81] A few decades after the Second World War, Germany's weak diplomatic influence could be partly balanced by the international presence of its economy: German firms became essential actors in restoring the reputation of their country on the basis of its new image as a generous industrial nation eager to share its expertise with the needy "Third World."

From German to Brazilian members of government, Sauer was able to efficiently mobilize his personal networks to guarantee the best political conditions for the making of his "model ranch." The CVRC was in a certain sense "his" ranch. Opening it was Sauer's first major decision after he took the leadership of VWB in 1973. Guided by both passion and the search for personal prestige, he was ready to defend the project against pessimistic minds.[82] As a collaborator remembers, Sauer felt in the Amazon forest like a fish in water. No sooner had he arrived at Cristalino than he had great ambitions for the place:

We were standing in the place of the project, where there was nothing apart from forest and the river that cut through this huge portion of land. Sauer was walking with a knife kept in a thick belt, because there were many jaguars prowling around. He pulled it out of his belt and, holding it firmly, sat down on the ground. With this knife, he sketched the project. It was as if he had it designed in his mind. He pointed to the place of the pasture, the buildings, the housing, the bridges, the slaughterhouse.[83]

Sauer loved the Brazilian countryside and was fascinated by agronomic innovations.[84] He owned his own *fazenda* in the hinterland of São Paulo,

---

[81] Corinna Unger, "Export und Entwicklung: westliche Wirtschaftsinteressen in Indien im Kontext der Dekolonisation und des Kalten Krieges," *Jahrbuch für Wirtschaftsgeschichte/ Economic History Yearbook* 53, no. 1 (2012), 77.

[82] BArch B116/61917, Sauer to Ertl, September 3, 1975.

[83] Doretto, *Wolfgang Sauer*, 344.

[84] Coen, "Les multinationales rêvent aussi."

where he raised 580 head of Nelores cattle and rode his purebred horse, Tabasco.[85] Enthusiastic about participating in the Amazonian colonization, he could hardly hide his pride as the ranch began to take shape.[86] He liked to repeat in interviews that agriculture was the best trump card for the future of the Brazilian economy.[87] He began to bring his friends to Cristalino regularly, enjoyed organizing and attending events such as the rodeo taking place yearly at the ranch, and grew much more excited in showing the ranch than the São Bernardo do Campo car factory to visitors.[88]

His assistant Christian Bruno Schües remembers how Sauer excelled in transmitting to others the idea that Cristalino would be the place of an exceptional historical experiment: "This piece of land was gigantic and it filled us with courage and bravery. I was very young and imagined transplanting to this lost place progress, civilization, social and economic growth. Impossible not to catch the contagion of the creative exaltation that seized Sauer every time he set foot there."[89] This is not to say that the CVRC was like a giant toy at Sauer's disposal for his entertainment. On the contrary, Sauer took his new role as a ranching businessman very seriously, taking positions at the national level with respect to Brazilian agricultural policy. In August 1974, he spoke in favor of a green revolution in Brazilian agriculture. During a meeting of a business club over which he presided, the Clube dos Exportadores, he said to Minister of Agriculture Alysson Paulinelli that "The time has come to speak seriously about the increasing necessity of transforming merely agricultural enterprises into industrial companies, endowed with industrial planning, industrial management, industrial mentality and, above everything, industrial engagement."[90] Sauer's point was to massively re-equilibrate Brazil's balance of payments through a dramatic increase in agricultural production. He had no sooner arrived into the business than he was already teaching the federal government how to make agriculture a pillar of Brazilian economic policy.

The other motor of Sauer's overactive motivation was prestige: the prestige of associating his name to what he saw as a major step in Brazilian

[85] "O novo homem da volks," *Veja*, July 11, 1973; "Interview," *Quatro rodas*, January 1974. Nelores were a breed of cattle raised at the Cristalino ranch.
[86] BArch B116/61917, Vanselow to Hoffman, February 14, 1978.
[87] *Quatro rodas*, January 1974.
[88] *Die Welt*, August 30, 1977; Geraldo Moser, "Besichtigungsobjekt für Gäste: Cristalino mit seinen 110 000 Rindern," *Die Welt (Supplement)*, August 30, 1977.
[89] Doretto, *Wolfgang Sauer*, 344.
[90] *Correio da Manhã*, August 12, 1974.

history. Sauer was not "only" German. He had lived in several places in the Iberian (including Portugal) and Latin American worlds (his wife was Venezuelan), and in Campinas, São Paulo state, since 1963 as the chief executive of Robert Bosch do Brasil.[91] He sincerely identified himself with a South American national project. Celebrated by the Brazilian media as an authentic *líder Latino* since his arrival at Volkswagen, Sauer grew even more famous in the country in 1974, as the press reported on his visionary Amazonian plans.[92] The CVRC was the personal masterpiece that would lend his name to Brazilian history. To make this clear, Sauer not only became president-director of the Companhia Vale do Rio Cristalino board of management. He also represented the CVRC personally in the diverse steps of negotiation with SUDAM, which meant traveling regularly from São Paulo to Belém.[93] His portrait was hung everywhere in the buildings of the *fazenda* – even on the fridge behind the bar in the ranch's club.[94] The school that opened in 1978 on the ranch to teach the employees' children was named "Escola Wolfgang Sauer." But tribute was not only paid to Sauer inside the VW *fazenda*. The Brazilian authorities rewarded him in 1982 with Brazilian citizenship, five years after bestowing upon him the highest national decoration, directly delivered by the president of the republic.[95]

Without Sauer's pugnacity, the CVRC would probably never have come into existence. Indeed, the man was well known for his stubbornness in pushing through the ideas he believed in. He had gained this reputation in the 1960s through his obstinacy in producing car radios at Bosch do Brasil while everybody around was telling him that this market was saturated – an operation that turned out to be a great success in the end.[96] Sauer's eccentric ideas as the head of VWB could only be concretized because someone gave them a chance: this "someone" was his friend Leiding in Wolfsburg, who seemed to trust each of Sauer's decisions about VW's Amazonian investments. Leiding himself had directed VWB from 1968 to 1971, the period during which the two men developed a friendly relationship, and he thus shared with Sauer a certain identification with Brazil.[97] All along, Leiding also proved mysteriously stubborn

[91] Econorte, *Cia Vale do Rio Cristalino Agropecuária Indústria e Comércio. Processo de avaliação* (Belém: SUDAM, 1974).
[92] "O novo homem da Volks," *Veja*, July 11, 1973.
[93] *A folha de São Paulo*, March 18, 1975.
[94] Coen, "Les multinationales rêvent aussi."
[95] "VW Konzern. Durchgewirbelt."
[96] *Veja*, July 11, 1973.
[97] "Interview," *Quatro rodas*, January 1974.

in advocating the CVRC project, to the exaggerated point of risking his position for it.

Internal Polemics at VW

When in 1973, Leiding presented the land transaction effected in the Amazon to the VW managing board, he found himself advocating the project alone.[98] The other council members were divided between skepticism and indifference – or even in one case, indignation. No clear support was to be perceived among board members, who only seemed to agree on validating the project because they considered it a minor topic. In addition, Leiding had already purchased one-third of the property before consulting the board anyway. He justified this by arguing that he was under time pressure to buy the *fazenda* as he was traveling in Brazil and, thus, felt confident to settle for the sole agreement of Rust, as was permitted by VW statutes. The ranch was bought by the two men and their colleague Hermsdorf without any consultation with other VW executives – except Sauer – and without drawing up any detailed plan of what would happen with it afterward.

For many German executives, the project made no sense, and Leiding's decisions in its regard were simply inexplicable. Even those who had sympathy for the project, like the German General Consul in Brazil, expressed serious doubts about its long-term viability.[99] In this case, why did Leiding, Sauer, and Rust make this unexpected deal with the Lunardelli family? In addition to the causes already addressed in these pages, was there not a certain amount of irrationality in the establishment of the VW model ranch? As Brazil enthusiasts, were Sauer and Leiding not intoxicated by the growing Amazon mania that affected entire sectors of the Brazilian elite since the launch of Operação Amazônia? There was a gap between the enthusiasm of Sauer, Leiding, and Rust on the one hand, and the lack of credit that other VW chiefs gave to the project on the other hand. It seems that, aware of the very peculiar character of their project, the three men bought the ranch without informing anyone, only because they feared that the VW board of directors might veto the transaction if the board members were not faced simply with a fait accompli.

---

[98] VW Unternehmensarchiv 373/169/1, October 5, 1973, "Sitzung des Vorstands der Volkswagenswerk-AG."

[99] PA AA, Zwischenarchiv, Bd. 102.024, "Protokoll der 1. Konsularkonferenz in Brasilia vom 23. bis 25. September 1974."

In one sense, they might have been right to do so. The cattle ranch was launched without too much formal resistance from the board, since the Amazonian property already belonged to VW anyway. In another sense, Leiding and Rust's method of not asking company executives and shareholders for their opinion provoked harsh informal reactions from some VW insiders, and contributed to tarnishing, at least internally, the image of the company's management. According to *Die Zeit*, the acquisition of the cattle-raising estate in Brazil triggered a "palace revolt" against the head of the VW supervisory board, Josef Rust.[100] While he was traveling in Brazil and buying the Amazonian estate together with Leiding, other members of the board, having heard of the operation, engaged in intrigue to force Rust out of the leading position he had occupied for seven years. To sum up the situation, one board member told *Der Spiegel* that "the cattle-raising project in Brazil really showed that it's time for Rust to go."[101] Rust, having been made responsible by the new chancellor and rival party leader, Helmut Schmidt (SPD), for the financial losses VW suffered during the sales crisis of 1974, was dismissed a couple of months later.[102]

However, the Amazonian episode also weakened Leiding's reputation as company chief. Eugen Loderer, the workers' representative on the board of directors and federal president of IG-Metall, the main German trade union, strongly protested against Leiding's way of dealing with the ranching project. He stated to Leiding that it was not enough that the president of the supervisory board only inform the president of the managing board about his decisions.[103] He added that in the future, approval would no longer be granted by the workers' representatives if an important decision was processed in that manner, and insisted that he and his union colleagues did not appreciate having been informed of the ranching project through the press. However, Loderer did nothing to stop the project, in spite of the perplexity various VW insiders shared about it.

One senior VW executive, for example, told *Der Spiegel* that he did not understand the utility of the project, guessing with irony that it was "probably a place where to send our fired managers."[104] Others were

---

[100] *Die Zeit*, December 14, 1973.
[101] "VOLKSWAGEN. Freier Austritt," *Der Spiegel*, November 19, 1973.
[102] "VW-Ausichtsrat soll gehen," *Der Spiegel*, August 19, 1974.
[103] VW Unternehmensarchiv 174/533/2, November 14, 1973, "65. Sitzung des Aufsichtsrats der VW-AG."
[104] "VOLKSWAGEN. Freier Austritt."

worried about Leiding's alleged nonchalance. Engineer H. S. Stremme, for example, warned Leiding that the project was unsustainable.[105] Stremme mentioned the monumental failure of Fordlândia a number of decades earlier, with the reminder that Ford's experience was built on much better plans and in much more favorable geographical conditions than the VW ranch. Besides, he said, whereas it was coherent for a car company to grow rubber, seeking to raise cattle made no sense. He was no more indulgent about what he saw as poor consideration, by the project's designers, of the region's environmental conditions, for "in the Amazon high forest it is impossible to create pastures and to resolve the issue of transportation costs; these things are only possible in the steppes region which lies a thousand kilometers to the south. Yet, even these regions very much lack water and rain and are threatened by ever recurring droughts." Greatly disappointed by the "evasive answers" Leiding gave to his criticisms, Stremme complained directly to the German Finance Ministry in February 1974, characterizing the Amazonian ranch as a "squandering of VW finances." He argued that the reinvestment of savings made on Brazilian taxes did not provide a sufficient amount of money for creating such a large-scale agro-industry and that the project necessitated a much greater amount of supplies than "what Mr Leiding wants to make believe." What irritated Stremme the most, however, was Leiding's incomprehensible stubbornness in defending the project without considering the objections made against it, and without even seeing it necessary "to justify these plans of his."

In fact, Leiding's behavior was particularly difficult to understand, especially in the years 1973–4, during which he was traversing a very uncomfortable period as VW chief executive. The company's poor results and growing deficit were already increasing shareholder protests against him.[106] In this context, insisting on such a risky and apparently incoherent project as the CVRC contributed to Leiding losing his job. The year 1974 was to be his last as board director. Called into question for his governing style, the CVRC plan being a significant example, he had to leave at the end of December.[107] For the VW Company, it was already too late to step back: a deal with the Brazilian authorities had just been signed; the cattle project was firmly on its way, even if the new Wolfsburg management board was not particularly delighted with this legacy. At the very

---

[105] NLA-HstAH Nds. 200 (125/99) Nr 319, Stremme to Kropff, May 30, 1974.
[106] *Handelsblatt*, September 10, 1974.
[107] "Gearbeitet wie ein Berserker," *Der Spiegel*, December 30, 1974.

least, it is certain that Leiding's successor, Toni Schmücker, did not share Sauer's enthusiasm for the "ranch of the future." Asked by the German press about this topic, he said he had no time to care about it and finished with a cold "I have the feeling; there are more important things to do."[108]

A Project Revealing the Ambiguities of Brazilian Nationalism

The CVRC had the potential to provoke strident opposition not only in Germany, but also in Brazil, because it contradicted certain principles of Brazilian nationalism. Support for the participation of foreign groups in developing Brazil had never been unanimous, even within the military regime. Delfim Netto, minister of finance in several successive governments and the leading figure behind the regime's economic policy, was convinced that only a massive capital inflow from abroad would enable Brazil to develop quickly. From his nomination in 1968 he continued to advocate a policy of high interest rates in order to attract foreign loans. He also adopted a monetary policy based on frequent mini-devaluations to prevent the Brazilian currency, the cruzeiro, from being overvalued or speculated against, while keeping the rate of devaluation substantially lower than the domestic inflation rate.[109] This strategy succeeded in boosting exports, but it also made borrowing from abroad particularly attractive for Brazilian firms. While Brazilian foreign exchange reserves increased tenfold under Medici's mandate, the country's foreign debt also doubled.

Since the early years of the military regime, certain factions of the political majority had expressed their opposition against this foreign-friendly economic policy. In 1969, a key figure within the nationalist arena, General Albuquerque Lima, resigned from his position as minister of the interior in protest against Delfim Netto's policy, which he rejected as too favorable to foreign capitalism.[110] Among those who criticized the opening up of the Brazilian economy, an important current, composed of both majority and opposition politicians, was firmly opposed to the opening of Operação Amazônia to the *estrangeiros*. This current spread many rumors about supposed U.S. capitalist villains, depicted as professional speculators in forest land. The most prominent political representatives of this point of view were active in the Comissão Nacional pela Defêsa da Amazônia (CNDDA), which had been especially created during

---

[108] "Die tödliche Gefahr ist vorbei," *Der Spiegel*, September 8, 1975.
[109] Baer, *The Brazilian Economy*, 75–8.
[110] Skidmore, *The Politics of Military Rule in Brazil*, 89.

the Operação Amazônia wave, with the added support of high-ranking nationalist military personnel.[111] Many members of the CNDDA were partisans of colonization, but promoted larger state investments and a very restricted opening to foreign capital. They denounced the privatization of Amazon resources as an "antinationalist policy." Allied with prestigious intellectuals and supported by certain government members, they secured the establishment of an official inquiry commission to investigate irregularities committed by foreign groups in land purchase. The question of opening up the Amazon was a veritable source of division within Brazilian politics: pro-opening actors were no less aggressive than their counterparts. As early as in 1967, the new director of SUDAM warned the nationalists that "a maximum of realism" was demanded in order to get the Amazon out of the "develop or disappear" dilemma. To refuse foreign capital, he said, was nothing other than to express the "dishonesty of pseudonationalism," which resulted in keeping underdeveloped areas in situations of stagnation. Far from the xenophobic discourse of the intellectuals who had inspired Operação Amazônia, he concluded that "all those who desire to help us in this developmentalist crusade" had to be received "without fear or mistrust."[112]

Composed of representatives from about thirty different public institutions, CONDEL (SUDAM's high council) reflected the military regime's diverse sensibilities. As such, it may well have become the theater of a political conflict on the subject of foreign participation. Projects like the CVRC may have had to pay the price for such a conflict, since divisions within CONDEL could jeopardize the solidity of their partnership with SUDAM. True enough, Volkswagen was not a North American firm, whereas the move against foreign investments in Brazil, and particularly in the Amazon, consisted essentially of attacking so-called U.S. imperialism. The case most emblematic of this anti-U.S. movement was the opposition voiced by certain military men to the Castelo Branco government's approving concessions to the U.S.-owned Hanna Corporation so as to mine and export iron ore.[113] At a certain point, fear of U.S. domination among nationalists grew so strong that it drew their attention

---

[111] "A Amazônia em foco," ed. Comissão Nacional de Defesa e pelo Desenvolvimento da Amazônia (1967), 31–7.

[112] SUDAM, ed. *Operação Amazônia*, 132–3.

[113] Raymond F. Mikesell, "Iron Ore in Brazil: The Experience of the Hannah Mining Company," in *Foreign Investment in the Petroleum and Mineral Industries: Case Studies of Investor–Host Country Relations*, ed. Raymond F. Mikesell and William H. Bartsch (Baltimore, MD: Johns Hopkins University Press, 1971).

away from the actual influence coming from other foreign countries. The Brazilian government, under the presidency of Ernesto Geisel (1974–9), even implicitly utilized Brazil's partnership with non-U.S. foreign firms or official institutions as proof that its policy was not dictated by its powerful North American ally.

Concerned with demonstrating that it was not acting in the pay of U.S. rule, Geisel looked particularly at "Germany as one of the poles in the structure of Brazil's new geopolitical relations."[114] Germany had the advantage of representing an economic and technological model, but without the neocolonial connotation that existed in the case of the United States, German economic and political actors were aware that they could benefit from being citizens of a (historically) "forgotten colonial power" and as such partly immune from suspicions of imperialism.[115] German authorities cultivated this positive image by actively promoting technological exports to Brazil, while at the same time they refrained from intervening directly in Brazil's governmental decisions. The question of nuclear technology illustrated this clever tactic. In the aftermath of the 1973 oil shock, Geisel turned toward alternative sources of energy and decided that Brazil needed to increase its recourse to nuclear energy tenfold. While Brazil had previously contracted the U.S. Westington Electric Company to construct its first nuclear power plant in 1972, Geisel declined to renew this partnership in 1974. This was due in part to the political conditions set by the U.S. government, which wanted to frame the nuclear contracts with a series of measures preventing Brazil from moving toward the acquisition of nuclear weapons technology. The West Germans used this opportunity to open negotiations in order to become Brazil's new atomic industry provider.

This opening toward Germany – but also other European countries and Japan – which had been increasing since 1964, resembled a compromise between the nationalist area of the regime (which wanted to avoid foreign intervention in Brazilian affairs) and the military's dominant economic doctrine (which prioritized opening toward world capitalism). Therefore, from 1965 to 1974, German imports increased from a share of 9 percent to 12.5 percent of total foreign imports. At the same time, U.S. imports decreased from 30 percent to 24 percent.[116] While between 1969 and 1974 U.S. investments declined from a share of 47.7 percent

[114] Skidmore, *The Politics of Military Rule in Brazil*, 194.
[115] Unger, "Export und Entwicklung," 77.
[116] Uncomtrade, http://o-comtrade.un.org.biblio.eui.eu/db/dqBasicQueryResults.aspx?cc=TOTAL&rg=1&px=S1&r=76&y=1974, access date April 18, 2012.

to 33.5 percent of total foreign investments in Brazil, German investment increased from 10.4 percent to 11.8 percent, in spite of a context of widening competition. German companies were leaders in key sectors of the booming Brazilian industry, such as pharmaceutics (Bayer), electromechanics (Siemens), metallurgy, and machinery (Bosch, Mannesmann and Thyssen). These brands had all been expanding since the coup of 1964, and the Brazilian press often praised them as commercially audacious, technologically advanced, socially generous, and culturally adapting to Brazilian expectations.[117] However, it would be wrong to assume that this positive picture was bound to last forever. It was unsure how long the German label could be spared from the accusation of imperialism frequently raised against U.S. companies. Although Volkswagen enjoyed excellent backing within the government, the risk that the more nationalist parts of the regime would become critical of Volkswagen's project in the Amazon could not be discounted.

The ranching project submitted by Wolfgang Sauer was discussed three times within CONDEL before approval: in June, November, and December 1974. This was a surprisingly long period of probation, so long that at the end of 1974 General Geisel himself had to intervene and ask SUDAM to approve the project.[118] The truth is that this project embarrassed SUDAM because it threatened to gain symbolic significance showing that Brazil was selling off valuable resources to the *estrangeiros*. Although the federal government's obvious support of Volkswagen did not leave much room for protest by CONDEL members, a part of the high council sought to show its irritation by more subtle means. Instead of rejecting the project, they criticized certain significant aspects of it, demanded its revision, and delayed its validation.

CONDEL's role was not only to approve or reject a private development project, but also to decide on its level of "priority." Projects awarded "priority 1" status could benefit from a state subvention amounting to 75 percent of their capital, while the remaining 25 percent should consist of the private investor's own funds. "Priority 2" meant that SUDAM made available 50 percent of the capital, while a project labeled "priority 3" could not lay claim to more than 25 percent of incentive credits, the investing corporation having to provide 75 percent of the capital. Not surprisingly, SUDAM's executive secretary proposed to CONDEL that the CVRC

[117] "Einige sozioökonomische Auswirkungen des deutschen Kapitals in Brasilien," *Brasilien Nachrichten* (85), 1984.
[118] Buarque, "A capitania da Volkswagen."

be granted the highest priority.[119] However, the National Development Bank (BNDE) representative sparked a fire as he made his CONDEL colleagues aware that the CVRC project was both one of "exceptional profitability" and "foreign" – for him a problematic combination.[120] Although the main official shareholder of the CVRC was a Brazilian company called Transalme, this company belonged in reality to the VW-Aktiengesellschaft, with headquarters in Germany. Subsidizing this project to a level of 75% percent of its capital would even contradict the words of SUDAM's general director who, in a previous meeting, had reminded CONDEL that "priority 1" should put companies that were "eminently national" first. As a consequence, BNDE's representative asked that the CVRC be offered only a "priority 3" subvention. Although this intervention did not convince the director of SUDAM, it was followed by a long technocratic dispute, which divided CONDEL into two blocs. Quoting various SUDAM regulations, as well as paragraphs and amendments of the Operação Amazônia laws that partially contradicted each other, the council members debated whether the highest category of state subvention could be applied to a project whose main private investor was not "eminently national." This somewhat Kafkaesque controversy illustrated the ambiguities of the entire Operação Amazônia package, which could become a tricky piece of legislation when it came to its application in concrete cases. On the one hand, Operação Amazônia was a product of nationalist inspiration. On the other hand, one of its main political innovations was to open the door to foreign capital.

The question of natural resources emerged as a sticking point during the examination of the VW project. Various members of CONDEL feared that VW's economic interest might not lie in the cautious exploitation of resources. They were not anxious about the overexploitation of the forest, rather about its possible squandering. They saw deforestation as a useful process, but only as long as it was rationally planned, so that no valuable resources ended up destroyed or unexploited. Bento Souza Porto, a representative of the minister of agriculture, was embarrassed by a phrase he found in the dossier submitted to SUDAM by VW: "Clearing: after cutting down the trees, the fallen vegetation is bundled, when then its burning can be carried out." To Souza Porto, the right way would be to first engage in a program of evaluation of the valuable resources, so that the clearing could be meticulously processed, without destroying potential

[119] Arquivo da SUDAM, *Reuniões do Condel. Atas ordinárias. Jan./Jun. 1974.*
[120] Ibid., *Jul./Dez. 1974.*

primary products that could be lucratively made available in a cycle of production. By suggesting – he thought – the indiscriminate clearing of the vegetation, VW was proposing an approach that might lead to the squandering of certain valuable species, especially rare timber species such as the mogno, jatobá, and babaçú. He thought that the VW project was far too focused on cattle raising and did not give enough place to timber harvesting, although, he said, VW's country of origin had one of the best technological levels in the world regarding forestry.

This argumentation convinced the rest of CONDEL, which feared that VW's only intention was to produce cellulose from Cristalino's least valuable woods while neglecting to use valuable woods. The council members agreed that it should be avoided that the CVRC become a project of mere forest devastation. The president of SUFRAMA, a state organization selecting projects for the tax-free zone at Manaus, used the opportunity to deliver a vibrant speech in support of the preservation of Amazon biodiversity. It was November 1974 and the discussion on the CVRC, which had been going on for months, was not yet over. The council voted a resolution that forced Volkswagen to emphasize the dimension of timber exploitation in its farming project, and to give it more technical precision. Only under this condition would the project be accepted by SUDAM.[121]

The following CONDEL session at the end of December 1974 finally saw the CVRC project validated under the "priority 1" category, guaranteeing subventions and tax exemptions for a period of eleven years (renewable), on the basis of greater involvement by VW in timber exploitation. For juridical reasons, the VW ranch also had to change its status and become a public limited company, taking the new name of Companhia Vale do Rio Cristalino Agropecuária, Comércio e Indústria. It was time that SUDAM recognized the project. On the ranch, 4,000 hectares had already been cleared, and the first 3,000 head of cattle were expected by February 1975.[122] Once again, however, the debate at CONDEL hardly proceeded harmoniously. Councilors from both the minister of employment and BNDE threatened to vote against the resolution, and they were supported in this by the representative of the minister of finance. The latter did not see why foreign capital, which already had a strong position in the country, needed financial support.[123] The director of SUDAM attempted to calm the nationalist zeal of his colleagues. He insisted that

[121] Ibid., *Jan./Jun. 1974*.
[122] "Volkswagen züchtet Rinder."
[123] Ibid., *Jul./Dez. 1974*.

the CVRC was a very special project, specifically wished for by the federal government and demonstrating the success of Operação Amazônia, since the CVRC was the first concrete result of the famous entrepreneurs' visit organized in southern Pará by BASA in 1973.

The discussions about the VW project during different CONDEL meetings of 1974 provide a view of the gap existing between the two poles within the institutions of the regime. One pole was nationalist, wishing to limit control by foreign investors over Brazilian forest resources. It did not hesitate in mobilizing conservationist considerations to defend its point of view. The other pole was pragmatic, convinced that foreign participation would add precious capital, as well as technological value to the development of the Amazon. Nevertheless, there was no clear-cut division between the nationalist and pragmatic groups: the two sensibilities often emerged in the discourse of the same CONDEL member. In this regard, the debate on timber exploitation at the CVRC had an element that may be deemed inconsistent. Let us look again, for example, at the position of Souza Porto, the representative of the Ministry of Agriculture, regarding the question of timber exploitation. He insisted that SUDAM, as representative of the national interest, should be sovereign over "the rules of the game" and impose its view on Volkswagen. He was worried that VW might clear the vegetation indiscriminately. But, at the same time, he argued that SUDAM should push VW to exploit the forest's resources even more, so that "the Amazon could be occupied on a more economic basis, with greater technological density and a more rational benefitting from these immeasurable riches."

In view of this hardly coherent stance, one can legitimately raise doubts about the nationalist strain, which was expressed during CONDEL debates. How much sincerity can be interpreted from this nationalist discourse? How much posture? Everybody in the high council knew that the project was supported by President Geisel anyway. It was possible to ask VW to revise the project's modalities, but SUDAM could not reject the CVRC. All in all, it seems that the main preoccupation of some of the council members was to show VW the muscles of Brazilian sovereignty. The point was to make clear that the Brazilian state had its word to say in the making of the development projects it subsidized. The only problem in this strategy is that SUDAM, and behind it the entire military regime, did not think as a bloc, at least regarding the Amazonian question. In fact, since the launching of Operação Amazônia, capital-friendly, pragmatic positions cohabited with national populist invectives; productivist discourses inviting Brazil to a "war against nature" were balanced by conservationist approaches claiming the necessity of handling the rain forest's natural resources with caution. Consequently, VW, as it engaged in its partnership with SUDAM, not only implicitly agreed to produce a multifunctional project that would integrate, in addition to VW's own objectives, features responding to nationalist aspirations. It also exposed the CVRC to becoming (at least occasionally) a hostage of the military regime's internal divisions over the question of opening toward the outside world.

A Multifunctional Model of Development

Nationalist hesitations in approving the CVRC say much about the ambiguity of the regime's Amazonian policy, but they represented no serious threat to the project's immediate implementation. Even the most skeptical CONDEL members did not hesitate to praise the CVRC as a model ranch. During the meeting that voted "priority 1" status for the CVRC, Souza Porto insisted that VW had "contributed in a very meaningful way to the process of Amazonia's development" and stated that he had "absolutely no doubt that Volkswagen is a company which has deserved all the trust of this country."[124] After a few weeks, all opposition to the CVRC seemed to have vanished from CONDEL, as Souza Porto, without raising any dissenting remarks from the other councilors, reported very positively about a visit he had just made to Cristalino. During a council meeting at the end of January 1975, he explained that the deal on timber exploitation, which had been made with VW, had brought excellent results.[125] In Cristalino, he had noticed an optimal use of timber and a desire to exploit the valuable wood in a rational manner. He remained impressed that even the rotten wood was recycled for building fences or for provisional farm installations.

VW had good reason to respect its commitments to SUDAM: CONDEL had voted to invest more than 116 million cruzeiros (about US$19 million) in the CVRC project.[126] Amounting to more than one-fourth of SUDAM's total investments in cattle breeding, this sum stood largely above the average subvention the agency granted to private projects.[127] With a property about five times the size of Cristalino and greater

---

[124] Ibid.
[125] Ibid., *Jan./Jun. 1975*, 15.
[126] Arquivo do FINAM, SUDAM, Resolucão n° 2067, December 20, 1974.
[127] Pompermayer, "The State and the Frontier in Brazil," 186 – author's own calculation.

objectives in terms of quantity of cattle, the Agropecuária Suiá Missu, located in the same region and subject to similar ecological conditions, did not receive even half the same.[128] It is clear that CONDEL saw the CVRC as a good business opportunity to enhance SUDAM's reputation, in order to attract southern Brazilian and foreign investments in Amazon colonization. When the CVRC was launched, it seemed that SUDAM had made an excellent choice. The "model ranch" (a term used by both SUDAM and Volkswagen) created a stir in the Brazilian press, beginning with the major pro-regime political magazine *Veja*, largely read by São Paulo's economic elites.[129] But the project also raised enthusiasm in developed countries, particularly in Germany and the United States, where the *New York Times* identified it as the start of a new trend in tropical agriculture.[130]

A Win-Win Partnership

Understandably, the Germans were the most inspired by VW's Amazon novelty. Their embassy in Brazil was the first to react to the news, in September 1974, as during a conference in Brasília the head of the embassy's farming division stated that projects like the CVRC were the only ones capable of achieving a systematic clearing and cultivation of the "virgin forest." Multinational firms, he argued, were in a position to apply scientific findings and practical experiences to the Amazon, which they had collected elsewhere in the world.[131] German business circles were also seduced by VW's Amazon promise, celebrated in the national business newspaper of reference, *Handelsblatt*.[132] The *Deutsch-Brasilianische Hefte* (*DBH*), the newssheet of German investors interested in Brazil, stated in an laudatory article of January 1975 that "VW's business in the Amazon can show new and original ways for Germany to participate in the Brazilian development process. It offers Brazil a model, which can have great impact and effect for economically making the most of the Amazon region; it brings the country new sources of protein; it brings new goods and new markets for exports."[133]

---

[128] SUDAM, *Amazônia legal: manual do investidor* (SUDAM, 1972), 70.
[129] "O gado do futuro," *Veja*, December 31, 1980; "Pecuária. Projeto VW."
[130] Howe, "VW Adding Cattle to Beetle in Brazil."
[131] PA AA, Zwischenarchiv, Bd. 102.024, "Protokoll der 1. Konsularkonferenz in Brasilia vom 23. bis 25. September 1974."
[132] "VW auf vier Beinen."
[133] *Deutsch-Brasilianische Hefte*, January 1975.

The CVRC did not only interest businessmen or elites with a special knowledge of Brazil, but it also appeared in German large-circulation newspapers as an unexpected, somewhat curious, but still promising project. Publications linked to the two main West German political blocs encouraged VW in its plans. While the moderate conservative *Frankfurter Allgemeine Zeitung (FAZ)* issued a very positive report in its business supplement, the *Neue Rhein Zeitung*, (very) close to the governing center-left party SPD, depicted the CVRC as a subject of national pride.[134] Saying that "The *Volkswagenwerk* has a pilot function in the battle for the North of Brazil," the newspaper stressed that VW had taken the lead in a state-subsidized development area of 1 million hectares and 400,000 head of cattle, to produce "meat for the world." VW, according to the article, had the support of Germany in this adventure: "Here again: the Germans are present. The middle class is following the firms." Only a few far-left publications questioned the CVRC as an unethical enterprise enriching European investors at the expense of nature and the poor.[135] The newssheet *IZ 3.W* (an abbreviation for *Third World Information Center*), was scandalized by the laudatory articles published in the German press about the VW ranch. It stated that "VW contributes millions to land speculation in the Amazon region. After the state invested billions to open that region to transportation with the Transamazonian, capital can now make its profit. VW builds giant cattle farms managed by only a few workers. Even the beef adheres to the 'Produced in Brazil – Consumed in Europe and the USA' framework."

IZ 3.W's analysis represented a lonely voice in the desert. German multinational companies, and Volkswagen particularly, were seen by many as an efficient vehicle for German social-liberal values, overcoming the prejudice that had tarnished Germany's global reputation since the end of the Second World War. This is probably one explanation for the positive welcome given to the CVRC in the German media. Increasing German involvement in the booming Brazilian economy amplified interest in the project. Indeed, the German press was not only infatuated with VW do Brasil, but also with Brazil's high growth in general and the economic policy of the military regime. *Die Welt* praised Brazil and "its head

---

[134] Martin Gester, "4000 Hektar Volkswagen-Weiden wurden bereits aufgesät," *Blick durch die Wirtschaft*, December 12, 1974; Neue Rheinzeitung, November 7, 1974.

[135] "Multis," *Berliner extra Dienst*, March 11, 1975; "Brasilien. VW do Brasil," *Blätter des IZ 3. Welt*, November 1974.

of state of German decent, Geisel" as "a model for the development of Latin America," and was so fascinated by the country's economic growth that it came to the point of minimizing the violence of the dictatorship.[136] Brazil, the newspaper wrote, "compared to the communist countries and socialist states of the Third World, has a free society. In comparison with the other military governments in South America, Brazilian law makes itself appear very generous and soft."

Die Welt also complimented Brazilian policy for the Amazon, which it saw as making "the 'green hell' com[e] back to life." The positive reception of both Amazonian colonization and the CVRC by the German press fit the plans of the project's designers, who wanted to make it a model of agricultural development for the world. The plot of the CVRC was written as the success story of a win-win partnership between a "northern" company sensitive to the improvement of Third World economies, and a "southern" state open to the business spirit of the developed world. This model ranch served as a showcase to attract investors for SUDAM, which asked VW to produce advertisements for the colonization program. For example, in 1977, VW published in business magazines an advertisement illustrated by a picture of a grazing cow, subtitled "Volkswagen Sudam, model 77." Explaining that VW was using SUDAM's incentive program, the text talked about the "excellent returns on investments" of such an operation. It concluded by inviting potential investors to "apply your fiscal incentives in the area of Sudam, and come to the Amazon [and] be our neighbour. You would be giving your company a place in this task of national interest, which is the creation of new poles of progress. And this way, you will be proving your love for this country, and you will also earn more money."[137]

As for VW, it had excellent strategic reasons to place itself at the head of Amazonian colonization and mark the region with the positive image of a cutting-edge model. As the *DBH* rightly stressed, in the long term, such a project meant a secure presence for VW in a region that might soon witness a dazzling growth process.[138] The company also hoped to reap benefits in terms of image. The CVRC's symbolic reputation, framed within a national unifying colonization project, signified a further step in VW's cultural implantation in Brazil. Showing good will in contributing

---

[136] "Brasilien," *Die Welt (Supplement)*, December 4, 1974.

[137] *Amazônia*, April, July 1977. A new, similar advertisement appeared the next year: *Amazônia*, April–May 1978.

[138] *Deutsch-Brasilianische Hefte*, January 1975.

to the modernization of the nation's interior could become particularly advantageous, if not necessary.

A Way Paved for the Modernization of Brazilian Agribusiness

The Brazilian government did not want Volkswagen to appropriate the whole region surrounding Cristalino for its own corporate interest, but rather to be an economic motor, pushing local agro-industry. According to SUDAM, the project was likely to attract financial and technological resources at a high level, which would revitalize a region considered economically inactive and culturally stagnant.[139] By creating a previously unseen workforce, services, and primary products demand, Volkswagen should also accelerate the socioeconomic development of the southeastern Amazon, one of the strategic pioneer areas from which the Brazilian state sought to start the colonization process for the entire Amazon region. A report by the state agency stated that the "effects of the enterprise are unquantifiable," quoting its probable impact in increasing the revenues of the state of Pará and the county of Santana do Araguaia and improving the Brazilian herd through zoo-technical measures, "in rupture with traditional practices."[140] In sum, VW's "modern" skills were needed to improve a "nonmodern" region.

Most importantly, VW should introduce a model of livestock-raising and, as the company itself announced in advertisements, create the "ox of the future."[141] Cristalino's pastures were "planned to feed a herd expected to be standard for the Amazon."[142] Everything, in Cristalino's cattle-raising model, seemed to obey ultra-modern technical standards and extreme scientific rigor. The pastures and herds were monitored by a computerized system based at VWB's headquarters in São Bernardo do Campo, supervised by renowned agronomists and veterinarians from the Federal Polytechnic College, Zurich and from the University of Georgia in the United States. Soil and fodder were analyzed annually to determine the level of minerals that should be supplemented by salt, while sowing and fertilizing were done by airplane. Three hundred radio transmitters were implanted among the herds so as to measure the animals' pulse rates, temperature variations, and respiration frequency.

---

[139] Arquivo do FINAM, SUDAM, Processo n° 04206/74, November 29, 1974.
[140] Econorte, *Cia Vale do Rio Cristalino Agropecuária Indústria e Comércio.*
[141] "O gado do futuro."
[142] Volkswagen do Brasil, *Cristalino.*

Often described as stagnant by FAO farming experts, the Brazilian livestock sector's productivity indicators were poorly ranked by international standards.[143] Whereas the Brazilian average for producing a ton of meat was fifty-two head of cattle, VW had the objective of reaching a number close to the European norm, about fourteen head of cattle for a ton of meat.[144] VW carried out research that it hoped would result in inventing the cattle breed best adapted to tropical ranching and at the same time similar physically to cows bred in temperate climates, in order to meet the habits of Western consumers and have a chance to break through in the export market.[145] The first cattle selected to be raised at the VW ranch were Nelores, an Indian breed of Zebu extensively tried by Brazilian farmers, and resistant to tropical infectious disease. The midterm objective was finding a breed that "joins the virtues of the hardy Zebu with the productivity of European breeds."[146]

The agronomic study supposed to achieve this objective was undertaken together with a German private laboratory, the Rinderproduktion Niedersachsen, which specialized in artificial insemination, and the College of Veterinary Medicine in Hanover, the oldest veterinary school in Germany, ranked as one of the most productive in the world. The research began concretely in 1979 with a selection of 500 Zebus receiving semen from five of the best European breeds. Afterward, Zebus crossed with different European breeds were tested in the Cristalino *fazenda* and classified according to a complex selection program. The research was processed as in the European scientific tradition and consisted of identifying the superior animals and separating them into groups that provided the parameters for the parents of subsequent generations. Following a precise agenda running over fifteen to twenty years, the ranch would "obtain its own stock of improved Nelores bulls and cows, superior in all aspects to those of the region."[147] Interestingly, Cristalino's Nelores of the future, crossed from European cows and Brazilian Zebus in order to achieve an exceptional rate of productivity, appear as a metaphor for the multifunctional development model proposed within the framework of the entire CVRC project: an alliance between European techno-scientific

[143] Hecht, "Cattle Ranching in the Eastern Amazon," 28.
[144] Volkswagen do Brasil S. A., *Cristalino. Eine Rinderfarm im neuen Viehzuchtgebiet* (Volkswagen A. G.: Wolfsburg, 1983). In: VW Unternehmensarchiv.
[145] Robert Wilton Wilcox, "Cattle Ranching on the Brazilian Frontier: Tradition and Innovation in Mato Grosso, 1870–1940" (New York University, 1992), 5.
[146] Volkswagen do Brasil, *Cristalino*.
[147] Ibid.

excellence and Brazilian elites, supposed to pull the rest of the country toward a process of growth in order to achieve the standards of developed countries.

The VW ranch rapidly became a place of excellence for Brazilian agro-industry. By the late 1970s, it was the theater of an annual trade show exhibiting the CVRC's results in terms of ox raising and gathering together the region's main businessmen, farmers, and cowboys.[148] But the Brazilian authorities were confident that besides achieving exemplary production rates, VW was capable of pushing boundaries in Amazonian agricultural research and enabling technological innovations to circulate within the Brazilian farming sector. In May 1975, Wolfgang Sauer, Brazilian Minister of Agriculture Paulinelli, and German Minister of Food, Agriculture and Forestry Josef Ertl discussed the first concrete project that went in that direction.[149] On the basis of providing qualified professionals for the VW ranch as well as importing European know-how to the Amazon, the three men projected to create a large research institute for agrarian and forestry techniques. The institute would be located on the VW estate and include an educational center training specialists for the region. Sauer saw the creation of this institute as a solution to the agronomic, veterinarian, and ecological difficulties that were bound to arise in Cristalino given the newness of the project and the general lack of human knowledge about the Amazonian ecosystem. Paulinelli and the Brazilians envisaged this research and training center above all as a unit of excellence that would produce the Amazon's future agronomic elite. The idea managed to raise the interest of the German Ministries of Technology and Economic Cooperation, as well as of the Austrian government, ready to participate financially and through the transfer of expertise. It received the full support of the Brazilian National Research Council or CNPq (Conselho Nacional de Pesquisa), Brazil's main public organ for research incentives.

Besides creating regional economic demand and introducing innovative farming techniques, large-scale ranching, if it was carried out with serious ambitions, could perceptibly expand infrastructural equipment in its areas of influence. Cristalino set up a complete weather station measuring temperature, humidity, pressure, and rainfall to help program planting on the pastures in spite of seasonal imbalances. Such meteorological equipment was exceptional for a cattle ranch in Brazil

[148] Arquivo do FINAM, SUDAM, 116.5.D – 74.013, 1986, "Processo n° 0659/86."
[149] BArch B116/61917, Sauer to Ertl, September 3, 1975.

and provided precious data about the Amazon region, which were put at the disposition of other farms.[150] The construction by VW of an airstrip and airplane base at Cristalino virtually offered a new airport to the county of Santana do Araguaia. To guarantee access to the CVRC at various entrance points – bearing in mind that the ranch was the size of Luxemburg – to enable the ranch to be connected with urban centers and to reduce transportation costs over the long term, VW built an efficient road network. By the beginning of 1980, the company had already constructed 141 kilometers of road and 452 meters of bridges.[151] As VW rightly stressed, "the road which has been opened and preserved by the large businesses is facilitating the settlement of smaller companies."[152] In fact, the Brazilian state used the mediation of the big companies it funded to achieve what it could not plan and implement alone: expanding infrastructure in the Amazon region and making formerly isolated areas accessible, not only to other private companies, but also to the state itself. The transport networks and facilities established by the big ranches would enable the army, police, and other public services to expand their presence and control in the Amazon region. At the same time, the state tried to signal (whether true or not) that it was not dependent on, but was supervising, the private projects it funded. As such, state organs made sure to render visible their presence, so as to stress their own roles in the creation of infrastructure and services that came along with the projects. This is why SUDAM demanded that, in exchange for its financial participation, all CVRC machines and vehicles carry the SUDAM logo.[153]

A Social Model: The Welfare Ranch

Volkswagen's expansion was useful for Brazilian development, and Brazilian development was useful to Volkswagen: this exchange underpinned the CVRC's allegedly benefiting all actors involved, from the international businessman to the Amazonian rural worker and the average Brazilian consumer. Development for the poor necessarily started with the concentration of capital as a condition for its rational investment. An undated VW poster advertisement, probably from the late 1970s, stated under a glittering picture of the ranch that "only strong companies can afford this pioneer work: the building of roads, the production of

---

[150] Volkswagen do Brasil S. A., *Cristalino*.
[151] VW Unternehmensarchiv 174/842/2, January 1980, "CVRC Agropecuária Comércio e Indústria."
[152] Volkswagen do Brasil, *Cristalino*.
[153] Arquivo do FINAM, SUDAM, Parecer n°037/74, November 29, 1974.

electricity, the building of a school for the children and the provision of all things necessary for the people."[154] In conclusion to this capital-focused representation of development, the poster asked: "Why is Volkswagen investing so much in this project?" It answered, "because only a positive future for Brazilians means a positive future for Volkswagen in Brazil." VW, together with the Brazilian actors supporting its ranch project, applied this discourse on the macro level by profiling the CVRC as a decisive contribution to the global fight against poverty. But they also staged their social model at a micro level by constructing the ranch into an idyllic social village, whose inhabitants' privileges were depicted as desirable standards for the future Brazilian middle class.

The CVRC's social vocation was rooted in a global rhetoric of Third World development aid, made explicit by Leiding in July 1974 as he explained that VW's farming undertaking was necessary because "this world not only needs cars, but also meat."[155] Providing protein to a hungry world was a constantly asserted goal of the CVRC, which had been oriented toward this mission by the Brazilian government itself. Minister of Agriculture Paulinelli used to say that only two countries on the earth had the potential resources to alleviate the hunger catastrophes that jeopardized the ever-increasing world population: Australia and Brazil; and Brazil, if it succeeded in transforming the Amazon into the world's biggest cattle-ranching territory, would play the largest role in saving the world from a lack of protein.[156] As a VW commentator in Wolfsburg stressed, Volkswagen's first contribution to feeding the Third World was the "*fazenda* at Rio Cristalino" as "a convincing answer to Brazil's needs in terms of food."[157]

Feeding a country that allegedly lacked protein was one of the humanitarian pillars legitimizing the CVRC project. But Uwe Holtz, a Federal Member of Parliament from the SPD and president of the Commission for Cooperation in the Bundestag – the German Federal Parliament – strongly doubted VW's philanthropic intentions. For him, as he expressed in 1974 in front of VW executive Backsmann, the CVRC project was not conceptualized for the Brazilian market; it was just a capital-intensive and industrial form of farming, designed for export, unhelpful for small Brazilian farmers, and not corresponding to the priorities of Third World development. Holtz's

---

[154] In VW Unternehmensarchiv.
[155] "Interview," *Autogramm*, July 1974.
[156] *Deutsch-Brasilianische Hefte*, January 1975.
[157] Adams to Hax, August 2, 1982, in: Dritte-Welt-Haus e.V. Arbeitsgruppe Brasilien, ed. *Die Farm am Amazonas: Von Volkswagen lernen* (Bielefeld: Dritte-Welt-Haus, 1984).

position, obviously, was that of a politician who was particularly sensitive to the themes of fair cooperation and development aid.[158] However, it is easy to demonstrate a gap between VW's "feed the poor" discourse and the company's actual – and confused – commercial intentions.

For example, at the German embassy in September 1974, it was said that VW's primary commercial objective was the exportation of beef to developed countries.[159] In an internal communication emitted by VW's shareholding department (1976), it was also stated in bold print that VW in the Amazon should produce beef "principally for export."[160] During a party meeting at Cristalino at the end of 1977 involving half a dozen prestigious politicians belonging to Brazil's ruling majority, Sauer stated that Volkswagen, together with its partner farms in southeastern Pará, would slaughter 600 head of cattle a day "for exportation."[161] This is also what German journalist G. Moser understood during his visit to Cristalino.[162] Asked to clarify this point during the hearing he attended at Holtz's commission, VW representative Backsmann hardly answered whether his company would produce for the domestic or for the export market: "we will do both," he said, "we will produce for all sectors which will take delivery of our merchandise, so first for the domestic domain, obviously also for export."[163] Yet, at a public debate about social inequalities in Brazil, organized in the German city of Recklinghausen by a Catholic NGO, Otto Adams, the leader of VW's Brazil department in Wolfsburg, described the CVRC exclusively as a "meat producer for the Brazilian internal market."[164] In addition, articles dedicated to Cristalino in the *Autogramm* magazine, which was published for German employees, insisted on the ranch's contribution in feeding the Brazilian poor.[165]

It seems that VW answered differently about its commercial aims depending on the audience it was addressing. A German conservative journalist, a European businessman, or a Brazilian administrator worried about Brazil's trade balance would hear VW say that it was producing meat for export. A left-wing journalist or a German VW worker reading *Autogramm* would take away that the meat would end up on the tables

---

[158] Ausschuss für Wirtschaftliche Zusammenarbeit, *31. und 32. Sitzung*, 45.
[159] PA AA, Zwischenarchiv, Bd. 102.024, "Protokoll der 1. Konsularkonferenz in Brasilia vom 23. bis 25. September 1974."
[160] VW Unternehmensarchiv 373/190/2, August 18, 1976, "Brasilien-Schlachtprojekt."
[161] "O anfitrião Sauer," *A folha de São Paulo*, December 20, 1977.
[162] Moser, "Besichtigungsobjekt für Gäste."
[163] Ausschuss für wirtschaftliche Zusammenarbeit, *31. und 32. Sitzung*, 45.
[164] "Not in Brasilien schlägt Wellen im Revier," *Recklinghäuserzeitung*, December 1, 1982.
[165] *Autogramm*, October 1976.

of hungry Brazilian families.[166] And the German MPs on the Commission for Economic Cooperation, for they represented different parties and ideological sensibilities, would get a convoluted answer amounting to every possible meaning.

The truth is that VW had no long-term business plan. Not a single company document – unless it has been kept secret until now – gave details of the CVRC's sales objectives, be it for the import or the export market. In any case, it was very unlikely that CVRC beef directly contributed to filling the lack of protein experienced by the poorest sectors of the Brazilian population.[167] Since the CVRC set out to produce meat of exceptional quality and resorted to high technical investment, its meat would probably end up being sold at a high price and, even if in the domestic market, addressed to upper-class consumers. The CVRC project was aborted before it really established itself in an identifiable business cycle. Production from the VW ranch, in its first and only thirteen years of life, was principally consumed in the VW canteens at São Bernardo do Campo and by the farm's inhabitants, while the CVRC's profits essentially came from the export of timber and cellulose.[168] However, numbers unveiled by the Brazilian organization of slaughterhouses in May 1986, when the CVRC was just beginning to establish itself on the beef market, revealed that the company offered ready-to-slaughter cattle at more than 1.5 times the price normally paid in the country.[169] This figure confirms the tendency suspected by Schölermann that VW would essentially produce meat for socially more affluent classes.

Releasing Brazilian society from hunger, at any rate, was only one side of VW's humanitarian coin. The other was the allegedly privileged treatment offered to the farm's 450 employees, who with their families composed an "employee village" of about 800 inhabitants in 1974–5.[170] Unlike the administrative staff, mainly coming from São Paulo, the employees came predominantly from the states of Amazônia Legal and had grown up in frontier areas. A great majority of them came from Goiás, an Amazonian state with low socioeconomic ratings bordering the eastern side of Pará.[171] Since Goiás was historically a weakly populated

[166] *Autogramm*, July 1974.
[167] Schölermann, "Volkswagen do Brasil," 86.
[168] Econorte, *Cia Vale do Rio Cristalino Agropecuária Indústria e Comércio.*
[169] "Para a Sunab, pecuaristas retêm o gado e prejudicam abastecimento," *A folha de São Paulo*, May 28, 1986.
[170] Öffentlichkeitsarbeit Volkswagenwerk A. G., *Volkswagen*, 41.
[171] Buarque, "A capitania da Volkswagen."

forest region, many of its inhabitants came from migrant (frequently northeastern) families. Volkswagen often insisted that the company had pulled these people out of a precarious, nomadic life marked by poverty. "In this huge project," so went a company document on the CVRC, "there is included, and this is not a secondary feature, a big social engagement on the part of an industrial enterprise for the people working for it."[172]

The CVRC comprehended a series of social services, presented as advantages offered to the farm workers. One of these was the "Wolfgang Sauer Grammar School," featuring modern, audiovisual teaching equipment, and benefiting not only the Cristalino children, but also the children of employees in certain neighboring *fazendas*.[173] From 1978, a VW vehicle traveled more than 300 kilometers daily to transport the students. The children received "medical assistance" and "free snacks." Even the farm workers could go to school and attend literacy classes. For VW, the school was an important contribution to the process of "settling man on the ranch, where he receives a good salary, modern functional housing and an excellent social structure." The ranch's employees, indeed, could count on basic comfort, which, compared to the living standards of the Amazon region at the time, was exceptional. They lived in small personal or family houses fitted with electricity and running water. They had – at least according to VW public documents – good salaries, leisure schedules, and spaces – a soccer field, a bar, a dancing club, cinemas, and swimming pools, including other distractions – as well as free medical and dental services. They could buy essential goods like milk, meat, or rice at prices below their standard market value, and vegetables, grown on the farm itself, were distributed free of charge.[174] VW publications stressed that all these social-friendly principles were imported from the welfare policy already applied in its German factories. This was the case, for example, as regards the low prices of products sold in the farm canteens and shops, which, according to "an age-old instruction from Wolfsburg, are only allowed to be sold at cost rates, hence they cannot make a profit."[175]

As if to prove the sincerity of its social commitment through an argument based on coherence, most VW company communications about the privileges of farm employees were concluded by statements about the common interests between firm and workers – such as: "Workplace turnover

[172] "Der Friedensrichter kam zur Sammelhochzeit," *Autogramm*, March 1982.
[173] Volkswagen do Brasil, *Cristalino*.
[174] "O gado do futuro."
[175] "Der Urwald überwuchert Alles."

among the farm's collaborators is low. This shows how worthwhile it is to familiarize the worker with the comfort of a house with electric light and running water, and pay him well, build schools for his children, afford him medicinal and dental care."[176] A confidential document consigned to SUDAM by VW in 1974 detailed the nature of this common interest in somewhat more corporate-centered language: "To be effective and able for required productivity, the worker also needs to be well fed, healthy, strong and – as a human being – encircled, together with his family, in certain, though modest, conditions of dignity."[177]

That a business's financial interests automatically gave rise to corporate generosity is a debatable statement, making it worth asking the following question: could the CVRC's self-proclaimed social vocation be taken for granted? How far was the CVRC a model ranch with regard to the welfare structure offered to employees – leaving aside, for the moment, any possible practical deviations from the ranch's official welfare package? Looking at the details of this package, it appears that the generosity that the CVRC claimed to demonstrate toward its workers was limited. Wages, for example, were not as high as VW documents stated. The majority of CVRC workers (cowboys, mechanical workers, woodworkers) earned only about 14 percent to 15 percent more than the official Brazilian minimum wage, even if a number of tractor drivers, working team leaders, and bulldozer drivers received a more advantageous income (35 percent to 36 percent more than the minimum wage for the former, and approximately. 2.7 and 3.6 times the minimum wage respectively for the latter categories).[178] Although the numerous free or low-cost services available to the employees contributed to sharply reducing their cost of living, it is worth noting that the Brazilian minimum wage constituted a very low basis. In principle, it was calculated to cover the vital needs of a worker's family with four children (food, housing, clothing, transport, and hygiene). However, the cost of living that served as the official basis for determining the official minimum wage was largely underestimated by the government, which only partially took the ever-rising inflation into consideration. According to a German NGO, the Brazilian minimum wage did not even cover the daily needs in calories for an individual rural worker – hence, it was far from enabling a decent livelihood for an entire family.[179] Besides, the material advantages listed in VW advertising

[176] Ibid.
[177] Econorte, *Cia vale do Rio Cristalino agropecuária indústria e comércio.*
[178] Schölermann, ‚Volkswagen do Brasil."
[179] Arbeitsgruppe Brasilien, ed. *Die Farm am Amazonas*, 17.

were only distributed to CVRC employees. The hundreds of seasonal, outsourced laborers employed in clearing and infrastructure building did not receive a single one of these advantages.

The exclusion of seasonal workers from social advantages testifies to how this welfare structure was reserved for a micro population and was in part limited to VW's legal obligations. What VW presented as privileges offered to its workers often corresponded to mere compliance with Brazilian law or with VW's contractual commitments with SUDAM. In the agreement, which was a condition for receiving SUDAM subventions for the project, it was listed under the "economic goals to achieve" category that the ranch should develop "additional services; social, moral and civic assistance; livelihood" for its human population.[180] It was also SUDAM that obliged the companies it funded to supply hospital services and guarantee access to school for the children, although Volkswagen alleged to the German public that these services were "set up without any legal obligation."[181] VW's prospectus boasted that "the Volkswagen ranch was also one of the first enterprises to set up an industrial safety structure and to organize an Internal Commission for the Prevention of Accidents in the rural zone of Pará," or that "cowboys receive pants, shirts and boots for their activities. Those that work in specific areas, as in mechanics or the sawmill, receive adequate clothing – boots with steel toecaps, gloves, hard hats and safety glasses."[182] These were certainly positive precautions that were part of improving the workers' conditions. Nevertheless, far from being spontaneous acts of protection granted by a firm to its employees, these measures were stipulated by Brazilian legislation. The setting up of commissions for the prevention of accidents was compulsory for every company of more than 100 employees in Brazil since 1944, and the labor law established under Vargas implied that working equipment could not be deduced from salaries.[183]

Did Volkswagen's social contribution to Amazonian development merely consist of respecting the ranch's legal obligations? After all, the firm bragged about "the new patterns of behavior" it was introducing in the Amazon, quoting in the first place its respect for "tax-paying and labor legislation": being faithful to the law was, in VW's eyes, a humanitarian innovation that deserved mention.[184] This point of view was

---

[180] Arquivo do FINAM, SUDAM, Parecer n°037/74, November 29, 1974.
[181] *Autogramm*, September 1985.
[182] Volkswagen do Brasil, *Cristalino*.
[183] Decree-Law n° 7.036/44, Art. 82.
[184] Volkswagen do Brasil, *Cristalino*.

not, in fact, absurd. Most of the southern Pará farms did not supply the services that VW provided for its employees. Many of these farms hardly took account of the minimum wage. Some of them did not even draw up legal employment contracts.[185] In this regard, the VW ranch was indeed a social friendly oasis in the middle of the jungle. Ironically, the unethical practices of the surrounding ranches legitimized the CVRC as a model.

Neither a "Tropical Wolfsburg" nor a "Brasília in Miniature"

As they began to elaborate their colonization plans, the VW executives in Wolfsburg started to define the Amazon as an "underdeveloped" region.[186] They surely meant it in an economic sense, but as Esteva describes, the allusions contained in the "underdeveloped" epithet go well beyond. The term points toward the "undignified condition" of not living according to the standards of industrial countries.[187] "Underdevelopment," according to Esteva, is a rhetorical construction that belittles an area and its population into a condition they are supposed to "escape" through development. In this regard, escaping underdevelopment does not only take place through economic transformation. It is also a process that aims to change mentalities, educate people to productive work, a spirit of initiative, and self-confidence. This was one of the tasks the CVRC undertook, which, as well as being a social and economic project, was also a civilization laboratory.

As the building of the ranch structure progressed, VW's discourse increasingly stressed the idea of creating a nucleus of civilization in the middle of the wild. Advertisements declared that the CVRC was "almost a city," "worthy of a city in the middle of the jungle," or, more explicitly, "the civilization which has arrived" in the Amazon.[188] The word "city," often placed with that of "civilization" or "development," meant something different for the traditional Amazonian villages and countryside communities of the Amerindians or Caboclos, which in comparison to the developing urban south were seen as living in a state of immobility. The "city" was a place in movement, striving for modernity, as opposed to the "village," symbolizing "timelessness and rooted traditions."[189] But the city was also a community of human beings, sharing the same way

[185] Brantord, *The Last Frontier*.
[186] VW Unternehmensarchiv 174/533/2, November 14, 1973, "65. Sitzung des Aufsichtsrats der VW-AG."
[187] Gustavo Esteva, "Development," in *The Development Dictionary*, ed. Sachs, 6–25, 7.
[188] *Veja*, December 31, 1980.
[189] Cullather, *The Hungry World*, 5, 78, 84.

of life framed by a collective imaginary. This project of a "city in the middle of the jungle" was reminiscent of different past experiments. For example, impressed by the modern infrastructure of the ranch's buildings, its airport, club, and swimming pool, a local Brazilian priest saw the CVRC as a "Brasília in miniature."[190] Just like Brasília, the CVRC symbolized Brazil's national move toward development, and was erected from scratch in the middle of an unpopulated area in the interior of the country. This comparison stops where the CVRC's actual function begins, however: unlike Brasília, the colony at Cristalino was built to sustain an agro-industrial project. The small city was organized so as to connect the private fulfilment of the inhabitants with their duties as workers, and encourage them to identify with their employer, VW.[191]

In this aspect, Cristalino was in the lineage of the tradition in which Wolfsburg itself was founded almost out of nothing in 1938, to house the workers of the very first Volkswagen factory.[192] Wolfsburg is not the only historical example of a city created by and for a company. Henry Ford carried out several such experiments in the American Midwest and even built his jungle city Fordlândia as part of his search for the ideal North American small town. That Fordlândia served as a model for Cristalino is mentioned nowhere – probably, the legendary failure of Ford's project dissuaded Volkswagen from risking any such comparison. But there are some resemblances between the two colonies, in spite of the decades that separate the founding of Fordlândia (1928) and that of Cristalino (1973). Cristalino's housing complex, for example, is at least partially reminiscent of that of Fordlândia, with its small family houses with identical masonry, harmoniously aligned on regular, large avenues. In spite of architectural differences between these two cases, the way individual housing was organized invited the inhabitants to a similar, Westernized lifestyle, with a fence to demarcate the family's perimeter, a small, flower garden, and a private parking lot.[193]

---

[190] Ricardo Rezende Figueira, *A justiça do lobo: posseiros e padres do Araguaia* (Petrópolis: Vozes Ltda, 1986), 33.

[191] Company towns in which workers' control is intimately combined with measures of social welfare have been a frequent basis for the social engineering of multinational development projects in Latin America. See Thomas Miller Klubock, *Contested Communities: Class, Gender, and Politics in Chile's El Teniente Copper Mine, 1904–1951* (Durham, NC, and London: Duke University Press, 1998), 49–80.

[192] Wolfsburg's first official name was "Stadt des KdF-Wagens bei Fallerselben": Christian Schneider, *Stadtgründung im Dritten Reich: Wolfsburg und Salzgitter: Ideologie, Ressortpolitik, Repräsentation* (München: Moos, 1978).

[193] Source: Volkswagen do Brasil S. A., *Cristalino*.

FIGURE 2.3 Employees' house with garden at Cristalino.
Source: Image courtesy of Volkswagen Aktiengesellschaft. Volkswagen do Brasil
S. A., *Cristalino: eine Rinderfarm im neuen Viehzuchtgebiet* (Volkswagen A. G.:
Wolfsburg, 1983).

However, there was a major difference between the two jungle cities.
Fordlândia was a deliberate – and quite ingenious – attempt to transpose
the architecture and customs of an industrial U.S. city into a tropical
forest area. For example, the Midwestern-styled houses there, if they corresponded to Henry Ford's vision of American modernity, were "totally
inappropriate for the Amazon climate" for the choice to build metal roofs
lined with asbestos instead of the traditional Amazonian materials made
them "hotter than the gates of hell." A witness stated that they seemed
to be "designed by Detroit architects who probably couldn't envision a
land without snow."[194] Cristalino, on the contrary, was something other
than a tropical clone of Wolfsburg. In the ranch esthetic, organization,
and habits, there is no sign of any obsession from the management to
impose a "Germanized" way of life on the Brazilian inhabitants. Still,

[194] Grandin, *Fordlândia*, 274–5.

as an international experiment partly driven by Germans, conceived to consolidate the reputation of a private firm, neither was Cristalino a "little Brasília." It was a new invention, in which (mainly) European businessmen claimed to both import their industrial know-how and place their model into a genuinely Brazilian national project.

A draft of the project, which VW handed to SUDAM in 1974, described clearly that the CVRC was an enterprise, which not only envisaged revolutionizing agricultural techniques, but also the human mind. Making the workers aware of a common industrial objective, encouraging them to perceive themselves as an integrated part within a collective pioneer adventure, were key objectives of this civilizing mission. Thus, in the VW project, we learn that "the spirit of community will be first developed by strengthening the awareness of the inhabitants, and then maintaining it at the highest level, so that the community leans toward a gradual evolution, predisposing the men to labor," or still more that VW wanted to make of the ranch worker a "man aware of his value and responsible" because this was "the most important key to entrepreneurial success." In the context of geographic isolation, hard work, and the health risks that characterized life at the ranch, VW proposed establishing measures that could strengthen group cohesion and teach the workers to be socially responsible and capable of living in community. "Man will not be seen as a singular being," an administrative document said, "but rather as a socialized being, who thinks and acts according to the patterns, to the traditions of his group, adapting to the social situations that, at every step, take shape around him."[195]

For those who designed the project, the introduction of a solid settler mentality was a necessary condition for single individuals adapting to the spirit of community. Settlement, in turn, could be achieved only through a solid family life, as a guarantee of the workers' private stability. This meant that the Amazon workers had to renounce their previous life customs. As the company's communication service did not hesitate to explain in a public brochure, VW intervened in the workers' private lives, for example, by inciting cohabiting partners to marry: "*Living together*, the most common form of relationship in the region, does not give the family stability necessary for men to settle. As a result, the Companhia Vale Do Rio Cristalino encouraged the legalization of these de facto situations."[196]

[195] Econorte, *Cia Vale do Rio Cristalino Agropecuária Indústria e Comércio*.
[196] Volkswagen do Brasil, *Cristalino*.

In 1977, for example, CVRC management called a magistrate and organized a collective marriage ceremony to "regularize" the situation of the thirty nonmarried couples.[197] The company celebrated the success of this interventionist strategy in the following terms: "the man of the region, formerly of a nomadic disposition, began to put down roots, making for a low turn-over rate in the manual labor of the ranch." The company's regulation of private behavior had other aspects, sometimes approaching bodily control, such as to "enlighten about the dangers of consanguine marriages" or "making families aware of the advantages of having habits of body, house, clothing and even mental hygiene." Management paid attention to the capacity of the workers' families to run their homes. The ranch family keeping its house in the "most beautiful and ordered way" received a refrigerator as a Christmas present from the company. An education in the area of "balanced diet" was also planned. The establishment of familial norms compatible with the employees' working duties went so far as to provide "familial orientation, chiefly regarding the notions of child education, of relations between spouses, between parents and children and between brothers and sisters, aiming, as the highest point of this process, towards familial harmony."[198]

Not surprisingly, women, viewed as important contributors to the workers' stability and welfare, were taught how to become skilled housewives, receiving sewing, homemaking, and embroidery lessons.[199] The manner in which VW was concerned with influencing the family life of its employees in the Amazon, was not invented from a clean slate, but drawn from practices already applied in the giant VW plant at São Bernardo do Campo. The establishment of a maternity ward in the private VW clinic at São Bernardo, for example, was a way of strengthening the company's symbolic patronage of its employees' families. An advertisement explained that in this clinic, "a daily average of eight 'VW-babies' comes into the world; and the father who plans for the long-term sees in a baby, especially when it is of male gender, a future employee at VW do Brasil."[200]

---

197 "Der Friedensrichter kam zur Sammelhochzeit."
198 "VW als Viehzüchter," *Institut für Brasilienkunde e.V. Informationen*, January–April 1977.
199 Volkswagen do Brasil, *Cristalino*.
200 Volkswagenwerk A. G., *VW in Brasilien*. About the fabrication of gender roles in the Brazilian industry, see also Barbara Weinstein, *For Social Peace in Brazil: Industrialists and the Remaking of the Working Class in São Paulo, 1920-1964* (Chapel Hill, NC: University of North Carolina Press, 1996).

This form of managing private life illustrated how a modern company understood the process of transposing people from instable, nonmodern life to the legible rules of civilization. In this narrative, separating the human from the forest, as a condition for mastering the natural world at the service of an economic project, was primordial. In a document published in the early 1980s, VW told the epic story of the first pioneers who arrived during the "difficult times" of 1973–4, when the CVRC was not yet an organized ranch, but still a patch of forest.[201] Food sometimes had to be dropped by airplane, when the weather forbade the movement of vehicles, but still the VW employees managed to survive the difficult natural conditions. The first ranch headquarters were built with mud walls and covered by wild banana leaves, replaced after a few months by houses made of wood, and some time later by "third generation housing" in masonry. This was the story of pioneer men – women were inexistent in this narrative – overcoming the hard conditions imposed by nature to finally embrace a modern life. The way in which VW advertisements described family gardens in the ranch housing complex was a meaningful illustration of this detachment from natural contingencies: "Even the individual gardens of the houses are wrenched from the wild. And, of course, these gardens have a proper fence, so as to keep wild animals away."[202] What matters here is the physical distinction from the wild encouraged by VW, with the intention of the ranch families being solidly settled within the borders of civilization. The more ranch men and women were educated and prepared, according to the educational material outlining the CVRC project, the more they "will be able to decisively confront the obstacles of hostile nature, taming it, placing it more effectively at the service of the entrepreneurial community."[203] As may be seen, CVRC inhabitants were educated according to Operação Amazonia guidelines, which encouraged Brazilians to adopt a new, more offensive, and "rational" attitude toward nature. The CVRC needed workers who could dominate nature, unlike traditional peasants, who, according to a VW document, had failed to exploit Amazonian land because they "helplessly faced the climate, distances and soil conditions" of the forest.[204]

VW also inculcated a sense of loyalty in its rural workers and cultivated pride in belonging to the great multinational VW family. Constructing

---

[201] Volkswagen do Brasil, *Cristalino*.
[202] Volkswagenwerk A. G., *Volkswagen*.
[203] Econorte, *Cia Vale do Rio Cristalino Agropecuária Indústria e Comércio*.
[204] Volkswagen do Brasil S. A., *Cristalino*.

this emotional link could only have positive effects on the workers' productivity. The VW project outline stated that the duality of social supplies and education programs provided to the worker were aimed at conferring upon him "permanency and true integration into the company, as a factor and as a person."[205] In 1980, a VW brochure seemed to consider this goal as already accomplished, for it asserted that the workers had already found a "homeland" (*heimat*) in VW.[206] Besides encouraging the Cristalino laborers to perceive themselves as much VW workers as, for example, the car assemblers at Wolfsburg or São Bernardo do Campo, VW management sought to integrate the farm into the VW global community by bringing the urban automobile workers into – virtual – contact with the colonization process led by the company in the Amazon. The German VW workers regularly received, via *Autogramm*, news of the advancement of the clearing job and farming experiments in Cristalino. The magazine also relayed images of suntanned Cristalino cowboys in picturesque photographs that showed them riding horses, posing in front of cattle herds, or leaning on a pasture guardrail that carried the metallic VW brand logo.

The pictures were accompanied by captions insisting on these workers' belonging to the VW family, such as "even these four weather-beaten and adventurous-looking boys are VW-employees, who carry out their work under the same logo as all" – or still more "Strangers' faces, marked by life in the virgin forest, and still in the widest sense VW-employees."[207] As for the Brazilian car workers, the CVRC was rendered materially present in their social and working life. The meat and vegetables produced at Cristalino were served in the VW canteens of São Bernardo do Campo. Some of the Amazonian timber was recycled to build boxes and packaging the car workers used in their factory. In counterpart, new models or technical innovations produced by the VWB workers were tested by inhabitants of the ranch property before being put into commercial circulation.

The CVRC's mission, however, could not be limited to promoting the VW world community. In the economic integration of the Amazon, SUDAM saw a way to expand the authority of the Brazilian central state. Volkswagen was expected to help promote national values, as one of the

[205] Econorte, *Cia Vale do Rio Cristalino Agropecuária Indústria e Comércio.*
[206] Richter, *Die Fazenda am Cristalino*, 12.
[207] "Wir vertrieben keine Indianer," *Autogramm*, November 1978; "Der Urwald überwuchert Alles."

FIGURE 2.4 Ranch cowboys.
Source: Image courtesy of Volkswagen Aktiengesellschaft. *Autogramm*, September 1985.

FIGURE 2.5 Cowboys on horses. Original caption in *Autogramm*, March 1982: "Auch das sind VW-Mitarbeiter mit Cowboyhut auf kleinen, zähen Amazonas-Pferden" ("Even these are VW employees with cowboy hats on short and sturdy horses").
Source: Copyright license from Pictures Alliance – DPA.

FIGURE 2.6 Employees showing the VW logo. Original caption in *Autogramm*, October 1985: "Stolz zeigen die Gauchos das VW-Zeichen, unter dem sie gerne arbeiten" ("The *Gauchos* proudly show the VW logo under which they are happy to work").
Source: Copyright license from Pictures Alliance – DPA.

counterparts for the subventions it received. For SUDAM, "the Company Vale do Rio Cristalino was organized with the supreme purpose of contributing proficiently to the aspirations of the developmentalist movement in the Amazon."[208] A meaningful picture published by VW shows, for example, the children of the Wolfgang Sauer Grammar School gathered in line, standing at attention behind several flags being hoisted at the same time. Of the two central flags, one carries the emblem of VW, while another bears the Brazilian national colors. Jacky Mendonça, one of Sauer's collaborators, remembers the ritual immortalized by this picture: "The children were there, in front of us, all dressed in their uniforms, standing side by side, singing the national anthem, while the Brazilian flag rose along the mast, shaken by the movement of the wind."[209]

This was coherent with VW's commitments, in which it promised SUDAM to provide the ranch population with lessons in moral and civic education transmitting "respect for the authorities and laws of the

[208] Arquivo do FINAM, SUDAM, Parecer 037/74, November 29, 1974.
[209] Doretto, *Wolfgang Sauer*, 346.

FIGURE 2.7 The children of the ranch standing behind four flags representing, from left to right: the Cristalino Company, Volkswagen, the Brazilian nation, and the state of Pará.
Source: Image courtesy of Volkswagen Aktiengesellschaft. Volkswagen do Brasil S. A., *Cristalino: eine Rinderfarm im neuen Viehzuchtgebiet* (Volkswagen A. G.: Wolfsburg, 1983).

country, thus awakening the spirit of nationality and patriotism." The CVRC would also organize "civic celebrations on the most relevant national days," so as to keep the workers' national feeling alive in spite of their relative geographic isolation from the rest of the country's human population.[210] VW was bringing the national state into the deep interior, and thus delivering to the governing military regime and its civilian supporters a demonstration of its Brazilianization. In an advertisement for Cristalino published in 1976 in popular Brazilian magazines, VWB underlined its strong territorial presence, right up to the pioneer frontier of the rain forest: "We, who are here, can testify. Occupying the great empty spaces of Brazilian territory today is the most fascinating and promising undertaking in the whole world, contributing to turning into reality the motto of *integrar para não entregar*."[211] That a multinational firm could reclaim the xenophobic message driving the military regime's doctrine of national security, according to which Brazil had to "integrate" the Amazon in order to protect the region from foreign greed, illustrated the deep paradox of Operação Amazonia.

[210] Econorte, *Cia Vale do Rio Cristalino Agropecuária Indústria e Comércio*.
[211] *Manchete*, May 8, 1976.

Another demand of the military regime, which held to Christianity as a force cementing national cohesion, was embraced by VW: that of spiritual education. This education would have its place in the ranch "as pinnacle of the educational process, staging man as God's creature, moulded after his own image and likeness."[212] For this purpose, a church was built at Cristalino as early as in 1976. Most probably, this initiative also aimed at framing the workers' religious practices within the borders of the Cristalino company. Faith should be expressed with the help and under the supervision of CVRC management, so as to prevent the workers from being influenced by Marxist priests supporting the liberation theology movement. Throughout the 1970s, the latter became increasingly popular among rural laborer communities in the county of Santana do Araguaia. As a later chapter will elaborate, these priests depicted large Amazonian ranchers as enemies of the workers' interest. Various organizations close to liberation theology were attentive to the unfolding of the VW ranch and its consequences for the social equilibrium of the region.

As in the case of religious education for the workers, the CVRC's implementation program combined the concerns of the military regime with those of Volkswagen. This historical example shows that development cannot be reduced to a discourse that established patterns of domination from North to South. The success of the VW project depended largely on SUDAM's decisions. An annual report as well as frequent visits to the ranch by SUDAM administrators, veterinarians, economists, and agronomists decided whether the CVRC still deserved the entire array of financial incentives.[213] At the same time, this partnership supposed that the weaknesses of the Brazilian state apparatus also had an influence on the feasibility of the CVRC project. Volkswagen executives complained that they had to slow down the implementation of their plans and sometimes mobilize unplanned financial funds because SUDAM, paralyzed by its labyrinthine bureaucratic structure, often had delays in distributing subventions.[214] The stipulations of SUDAM also contributed to balancing VW's ambitions with a more cautious way of handling nature, for example, by insisting that the CVRC maintain a reforestation project. Although modest in size (172 hectares per annum), reforestation was strictly obligatory and obeyed precise and ample objectives with regard to

[212] Econorte, *Cia Vale do Rio Cristalino Agropecuária Indústria e Comércio.*
[213] Apesteguy, "L'intervention fédérale en Amazonie," 172.
[214] VW Unternehmensarchiv 373/190/2, August 18, 1976, "Beteiligungen."

biodiversity.[215] As contradictory as it may seem in the context of the regime's proclaimed developmentalist goals, voices existed within the Brazilian institutions that spoke in favor of a balanced exploitation of the forest and a careful handling of its ecosystems. As the next chapter will demonstrate, these voices also called for alterations to the CVRC project.

VW perfectly understood that SUDAM was the place from which to influence economic policies in the Amazon. In this respect, Sauer opted for a strategy of personal engagement. In negotiations about the setting and implementation of the CVRC, he preferred to meet SUDAM's director, Hugo de Almeida, personally, and chose to face SUDAM's cold administrative machine with his usual warmth and enthusiasm for human relations.[216] In his enterprise of charming SUDAM, Sauer was allied with the AEA business organization, which included the Amazon's biggest and most powerful ranchers. Although the AEA always fell short of its main claim – to have a certain number of seats for business representatives within CONDEL so that the private sector could monitor the planning of Amazonian colonization – the organization enjoyed influential networks and direct access to governing organs at state and federal levels.[217] The directing board of AEA, of which Volkswagen became a member immediately after the establishment of the CVRC, was in permanent contact with the Ministries of Agriculture and of the Interior. It regularly organized events attended by prestigious guests such as government representatives or SUDAM administrators. In 1975, Sauer led AEA's new campaign of claims and, as such, handed Hugo de Almeida a list of AEA-recommended measures. It included the end of payment delays in SUDAM incentives, administrative simplification, and greater flexibility in the funding criteria of SUDAM.[218] Moreover, Sauer was aware that the ranch's future depended on its identification with the Brazilian national project as a whole. In order to secure government support, and to win over Brazilian public opinion, he used to say in public interviews that VW wanted to "use fiscal incentives, together with industrial and administrative know-how, in order to help the government to integrate the north. It is with this motivation that we took up the challenge of livestock farming."[219]

[215] J. M. Condurú, *Projeto florestal Cia Vale do Rio Cristalino* (Condurú Agrimazônia LTDA, 1975). In: Arquivo do FINAM, Belém.
[216] "Volks ultima seu projeto na Amazônia," *A folha de São Paulo*, March 18, 1975.
[217] Apesteguy, "L'intervention fédérale en Amazonie," 176–7.
[218] "AEA elege diretoria," *Amazônia*, March 1977.
[219] "Interview," *Quatro rodas*.

In the end, there was neither a multinational nor a nationalist project at the Vale do Rio Cristalino: there were state authorities and nationalists trying to retain control over multinational investments and to orient the project according to the regime's goals. There was also a multinational company trying to influence Brazilian federal policies in order to defend its own interests in the process of Amazonian colonization. The CVRC was nothing but the result of the interaction between these two poles. Neither of the sides permanently and clearly had the upper hand in the project. This situation shows how fragile the concept of development was, in spite of its appearance of being absolute, covering all domains of life and deciding the direction in which the country should move. Development was presented as the path to follow for everyone, the only possible road out of poverty and dependency. However, it served interests that were sometimes opposed.

During its first years of life, the CVRC was politically successful because VW and the SUDAM managed to conceal these divisions behind an enthusiastic developmentalist rhetoric. Admittedly, the form in which the project was implemented raised some doubts and provoked minor controversies: Sauer and Leiding could have involved their VW colleagues more in their plans and the coordination between VW and SUDAM could have been somewhat better prepared. But the core idea of the project, that the Amazon needed a high level of technology and rationally managed farming, and that big capitalist groups were best suited to accomplishing such tasks, remained nearly uncontested. The period between 1976 and 1983, approached in the following chapter, was not as peaceful for the CVRC, principally because the idea that the forest should be massively altered for the service of human development grew ever less evident.

3

Development in the Age of Scarcity (1976–1983)

To understand how the question of the finitude of natural resources affected the developmentalist consensus, let us for a moment accelerate time and look at an episode that occurred in 1983. At this point, the VW ranch had added a slaughterhouse, located further east in the county of Santana do Araguaia. A new manager coordinated the CVRC; he was a Swiss agronomist named Friedrich Georg Brügger. He received the visit of a journalist from the German magazine *GEO*, writing a feature on endangered biodiversity in tropical forests. As they were visiting the slaughterhouse, the latter asked Brügger how it felt to clear 6,000 hectares of forest year after year, burning the woods to gain pastures.[1] "Understand me," the journalist insisted, "an ecologist would describe the circumstances as follows: yesterday, rangy centuries-old rain forest was still standing in that place, and today grey oxen are grazing there." Staring at his interlocutor as if the latter were a madcap, Brügger replied, horrified: "Every day, 200 million people are starving in the world – and you're talking of protecting the virgin forests!" The journalist, in turn, held these words for nonsense, saying: "but the two things have nothing to do with each other. The starving people in the Brazilian northeast, in the slums of Manaus or Altamira [two rapidly growing northern Amazonian cities] are just far too poor to buy meat." As the conversation went on, the journalist realized that he and Brügger simply could not agree. He always saw "rain forest," where Brügger systematically understood "beef."

Brügger's point of view, in this scene, was that nature could in no way constitute an obstacle to human progress, and that the destruction of the

---

[1] Peter Schille, "Angriff auf die Wildnis," *GEO (Germany)*, February 1984.

forest was a condition for helping humanity out of poverty. This opinion corresponded to the developmentalist consensus that underpinned the agreement between state and private companies resulting in the CVRC project in 1973. At that time, the official discourse of the military regime was to see environmental protection as an enemy of progress. This was at least the developmentalist visage the Brazilian delegates exhibited at the first Conference of the United Nations (UN) on the Human Environment held in Stockholm in 1972. These delegates argued that environmental measures should not be allowed to slow down the march of developing countries toward industrialization.[2]

At the same time, the Stockholm conference signaled the arrival into world politics of the new awareness that natural resources were not infinite. As the Amazon policy in Brazil was intimately linked with a process of accelerated appropriation of resources, it was concerned in the first place with this finitude. A couple of years later, the consequences of the quadrupling of global oil prices put an end to economic optimism in Brazil by sweeping away the belief that development had no limits. In the light of this new context, national developmentalism started to be unsteady on its feet, and state-financed projects implying the mobilization of natural resources by foreign actors – like the CVRC – to be observed by Brazilians with a watchful eye. As collective belief in an irresistible and endless development vanished, the worry grew that waste and destruction of resources might lead to their scarcity. Including at the global scale, many actors ceased seeing the Amazon as an endless reserve of primary goods, and grew concerned with forest preservation.

This chapter depicts how this shifting vision of the Amazon, influenced by rising ecological concerns and a growing awareness of the limits of human progress, affected the CVRC project. However, as we grasp from Brügger's difficulties in discussion with the *GEO* journalist, it was not an easy task to make the CVRC compatible with the principles of environmental care. Indeed, the ranch project was born out of the will to colonize nature, independent of any kind of thought for the forest's ecological equilibrium. In the following, I show how, through ecological debates and conflicts involving the distribution of land, in an increasingly disputed Amazon region, the VW ranch would cease to be an utopian, ground-breaking model, and began to experience the limits of development.

---

[2] Ferreira and Tavolaro, *Environmental Concerns in Contemporary Brazil.*

VW's "Environmental Sins": Facing the Issue of Natural Resources

The clearing of the Cristalino estate was carried out through a mix of four techniques applied one after the other. Logging was first effectuated by bulldozers according to the "thick chain" method, developed by the U.S. Army to clear the forests where Viet Cong soldiers hid during the Vietnam War.[3] Two 400-horsepower tractors, driving at a short, parallel distance from each other, pulled a heavy, ninety-meter-long metal chain, uprooting the trees in their path.[4] After this, a defoliant was spread on the just logged area to eliminate weeds and shrubs. In a last step, the remaining trees and bushes were felled manually by seasonal workers over periods of three or four months. The cleared area remained untouched for two to three months, when then it was burnt during the dry season. After this, grass was planted on the ashes so as to form separated pastures of approximately 120 hectares, which were then delimited by fences.

Clearing as practiced by the CVRC damaged the soils at least twice: first by eroding them through the passage of bulldozers and second by overheating them through the application of defoliant and fire – according to the words of a CVRC worker in 1978: "It looks as if a huge thunderbolt has just fallen."[5] In order to avoid soil sterilization, other big farms, such as the Jari Agropecuária, property of a U.S. businessman, relied exclusively on the mechanical abatement of trees by ample groups of workers equipped with chainsaws.[6] VWB argued for burning as the most economical way to eliminate the vegetation undesirable for pasture, which could still develop rashly even during the clearing process.[7] Burning also destroyed larvae and other potential endoparasites. What is more, the nutrient properties of ashes enabled livestock fodder grass to germinate and sprout rapidly.

At the beginning, VW managers were not aware of the opposition that their choice in favor of slash-and-burn might generate. Company management did not even grasp clearing *per se* could be seen as a negative

[3] José A. Lutzenberger, Brasilien: "Wo die Viehfarmen kommen, da kommt der Hunger" – Teil I," *Frankfurter Rundschau*, October 4, 1982. The CVRC clearing methods are listed by Sauer in Arquivo do FINAM, SUDAM, Sauer to SUDAM, December 2, 1980.

[4] "VW als Viehzüchter," *Institut für Brasilienkunde e.V. Informationen*, January–April 1977; Scheifele, "Erschliessung des Amazonasgebietes."

[5] Buarque, "A capitania da Volkswagen."

[6] Pinto, "*O garrancho amazônico.*"

[7] "A Cristalino apenas cumpriu o que prometeu," *O estado de São Paulo*, September 5, 1976.

thing. In commercials, VW naively boasted about the deforestation undertaken at Cristalino, as a sign of progress and human victory over the wild.[8] In 1974, the VWB press committee proudly informed its public that the company had burnt 4,000 hectares of Amazonian woods in a few months, "a record never equaled until now by any other similar project implemented in the region."[9] A couple of years before, this rhetoric, borrowed from the spirit of conquest inherent in Operação Amazônia, would probably have been consensual. But since the early 1970s, an important intellectual shift in the human vision of nature was starting to take place on different geographic scales. A succession of internationally successful books had made technological progress and agro-industrial growth responsible for destroying nature at the expense of human life.[10] Popular demonstrations like Earth Day for environmental reform in the United States (millions of participants in 1970) and the creation of Green electoral coalitions in New Zealand (1972), the United Kingdom (1973), and France (1974) made environmental protection a political value. While most of these events occurred in industrialized societies, they were given a global impact in 1972 during the Stockholm UN Conference, which brought nation-states of the Global North and South to discuss the consequences of and the solutions to environmental degradation.

The "World's Biggest Fire": A Scientific Controversy

Networks of natural scientists played a major role in Stockholm's preparation.[11] As Keck and Sikkink recall in their analysis of the mobilization, which took place around Stockholm, epistemic communities were already closely linked on an international scale in the early 1970s.[12] Numerous contacts existed between scientists of the world's northern and southern countries. Probably one of the most transnationally networked sectors of Brazilian society, the Brazilian community of scientists and academic researchers, united in the Sociedade Brasileira pelo Progresso da Ciência (SBPC), showed themselves to be sensitive to the conservationist

[8] Würtele and Lobgesang, *Volkswagen in Brasilien*, 72.

[9] J. Casado, "Volkswagen. Devastação com incentivos," *Opinião*, August 6, 1976.

[10] Rachel Carson, *Silent Spring* (Boston, MA: Houghton Mifflin, 1962); Meadows et al., *The Limits to Growth*; Ernst Friedrich Schumacher, *Small Is Beautiful: A Study of Economics as if People Mattered* (London: Blond & Briggs, 1973).

[11] Peter M. Haas, "UN Conferences and Constructivist Governance of the Environment," *Global Governance* 8, no. 1 (2002).

[12] Sikkink and Keck, *Activists Beyond Borders*, 122–6.

movement affecting scientists at the global level. The SBPC, an organization of more than 10,000 members, enjoyed recognition and respect from
the government, the opposition, and Brazil's foreign partners.[13] It invited
hundreds of Brazilian and international researchers to its Congress of
Science, a yearly forum including a multitude of conferences on all fields
that were the subject of research in universities.[14]

The twenty-seventh Congress of Science, held in July 1975 in the city
of Belo Horizonte, proved an illustration of the "global environmental
moment" and of the growing concern of Brazilian scientists for the fate
of nature.[15] That year, the logo of the meeting was a dying bird, recording
the scientific poetry of American biologist Rachel Carson who, in her
best-seller *Silent Spring*, had condemned the effect of agro-pesticides on
the diminution of bird populations ("the early mornings are strangely
silent where once they were filled with the beauty of bird song").[16] The
title of the SBPC meeting, situated in the same catastrophic rhetoric,
was "Porquê"? ("Why?" or "What for?"), referring to the supposed
destructive madness of the modern world. A great emphasis was given
in the Congress programs to topics related to the endangered environment. In his opening speech, the president of the organizing commission
announced that the conference would proceed in the objective of building a "mentality of conservation" in Brazil and confirmed that the SBPC
also identified themselves with a global epistemic anxiety for the earth's
future.[17] Since the Congress of Belo Horizonte, with its 2,000 papers,
was the largest scientific meeting ever organized in Latin America, and
maybe also a sign that environmental problems were starting to interest
Brazilian society, it benefited from impressive media coverage. Most of
the Brazilian newspapers dedicated daily articles to it during the entire
week of the event.

---

[13] José Maurício de Oliveira, "SBPC quer ser a ponte de diálogo," *A folha de São Paulo*,
May 9, 1975.
[14] SBPC, *27° Reunião anual – resumos* (São Paulo: SBPC, 1975). José Paulo Netto, "Em
busca da contemporaneidade perdida: a esquerda Brasileira Pós-64," in *Viagem incompleta. A experiência Brasileira (1500–2000). A grande transação*, ed. Carlos Guilherme
Mota (São Paulo: SENAC, 2000), 233.
[15] I borrowed this expression from Roger Eardley-Pryor, "The Global Environmental
Moment: Sovereignty and American Science on Spaceship Earth, 1945–1974" (University
of California, Santa Barbara, 2014).
[16] Carson, *Silent Spring*.
[17] Angelo B. Machado, "Mentalidade conservacionista" – discurso proferido no 9 de Julho
de 1975 na abertura da XXVII Reunião annual da SBPC em Belo Horizonte," *Ciência e
cultura* 27, no. 9 (1975).

One of the most tumultuous symposia of the Congress was dedicated to the "Vicissitudes of the Colonization in the Amazon."[18] Geneticist Warwick Estevão Kerr launched the controversy. Kerr enjoyed solid authority in the scientific milieu and was also the honorary president of the SBPC. Since March 1975, he was the director of the Instituto Nacional de Pesquisas da Amazônia (INPA), an organism located in Manaus and financed by the federal government. Set up in 1952 by Vargas as a nationalist answer to a UNESCO idea of creating an international research institute in the Amazon, the INPA was by far the main research center in the region.[19] It could count both on frequent contact with North American and European specialists and on locally grounded research conducted in its field stations throughout the Amazon. After Kerr, during the conference in Belo Horizonte, attacked the policy of the multinationals, he was immediately approved by another forest specialist, Carlos Thibau, who accused the projects funded by SUDAM of "criminal deforestation."[20] Sociologist Fanny Tabak alleged that everything started because of the state, which did not properly consult scientists before taking the decision to invite big companies to settle in the Amazon.

In another Congress meeting, a number of participants addressed these grievances directly to chemist Clara Pandolfo, who was representing SUDAM at the conference. She coldly replied that it was impossible for the state to stop supporting big private colonization projects. Furthermore, she argued in favor of the transformation of forest into pastures and stated that some kinds of woods "will be devastated indeed, since they do not have any economic value for the government, which, besides, has the intention to lead world tropical timber production within a few years."[21] The conference members strongly disapproved of Pandolfo's words, and the Congress of Science at Belo Horizonte turned out to be the first public rebellion of Brazilian scientists against the joint colonization of the rain forest by the Brazilian state and big private companies. On this occasion, in Belo Horizonte, the name "Volkswagen" was on the lips of every Brazilian and foreign guest.[22]

---

18 *O estado de Minas*, July 15, 1976.
19 Hochstetler and Keck, *Greening Brazil*, 156.
20 *O estado de Minas*, July 15, 1976.
21 Ibid.
22 Irene Garrido Filha, "Capitais estrangeiros na Amazônia Brasileira," *Amazônia Brasileira em foco (Comissão Nacional de Defesa e pelo Desenvolvimento da Amazônia)* 11–12 (1976).

To understand why a call for a new forest policy took place at Belo Horizonte, in a country dominated by developmentalist thought, it is first necessary to underline that the SBPC's conservationism fell within a certain national tradition. As various historians have shown, there had been a conservation-minded circle of influence overlapping with top sectors of scientific research in Brazil, especially among natural scientists, since the colonial period.[23] From the 1920s to the 1940s, institutions like the National Museum in Rio de Janeiro, the Geographic Society, and the Brazilian Academy of Sciences were the strongholds of such thought.[24] A following generation of renowned engineers, agronomists, biologists, and chemists gathered in the 1950s in the Fundação Brasileira para Conservação da Natureza (FBCN), a member of the International Union for the Conservation of Nature. Continuity existed between these initiatives. For example, the first Brazilian symposium for the conservation of nature, taking place in Rio de Janeiro in January 1967 and jointly organized by the FBCN and the Brazilian Botanical Society, displayed personal networks very similar to those of the first conference for the protection of nature, held in 1934, also in Rio.[25] In part, the two conferences brought together the same participants, including many of the students and followers of the main personalities of the 1934 conference who showed up in 1967. This example indicates that the interest in environmental protection in Brazil was not a new phenomenon. It was rather the product of a small but consistent network of conservation-minded personalities, which had managed to reproduce over the developmentalist decades.

Having recognized this tradition, we still need to ask why the Brazilian concern for native forest at the SBPC conference in 1975 took the form of a discourse critical of the government and the multinationals. Needless to say, Brazilian scientists in the 1970s were partially influenced by the politicization of environmentalism taking place in the industrialized world, where provocative theses against industrial growth were transforming traditional conservationist lobbying into a socially critical ideology. In

[23] Dean, *With Broadax and Firebrand*; José Augusto Pádua, *Um sopro de destruição. Pensamento político e crítica ambiental no Brasil escravagista (1786–1888)* (Rio de Janeiro: Zahar, 2002).

[24] José Luiz de Andrade Franco and José Augusto Drummond, "Wilderness and the Brazilian Mind (II): The First Brazilian Conference on Nature Protection," *Environmental History* 14, no. 1 (2009).

[25] José Luiz de Andrade Franco and José Augusto Drummond, "O cuidado da natureza: a Fundação Brasileira para a Conservação da Natureza e a experiência conservacionista no Brasil: 1958–1992," *Textos de história* 17, no. 1 (2009).

addition, since *Silent Spring*'s publication, European and North American scientists had adopted an apocalyptic tone in their warnings that biodiversity loss represented terrible dangers for humanity.[26] Why should this contagious pessimistic discourse, which contributed to the radicalization of the scientific world, not reach Brazil? As Keck and Hochstetler indicate, Brazilian conservationists had "long participated in international associations and conferences, studied abroad, and associated with expatriate scientists in Brazil."[27] SBPC conferences comprised dozens of foreign guests and the INPA regularly collaborated with distinguished U.S. scientists such as biologist Thomas Lovejoy, program administrator at the World Wildlife Fund.[28]

Yet, domestic political evolutions can also explain the radicalization of the SBPC. After 1964, the repressive atmosphere led to state pressure on various scientists. Some cases of torture affecting its members pushed the association to adopt several resolutions that criticized the government.[29] The Médici mandate (1969–74), during which state repression reached its highest stage in Brazil, became a period of tense relations between the regime and the SBPC. On the contrary, Ernesto Geisel, who succeeded Médici in 1974, under the impulsion of the moderate wing of the military, announced that his mandate would be a period of *distensão* (a Brazilian equivalent to *détente*). This process turned out to be uneven and hampered by repressive forces gone out of control, as was shown by tragic events such as the death of journalist Wladimir Herzog under torture in 1975, which the police tried to cover up by making it look like a suicide.[30] Still, and to a certain extent also in reaction to these acts of violence that tarnished the regime's reputation abroad and threatened its popular support at home, Geisel's *distensão* gradually opened the valve of political participation. In this new context of partial suspension of censorship, controlled liberalization of electoral politics, and decreasing repression of political activists, the SBPC

---

[26] Kai F. Hünemörder, "Kassandra im modernen Gewand. Die umweltapokalyptischen Mahnrufe der frühen 1970er Jahre," in *Wird Kassandra heiser? Die Geschichte falscher Öko-Alarme*, ed. Frank Uekötter and Jens Hohensee (Stuttgart: Steiner, 2004).

[27] Hochstetler and Keck, *Greening Brazil*, 64.

[28] Ibid., 30; Foresta, *Amazon Conservation in the Age of Development*, 32.

[29] José Goldemberg, "A Sociedade Brasileira para o Progresso da Ciência (SBPC). Seu contorno político," *Interciência* 6, no. 1 (1981); SBPC, ed. *Ciêntistas do Brasil: Depoimentos; Edição comemorativa dos 50 anos da SBPC* (São Paulo: SBPC, 1998), 13.

[30] James N. Green, *We Cannot Remain Silent: Opposition to the Brazilian Military Dictatorship in the United States* (Durham, NC, and London: Duke University Press, 2010), 330–1.

became a forum for free political debates, where "scientific" expertise often served as a pretext to criticize the government. The meeting of 1975 in Belo Horizonte emerged at this moment of a highly politicized practice in the sciences.

In particular, governmental guests served as receptacles for scientists' anger against deforestation. In a symposium taking place on July 11, government member Paulo Nogueira Neto had to face the indignation of a group of Brazilian, German, and North American Congress guests, accusing VW of mounting "the most antiecological project in the world."[31] Himself a natural historian, Neto was at the head of the Secretariat of the Environment (SEMA), an organ created in 1973 as a diplomatic initiative to counterbalance Brazil's intransigent attitude at the Stockholm summit. Nogueira Neto's position at Belo Horizonte was embarrassing. According to his own words, he was "a conservationist at heart" and one of the cofounders of FBCN.[32] As member of a developmentalist government, he practiced as a discreet "environmental guerrilla" within the institutions, as he later described his efforts to promote regulations on water and air pollution. Brazilian environmentalists had placed certain hopes in his person. At the same time, forest policy was not the competency of the Secretariat of the Environment, Nogueira Neto could not contradict state policy publicly, and at the personal level he also happened to be a good friend of Wolfgang Sauer.[33]

Whether or not because of this friendship, Nogueira Neto dismissed scientists' worries about the environmental consequences of the CVRC as a misunderstanding.[34] He added that SEMA was not given information about the extent of the fire set by VW in the forest. Referring to the – forthcoming but not yet launched – Brazilian radio-detection project, he said in order to pacify his scientific peers that "everything will be much easier when the satellite survey program starts."[35] Ironically, five months later, it was the United States' National Aeronautics and Space Administration (NASA) that, thanks to its Skylab satellite, detected in the southeastern Amazon a calefaction of particular intensity and width,

[31] Roberto Godoy, "Satélites vão auxiliar a SEMA," *O estado de São Paulo*, July 12, 1975. BArch B116/61917, Generalkonsulat der BRD (Recife) to Auswärtiges Amt, December 10, 1976.

[32] Hochstetler and Keck, *Greening Brazil*, 27–9.

[33] "O anfitrião Sauer."

[34] "Sema apura denúncia de devastação na Amazonia," *O estado de São Paulo*, July 15, 1975.

[35] Godoy, "Satélites vão auxiliar a SEMA."

similar to that of an erupting volcano.[36] NASA later found out that the Skylab picture actually betrayed the existence of a continuous fire over an area of about 25,000 square kilometers, situated at the intersection between several cattle ranches.[37]

Volkswagen had not burnt this entire area. After NASA transmitted the picture to the Brazilian National Institute of Spatial Research (INPE), it appeared that of the total surface affected by the fire, only 9,383 hectares were situated on the property of the German company. But fantastic rumors multiplied within the community of researchers on the Amazon after, in a meeting in Belém in 1976, Kerr evoked publicly the Skylab picture. Under the impetus of indignation, he absurdly reproached VW for having burnt "one million hectares."[38] Another personality of Brazilian naturalism, internationally renowned landscape architect Roberto Burle Marx, repeated the "one million hectares" figure during a hearing at the federal Senate in June 1976. Volkswagen, Burle Marx said, destroyed a forest "the size of Lebanon" and "produced, in the Amazon, the biggest fire in the whole planet's history."[39] He also talked about the growing use among big Amazonian ranchers, of the powerful defoliant "Agent Orange," which many environmentalists suspected could provoke cancer.

Although it was not clear whether Burle Marx meant to accuse VW, in particular, of resorting to Agent Orange, it seems that a similar defoliant was indeed used to clear the Cristalino estate. In fact, three months later, a state deputy claimed at the assembly in Pará to be in possession of evidence in this regard.[40] In 1978, journalists who visited the ranch and talked to CVRC technicians reported that the company was defoliating using Tordon-155.[41] Tordon-155 contained a quantity of 2,4,5-Trichlorophenoxyacetic, the most toxic component of Agent Orange, used by the U.S. Army to destroy rice fields and forest shelters during the Vietnam War. The undifferentiated airplane spreading of more than 100 million liters of Agent Orange in Vietnam between 1961 and 1971 caused toxic exposure to millions of people, the majority Vietnamese, but

---

[36] Cary Fowler and Patrick R. Mooney, *Shattering: Food, Politics, and the Loss of Genetic Diversity* (Tucson: University of Arizona Press, 1990), 98.

[37] Frances Moore Lappe, Joseph Collins, and Cary Fowler, *Food First: Beyond the Myth of Scarcity* (New York: Ballantine Books, 1979), 50.

[38] Ibid.

[39] Roberto Burle Marx, "Depoimento no Senado Federal," in *Arte e paisagem. Conferências escolhidas*, ed. José Tabacow (São Paulo: Nobel, 1987), 71.

[40] *Diário do Congresso Nacional. 15 de Outubro de 1976* (Brasília: Câmara dos Deputados, 1976), 10,431.

[41] Buarque, "A capitania da Volkswagen."

also U.S. soldiers.[42] After the latter returned home with hormonal disturbances, the use of Tordon-155 in farming was strictly limited by law in the United States. Remaining stocks of 2.3 million gallons of the defoliant were transferred to be sold on the Brazilian territory in 1973.[43]

Although Tordon-155 was not prohibited by Brazilian legislation, its use worried local scientists. Biologist Waldemar Ferreira wrote that the defoliant carried "risks of foetal mortality and congenital anomalies, even when used in very small quantities."[44] Besides, global media reports and shocking photographs depicting U.S. war crimes had turned the Vietnam War into a symbol of imperialism. Agent Orange illustrated the presumed cruelty with which the industrialized world sought to extend its domination over poorer countries. In this context, the association of the Cristalino project with Agent Orange indicated a recrudescence of nationalist resentment against the Amazon's appropriation by multinationals.

Denunciation of the use of toxic defoliant raised the issue of the risks of deforestation for human health, but also for the climate, water cycle, and biodiversity. Brazilian Senator Paulo Brossard believed that the "transformation of the Amazon into a desert will have extremely grave implications for the climate of northern and southern America."[45] This affirmation had to do with the role of the Amazon in the global cycle of carbon. Although this role was not clear to scientists, it was known that the rain forest held a tremendous amount of carbon, which meant that reducing the forest areas could result in disruptive effects for the world climate.[46] Another issue on which scientists agreed was that precipitation in the Amazon region was partly dependent on the forest's density. The disappearance of the vegetation could thus lead to limited rainfall, and consequently diminish the level of the river, which in turn would reduce rainfall and prevent the forest from regenerating itself. As another Brazilian senator, Evandro Carreira, synthesized: "Without rain there is no river, without river there is no rain, without rain there is no forest and without forest there is neither river, nor rain."[47]

[42] André Bouny, *L'Agent Orange: Apocalypse Viêt Nam* (Paris: Demi-Lune, 2010), 33, 143.

[43] Evandro Carreira, *Recado Amazônico*, 155.

[44] Buarque, "A capitania da Volkswagen."

[45] Carreira, *Recado Amazônico*, 151.

[46] Thomas E. Lovejoy and Herbert O. R. Schubart, "The Ecology of Amazonian Development," in *Land, People and Planning in Contemporary Amazonia*, ed. Françoise Barbira-Scazzochio (Cambridge: Cambridge University Press, 1980), 21–6, 24.

[47] Carreira, *Recado Amazônico*, 153.

If these questions were discussed in Brazil, none of them grew as acute as the debate on soil quality, which offered the most concrete link between the issue of environmental stability and the economy of resources. The fight against soil erosion was compatible with a utilitarian approach to conservation, interested in the possibilities of expansion of Brazilian farming. As such, it was coherent to express concern for the soil even within the national-developmentalist logic that underpinned Brazilian politics. It should be added that Brazil was still a farming country in the 1970s: at the beginning of the decade, more than 44 percent of Brazilians lived in rural areas where farming played a structural role.[48] The question of soil appealed to the Brazilian people. They knew too well the case of the northeast, a once fruitful land turned sterile by centuries of sugarcane planting.[49] In 1948, President Eurico Gaspar Dutra, aware of this national trauma, raised an "alarm call" in a vibrant speech at Itaperuna.[50] He underlined that the foundation of Brazilian agricultural production was "the soil, this same soil that we have mistreated during our whole life, we who are harvesting today the rotten and bitter fruits of this lack of care." He called on the farmers to adopt "conservation practices, in order that our children and the children of our children do not address to us the same accusation that we are throwing today to our elders: the accusation of making deserts." The soil was a major element of the Brazilian economy and in the case of the Amazon, it was an issue dividing the political scene along opposing scientific (or pseudoscientific) arguments.

It was widely accepted that Amazonian soils were nutrient poor, the available nutrients being locked up in the vegetation rather than in the soils.[51] The latter hardly possessed its own humus layer (the organic matter in soil that furnishes nutritive components). Therefore, the main dividing point between partisans and opponents of deforestation lay in

---

[48] Ana Amélia Camarano, "Êxodo rural, envelhecimento e masculinização no Brasil: panorama dos últimos cinqüenta anos," *Revista Brasileira de estudos de população* 15, no. 2 (1980), 47.

[49] Gilberto Freire wrote a magisterial, historical study of this case, based on the tools of human ecology, as early as in 1937: Gilberto Freire, *Nordeste: aspectos da influencia da canna sobre a vida e a paizagem do nordeste do Bracil* (Rio de Janeiro: J. Olympio, 1937).

[50] Eurico Gaspar Dutra, "'O solo: a sua conservação,' discurso proferido pelo Presidente Eurico Gaspar Dutra em Itaperuna, em 19-9-1948," *Conjuntura econômica* 27, no. 12 (1973).

[51] Françoise Barbira-Scazzocchio, "From Native Forest to Private Property: The Development of Amazonia for Whom?" In *Land, People and Planning in Contemporary Amazonia*, ed. Barbira-Scazzochio, iii–xv, iii.

the question of whether pastures could durably replace rain forest as a reserve of nutrients to prevent soil erosion. As a basic measure to preserve soils, Brazilian legislation obliged ranchers in the Amazon to recreate a certain amount of "arboreal coating" – in principle, trees – on the cleared land. The military regime's favorite agronomist, Pimenta, considered this a useless measure, as for him any kind of vegetation could assume the nutrient role of arboreal coating.[52] Drawing on such counter-expertise, the ranchers' organization AEA demanded that any type of vegetation, including pastures of grass and legumes, be legally recognized as arboreal coating. Besides, Pimenta contended that grass and legumes were the most adaptable vegetation for carrying out the process of photosynthesis because, he hypothesized, they might produce more oxygen than trees. Most ecologists dismissed this theory, as it ignored the vital role of tree leaves in maintaining the stability of soils. In a native forest, a layer of about half a meter composed of organic matter, principally dead and rotten leaves, settles around each tree. This decomposing material, besides producing a thin humus layer, nurtures a population of microscopic animals, insects, and plants that protect and fertilize the soil. Ecologists believed that this protective layer would disappear together with deforestation. The vanishing of the canopy would also leave the soil impoverished, insofar as this heavy vegetative cover enables the forest to capture incoming nutrients in rainfall from stem flow.[53]

These arguments help to explain why those who blamed VW for deforesting also accused the company of ruining the soil. But a further problem is whether the soil question really concerned the region of Cristalino. First, the Amazon region was composed of various typologies of soils. Even according to conservationists like Kerr, some of these typologies, characterizing a small portion of the Amazon, were actually estimated to be rich enough and suitable, if not for cropping, at least for cattle raising.[54] Second, Cristalino could be envisaged as a specific case because it was located in the transitional rain forest, a hybrid area separating the rain forest in the north from the savanna in the south. This type of region had not been scientifically researched. Besides, no systematic farming had been undertaken there, hence the impossibility of ascertaining if Cristalino's soils were as fragile as the majority of rain forest soils.

---

[52] *O estado de São Paulo,* November 11, 1975.
[53] Lovejoy and Schubart, "The Ecology of Amazonian Development," 21.
[54] José Antônio Dias Lopes, "A Amazônia tem salvação," *Veja,* March 31, 1976.

Volkswagen, which did not prepare its arrival in the region on the basis of soil quality research, had been warned about this incertitude. In 1974, the German embassy in Brazil informed the Ministry of Foreign Affairs in Bonn that the ecological consequences of the VW ranch were unclear: they could be as probably negative as positive.[55] In January 1975, the German general consulate in São Paulo sent an observer to Cristalino, who, in the aftermath of his visit, asked whether it was serious "to undertake such gigantic projects without very detailed studies about their future perspectives."[56] He also warned that every kind of cropping or livestock-raising attempts at Cristalino might fail for ecological reasons, leaving VW with timber exploitation as the last possibility for benefiting from its ranch.

Against the background of emerging global concerns with rain forest preservation, the criticisms of Cristalino hit an essential nerve of modernization discourse. Volkswagen and SUDAM had repeatedly justified their projects through their capacity for mobilizing scientific networks and acquiring up-to-date agronomic tools. Yet, the very persons they respected, the scientists, specialists in farming, forestry, ecology, and landscapes, were opening a debate about uncertainties and risks. This amounted to scientists recognizing that scientific research was not advanced enough to cope with the Amazon's infinite complexity. It was simply impossible to say yet whether Amazonian soils would stand the expansion of cattle ranching and what consequence the clearing of large areas could have on the ecosystem. The experts themselves, in sum, were denying the power of expertise, and developmentalism was losing one of its main arguments: that techno-scientific progress could provide an answer to all problems.[57]

Warwick Kerr was the most explicit representative of this wave of doubts. Preoccupied with the risk of "foreign greed" in the Amazon region, he was in no way a preservationist, rather a national conservationist.[58] His greatest concern was to develop Brazil in order to improve the living conditions of lower social classes; hence he did not think that forests should be "untouchable." However, Kerr thought that the development of the region had to proceed cautiously, so as to save its natural

---

[55] BArch B102/8643, Botschaft der BRD to Auswärtiges Amt, November 4, 1974.
[56] BArch B116/61917, Georg Trefftz, February 14, 1975, "Landwirtschaftliches Großprojekt der Volkswagen do Brasil."
[57] Bruno Latour, *Nous n'avons jamais eté modernes. Essai d'anthropologie symétrique* (Paris: La Découverte, 1991).
[58] Lopes, "A Amazônia tem salvação."

resources for future use. Above all, Kerr used to repeat that "nobody knew" what would happen if fires in the Amazon forest went on. He insisted that precisely because of this ignorance, humans should consider the worst prognostics "after reaching the superior layers of the Earth, the excess of oxide and monoxide of carbon could even melt the polar icecap and raise the sea to many meters. Manaus would simply remain under water."[59] This discourse expressed the overlapping of scales, which characterized the issue of tropical deforestation. Kerr specifically accused multinationals of being co-responsible for a regional phenomenon of environmental degradation in the Amazon. He warned that this regional degradation could, in turn, have global climatic consequences, and from this risk of global deregulation he came to the potential local consequences in the Amazon city of Manaus, where he worked as a researcher. As appears here, the environmental risks brought about by the colonization of the Amazon, and illustrated by projects such as the CVRC, had created a strong sense of global connections among Brazilian scientists.

The Institutional Controversy

In the aftermath of the Stockholm conference, the tendency to depict Brazil as a country lacking environmental awareness was strong.[60] Yet, local legislation in the domain of environmental conservation was not that poor in comparison to international standards, especially in relation to other Latin American military regimes. While the Argentinean junta tended to destroy the conservationist structures created by the previous governments and the Chilean regime simply remained inactive in the area, Brazil's military governments at least built up existing legislation.[61] Even worldwide, only eleven countries possessed a secretary of the environment, like Brazil. Surprisingly, the military regime did not undermine the preparative work done by the conservationist civil servants of the Federal Forestry Council under Goulart to extend and reinforce forest protection law. The endurance of conservationist thought within a faction of the Brazilian public administration, which, cleverly, abstained from taking a political side in order to survive power change, might explain this paradox.

---

[59] Ibid.

[60] André Aranha Corrêa do Lago, *Stockholm, Rio, Johannesburg: Brazil and the Three United Nations Conferences on the Environment* (Brasília: Instituto Rio Branco, 2009), 108, 16, 27.

[61] Hochstetler and Keck, *Greening Brazil*, 24.

The Brazilian Forest Code, adopted in 1965, comprised major protective measures. It required, for example, that 50 percent to 80 percent of any land property in Amazônia Legal be maintained as forest reserve, in addition to which there had to be "permanent preservation" of riverbanks, slopes, and other fragile areas.[62] The Code's main virtue, from an environmentalist point of view, was to proclaim that forests were a common good and to recognize the necessity of limiting private property in order to favor natural preservation.[63] It instituted the principle of endangered, non-clearable timber species – although the Code itself did not contain a concrete list of these.[64] It also foresaw the creation of national parks and biological reserves, which would have entrance fees to finance policies of preservation. It submitted the "use of fire" in forest areas to the authorization of the federal government.[65] In sum, the Forest Code contained legislative tools for a conservationist policy and a basis of legal arguments for environmentalists to oppose forest-destructing projects.

However, the state did not equip itself to comply with these ambitious prerogatives. Ten years after the adoption of the Code, Paulo Berutti, head of the Instituto Brasileiro de Desenvolvimento Florestal (IBDF), recognized that due to a lack of financial resources, nothing had been done to open natural reserves.[66] The state of Pará, whose area – essentially composed of forests – was five times bigger than that of the Federal Republic of Germany, had only five forest guards to ensure that farmers respected the forest protection laws. Legislation itself was highly complex, as besides conservation measures it also contained incentives to deforest. Article 19 of the Forest Code amounted to a license to cause disturbances to the ecosystem: "aiming at the highest economic return," it authorized "owners of heterogeneous forests to transform them into homogeneous forests."[67] Besides, the Brazilian laws linked deforestation with the legitimacy of property. Farmers cultivating land without being its official owner could obtain a property title corresponding to a finite amount of land, which was a multiple of the area of forest already converted to pasture.[68]

---

[62] Ibid., 149.

[63] Ganem and Lima, "Código Florestal," 254.

[64] Law n°4.771.

[65] Ibid.

[66] Câmara dos Deputados, *Política florestal e concervacionista do Brasil. Conferência pronunciada pelo Dr. Paulo Azevedo Berutti na Comissão da Amazônia* (Brasília: Câmara dos Deputados, 1975), 9–10.

[67] Law n°4.771.

[68] Binswanger, "Fiscal and Legal Incentives with Environmental Effects on the Brazilian Amazon," 18.

In comparison to such incentives, the Forest Code's conservationist articles seemed in some aspects inefficient. The rule stipulating that at least 50 percent of an Amazonian property should not be cleared did not convince all environmentalists. INPA thought that this provision would be meaningless as long as it did not specify the distribution of this 50 percent according to vegetative types, soil quality, or relief.[69] The 50 percent that ranchers chose to preserve were often areas that were impracticable for farming anyway. For example, about half of the Cristalino property consisted of small mountainous areas, where cattle productivity would have been considerably reduced, as the animals would have lost energy through additional physical efforts.[70] It is primarily this consideration that guided VW in the choice of the 50 percent reserve area, rather than an attempt to conserve the ranch's biodiversity. Finally, the rule could be easily circumvented. Nothing, for example, forbade a landowner from clearing 50 percent of his estate and selling the other, untouched half, which in turn could be deforested by its new owner.

Another problem that handicapped the enforcement of environmental law was the multiplication of federal and interregional agencies having competencies in Amazônia Legal. The Brazilian military, in coherence with the cult of rationalization they practiced, had created a sprawling bureaucratic apparatus of planning and control administrations.[71] These had grown into autonomous structures, developing a culture of rivalry between each other. In the first half of the 1970s, there had been tense exchanges between INCRA and SUDAM, accusing each other of corruption and incompetence.[72] Both agencies competed to see their respective ideological visions adopted by the federal government. While INCRA favored small settlers' colonization, SUDAM recommended relying more strongly on a partnership with private investors.

This ideological confrontation moved to the background as INCRA's influence was neutralized, together with the end of President Médici's mandate. In the mid-1970s, the debate on how to adjust colonization policies in order to respond to forest squandering became the main dividing line between public agencies. Most SUDAM administrators

---

[69] Lopes, "A Amazônia tem salvação."
[70] *Suplemento agrícola (O estado de São Paulo)*, July 15, 1977.
[71] Faucher, *Le Brésil des militaires*, 191–2.
[72] Pompermayer, "The State and the Frontier in Brazil," 253–4.

were partisans of accelerated forest exploitation. They considered that their mission was to help build up a large primary goods export sector in the Amazon, as a lever for the accumulation of foreign currency. In this aspect, SUDAM's most embarrassing rival was the IBDF, a federal agency created by a decree of 1967, subordinated to the Ministry of Agriculture but expressly charged by the president of the Republic to "formulate the forest policy" of the country.[73] Its role was to "orient, coordinate and execute" the rational use of the forests, but also to ensure the conservation of their "renewable natural resources." In particular, IBDF had the power to tax private properties and to charge their owners with a financial penalty in case of infractions of conservationist laws. During the first years of its existence, IBDF's discourse did not differ from the developmentalist consensus of Operação Amazônia. Far from protesting against forest squandering, IBDF executives promoted a limitless subordination of the forest to the immediate needs of the economy.[74]

However, probably in part to exist within the bureaucratic landscape and to develop its own identity rather than fading in the shadow of SUDAM, IBDF grew more and more into a conservationist institution. Its president, Paulo Berutti, confirmed this ideological evolution as in 1975 he declared, in front of the Federal Congress Amazon Commission, that "it is impossible, while we are taking the most important measures to efficiently occupy the Amazon, on the same level, not to carry out objective research to indicate the way for conservationist measures."[75] Rather than transforming ever larger surfaces into farming areas, he estimated that the exploitation of the Amazon should be focused on realizing the value of the natural riches already available in the region, such as precious timber, or protein sources like fish or nuts. In order to both conserve and expand these extractive resources, IBDF recommended not only a strict supervision over clearing, but also the generalization of reforestation. In principle, IBDF's conservationist philosophy was supposed to apply to SUDAM-backed ranches, as every project involving forest exploitation in Brazil was obliged to receive a license from IBDF. In practice, however, never would SUDAM forward project files to the IBDF administration, nor even signal to funded firms the necessity of consulting IBDF before starting a project.[76]

---

[73] Decree-Law n°289/66.
[74] FAO, *Estado de la informacion florestal en Brasil* (Santiago, Chile: FAO, 2003), 48.
[75] Câmara dos Deputados, *Politica florestal e concervacionista do Brasil*, 6.
[76] Foresta, *Amazon Conservation in the Age of Development*, 162–3.

The Skylab satellite intervened at the most complicated moment for VW, precisely when the debate on forest conservation was splitting up two important development agencies. The VW affair highlighted the rivalry between IBDF and SUDAM, and illustrated how environmental conservation had become a powerful marker in the debates about Amazonian development within the military regime. Tired of being ignored by big ranchers, IBDF informed VW that the company had to ask for authorization before deforesting, and to pay a "deforestation tax."[77] Used to bargaining within the twists and turns of Brazilian bureaucracy, the company executives complained in a letter to SUDAM director Hugo de Almeida: "SUDAM and IBDF are obviously in a conflict, whose negative consequences are affecting companies in turn, making the development of projects of national interest difficult. We find it absolutely indispensable that this conflict between SUDAM and IBDF be concluded once and for all, without us having to be unfairly involved."[78] SUDAM, in reaction, renewed its support for the VW project, placing itself in contradiction *de facto* with the IBDF.

Now, if financial weight and ties with high-ranking politicians alone could decide the power struggle between institutions; if the military regime were an immobile, rigid, and hermetic political framework; then IBDF would probably have had to withdraw its demand to VW. However, the political climate of *distensão* promoted by the Geisel government, together with the weakening of the government's popularity, made many actors within the regime sensitive to another agent, public opinion, or at least its partial expression through the press. The Skylab factor, publicly relayed by the charismatic Warwick Kerr, offered IBDF an undreamt of argument. Indeed, public opinion had before its eyes the proof that VW was burning at least thousands of hectares of forest. It is in this favorable context that Paulo Berutti sent two IBDF agents to Cristalino in order to certify that 9,334 hectares had been cleared there, without previous authorization.[79] After doing this, he informed the press about his intention to fine VW 47 million cruzeiros for having destroyed 10 million trees.

VW defended itself by resorting to its two main channels of influence: political networks and public communication. It first succeeded in getting the Ministry of Agriculture, which was IBDF's legal superior, to

---

[77] "A Cristalino apenas cumpriu o que prometeu."
[78] Ibid.
[79] "Amazônia devastada," *Veja*, July 7, 1976.

deny that any fine against VW existed.[80] Representatives of the minister of agriculture argued that the surface of forest cleared by VW was much inferior to the 70,000 hectares permitted by law, corresponding to 50 percent of the Cristalino property. By taking such a position, the Ministry was ignoring the decree-law n°289/66 entitling IBDF to oversee ranches practicing deforestation. As if this decree did not exist, VW added that it only recognized SUDAM's role in implementing forest conservation laws.[81] The company even went so far as to attribute to itself a conservationist approach to clearing, preserving noble timber species and burning only "worthless plants, shrubs and parasite vegetation." This answer took into account the market value of resources without recognizing the criticisms of scientists, that forest burning might result in ecosystem disturbances. Besides, VW's argument appeared only moderately credible, given that in the Amazon large numbers of heterogeneous species cohabit within surface areas of only a few hectares. This makes it extremely difficult to distinguish individual plants or trees and preserve them during the intervention of powerful chemicals, bulldozers, and large-scale fires.

Despite VW's resistance, Renato Coral, an IBDF regional delegate in Pará, had decided to ensure that the law be fully respected. In the national press, he dismissed as "dumb" the possibility of any arrangement with VW and added maliciously, referring to the IBDF regulation: "IBDF is not closing anyone's company. I am just complying with article 1, item 3 of ordinance n°2."[82] Indeed, Coral was not ready to compromise in his duty to apply legal texts. He elaborated the fine against the CVRC on a strict basis: according to an official table of calculation, each hectare of forest contained an average of 1,000 trees, which meant that VW had felled 9,334,000 trees. Therefore, the fine would amount to 59,550,920 cruzeiros: 638.30 fixed fine, plus 1 percent of the regional minimum salary for every abated tree.

Coral's task was not especially easy. After he opened his inquiry at the end of June 1976, VW took advantage of Coral's holiday week to start negotiations with the Ministry of Agriculture in order to suppress the fine. As if to illustrate the financial misery of Brazilian conservationist policy, IBDF had no resources to substitute Coral during these days. On another occasion, the IBDF office in Belém had to renege on sending inspectors to Cristalino, because all agents were dispersed for duties in

[80] "Paulinelli ignora multa à Volkswagen," *A folha de São Paulo*, June 30, 1976.
[81] Ibid.
[82] "IBDF não cogita de acordo com a Volks," *O estado de São Paulo*, July 1, 1976.

the interior of the state of Pará.[83] In the previous year, fourteen of the nineteen serving agents had been dismissed for financial reasons. To solve this problem, the federal office of IBDF in Brasília sent two employees to Belém to back up Coral. But when they arrived, the regional delegacy of Pará realized that it did not possess the funds to rent an aerial vehicle for the two employees to reach the *fazenda*. Clearly, there was no way for Coral to count on IBDF finances to process his investigation. In view of the IBDF's weakness, the last obstacle for VW to cancel the deforestation fine was Coral himself. Thirty years later, in his self-edited reminiscences, Coral recounted in detail how he received the visit of a VW agent, offering him "a brand new car, tomorrow, in front of your house door, with all accessories, with the only condition that you make the process file magically disappear."[84]

As it became clear to VW that Coral was incorruptible, the company management decided to enter a discussion with the IBDF through legal means. It was a victory for the conservationist agency, which, thanks to the insistence of a single delegate, had become as unavoidable as SUDAM regarding questions of forest development. At the end of July 1976, VW sent its lawyers to engage in discussion with Paulo Berutti, who demanded not only a fine, but also that VW reimburse the administrative costs of Coral's inquiry.[85] IBDF technicians raised their voices in protest against SUDAM's role in overseeing farming projects in the Amazon. Even Minister of Agriculture Paulinelli conceded to the IBDF the freedom to attribute a fine to VW. At the end of the inauguration of an agro-scientific project in Belém, the minister was circumvented by journalists asking him about the Cristalino affair. Paulinelli used this occasion to express, for the first time, concerns about recent deforestation data, and said that the Ministry was developing a plan for selecting Amazonian areas that would remain "untouchable."[86]

The CVRC affair was highly embarrassing for Paulinelli because it touched a nerve of the political troops supporting the government: the defense of the natural resources "belonging" to the Brazilian nation. That VW was caught red-handed "destroying" them, and might pay a fine for this offence, was a highly desirable symbol for those who, within the regime, had always viewed the alliance with international capital in

[83] "Férias," *Opinião*, July 16, 1976.
[84] "Lucio Flávio Pinto, "Quando a volks virou fazenda," quando a volks virou fazenda," www.lucioflaviopinto.com.br/?p=1247, access date January 27, 2013.
[85] "Area devastada na AM pode ser maior," *O estado de São Paulo*, July 23, 1976.
[86] "Paulinelli garante multa à Volkswagen," *A folha de São Paulo*, July 23, 1976.

Amazonian colonization with mistrust. These nationalist positions were illustrated on August 10, 1976 at the national Congress by an incident that occurred during a session having nothing to do with the Amazon.[87] That day, Sauer was invited to a hearing about VW Company motor products. To the surprise of the other participants, ARENA congressman Nino Ribeira intervened with a question out of the scope of the discussion: "In the end, Mister Wolfgang Sauer, for what purpose did you come to Brazil, produce automobiles or set fire in the jungle?"[88] Very embarrassed, Sauer went to find the minister of agriculture immediately after the hearing to tell him that the controversy had lasted too long, and was starting to threaten VW's support within the political ranks. As he left Paulinelli's office, hordes of journalists were waiting for him outside. Once again, he depicted VW as a victim of bureaucracy, and said: "we were invited by the government to carry out a project in the Amazon and we are doing everything according to the legal requirements. If we do not comply with the deforestation agenda, we will lose the SUDAM incentives."[89]

Sauer, in the end, did not obtain the symbolic declaration of innocence he hoped from the Brazilian public powers. Volkswagen obviously did not receive the maximal penalty, the 59 million cruzeiros once envisaged by Coral. Above all a bargaining weapon for IBDF, this 59 million would have meant the official denial of a project, the CVRC, which was a showcase of the federal policy for the Amazon. The Brazilian state could not allow itself to contradict itself on this point. Still, IBDF served VW with a fee of 367,139 cruzeiros.[90] Part of this sum, 225,000 cruzeiros, fined the "production and profits of timber" – it was a circuitous way to sanction forest burning. A further 139,842 cruzeiros was supposed to compensate for the administrative expenses generated by the CVRC's disrespect of IBDF rules.[91] The icing on the cake was the tiniest fraction of the fine: 2,497 cruzeiros reproving the opening of a sawmill at Cristalino without IBDF's authorization. This 2,497 cruzeiros amounted

---

[87] *Diário do Congresso Nacional. 29 de Outubro de 1976* (Brasília: Câmara dos Deputados, 1976).

[88] *Diário do Congresso Nacional. 19 de Setembro de 1978* (Brasília. Câmara dos Deputados, 1978), 8146–7.

[89] "Volkswagen defende-se e alerta para a devastação," *O estado de São Paulo*, August 11, 1976.

[90] "Volkswagen nega desmatamento; só admite as multas."

[91] "Volks desmente multa do IBDF por desmatamento," *O estado de São Paulo*, August 20, 1976.

to a symbolic revenge by the IBDF on SUDAM, as in 1974 the latter had conditioned its support for the CVRC on the opening of this sawmill.[92]

This compromise infuriated big Amazonian ranchers, because it confirmed the rise of conservationism as a major variable within the developmentalist debate. The AEA was afraid that this affair might set a precedent applicable to other ranches.[93] German diplomats felt concerned with the consequences of this episode for the image of foreign companies in Brazil.[94] A paper in the General Consulate in Recife regretted the lack of transparency of this "typically Brazilian arrangement" and bitterly noted that "VW only did what all its neighbors continuously do without being penalized." The German embassy also expressed its concern, defending slash-and-burn as the "only economically rational method" of clearing, deploring the political seizing of this environmental scandal, and denouncing the "strongly emotional" campaign organized against VW on this occasion.[95] As a result of an administrative conflict, VW had been made an "environmental sinner," to quote a term coined in a German environmentalist publication.[96]

While through their denunciation of the fire at Cristalino, scientists had underlined the necessity of politicizing the problem of forest management in Brazil, the IBDF "coup" against VW and SUDAM made this politicization happen. Last but not least, a widespread media coverage of the affair gave Brazilians the opportunity to appropriate the issue of deforestation and discuss it. This meant that the war against nature proclaimed by Operação Amazônia was losing its hegemonic position in the Brazilian political framework: forest destruction became discussable beyond a small elite of conservation-minded scientists. Ironically, this affair turned out to be VW's contribution to environmental protection. It is difficult, indeed, to imagine IBDF showing the same offensive behavior toward other Amazonian development projects, which were state-led or financed by domestic capital. This is where the bitter comments of the German diplomats made sense. Volkswagen paid for all the others, because it was a multinational company and a bit of xenophobia was necessary to convince the national-developmentalist state to listen to its conservationist institutions like IBDF. In consequence, this

[92] Richter, *Die Fazenda am Cristalino.*
[93] "Pastagens e preservação florestal," *Amazônia*, November 1976.
[94] BArch B116/61917, Generalkonsulat der BRD (Recife) to Auswärtiges Amt, December 10, 1976.
[95] BArch B116/61917, Hoffman to Bundesminister, February 23, 1979.
[96] Arbeitsgruppe Brasilien, *Die Farm am Amazonas.*

episode signaled the beginning of the end for VW's, until then successfully, Brazilianized image.

An Early Case for the Rain Forest Protection Movement

Not only had the conservationist forces of the Brazilian administration
found in VW the "sinner" they needed in order to enhance their position
in the regime's internal power games, so also did the Brazilian environmentalist movement use this ideal "villain" as a cement for its consolidation. The fire at Cristalino worked as a catalyst for Brazilian scientific,
associative, and political actors sympathetic to environmentalist ideas. It
revealed what kind of coalition could be mobilized in the country behind
the banner of forest protection, and for what reasons. The Brazilian
environmentalist movement, essentially concentrated in urban centers of
the south and southeast, had entered into a new stage of existence in
the early 1970s.[97] The foundation in 1971 of the Associação Gaúcha de
Proteção ao Ambiente Natural (AGAPAN) in Porto Alegre marked the
beginning of the movement's politicization. Since the 1950s, whistleblow-
ers of environmental pollution had been above all biologists, geneticists,
agronomists, in sum, nature "professionals."[98] FBCN, founded in 1955
by Nogueira Neto, saw its role as that of an organization of experts entitled to orientate governmental policies with their knowledge of natural
sciences. The association was more concerned with avoiding the waste of
economic resources than with a political critique of predatory relations
to nature.

AGAPAN was very different. It was composed of distinguished natural
scientists as well, but it also included students animated by a libertarian
ideal, still influenced by the antiauthoritarian youth protests, which as
in other places in the world had filled the streets of Brazilian cities in
1968.[99] The association, whose first president was charismatic chemist
and agronomist José Lutzenberger, criticized the foundations of a waste-
ful economic system, which threatened the means of subsistence of the
poor through the progressive annihilation of their living resources. The
organization, small by member size but loud in its actions, also adopted
provocative styles of protest. The climbing of a tree in a central avenue
in Porto Alegre by an AGAPAN activist on February 25, 1975 to impede

---

[97] Hochstetler and Keck, *Greening Brazil*.
[98] Ibid., 66–70.
[99] Madeleine Brocke, "Die brasilianische Ökologie-Bewegung zwischen Utopie und
Pragmatik: das Beispiel der AGAPAN in Porto Alegre/Brasilien," *Arbeitshefte des
Lateinamerika-Zentrums, Münster*, 15 (1993).

the tree's destruction in the framework of a viaduct being built has been viewed as the founding act of political ecology in Brazil.[100]

It was coherent with this combative approach that, during the controversy over the fire at Cristalino, AGAPAN started a campaign addressed to VW and the national government.[101] The aim was to "stop deforestation and the creation of cattle ranches in the Amazon as well as the fiscal incentives for investing in this region." It was a joint campaign with another association in Porto Alegre, Ação Democrática Feminina Gaúcha (ADFG). The history of this women's group illustrated the emergence of an interest for environmental problems in the southern Brazilian middle class. Founded on March 13, 1964, ADFG was one of the anticommunist women's groups that demonstratively supported the military coup. To be sure, ADFG's founding motivation was to defend the "Fatherland" against Brazil's political class – a discourse that recalled the allegedly "apolitical" claim of the military's rhetoric.[102] However, the association rapidly shifted away from its original message. One of the ADFG founders recently claimed that as the association's members traveled to a federal meeting of Brazilian women's leagues in the wave of the installation of military rule, they took measure of the violence that was hiding behind the new regime:

We went there full of ideals and enthusiasm, but what we saw was a closed group of men standing in a corner, a revolver at their waist and a jeer on their face. Nobody was talking about the Fatherland. It was a shock in my life. We, there, … willing to improve the country, and discovering who really was at power. We came back to Porto Alegre [and] decided to trace our own way, [our own] struggle for democracy. We had seen very well that there could be no democracy surrounded by tanks.[103]

The women in ADFG already possessed an environmentally friendly vein, which expressed itself on a practical basis by organizing neighborhood tree-planting operations.[104] Without a clear idea of what "ecology" actually meant, the most active ADFG members once went together to

[100] Elenita Malta Pereira, "A voz da primavera. As reivindicacões do movimento ambientalista gaúcho (1971–1980)," www.revistahistoriar.com 1 (2008).
[101] Brocke, "Die brasilianische Ökologie-Bewegung zwischen Utopie und Pragmatik," 32–3, 38–9.
[102] Elmar Bones and Geraldo Hasse, *Pioneiros da ecologia: breve história do movimento ambientalista no Rio Grande do Sul* (Porto Alegre: Já, 2007), 169–70.
[103] Ibid.
[104] Lilian Dreyer, *Sinfonia inacabada: a vida de José Lutzenberger* (Porto Alegre: Vidicom Audiovisuais, 2004), 151–3.

attend a conference held by Lutzenberg, after which they introduced themselves to him. AGAPAN and ADFG became partners in activism and the latter progressively evolved into a left-oriented organization, calling itself "feminist" and particularly interested in environmental issues.[105] Magda Renner and her friends started to engage in street protest, take legal actions against polluting companies, and criticize governmental decisions. Once considered as harmless housewives by the regime's local representatives, ADFG activists started to be scrutinized with watchful eyes and even receive death threats.[106]

In the protest writings of the association against the CVRC, it is possible to distinguish a critique of the development model dominant in Brazil. This appears in a letter published in the Brazilian press by Magda Renner: "Our struggle is against the *immediatist* mentality, which in the name of progress irrecoverably destroys basic resources. We do not contest the CVRC from the technical or financial point of view but it is an ecological absurdity to substitute the complex and magnificently equilibrated Hiléia [Amazon basin] by pastures in monoculture, whose sustainability is still unknown."[107] As shown through these words, ADFG resorted to the emerging scientific discourse already applied during the SBPC meeting in Belo Horizonte, saying that the Amazon was still widely unknown to science. In fact, although the various actors showing public indignation for Volkswagen's clearing practices did not join together in a commonly coordinated protest campaign, they used similar argumentative lines. ADFG also made arguments that overlapped with the discourse of actors working in favor of environmental protection within governmental institutions. Just as a civil servant like Coral, ADFG legitimized its criticism of VW through references to Brazilian conservationist legislation: "It is impossible that VW resort to the most primitive and destructive technique to liquidate the forest. Article 27 of our Forest Code is clear in this respect." This declaration also demonstrates that Brazilian legislation contained enough arguments for environmentalists to criticize the programs for colonization of the Amazon.

Lutzenberger, for AGAPAN, was as severe as ADFG about VW's actions in the Amazon, which he called an "orgy of destruction." However, he was more pessimistic about the instruments the institutional system offered to stop such a tendency.[108] What VW was doing, he said, was

[105] "Feministas gaúchas contra a devastação," *A folha de São Paulo*, September 25, 1976.
[106] Dreyer, *Sinfonia inacabada*, 151–3.
[107] "Feministas gaúchas contra a devastação."
[108] Ibid.

legal and approved by SUDAM, whose developmentalist "focus" was "fought against by all the natural scientists who know the Amazon." The AGAPAN-ADFG campaign against Cristalino consisted essentially of the distribution of letters of protest, and only a few newspapers published these grievances. Still, it was the first national campaign by the two associations, whose activities had been until that point confined to the state of Rio Grande do Sul.[109] Whereas until the mid-1970s environmentalism in Brazil had only been represented in the framework of regional controversies, the VW affair created one of the first environmental problems debated at the national scale. In the following years, deforestation by big companies in the Amazon would progressively become a federating theme of the ecologist movement.

The VW affair was also the occasion for personalities who were famous throughout the entire country to address the environmentalist thematic, not least Burle Marx. He was familiar to Brazilians, as since the 1930s he had designed many major squares and gardens in the country's cities.[110] At the core of his art stood the objective of merging nation and nature, particularly through the systematic use of native vegetation. This transposition of tropical plants into the urban areas was part of his research for a true Brazilian urban landscape, in rupture with the previous tradition of imitating European gardens. Burle Marx's innovative architecture and the nationalism of his artistic approach granted him the respect of the developmentalist state, including that of President Médici, who had appointed him as a member of the prestigious Federal Council of Culture.[111]

As one of the designers of Brasília, his name was also associated with modernity – although he was actually opposed to the colonization of natural spaces. Burle Marx had connections with Lutzenberger and ADFG, and supported the campaign against VW.[112] His speech at the Senate in June 1976 as well as his intervention at a conference at the University of São Paulo on October 10, 1976 had greatly contributed to nurturing the general indignation against Cristalino.[113] Burle Marx was literally in love

[109] Brocke, "Die brasilianische Ökologie-Bewegung zwischen Utopie und Pragmatik," 32–3, 38–9.

[110] Valerie Fraser, "Cannibalizing Le Corbusier: The MES Gardens of Roberto Burle Marx," *Journal of the Society of Architectural Historians* 59, no. 2 (2000), 180.

[111] Lia Calabre, "O Conselho Federal de Cultura, 1971–1974," *Estudos históricos* 37 (2006).

[112] Bones and Hasse, *Pioneiros da ecologia*, 122–3.

[113] Giulio G. Rizzo, "Maiêutica de uma nova estética," in *Arte e paisagem: a estética de Roberto Burle Marx*, ed. Lisbeth Rebollo Gonçalves (São Paulo: USP/MAC, 1997), 45.

with Brazilian landscapes, having written much about the aesthetic of nature and the respect it deserved from human beings. He did not see the relationship of humans with nature as that of a subject (humanity) having to conserve an object (nature) for the sake of economic necessities. He actually saw this relationship as a form of *convivência* (living together) in which both humans and nature were actors.[114] Because it despised such *convivência*, VW's policy in the Amazon was, to him, "either rapacity or ignorance."[115] For Burle Marx, the proof of it was that VW, rather than dedicating a portion of its profits to the conservation of nature, preferred to spend them for the maintenance of a department of public relations in order to argue in favor of natural destruction.

At the highest point of the environmental dispute involving the CVRC, Sauer and Burle Marx had an exchange of private letters, which admirably illustrated their irreconcilable points of view on the relationship between humans and nature. First, on July 8, 1976, a letter from the VW Public Relations Department invited Burle Marx to reflect about the declaration he had made at the federal Senate: "The version saying that Volkswagen produced in the Amazon the greatest fire in the whole history of the planet has gained impetus in the recent past. We believe that it first appeared in the North American press, to then spread throughout the world. And the most curious – and for us, highly frustrating – is that apparently nobody tried to verify seriously the veracity of this information."[116] The letter's mentioning that the criticisms of Cristalino originated in North America is worth brief discussion. Although I did not find any trace of it, I obviously cannot exclude that a first report of the Cristalino fire was published in the United States. Nonetheless, it is clearly in Brazil that the affair had the biggest media impact. In their letter to Burle Marx, VW interlocutors sought to place the company in a Brazilian nationalist perspective by dismissing environmentalism as an ideology coming from the northern hemisphere and consequently alien to Brazilians' preoccupation with development. This implicit fusion between anti-imperialism and anti-environmentalism amounted to a strategic recuperation by VW of the Brazilian governmental discourse expressed at Stockholm in 1972.

Behind these words, the two authors of the letter strove to relieve Burle Marx with classical conservationist arguments: VW would maintain

---

[114] Roberto Burle Marx, "Conviver com a natureza," in *Arte e paisagem: a estética de Roberto Burle Marx*, ed. Lisbeth Rebollo Gonçalves (São Paulo: USP/MAC, 1997).
[115] Ibid., 65.
[116] Hatheyer and Dierkers to Burle Marx, July 8, 1976, in ibid.

50 percent of its estate as a forest reserve, work for the "maintenance of the region's ecological equilibrium," burn exclusively "shrubs, damaging plants and *other kinds of forest* [*sic*]," and preserve all "noble timber species." The letter further argued that VW's clearing methods were that of "all the other farming projects in the region" and that VW's investments in the Amazon "contributed to the development of the country." Apparently unable to understand Burle Marx's preservationist position – just as Burle Marx, in his speeches and writings, had no consideration for economic problems – Sauer insisted on August 18 with a letter containing the same arguments, addressed to both Burle Marx and ADFG. In the letter, Sauer reproached them for defaming VW and asked Burle Marx to produce a public denial of his accusation that VW committed the largest forest fire in world history. This letter made Burle Marx even angrier, and his answer in a private letter to Sauer on November 4, 1976 proved biting:[117]

> I will never make such a denial....
>
> I am more interested in using my time trying to convince the authorities, because only they can change monstrous laws like these ones, which allow firms to realize, on behalf of their ideas about progress, genocides, which in other places would be punished by jail.
>
> I do not believe in domesticated fires. Besides "damaging plants," you probably also burnt "noisy" parrots, "dirty" armadillos, "fierce" jaguars, "wicked" cobras, certainly tall trees and maybe also some "perfidious" Indian. You have to know that the "shrubs and other kind of forest" you mentioned were once objects of admiration and fascination for illustrious Germans, Martius and Humboldt, who went to the Amazon in the nineteenth century; and as early as in 1810, Martius, revolted, denounced the massacre of such precious flora. You have to understand that it is my duty to resist against everything that I consider ecological crime, and therefore I do not agree with a forest code, which allows the deforestation of 50 percent of a glebe, independently of its size, flora, fauna and all the rest. I am against this law that you are using as shelter, although you were not even able to observe it correctly, since, as far as I know, your company has been fined. And I do not even care about the amount of the fine, and about whether this damaged the image of your company. For me, the important thing is that the sacrifice of nature is irreversible.

As Burle Marx was known to be a hot-headed artist, his impassioned reaction was not surprising. More puzzling was the active participation of congressmen and senators in the movement of environmentalist denunciation against VW. In their interventions, these politicians often

---

[117] Burle Marx to Sauer, November 4, 1976, in ibid.

linked the topic of ecology with that of nationalism (the protection of the national territory and resources), democracy (the application of law through a financial sanction against the CVRC, the rejection of an oligarchic appropriation of the Amazon), and social justice (indignation before the appropriation of fiscal incentives and land by one business group, while millions of subsistence farmers were struggling to survive).

The long parliamentary proceeding against the Cristalino fire started on June 23, 1976, as from the hemicycle Senator Dirceu Cardoso (MDB) briefly condemned "the greatest fire on earth."[118] It took on the dimensions of an entire speech six days later in the mouth of his colleague Paulo Brossard, leader of the Senate opposition, talking of an affair of "extreme gravity." Regretting the "thousands of hectares criminally devastated," he demanded "the federal authorities to be vigilant about how this area of our country is being ruined by big foreign companies." Besides defending the environment ("We did not make the Amazonian forests; we have no right to destroy them"), he placed his message within two major struggles of the Brazilian opposition. The first struggle was against the attacks to legality practiced daily by the military regime "I first want to see whether this company will actually pay the fine we are now talking about.... I am commenting [on] the fact to demand of the government a greater vigilance. I will not ask for rigor because I consider that compliance with the law should not be rigorous, it should just be exact."[119] The second struggle was that of nationality. In the context of this environmental debate, claiming nationality ironically responded to the military claim of "national sovereignty," brought by the Brazilian government at Stockholm in 1972 to oppose the adoption of an international regulation for biodiversity protection. It seemed to Brossard "that a crime against nationality is being committed [by VW], and we cannot indifferently watch such acts being practiced, with unquantifiable damage to the national community.

The senator of the Amazonas, Evandro Carreira, also from the MDB, made another speech, titled "Multinational Volkswagen and Devastation," on August 20.[120] The speech delivered Carreira's forecast of the "unquantifiable damage" feared by Brossard, by comparing what was happening in the Amazon with another environmental drama in Brazilian history. Indeed, Carreira recalled the example of the country's northeastern

[118] Carreira, *Recado Amazônico*, 282.
[119] Paulo Brossard, *O ballet proibido* (Porto Alegre: L&PM, 1976), 211–22.
[120] Carreira, *Recado Amazônico*, 137.

ecology, ruined by sugarcane culture. Left-wing MDB senator Benjamin Farah, a partisan of ex-President Goulart, added that by "killing plants," modern ranchers in the Amazon were "killing human beings," just as sugarcane planters had done in the northeast. Senator Lázaro Barboza (MDB) concluded that no fine would ever be sufficient to pay for "such a devastation, such a crime" committed by VW, which consisted of "breaking the entire ecological equilibrium of a whole region."[121]

In September, this parliamentary front against VW continued to grow, this time in the national Congress, with a speech by ARENA Congressman Carlos Wilson. The latter evoked a project marked by a "dominator appetite," "predatory action," and "attacks" against "flora and fauna."[122] He said that VW wasted "the resources of SUDAM" to "export timber at a scandalous price." Four days later, Congressman Antônio Pontes (MDB) of the Amazonian state of Amapá in turn condemned the destruction of 16,000 hectares of forest by VW during the first half of 1976.[123] Not corroborated by any source, these figures testified above all to the surrealist proportions of the hostile movement that had mobilized Brazilian politics against VW within a few weeks. Even years after the conflict between VW and IBDF stopped making press headlines, the fire at the CVRC remained a regular object of (always greatly applauded) speeches defending the Amazon in the Brazilian parliamentary assemblies. These speeches generally mixed ecological concerns with patriotism and claims for social justice: for example by ARENA Congressman Nino Ribeira in September 1978 or by his colleague Arnaldo Schmitt in October 1981.[124] Only rarely had parliament members the courage to contest such attacks, as ARENA Congressman Joacil Pereira did when he accused Schmitt of "xenophobia" and said that the CVRC brought to Brazil "the know-how that we do not have, the signs of civilization and development which comes to enliven our homeland."[125]

The succession of political speeches against the CVRC revealed the existence of a strong ecological voice within the Brazilian political institutions. That a few members of the MDB had a socio-environmentalist

---

[121] Ibid., 149.

[122] *Diário do Congresso Nacional. 11 de Setembro de 1976* (Brasília: Câmara dos Deputados, 1976), 8854–5.

[123] Ibid., *16 de Setembro de 1976* (Brasília: Câmara dos Deputados, 1976), 9128.

[124] Ibid., *19 de Setembro de 1978*, 10933; *Diário do Congresso Nacional. 3 de Outubro de 1981* (Brasília: Câmara dos Deputados, 1981).

[125] Ibid.

sensibility was already well known: someone like Evandro Carreira had not waited for the Cristalino scandal to be the voice of tropical forest preservation in the Senate. However, that a left-nationalist leader like Paulo Brossard started to discover political ecology as an ideological vehicle to argue in favor of democracy was an unexpected outcome. The environmentalist eloquence of parliament members coming from pro-regime political circles, such as Arnaldo Schmitt, was even more striking. Arnaldo Schmitt's favorite battlefield in the federal assembly was the defense of poor peasants and the promotion of subsistence agriculture as a more viable model than soil squandering by big firms.[126] He was often more inflexible and critical of government than his colleagues of the opposition banks when it came to the defense of soil sustainability. Admittedly, a handful of ecologically sensitive parliament members does not make up an environmentalist faction in a parliament. Still, I am not sure that at the end of the 1970s the environment would find the same handful of defenders in the legislative assemblies of most of the industrialized countries.

Several reasons explain the existence of a significant ecological voice within the Brazilian parliament at that time. First of all, the period of *distensão* Geisel had started in 1974 opened the perspective of a possible return to a plural political landscape. Therefore, the time was favorable for a general repositioning of the country's politicians as well as for maneuvers from part of the opposition to accelerate the democratic transition. This created a context of large political alliances (often circumstantial and around specific causes) and a great ideological porosity within the big "democratic opposition" camp, including between the political and associative spheres.[127] The poor ideological platform of the MDB, a party virtually sheltering all kinds of political traditions, left room for emerging ideas such as political ecology. Many MDB (and sometimes also ARENA) members were actually in search of new political ideas with which to identify themselves, so as to find a future political space in the perspective of the end of the polarization between authoritarianism and democracy. Such a political framework produced opportunities even for marginal ideas to gain surprisingly wide support, including among high-ranking politicians.

---

[126] Schmitt's parliamentary speeches can be heard on the online page of the Brazilian Congress archive: http://imagem.camara.gov.br/internet/audio/default.asp, access date January 12, 2013.

[127] Hochstetler and Keck, *Greening Brazil*, 70–83.

At the same time, *distensão* inspired both hope and uncertainty, due to the pressure from the military regime's hardliners and the occasional signs of authoritarianism still sent by those in power. For example, the municipal elections of 1976 raised the fear of a setback in the process of *distensão*, as the regime made sure to limit the opposition's freedom of speech with the help of the intelligence service.[128] Political ecology was not a bad concept to struggle with in this hesitating context, given the relatively inoffensive image of environmentalists in the eyes of the military leadership. The government and the secret services actually did not really understand what environmentalism was. To put it simply, environmental activists enjoyed a very ample margin of action because the military ignored them or at best saw them as harmless nature lovers. Although environmentalism deeply interrogated the dominant economic model, it was a privileged basis from which to safely criticize the authoritarian regime.[129]

In the mid- to late 1970s, many influential politicians joined campaigns against the building of an airport in São Paulo, the extension of the Brazilian nuclear park, and the distribution of timber concessions to private groups in the Amazon.[130] These environmentalist struggles were weaker in militant intensity than, for example, antinuclear mobilization occurring in certain Western European countries in the same period. But they often earned similar media and political success, precisely because of the support of well-known personalities coming from all corners of the political landscape. The global environmental moment probably helped to make environmentalism an intellectual trend in Brazil, but the translation of this trend into politics became possible because of the specific framework introduced by the process of *distensão*.[131]

The opportunities generated by *distensão* partly explain the surprising political impact of the fire at Cristalino. At the same time, the more the ecological movement against VW grew diverse, the more its message became blurred by a series of exaggerations and fantasies. This is at least what the Brazil correspondent of the German newspaper *FAZ* Martin Gester thought, as he wrote that "besides the attacks of the ideologues, there come the protests of the ecologists. The 'nature defilers' from

---

[128] Alves, *Estado e oposição no Brasil*, 230–1.
[129] Hochstetler and Keck, *Greening Brazil*, 159.
[130] Ibid.
[131] Interestingly, the ecological movement did not repeat these successes during the 1980s, when Brazil returned to the democratic system, and environmentalism lost its ability to penetrate different political movements. This evolution is captured in ibid.

Volkswagen became their scapegoat. Today, when someone talks about depletion in the Amazon, Volkswagen do Brasil (VWB) is mentioned in the first place. A 'Multi' in the virgin forest is for too many people like a devil making itself space in the sacred domain."[132] *FAZ*, a conservative-liberal paper convinced by the values of entrepreneurship, used to stick faithfully by VW. At the same time, Gester's point was not completely wrong. Few critics of the Cristalino project themselves came from the Amazon; most of them had never traveled to the region. In spite of their sincere adhesion to the vague principle that "forest should not be destroyed," environmentalists did not know the tropical forest much better than the developmentalist technocrats of the military regime did. Instead of drawing from a concrete experience, they often relied on collective imagination, drawing a pathetic portrait of the Amazon forest and its indigenous populations as powerless victims persecuted by modern technology.

This victimizing vision of the Amazon started with absurd figures on the quantity of the area cleared by cattle ranchers. The myth, propagated by Kerr and Burle Marx, that VW had cleared "one million hectares," belonged to this category of exaggerations. Although such figures were likely to have the immediate effect of shocking public opinion, it is not sure whether they had positive consequences in the long run. As Pinto underlined, the Cristalino case demonstrated that false figures on deforestation gave to environmentalism an unserious reputation, for "anybody with field knowledge of the Amazon would know it is impossible to burn one million hectares in only one go."[133] Besides, VW owned far less than 1 million hectares in the region. Sauer did not hesitate to exploit this contradiction in order to dismiss Kerr's and Burle Marx's accusations as absurd: "how could we burn one million hectares if we have only 140 thousand?" he asked journalists.[134]

In fact, most VW critics had no notion of the dimensions of ranches in the Amazon. The famous anthropologist and champion of the Indians Darcy Ribeiro thus asserted, in an attempt to mobilize emotions against the appropriation of the forest by a foreign group, that the size of the VW ranch was 300,000 hectares.[135] AGAPAN's leader, Lutzenberger,

---

[132] Martin Gester, "Volkswagen hat Ärger mit dem 'grasgetriebenen Modell,'" *Frankfurter Allgemeine Zeitung*, September 25, 1979.

[133] Lúcio Flávio Pinto, "O fogo visto do céu: advertência esquecida," *Agência Amazônia de notícias*, August 6, 2011.

[134] "Volkswagen desmente a queimada," *Jornal do Brasil*, February 7, 1980.

[135] Edilson Martins, *Amazônia, a última fronteira* (Rio de Janeiro: CODECRI, 1981), blurb.

furnished the same figure during a conference in Germany.[136] For Pinto, these exaggerations explain why the 1975 fire at Cristalino angered environmentalists and politicians without succeeding in durably shocking the population.[137] After Warwick Kerr announced that VW had burnt 1 million hectares, the later revelation that the company had cleared "only" little more than 9,000 hectares made the event appear harmless. Although burning 9,000 hectares in a single summer is a rarely equaled performance, it seemed a minor sin in comparison to the previously given figure. During a parliamentary session, some Brazilian senators even laughed out loud about the words of Burle Marx that VW was responsible for the "biggest fire of the planet."[138] But even senators struggled with numbers and proportions in the Cristalino affair, as, for example, some of them were convinced that VW's capital was limitless. Brossard contended in August 1976 that "as big as the fine can become, it will have no consequence for a company the dimension of Volkswagen."[139] This was not true: at some point, the IBDF threatened to apply a fine of 59 million cruzeiros, amounting to about half of the investments made until then in the CVRC.[140]

Politicians were encouraged to propagate such rumors by the caricatured image of Cristalino depicted in the press. For example, a comic by the illustrator Claudius in the satirical leftist weekly *Pasquim* depicted an Amerindian in traditional outfit, whose village was destroyed by bulldozers to give place to a giant pasture full of VW cows.[141] The end of the comic was even more fantastical, as the Indian character pointed at a huge surface filled with VW minibuses. In fact, rumors circulated that VW had deprived Indians of their land in order to build the CVRC, but these accusations were never founded on concrete evidence. However, they spread so quickly that VW felt obliged to publish a defensive article on the title page of its German company newspaper to belie them, titled "We Did not Expel any Indian."[142] Later, the newspaper even carried an advertisement about the fact that a neighboring Indian tribe had nominated ranch manager Friedrich Georg Brügger as its chief emeritus.[143]

[136] Lutzenberger, "Brasilien."
[137] Pinto, "O tamanho do fogo."
[138] Brossard, *O ballet proibido*, 211–22.
[139] Carreira, *Recado Amazônico*, 4, 150.
[140] Casado, "Volkswagen. Devastação com incentivos."
[141] Reproduced in *Brasilien Nachrichten* (82), 1984.
[142] "Wir vertrieben keine Indianer."
[143] "Durch jede Weide fließt ein Bach," *Autogramm*, October 1985.

Through the accumulation of spectacular representations of the CVRC by environmentalists, the idea that VW had perpetrated the biggest forest fire in world history soon crossed the Brazilian border. The Cristalino fire became a global negative reference of the rain forest cause, making VW do Brasil an environmental villain. The Germans, obviously, were interested in the Cristalino story. Important Bundesrepublik publications carried articles about the fire, while nature-friendly associations such as the Schwäbischer Albverein (Germany's oldest hiking society) and politicians like social-democrat Johann Bruns urged governmental actors to force VW to stop deforestation.[144] Between 1979 and 1980, the fire on the VW ranch was even briefly addressed in the German Bundestag (federal parliament) as well as in the European Parliament on the initiative of German deputies.[145]

Outside Germany, the British review *The Ecologist*, a publication of reference for the environmentalist movement worldwide, especially targeted the Volkswagen ranch and its Italian-owned neighbor, the Liquigás ranch, in attacks against those destroying the rain forest.[146] In one issue, *The Ecologist* even accused VW of participating in a "Holocaust in Amazonia" (understanding: an ecological holocaust, annihilating populations of nonhuman beings).[147] Even in Japan, the *Asahi Shimbum* newspaper, with a circulation of 7 million, dedicated columns to the Cristalino fire, so that, as a journalist of the publication said, "this serves as a warning for Japanese companies, for nobody has the right to destroy the land of others."[148] What had started as a small rivalry between two Brazilian development agencies had become a global example of the excess of modern civilization, to the point of taking on a pedagogic dimension.

In spite of these international reports, it was by far in Brazil that the controversy about the VW ranch reached the earliest and highest degree of politicization. The Cristalino fire was not an exception in the Amazon, where numerous big ranches practiced clearing. But it became

[144] Christian Küchli, "Feuer und kaltes Geld," *Natur*, July 1982; PA AA, Zwischenarchiv, Bd. 125.101, Scheerer to Ministerium für Auswärtige Angelegenheiten, February 4, 1982, "Abholzung in den tropischen Regenwäldern von Brasilien durch die Volkswagenwerke"; Niedersächsischer Landtag, 10. Wahlperiode, Drucksache 10/3128, Johann Bruns, August 29, 1984, "140,000 ha Farm des VW-Konzerns in Brasilien."

[145] *Deutscher Bundestag. Stenographischer Bericht. 183. Sitzung. Bonn, den 8. November 1979* (Bonn: Deutscher Bundestag, 1979), 14408–9. *Amtsblatt der Europäischen Gemeinschaften. 31.12.80* (Brussels: Europäisches Parlament, 1980), 27.

[146] *The Ecologist* 10, nos. 1–2 (1980), 17.

[147] *The Ecologist* 12, no. 6 (1982), 249.

[148] "Brasil-Japão," *O estado de São Paulo*, June 18, 1978.

a collective reference among Brazilians in the fight against the destruction of the rain forest. The VW precedent was widely cited as, in the late 1970s, several successful campaigns mobilized the country in defense of the Amazon: around the movement of rubber-tappers against the deforestation bulldozers in Acre, against the distribution of timber concessions in the region, finally also in 1979 with the creation of the Movement of Defense of the Amazon, a pressure lobby gathering together dozens of organizations of the Brazilian movement for democratization.[149] The VW case even played a role in modifying the optic of Amazonian colonization within the government. Not that the military regime abandoned its triumphalist vision of the conquest of nature, but still the forest policy became a space of lively debate, where the conservationist option gained a heavier weight than before. Even the former minister of industry and commerce of the Geisel government, Severo Gomes, spoke in 1982 for the end of the fiscal incentive policies in the region.[150] To demonstrate that the political crisis created by the fire at Cristalino would not remain without legislative consequences, Minister of the Interior Andreazza convoked Sauer for a talk in February 1980, in the frame of the preparation of a more conservationist forest law.[151] Although efficient lobbying of the AEA succeeded in emptying this forest law project of its conservationist substance, slight changes of vision occurred within developmentalist institutions. In September 1981, the CONDEL of SUDAM used the opportunity of a discussion on the CVRC to recommend more measures about environmental conservation within SUDAM-funded projects.[152]

These evolutions confirm that the case of the fire at Cristalino deserves attention. It not only proved politically and institutionally influential, it also called into question many clichés about rain forest politics and the environmentalist movement in Brazil:

First, contrary to a widespread idea (especially among the Brazilian right wing), the forest protection movement in Brazil was nothing like a movement from abroad and even less an antinational movement.[153] Although historically this movement has been internationally networked,

---

[149] Hochstetler and Keck, *Greening Brazil*, 154–60.
[150] "Ex-ministro sugere fim dos incentivos," *O estado de São Paulo*, March 11, 1982.
[151] "Volkswagen desmente a queimada."
[152] "Reduzir área de pastagens," *Jornal de Brasília*, September 26, 1981.
[153] Gélio Fregapani, *A Amazônia no grande jogo geopolítico – um desafio mundial* (Brasília: Thesaurus, 2011); Rosineide Bentes, "A intervenção do ambientalismo internacional na Amazônia," *Estudos avançados* 19, no. 54 (2005); Lorenzo Carrasco, ed. *Máfia verde: o ambientalismo a serviço do governo mundial* (Rio de Janeiro: Capax Dei, 2008).

it has also managed to mobilize on a national basis and with nationalist arguments. As I have shown by reporting some of the debates taking place about Cristalino in the Brazilian parliament, defense of the Amazonian landscape took its place inside a discourse favoring the forest commons as national heritage. It is not by chance that the scandal involved a multinational firm, while at the same time dozens of other big *fazendas* of direct Brazilian ownership were practicing massive deforestation in the Amazon without provoking the same impassioned reactions.

Second, Brazilians did not become aware of rain forest degradation because European or U.S. environmentalists taught them so. The Cristalino scandal demonstrates quite the reverse movement. In Brazil, it was a highly mediatized and politicized rain forest controversy, raising intensive environmentalist engagements back in the years 1975–6. Yet, according to Moran, the first mainstream media reports on rain forest destruction in the United States and Europe were issued several years after, principally around the late 1970s–early 1980s.[154] In fact, it is not particularly illogical that the topic of tropical forest interested in the first place the people of a country that had tropical forest in its own territory.

Third, it is impossible to understand the Brazilian ecological issue as an isolated area within politics. As we see through the Cristalino controversy, the environmental question mobilized very different social actors. Many of them were not even "full-time" political ecologists. They rather understood their environmental engagement as part of the wider antiauthoritarian agenda developed by the opposition during the *distensão* period. In this context, Brazilian environmentalism was often mixed with the values of social justice, democratization, or nationalism. Environmentalism promoted socioeconomic models that differed radically from the policies of the military regime, without having a subversive reputation. In the specific moment of *distensão*, it served some politicians and activists as an innovative ideological vehicle for safely criticizing the authoritarian system.

Fourth, as we see through the role played by Coral and IBDF, the environmentalist/conservationist struggles of the 1970s had one foot in society and the other within governmental institutions. These struggles sometimes even started from actors who were admired and respected by the military, for example, technocrats and natural scientists. Many VW critics were actually conservationists before being preservationists (with the

---

[154] Emilio F. Moran, "Deforestation and Land Use in the Brazilian Amazon," *Human Ecology* 21, no. 1 (1993), 9.

exception of personalities like Burle Marx): therefore, environmentalism was not necessarily a movement challenging the principles of modernization *per se*. What environmentalism actually did was to shake the certitudes carried by the dominant modernization discourse. It did not, in sum, fundamentally reject the concept of development, but challenged developmentalism as an all-encompassing ideology justifying all policies.

VW's *Answer between Anti-ecological Discourse and Greening of the* CVRC

Environmental controversies did not dissuade the company from continuing to present the ranch project as a model. To make this clear, VW sent a film director, Harald Schott, to Cristalino for the purpose of making a documentary movie.[155] The movie, called *The Fazenda at Cristalino*, was ready in 1980 and Wolfsburg, which saw pedagogic value in the ranching experience, distributed the video to German middle and high schools. Accompanied by a booklet for teachers, it was intended to serve as material for classes of geography, biology, or civic studies.[156] The film was filled with spectacular landscapes, especially accentuating the contrast between the perfectly cared-for living and agricultural areas of the ranch, and surrounding nature. Also placed at the disposal of the news media, it provided answers to all the criticisms leveled until then against the Cristalino project. One of the movie's functions was probably to prevent the campaign against the ranch reaching in Germany the proportions it had taken in Brazil, for this would have been disastrous for the company's image.

The first shot displayed an impressive airplane forest panorama of seemingly endless scale, free from any sight of human civilization and traversed by a large river. It was a classical representation of the Amazon as one could find it in Western TV reports. A narrator immediately announced the fate reserved for this natural space: Brazil, because of its many socioeconomic problems, had no option but to exploit this region economically. Thus the film started with the idea that nature was a problem, and its transformation into a space of production a solution. As if to show under what conditions this exploitation could be put into practice, the next sequence of the movie, this time shot from ground level, featured a bulldozer and chainsaw-equipped men felling forest trees one by one while the narrator said: "A land without settlers. But full of challenges.

[155] Harald Schott, "Die Fazenda am Cristalino" (Germany, 1981).
[156] Richter, *Die Fazenda am Cristalino*, 7.

Chances. Risks." Another sequence of forest destruction followed, depicting a fire and explaining that it took four weeks to transform forest into pastures. A further sequence, coming back to the airplane view, showed perfectly finished pastures, housing villages, and farm installations. These various sequences served a schematic, three-step narrative of progress: first wild and unpopulated nature, then nature being destroyed, finally the result of human work – victory over nature.

This narrative recalled the progressive conquest of the Brazilian wilderness by the mythical *Bandeirantes*, placing VW in the scope of nation-building propaganda. But the movie added a modern touch by presenting Cristalino as a scientifically controlled operation of landscape transformation, in contrast with the spontaneity of the *Bandeirantes'* epic. Several of the film's scenes took place in a laboratory, showing test tubes and all sorts of sophisticated, science-dedicated objects manipulated by experts in white coats: a feeling of scientific thoroughness was given to the spectator. This was actually the general impression transmitted by the rest of the documentary: everything was under control, no professional, ecological, or social detail escaped the organization of the *fazenda*. Every cow was registered and its blood analyzed.

Better even: this perfect organization was not a cold production machine. It had a human face, as the ranch was also a project for populating the forest – even, the film said in a moment of megalomania, to solve the problem of the confining of Brazilian poor within urban slums. As the narrator said, "people came from every part of Brazil" to Cristalino "to work for a common task together. Everybody at their right place." Indeed, the movie then showed a succession of sequences displaying the human actors of the farm and their function in the business: the wood burner furnishing electricity to the farm, the doctor healing the workers, the teacher teaching basic mathematics to children, the administrators, and the supermarket workers. In the middle of the wild, VW had managed an optimal division of labor: each worker appeared as a wheel in the "civilization" machine. The movie ended by staging the employees relaxing in the *fazenda* bar at the end of a hard day's work. A cheap metaphor for technical progress (a close-up of the electric bulb hanging over a group of chatting workers) closed this last scene to illustrate the narrator's concluding sentence: "Has anything in humanity ever been made without the courage to take risks?" VW, in sum, instigated ambition into the minds of Brazilian rural workers, and showed them the path of progress, which they deserved in reward for their hard work.

Despite this triumphalist tone, the movie was underpinned by VW's need to withstand environmentalist and nationalist critiques: its role was to build the ranch an ecological and national legitimacy. It said a lot about the "pioneering" work of the CVRC and made allusions to the incapacity of the Brazilian state to realize colonization alone. The movie demonstrated that the VW people were the first human actors to arrive at Cristalino, that they made it a space of labor and production. This is why they were entitled to stay: as the narrator asserted: "Here land will be made habitable. Forever." To dismiss the reproach that VW concentrated land and fiscal funds at the expense of hundreds of thousands of subsistence farmers in search for land to grow food crops, the movie made clear that "Against the attacks of nature, only planned scientific methods help." This was a recuperation of the SUDAM discourse depicting big private capital as the most suited actor to mobilize knowledge for taming nature.

This representation of nature as the enemy of humans was one of the main narrative features of the movie. At the same time, Schott unwillingly displayed a ranch besieged by environmentalist suspicions, and compelled to clumsily appropriate the language and codes of its critics. A sequence expressing ecological doubts followed the hyper-developmentalist introduction of the movie: "Ecological risks," said the narrator, "how far do we have the right to clear?" As a possible solution to this question, the movie depicted a personalization of scientific authority, Winfried Blum, a professor of the University for Soil Culture in Vienna, carrying out analyses to evaluate the fragility of Cristalino's soils. Later on, he was shown discovering the existence of a thick humus layer in the soil of a part of the *fazenda*, as if to prove to the ecologists that VW was not damaging the equilibrium of a fragile area. After having being harshly attacked by natural scientists, VW attempted to show that it submitted to their scientific expertise.

As in the film, VW's answer to the environmental controversies was ambiguous. The company hesitated between evidence of ecological responsibility (a "greening" of the project) and contestation of the environmentalists' core arguments. The "greening" operation started in October 1976, when VW invited a group of journalists to the *fazenda* to show them "examples of how noble trees are preserved and used for improvements."[157] The guests were guided into the sawmill, where the management showed them how timber was recycled in the building of prefabricated components for the workers' houses. Conservation,

---

[157] "Pastagens e preservação florestal," *Amazônia*, November 1976.

concern for biodiversity, recycling: VW, which was once proud of its clearing bulldozers, was unveiling to the public a brand new perspective on forestry. The fact that 50 percent of the Cristalino area would remain preserved, that the ranch included a small program of reforestation, and that "mountains and hillsides remained conscientiously intact in order to prevent erosion and ensure water circulation" were repeatedly advertised in the context of this new argumentation.[158] These measures, actually imposed by the SUDAM rules, were completed by declarations about how VW cared about the sustainability of the Amazonian soil. In a publication defending the project, the AEA underlined: "It is important here to remember a little divulged piece of data about the Project at Rio Cristalino: these areas are being seeded with guineagrass, alongside leguminous 'pueraria' and 'centrosema,' which, according to the specialists, are rich in protein and green mass, of great value for enriching the soil with nitrogen."[159]

The controversy that occurred in 1976 not only incited VW to "discover" that its ranching project had ecological virtues, it also led to alterations in company practices. For the first time, the CVRC started to carry out a number of soil analyses, in order to evaluate the sustainability of its pasturing techniques.[160] In the early 1980s, VW introduced a new computer program to the international and Brazilian press.[161] It determined the ideal number of animals to graze on the different pastures, and selected adequate species of grass, as measures to avoid soil erosion. This early case of green washing – which, instead of interrogating modern modes of production, resorted to scientific progress in order to correct their negative effects – obviously needed willing media organs to propagate it. Conservative newspapers did it in Germany, transforming the "environmental villain" VW into a model of environmental responsibility. According to *FAZ*, "A great step would be reached, if this invasion of the world's biggest forest region did not become a profit-greedy destruction, but a scientifically controlled development, as to all appearances is the case at Rio Cristalino."[162] Several newspapers played a similar role in Brazil, as they congratulated the company for its new commitment, announced in September 1981, to reformulate the topographic planning of the CVRC.[163] As a measure of "natural preservation," only 40 percent

[158] Scheifele, "Erschliessung des Amazonasgebietes / Exploração da Amazônia."
[159] *Amazônia*, November 1976.
[160] Richter, *Die Fazenda am Cristalino*.
[161] "Volkswagen cria ganado en medio de la selva Amazonica," *ABC*, November 3, 1982.
[162] "Gefrierfleisch aus der 'Grünen Hölle' Brasiliens."
[163] "Reduzir area de pastagens"; "Volks reduz área desmatada no Projeto Rio Cristalino."

of Cristalino's 140,000 hectares (instead of the initial 50 percent) would be turned into pasture; the rest would remain untouched forest. Volkswagen named this "practiced environmental protection": while "self-proclaimed environmentalists" were raising "very imaginative, but unfounded suspicions," VW was acting to protect the forest.[164] In reality, the critiques of environmentalists had not been as sterile as the company insinuated, for they had directly influenced the CVRC's partial conversion to conservationist thinking. In a note of February 1981 to SUDAM, the CVRC's management wrote that the reduction of the pasturing area to only 40 percent was a direct response to the concerns of "Brazilian and international environmentalists."[165]

Nonetheless, these concessions stood in contradiction with the company's action as a member of the ranchers' lobby, the AEA, on whose managing committee Sauer was sitting. While VW publicly developed a discourse that partially adopted the patterns of expression of the environmentalist movement, the AEA lobbied to render conservationist legislation more flexible.[166] Afraid of the consequences for cattle ranch projects of recent debates about ecological protection, the organization set up its own plan for reforming the colonization laws. It recommended a massive expansion of Amazonian road networks, and demanded the suppression of the legislative provision of the Forest Code stipulating that 50 percent of the forest territory of single private land estates should be spared from clearing. Instead, they suggested that the 50 percent principle become a governmental objective for the total area of Amazônia Legal. According to the AEA project, the state would make sure to reach this objective through the establishment of giant natural reserves, while existing private properties could be cleared according to the wishes of their owners.

The CVRC was squeezed between the ecological variable, newly influential in politics, and the founding engagement for economic development that cemented the association between SUDAM and Volkswagen. In this context, VW adopted the uneasy stance of giving itself the image of an "eco-responsible" enterprise while at the same time it stuck to the idea that deforestation was a necessity. As it stood in the booklet accompanying the movie *The Fazenda at Cristalino*, the Amazon, in spite of all the ecological issues, remained for VW a fantastic challenge for the Brazilian

---

[164] "Der Friedensrichter kam zur Sammelhochzeit."

[165] Arquivo do FINAM, SUDAM, February 25, 1981, "O projeto Rio Cristalino e os pressupostos de uma nova tecnologia para a pecuária amazônica."

[166] "Modelo para implantação de uma nova fronteira," *Amazônia*, April 1977.

nation: "A continuously growing population on the Atlantic coast faces this tremendous natural space in the country's interior. Forest is land; this land reserve is a challenge to the fifth biggest state on earth."[167] Praising VW as a leader of this national movement toward the interior, booklet author Richter defended the extension of "the new frontier of ox" as an inevitable movement of progress: "moving as a semicircle from the east and south into the rain forest. Clearings, highways and airports are the outpost of the land conquest; pioneer work is being done here." According to the text, environmental degradation might be regrettable, but the appropriation of forest by humans was just going in the natural direction of world history:

This process can be compared with the land-grabs by the Europeans in North America or with colonization in medieval central Europe. In the end, these were successful attempts by man to improve his living conditions and extend his homeland, even though damage to the regional ecosystems [is] noticeable. Through the continuously advanced ability of man, this process of cultural, social and spatial change has now become possible in tropical rain forests as well. The incitement of his action has always been the desire to ensure survival, to improve individual living conditions. For this reason, natural resources were and continue to be tapped [and] natural landscapes reshaped.

Sauer similarly tried to convince Brazilians of the benefits of deforestation, as he declared that "if we [as usual, he included himself in this national 'we'] did not deforest the states of São Paulo and Parana, the country would not enjoy its current development."[168] In interviews and press conferences, Sauer essentially stuck to the national-developmentalist consensus, the "Order and Progress" motto featuring on the national flag. Aware of the power and potential excesses of communication, he did not attack the environmentalists frontally.

Ranch manager Mário Thompson did not take these diplomatic precautions. Ecological grievances revolted him, as British journalist and long-time Amazon traveler Sue Branford remembered: "When we visited his ranch in November 1977, he told us with rancor that ecology was 'a new-fangled profession, recently invented by out-of-work intellectuals who have nothing new to say.'"[169] Brügger, his successor from 1978, who was a hot-tempered personality taking offense easily, was even more aggressive when it came to the topic. For him, criticisms about the

[167] Richter, *Die Fazenda am Cristalino*, 4.
[168] "Volkswagen defende-se e alerta para a devastação," *O estado de São Paulo*, August 11, 1976.
[169] Branford, *The Last Frontier*, 75.

climate and the environment were based on ignorance and superficiality. Most of the critics of clearing, he supposed, had been at best to Manaus; they did not know the forest and "sat in front of European pans full of meat."[170] Brügger symbolized the mental difficulty of the people engaged in the CVRC project to switch into an even slightly greened conception of Amazonian development. Branford witnessed one of his sudden mood swings when he heard about something related to environmental protection. As she timidly brought up the question of ecological viability, he banged on the table and said: "don't you speak to me about ecology!"[171]

As we see from such anecdotes, VW, even years after the conflict that opposed it to the IBDF, faced the new issue of the scarcity of resources hesitatingly, making steps toward the environmental ethic and steps backward. This was not simply due to the old-fashioned developmentalist vision of personalities like Brügger, Thompson, or Sauer. Much more, this hesitating behavior reflected the breakout that Brazil was traversing. Public policies still belonged to a conception of national development ignoring environmental problems: consequently, VW could not stop deforesting, unless it wanted to lose the SUDAM incentives. But at the same time, the question of nature, expressed in a movement defending the climate, plants, the forest, and fauna, was entering into world and Brazilian politics. In Brazil, the growing concern for nature went together with the promotion of values such as nationalism, democracy, or land equality. By including the protection of nature in a broad conception of the general interest, the environmentalists criticizing VW challenged the very notion of development and its claim to show the direction of "good change" for the whole human community.

The Revenge of Nature? Agro-ecological Difficulties at the CVRC

Between 1973 and 1983, VW invested nearly 34 million deutschmarks (DM) in the CVRC, which was an exceptional expense for what many observers saw in 1973 as a mere fiscal placement.[172] The Brazilian state spent twice that much (more than 63 million from the SUDAM fund), not counting the whole array of tax cuts from which the project benefited. At the end of 1979, the project had reached stratospheric costs, to the point of alarming SUDAM. In an internal report, the agency gave a very

---

[170] "Wie dem Urwald eine Hazienda abgerungen wird."

[171] Interview with Sue Branford in the documentary film by Fanny Armstrong, *McLibel: Two Worlds Collide* (1997).

[172] *GEO (Germany)*, February 1984; VW Unternehmensarchiv 373/48/9, July 1985, "Companhia Vale do Rio Cristalino, Agropecuária Comércio e Indústria."

positive evaluation of the technological level of the farm, but pointed at the high structural costs of the model and "warned the executors of the enterprise what might become of future profitability, since the actual value of the product is turning out to be very low and is not following the speed of the investment costs."[173] The prophecy proved accurate and costs exploded. The CVRC applied (and successfully obtained) various times for an increase in its funding from SUDAM, because of "actualizations": in 1978, 1980, 1981, and again on various occasions after 1983.[174] This means that many aspects had to be modified in the project, provoking an increase in the initially planned costs, always with a 75 percent participation by SUDAM through tax incentives. These reformulations were no marginal adjustments; they actually implied important sums. In 1981, for example, SUDAM approved an augmentation of 42.8 percent in the funds with which it financed the CVRC.[175]

To keep the maximal SUDAM participation of 75 percent authorized by law, VW had to increase its investments proportionally. This did not come at the right moment for VWB, which from 1979 faced the full brunt of the declining export demand linked to the oil shocks of the 1970s, the high interest rates of Brazilian loans and the fracturing of the domestic market.[176] In 1979, the profits made by VW's Brazilian branch dropped to only 1 million DM, while in 1980, the company registered losses of 56 million DM.[177] In 1981, it lost a record 452 million DM and in 1982, more than 200 million DM. In this context, where Wolfsburg was urging VWB to sharply contract its budget and reduce its investments, there were only scarce resources available for a reinforcement of the CVRC with the company's own capital. In order to increase the project's funds, Sauer started in 1981 to negotiate U.S.$12 million in the capital stock of the Companhia Vale do Rio Cristalino Agropecuária, Comércio e Indústria SA at the expense of Lebanese-Brazilian banker Edmond Safra.[178] Similar negotiations proceeded at the same time with a Kuwaiti investment bank.

There were two main reasons for the supplementary costs affecting the CVRC: the lack of infrastructure (VW had hoped that the state

---

[173] Arquivo do FINAM, SUDAM, Parecer 031/80, 1979, "Atualização financeira."
[174] Arquivo do FINAM, SUDAM, Parecer 037/84-AF, 1984.
[175] Arquivo do FINAM, SUDAM, Parecer 25/81, 1981.
[176] VW Unternehmensarchiv 373/421/1, February 1982, "Budget 1982/1983 Volkswagen-Konzern."
[177] VW Unternehmensarchiv 373/256/2, 1982.
[178] VW Unternehmensarchiv 373/239/1, December 7, 1981, "Protokoll Nr.42/1981 der Sitzung des Vorstands der Volkswagenwerk AG."

would construct roads or electricity lines in the region much faster than it actually did), and ecological issues. Unexpected natural occurrences, which VW had not foreseen due to a lack of initial studies on and experience with the region's environment, had the effect of slowing down the production agenda. The ranch management was poorly prepared to cope with the issue of soil. The project was conceived without precise knowledge of the area's topography. The only document preliminary to the elaboration of a settlement plan was a collection of photographs taken by airplane in 1973.[179] The fact that Sauer and Leiding organized the purchase of the estate in a few weeks, without previous internal consultation – not to mention external counseling, did not help any idea of convoking better expertise to evaluate the soil particularities of the terrain. As the clearing work and farming project concretely started, geographically uneven areas had not been properly detected and there was a lack of planning as regards the connection of future pasturing places with water points.[180] Besides, the hydrologic resources of Cristalino had been completely overestimated. There was no awareness about the lack of phosphate in the region's soils, although according to Congressman Schmitt, also a farmer this was something everybody knew in Brazil.[181] As Schmitt noted when he learned about the additional costs engendered in 1980 by the late inclusion of phosphate to fertilize the soils in the CVRC ranch, "if they had consulted a Brazilian agronomist, they would not have discovered such a necessity only after seven years."

According to Fearnside, phosphorus levels in the soil proportionally determine the nutritional quality of pasture grass, which means that they also strongly influence beef productivity.[182] When it started pasture organization, CVRC management probably counted on the effect of forest burning, known to multiply the phosphorus levels of Amazonian soils by six times according to certain experts.[183] Yet, it seems that they ignored a study published in 1976 by Ítalo Cláudio Falesi, an agronomist at the Brazilian Enterprise for Livestock Farming Research, a public institute affiliated with the Ministry of Agriculture.[184] As a result of

---

[179] Arquivo do FINAM, SUDAM, 1981, "Plano de reformulação. Cia Vale do Rio Cristalino Agro-pecuária Comércio e Indústria."

[180] Arquivo do FINAM, SUDAM, Parecer 25/81, 1981.

[181] *Diário do Congresso Nacional. 19 de Setembro de 1978*, 10933.

[182] Fearnside, "The Effects of Cattle Pasture on Soil Fertility in the Brazilian Amazon," 130–1.

[183] Ibid., 129.

[184] Ítalo Cláudio Falesi, *Ecossistemas de pastagem cultivada na Amazônia brasileira*, ed. CPATU, Boletim Técnico do Centro de Pesquisa Agropecuária do Trópico Húmido (Belém: CPATU, 1976).

analyses gathered on soils located along the Belém–Brasília highway, Falesi demonstrated that in spite of the initial peak subsequent to burning primary tropical forest, phosphorus levels sharply declined over a period of five years, to reach a plateau lower than the virgin value. The necessity of artificially augmenting the soil's phosphorus value had, according to VW itself, considerable repercussions on the CVRC budget.[185] The price of fertilizers in the Amazon, where, for example, superphosphate could be purchased in Belém at 0.30 U.S.$/kg-1, a very high value in world comparison, made failures in soil evaluations a perilous issue for the region's ranches.[186]

Next to these failings, mainly explicable by mismanagement, the CVRC had to face structural problems due to the regional characteristics. According to students of the Federal Polytechnic College of Zürich who carried out an analysis in the *fazenda* in the 1980s, the Cristalino soils had, in general, a weak exchange capacity.[187] The reasons for this were a low quantity of humus colloids as well as the dense presence of minerals with weak absorption capacity in the soil layers. Because of a very variable topography and bedrock, the *fazenda* actually comprehended many different soil types, from little weathered virgin soils to various types of latosols and poor sandy grounds. All of these types were hardly adapted for crop farming, very nutrient poor, easily desiccative, and strongly hampered by erosion.

VW used this as an argument to designate livestock-raising as the only adequate form of farming on the soils of Cristalino. With modern techniques of fertilization, company documents said, these soils that were unsuitable for crop culture could be made ideal for cattle.[188] However, the durability of the farming model put in place in the CVRC was uncertain. In a paper to the German foreign ministry, the German embassy in Brazil underlined that "Experiments by the Brazilian Society for Agricultural Research in the Amazon showed that even the guineagrass, seeded by VW, holds out as pasture grass for only a couple of years. In spite of artificial fertilization, it disappears after a certain time. For the moment, there exists no recommendation for a pasture plant that would be adapted to the region."[189] VW, the embassy thought, had penetrated *terra incognita*

---

[185] Arquivo do FINAM, SUDAM, Parecer 25/81, 1981.
[186] Fearnside, "The Effects of Cattle Pasture on Soil Fertility in the Brazilian Amazon," 131.
[187] Urs Holzmann, "Selektion auf erhöhtes Wachstum bei Nellore-Rindern" (Zurich: Eidgenössische Technische Hochschule Zürich, 1989), 15.
[188] Volkswagen do Brasil, *Cristalino*.
[189] BArch B116/61917, Vanselow to Hoffman, February 14, 1978.

by undertaking to exploit these soils; even with the help of up-to-date techniques, it was unsure whether the problem could be solved. It was also uncertain whether pastures could durably replace the function of humus maker and nutrient provider previously fulfilled by the forest canopy, and thus impede soil impoverishment. Pimenta's thesis that pastures ensured the continuity of the nutrient process much better than the "senile" tropical forest no longer enjoyed credibility in the 1980s. At this point, even a VW publication recognized that "only experience can teach us with certitude" whether pastures could guarantee the stability of soils on a sustainable basis.[190]

Other ecological obstacles proved more worrying, especially because their consequences were immediately visible. In 1974–5, many workers contracted malaria and consumed in a few months the ranch's entire reserve of quinine.[191] Year after year, jaguars settled around the cattle and, besides frightening the farms' inhabitants, regularly attacked the pastures and devoured a number of cows.[192] Many cows also died due to snake bites. In 1978, SUDAM showed itself concerned in a report by the "considerable number of deaths" of cattle in the CVRC, much above the normal limits.[193] The main cause of this mortality, however, was not attacks by wild animals, but that cows were "poisoned by toxic plants." A specialized farming publication, in an article about the CVRC, detailed the reasons for the presence of these plants and their spectacular effects on the cattle:

One of the region's biggest problems is mouse weed (formerly, its seeds were powdered and mixed in oil to fight against mice). [They] have the dimension of shrubs, with a three meter height when conditions are favorable to them; they prosper in greater intensity in humid areas and natural forests. They are taken by bovines and horses – during the first hours, these do not display any symptom of poisoning, but suddenly they start to feel tremors, fall to the knees, lie down and die without any possibility of attenuating their suffering and even less saving them. Death is certain and inevitable. 0.75g of the weed per kilogram of cattle is enough to provoke death. These weeds grow very rapidly, much more than other toxic species.[194]

In some areas of the Cristalino ranch, the presence of about 6,000 toxic plants was counted within only 120 hectares. According to a SUDAM

[190] Richter, *Die Fazenda am Cristalino.*
[191] Volkswagen do Brasil S. A., *Cristalino.*
[192] Gester, "Volkswagen hat Ärger mit dem 'grasgetriebenen Modell'; Buarque, "A capitania da Volkswagen."
[193] Arquivo do FINAM, SUDAM, Parecer 051/78, 1978.
[194] *Suplemento agrícola (O estado de São Paulo)*, July 15, 1977.

report, 5,848 head of cattle died poisoned by toxic plants at the CVRC between 1976 and 1981 – not much less than the 7,649 head killed for meat production during the same period of time.[195]

Another of the farm's problems was its geographic isolation. Contrarily to what VW and SUDAM boasted, large private businesses could stand powerless as they faced the huge distances, the harsh climatic conditions, or the low human density of the Amazon. Volkswagen claimed to be the most capable of dominating the "Amazonian proportions," but these could turn more problematic for a big ranch trying to find its place in the agro-food industry than for subsistence peasants, who did not have the same commercial objectives. The CVRC personnel rapidly discovered that they could do nearly nothing against the flood-bursting river and stream banks, flushing away the bridges built by the company and partially inundating pastures and roads during the rainy season.[196] For nearly one half of the year, no ordered production was possible at the *fazenda*, and vehicle travel within the whole region became a challenge.

Even during the dry season, the farm's poor connection to urban centers and national roads was one of the main obstacles to its daily business. Material and food supplies for humans and animals could be delivered by airplane, though at a price much superior to that of road transport. But what about the sale of the cattle? Sauer and Leiding did not think much about this problem as they acquired the ranch; they naively hoped that the expansion of road networks planned by the state and federal governments would become reality within a few years. However, it did not take three years before Sauer confessed to the media that "the company is facing difficulties because of the lack of roads."[197] Such a problem did not suffice to inhibit Sauer's legendary enthusiasm: the historical mission of colonization was the most important thing to accomplish; the economic outlets would appear naturally. Depicting his ranch once again as an episode in the national history of progress, he compared Cristalino with the construction of Brasília in the late 1950s: "something first has to be done, and just as Kubitschek decided first to build the new capital city, to then deal with the roads, VW is building its *fazenda* in Pará, and will think afterwards about the drainage of the production." A similar deficiency of infrastructure concerned electricity. The CVRC needed it

[195] Arquivo do FINAM, SUDAM, Parecer 25/81, 1981.
[196] "Wie dem Urwald eine Hazienda abgerungen wird."
[197] GPTEC V6.1., October 11, 1976, "Sauer diz que VW já investiu 65 mi na fazenda do PA."

in a significant quantity, particularly for the conservation of the cereals grown on the ranch, which during the rainy seasons had to be dried artificially.[198] The CVRC's only source of electricity was its own firewood power plant, but it did not suffice for such activities. To be sure, it was only a temporary installation, while the CVRC waited in vain for the region to be connected, as the government planned, to the big Tucuruí hydropower station on the Tocantins River, further north in Pará.[199] This did finally happen, but only after VW sold the ranch.

Despite the dramatic increase in SUDAM funding, the addition of (unforeseen) natural obstacles, together with the nonrealization of (expected) network infrastructure, made it impossible for the CVRC to keep up with the agenda of production elaborated in 1974. In September 1976, only about two-thirds of the pasture fields planned for this date had been created.[200] By the end of 1981, Cristalino barely reached 27,500 head of cattle for 19,620 hectares of pasture, whereas the initial objectives were to reach 56,000 head for 60,400 hectares that year.[201] This failure to match the initial objectives resulted in an occupation rate of about 1.4 head/hectare (head/ha), largely superior to the planned average of about 0.9 head/ha. This might appear as good news for forest conservation, because VW cleared at a slower rhythm than expected, but it was a negative evolution for the soil. In an information document to its incentive funds, SUDAM estimated that the maximal carrying capacity of rainforest areas amounted to 1 head/ha for breeding.[202] Computer simulations led by Fearnside and based on fieldwork processed between 1973 and 1978 in areas around the Transamazonian Highway unveiled figures closer to 0.4 head/ha for the first grazing year, 0.26 for the second and around 0.2 for the third year – the pasture grass in the samples was *caipim colonião*, used by VW at Cristalino.[203] According to Fearnside, exceeding this maximum stocking rate could provoke short-term degradations "resulting from the removal of grass through grazing and the invasion of some low weeds," medium-term degradation "resulting from invasion of woody second growth," and "longer-term degradation of soil

[198] Arbeitsgruppe Brasilien, ed. *Die Farm am Amazonas*, 16.
[199] Richter, *Die Fazenda am Cristalino*.
[200] "A Cristalino apenas cumpriu o que prometeu."
[201] Richter, *Die Fazenda am Cristalino*, 13; Econorte, *Cia Vale do Rio Cristalino Agropecuária Indústria e Comércio*.
[202] Philip M. Fearnside, "Cattle Yield Prediction for the Transamazonian Highway of Brazil," *Interciência* 4, no. 4 (1979), 221.
[203] Ibid.

nutrient and soil structure." Many years of excessive cattle trampling and excrement collection could reduce and even annihilate the soil's permeability to water by gradually hardening the undersoil while raising the ground level to several centimeters.[204]

Amazonian journalist Pinto, who has spent more than four decades investigating big farming projects and warning about their environmental consequences, drew in the late 1980s a pitiless state of the art of the CVRC's failures: "They never reached the herd of 110 thousand head [the initial objectives of the Cristalino project, supposed to be reached by 1983], plague attacked the pasture, and the market for this scale of production proved to be out of reach."[205] He further wrote that the ranch remained essentially characterized by "rudimentary techniques of soil preparation" and "incompetence in cattle management." VW, obviously, had a much more positive evaluation of the project: in 1981, the firm announced having reached exceptional rates of birth (80 percent), indicators of fertility (90 percent), and weaning (70 percent), standing largely above the national average.[206] Both Pinto's and VW's versions were ideologically biased. From the perspective of farming techniques and production results, the CVRC project was certainly not a complete collapse as other historical examples like the Ford or the Jari experiments were. Still, the misfortunes that happened over the years showed how displaced it was for VW and SUDAM to exhibit the certitude that the CVRC was a model. Yet, they had done it since the beginning, legitimized as they thought by the alleged superiority of the ranch's technology and its allegedly modern methods of management. To speak about a "revenge of nature" is obviously nothing but a jest. But it remains that VW paid the ecological price of not having taken environmental agency into account in its triumphalist conception of modernity.

Revival through Industrialization? The Atlas Frigorífico Slaughterhouse

In the 1970s, a ranchers' *bon mot* said that a cattle ranch in the Amazon was like marriage: everything went wonderfully in the first months, but once the dreamt-of project transformed into a daily business, it could only bring problems. In view of the unhappy encounter between the CVRC farmers and the ranch's complex ecology, these words seem to

[204] Wilcox, "Cattle Ranching on the Brazilian Frontier," 517.
[205] Pinto, "O tamanho do fogo."
[206] "VW AGRICOLA," *A folha de São Paulo*, September 9, 1981.

match their point. But with someone like Sauer, fascinated by the great Brazilian rural spaces, the honeymoon could survive a bit longer. On December 19, 1977, he organized a happy marriage anniversary, to celebrate the four years since the establishment of the Cristalino Company.[207] The *crème de la crème* of the politico-economic elites came to the ranch in their private airplanes to participate in a traditional Brazil *churras* (meat grilling): businessmen Plínio Salles Souto and Antônio Sobral, sugarcane magnate André Arantes, ARENA Congressman Sérgio Cardoso de Almeida, Secretary of the Environment Nogueira Neto, among other prestigious guests. Those in attendance discussed the role of the Amazon in overcoming the rising petroleum prices, defending the production of alcohol in the region as an energy substitute. Sauer used the occasion to boast about his own solution for fixing the disequilibrium in the commercial balance: the export of primary goods. This is when he announced a new step in Volkswagen's project of cattle production: the building of a slaughterhouse programmed to slaughter 600 head of cattle a day "for exportation."

The plan had been already discussed with the Brazilian authorities. In March 1976, the VWB boss informed Minister of the Interior Rangel Reis as well as the SUDAM director that VW was looking for investors, including foreign groups with recognized know-how, to launch a big complex of meat industrialization.[208] As Sauer wrote to Reis, a technical study for the realization of the project had already been undertaken by a respected European company. But Sauer insisted that this project also depended on the collaboration of the state: it would only be viable if the plan of road building in the region progressed. The need for a center to slaughter the cattle had always been in the mind of the investors in the CVRC project. Cristalino was so far from the centers of production that there was no other solution for selling the cattle. The next efficient slaughterhouses were about 1,000 kilometers away from the ranch.[209] A neighboring *fazenda*, belonging to the Centenco construction firm, made the choice of sending cattle to Belém by road, which financially ruined the project, as each head of cattle lost 26 kg during the trip. Volkswagen understood that it needed a slaughterhouse located at a reasonable proximity to Cristalino and took the initiative of creating it. Since it did not

[207] "O anfitrião Sauer."
[208] Arquivo do FINAM, SUDAM, Sauer to Almeida, March 19, 1976; Sauer to Rangel Reis, March 19, 1976.
[209] VW Unternehmensarchiv 373/190/2, August 18, 1976, "Brasilien- Schlachtprojekt."

want to assume all the investment for the project, it first found a German partner, the Atlas Company.

Atlas GmbH already had experience in the field, thanks not only to its five slaughterhouses in Germany, but also to a number of engagements abroad, including one slaughterhouse project in Thailand. It agreed to take on 40 percent of the investment in the Amazonian project and to be its leader, willing to bring its European "know-how" to optimize the installation of the industrial infrastructure and later the technical management of the enterprise.[210] The Atlas group had an excellent reputation in terms of quality management and would make sure that the industrial project conformed to the standards of hygiene of the European Community. Another foreign organization, the International Finance Corporation (IFC, a private-sector branch of the World Bank), would provide loans to finance the project. Volkswagen would provide 13 percent of the slaughterhouse's capital, the same amount as other big groups owning cattle ranches in the Araguaia, namely the Bradesco bank and two Brazilian insurance companies. That the ranch owners together made up the majority of the capital was a way of preventing them from falling as cattle providers into a disadvantaged relationship to cattle slaughters. As the project was expected to represent a regional monopoly, a substantial participation by VW in it was indispensable for the CVRC not to become dependent on alien companies for the exploitation of its meat products. The slaughterhouse, named "Atlas Frigorífico" ("Atlas Slaughterhouse"), was expected to cost U.S.$29.4 million. In 1978, SUDAM granted Atlas Frigorífico the title of "project of public utility" of the first-class category, deserving the maximum funding participation by the agency (75 percent).[211] The activities of the slaughterhouse were planned to start by mid-1982. The products were conserves, cooked frozen meat, meat extracts, beef cuts, initially planned at about 50 percent for export and 50 percent for the national market. The Atlas plant was built in the small town of Campo Alegre, founded in 1968 as a support base for the colonization project of Centenco, only one hour by car from Cristalino, and nearly fallen into disuse since the failure of the Centenco farm.[212] The cycle of meat production would thus be completed and Sauer's dream realized.

As often with big Amazonian projects, reality turned out to be much more complicated than the developmentalist dreams had predicted. The

[210] Ibid.

[211] Arquivo da SUDAM, *Resoluções e Atas do Condel. Jul./Dez. 1978* (Belém: SUDAM, 1979).

[212] "Der Friedensrichter kam zur Sammelhochzeit."

infrastructure was not ready at the planned date and the opening of the slaughterhouse had to be delayed until the end of 1983.[213] The costs of the project were grossly underestimated; by 1982, they had tripled to reach U.S.$97.5 million, $13 million of which was financed through an IFC/ World Bank loan. For reasons unconnected with Atlas Frigorífico, Atlas GmbH entered into a period of financial difficulties and first decided to lower its participation in the project capital from 40 percent to 29 percent. At the end of 1978, Atlas, which was the key actor in the project, announced its withdrawal from the capital. Another German meat producer, Heinrich Plambeck, agreed to replace Atlas as provider of the European "know-how" for the branch, though at a much lower level of participation (16 percent).[214] In these conditions, Volkswagen, which had given the impulse to the project, also had to take over its leadership, with 22 percent of the capital, above sixteen other investors, mostly Brazilian companies owning a ranch in the region.[215] As a result, Sauer was once again the project's representative in front of the state authorities. He became the CEO and president of Atlas Frigorífico while the company's second-in-command and managing director, Karl Heinz Theuer, was also a German VWB executive.[216]

As it had done with the CVRC, Volkswagen made of Atlas Frigorífico a grandiose development project in various senses of the term. Creating the largest meat industry facility in all of Amazônia Legal, with 700 to 800 workers, it implied not only the creation of a nucleus of industrialization, but also of civilization.[217] Planned to process 600 to 800 head of cattle a day, the plant comprehended a slaughterhouse and cooling, cold storage, tanning, meat processing, and canning facilities.[218] An extension of the plant was planned within a few years, so as to double Atlas Frigorífico's capacities due to the rhythm with which cattle ranching was expanding in the region. However, Atlas's main symbol of development was not the plant itself, but the town of Campo Alegre, which it caused to grow. Campo Alegre was boosted by its new role as a platform of services for the slaughterhouse.[219] A hospital, bus lines, an airport with daily

---

[213] Arquivo do FINAM, SUDAM, October 28, 1982, "Investment Agreement between Atlas Frigorifico S.A. & International Finance Corporation."

[214] Gester, "Volkswagen hat Ärger mit dem 'grasgetriebenen Modell.'"

[215] Volkswagen do Brasil, *Cristalino*.

[216] Arquivo do FINAM, SUDAM, Parecer 045/78, 1978.

[217] Arbeitsgruppe Brasilien, ed. *Die Farm am Amazonas*, 15–16.

[218] Arquivo do FINAM, SUDAM, October 28, 1982, "Investment Agreement between Atlas Frigorifico S.A. & International Finance Corporation."

[219] Arbeitsgruppe Brasilien, *Die Farm am Amazonas*, 15–16.

flights, swimming pools, bars, and restaurants started to grow in what had been until then a neglected urban stopover of migration toward the pioneer frontier. Running water and electricity arrived together with the plant, later also came squares, town gardens, and a garden belt supplying inhabitants with vegetables, fruit, and cereals.[220] This showcase of urban development was first and foremost due to Atlas Frigorífico's effort of creating a favorable climate for business agreements and exchanges in the town. The Atlas hotel, offices, and entertaining facilities became the business headquarters of southeastern Pará, where farmers and investors met to sell and buy cattle or discuss projects.

Nevertheless, social and environmental shadows undermined the ideal city and enterprise imagined by the conceivers of Atlas Frigorífico. The town of Campo Alegre grew faster than expected as the fame of the slaughterhouse project started to attract thousands of landless workers in search of a living.[221] In 1984, after the Atlas workers and their families had settled, the town had only 2,500 inhabitants, but the population more than tripled in only two years, to reach 8,000 in 1986.[222] Slums without basic supplies appeared at the margins of Campo Alegre, which became an illustration of the perverse social effects of the developmentalist ideology. In continuity with the criticism leveled against the Cristalino project, Atlas also raised environmentalist concerns. Suspicions arose that the plant might pollute the waters of the nearby river.[223] German publications noted that the surrounding woods were deforested daily to provide the Atlas temporary power plant with combustible material – like Cristalino, Campo Alegre was awaiting its connection to the hydropower plant of the Tucuruí dam in the north of Pará.[224] Tucuruí itself was at the heart of an ecological conflict because it was expected to provoke the flooding of 3,000 square kilometers of rain forest by overflow from the Tocantins River.

The issues raised by the Atlas Frigorífico project confirmed that industrial development carried risks, for human populations as well as for nature, and that VW in the future would have no choice but to consider these risks. The national-developmentalist framework according to which nature was passive in relation to humans had been fundamental in the original conception of the CVRC. As a result, the rise of environmentalist

---

[220] Volkswagen do Brasil, *Cristalino*.
[221] Arbeitsgruppe Brasilien, *Die Farm am Amazonas*, 16.
[222] Durval Rosa Borges, *Rio Araguaia, corpo e alma* (São Paulo: IBRASA, 1987), 383.
[223] Doretto, *Wolfgang Sauer*, 352.
[224] Arbeitsgruppe Brasilien, *Die Farm am Amazonas*.

thought caught VW unprepared in the mid-1970s, placing the company in an uncomfortable position. Volkswagen, which had been relying on the social authority of developmentalist certitudes, suddenly had to justify its project in an ecological perspective and rethink its relation to nature. Negligence toward environmental factors also created serious management problems on the ranch and brought the enterprise close to financial collapse – in fact, it was only saved by the indefectible support of SUDAM, institutional stronghold of developmentalism. In this new context, the idea of a limitless forest gave way to a feeling of scarcity, which, as I show in the following section, also expressed itself through the question of contested land properties.

From "Nature" to "Land": Cristalino Becomes a *Latifundio*

Darlene J. Sadlier argues that historically nature has been, together with race, one of the two key concepts that structured the Brazilian national imaginary.[225] At the same time, a number of funding works, like the writings of sociologist Gilberto Freire, structured the national construct on the grounds of two other key concepts: race and land.[226] One could say that the concepts of land and nature point at the same issue of disputing the national territory and its organic resources, only with a different approach. Volkswagen, indeed, was not only transforming nature, but also occupying land. This problem became clear from the second half of the 1970s as the ranch confronted its first social clashes and had to face the typical labor conflicts involving big landholders in northern Brazilian rural areas: conflicts over dismissals, loans, and working conditions. What happened at the CVRC was embedded in a context of transformation of the Brazilian rural conflict landscape, due to various factors. The beginnings of capitalist valuing of the Amazon region gave new significance and impact to the land conflicts. So did the particular place VW took in this process as a multinational company. The CVRC symbolized a new generation of technological, modern, and productive *latifundia*.

The renewal of the workers' strategies and expectations is a further point that characterizes the shifting rural context at the time of the CVRC.

---

[225] Darlene J. Sadlier, *Brazil Imagined: 1500 to the Present* (Austin: University of Texas Press, 2008), 4.

[226] Gilberto Freyre, *Casa-grande & senzala: formação da família brasileira sob o regime de economia patriarcal* (Lisboa: Livros do Brasil, [1993] 2001).

The landless peasants placed hope in the colonization of the Amazon because existing legislation and power balance made a redistribution of landownership in Brazil almost impossible.[227] Besides, the peasant movements were forced by the repressive conditions of the dictatorship and then helped by the *distensão* climate to adopt new forms of action. After 1978, the controlled liberalization of *distensão* was prolonged and deepened by Geisel's successor, President João Figueiredo, which increased the tools of protest at the disposal of social movements. In 1979, a law opening the possibility to create new political parties accelerated the return to a plural political life.

The following section shows why and how the CVRC became a *latifundio* in the political sense of the term: how, besides being a place of ecological controversy, it became a place of land conflict, which increased the hostility of the social movements against the project. It is important to understand this denomination as *latifundio* as a process: in fact, I have not noticed a single document in Portuguese naming the CVRC with this term before 1977. During the first years of its existence, the CVRC was presented as a solution for poverty. Only in small German left alternative circles was it criticized as a project that might worsen the social imbalance. It is progressively that a growing number of Brazilian actors saw it as a symbol of land inequalities.

The Issue of Land

The semi-feudal land structure that was predominant in Brazil during colonial times did not change after the abolition of slavery in 1888, which was not accompanied by measures of redistribution.[228] The result of this was chronic inequality as well as the emergence, in the twentieth century, of peasant movements supporting one main claim: land reform, in the sense of a massive expropriation and redistribution of property. From the mid-1940s to the mid-1960s, diverse movements organized around this claim, in the form of leagues, embryonic trade unions, and groups affiliated with the communist party, PCB.[229] In order to focus these diverse forms of protest, President Goulart encouraged the unionization of the workers in the early 1960s. He saw the unions as allies against a conservative parliament, and in fact, Goulart's sympathy for the land reform

---

[227] Martins, *Expropriação e violência*, 80.

[228] Pierre Dockes and Bernard Rosier, *L'histoire ambiguë: croissance et développement en question* (Paris: PUF, 1988), 277–8.

[229] Biorn Maybury-Lewis, *The Politics of the Possible: The Brazilian Rural Workers' Trade Union Movement, 1964–1985* (Philadelphia, PA: Temple University Press, 1994), 5–8.

movement turned out to be one of the reasons that caused the right to be afraid of a coming socialist regime.

With the military coup of 1964, a severe state repression neutralized all peasant and unionist leadership. In order to prevent insurrectional reactions to this repression, the regime mandated a team of experts favorable to land reform, asking them to elaborate the new Estatuto da Terra (Land Statute). At first sight, the Estatuto was an audacious law package, especially since it was written in the context of a conservative authoritarian regime. It guaranteed access to land property for everyone and set the principle of dispossession of unproductive estates in the name of social interest as a necessary tool for the state to enable social equality.[230] The land statute was not only considered as a social counteroffensive by the new regime to limit the influence of the left. The aim of the text was also to weaken the traditional, unproductive model of *latifundio* in order to replace it with dynamic land properties, following a model of "a modern export-oriented agro-industrial sector that could help Brazil redefine its role in the international economy."[231] The government wanted to break traditional monopolies on land so as to put Brazilian agriculture in the hands of new investors with a modern capitalist vision.

In spite of these ambitious objectives, the amendments and revisions to the Land Statute in the parliament, influenced by dozens of "ruralist" (prolatifundio and in general themselves landed) parliament members, resulted in a "complex, confusing and vague" legislative object, leaving "the maximum room for interpretation."[232] Concrete measures that could help to enforce the Statute's principles, like the creation of a judicial system specialized in agrarian questions, disappeared in the project's final version. Besides, there was no basis for the Estatuto to be applied in rural spaces precisely because these were politically dominated by big landholders. Yet, while the state proved able to efficiently repress the peasant movements, it did not furnish the material means to make local land oligarchs respect the law, especially in the Amazon, where state authorities were chronically underrepresented.[233] The tax on landowners

---

[230] Carlos Minc, *A reconquista da terra: estatuto da terra, lutas no campo e reforma agrária* (Rio de Janeiro: Zahar, 1985), 18.

[231] Peter P. Houtzager, "State and Unions in the Transformation of the Brazilian Countryside," *Latin American Research Review* 33, no. 2 (1998), 114.

[232] Marta Cehelsky, *Land Reform in Brazil: The Management of Social Change* (Boulder, CO: Westview Press, 1979), 208.

[233] Regina Bruno, "Le statut de la terre: entre réconciliation et confrontation," *Cahiers du Brésil contemporain*, no. 27–8 (1995), 41; Apesteguy, "L'intervention fédérale en Amazonie."

introduced by the Land Statute was made virtually inapplicable by the lack of a land registry that would have been necessary for the tax's assessment and collection.

After having undermined the social movement in rural Brazil and thus eliminated any possible basis of support for the Land Statute reforms, the government favored the emergence of nonsubversive trade unions. Similar to state agencies, they were responsible for administrative tasks like the management of social security and health care services, and also a medium for the state to oversee the workers.[234] These corporatist structures were depoliticized and enframed in a top-down organized confederation, CONTAG (Confederação Nacional dos Trabalhadores da Agricultura). Subordinated to the CONTAG national board were the state federations FETAGRI (Federação dos Trabalhadores Rurais), themselves coordinating the single rural unions, STR (Sindicato de Trabalhadores Rurais) that were active at the county level. Santana do Araguaia, for example, had its own STR, supposed to represent the interests of the workers of the CVRC and the region's other farms.

Although most of the trade union personnel was still favorable to land reform, their role in protesting against inequalities was limited by their relationship of submission toward the state. Their activities remained constrained into the field of possibilities existing within the dictatorship's legal frame. Providing assistance to union members in case of a conflict before the labor courts, and "sending official letters requesting resolution of a particular problem up and down the union hierarchy and to the *Ministério do Trabalho*" were the two main strategies in which the unions were involved for improving workers' conditions.[235] The unions' action, especially on a local level, exerted a corrective effect on some structural inequalities.[236] For example, on specific occasions, unions could be effective in helping workers' cases succeed in labor courts. But since the absence of any frontal critique of the regime's policy was the price for these small victories, unions were not in position to be efficient advocates of land redistribution. In these conditions, the decisive institution for advocating the cause of the rural workers turned out to be the Catholic Church.

[234] Houtzager, "State and Unions in the Transformation of the Brazilian Countryside," 105.
[235] Ibid.
[236] Ibid.; Regina R. Novaes, "CONTAG e CUT: Continuidades e rupturas da organizacão sindical no campo," in *O sindicalismo brasileiro nos anos 80*, ed. Armando Boito Juinior (São Paulo: Paz e Terra, 1991); Moacir Palmeira, "A diversidade da luta no campo," in *Igreja e questão agrária*, ed. Vanilda P. Paiva (São Paulo: Loyola, 1985).

The Church became a political shelter for the landless rural work-ers after the conference of Medellin (1968), where bishops from the entire Latin American continent agreed on a "preferential option for the poor."[237] The mobilization of young, relatively unknown priests in mar-ginalized rural areas at the service of landless peasants was a consequence of this renewal of clerical practices labeled "liberation theology." Socially minded priests played a leading role in the Comunidades de Base (CEB) organized in the 1960s in parishes to set up programs of education as well as to provide the workers with technical knowledge and moral sup-port in their fight against land injustice.[238] The help of the progressive Church to peasant farmers was structured in 1975 with the foundation of the Comissão Pastoral da Terra (CPT), backed by a number of char-ismatic Brazilian bishops. The CPT recruited lawyers specialized in rural conflicts, worked with intellectuals from the academic world, lobbied administrative and political institutions, and established contacts with human rights organizations at the international level.[239] On the one hand, the CPT aimed to favor the autonomy of the rural workers, encouraging them to engage in the unions or create their own networks of activism. On the other hand, it influenced the official trade unions in involving the worker base in their decisions, and adopting a combative political line that opposed the oligarchic policies of the dictatorship.

The CPT proved successful in both its objectives. After the priests of the organization had actively helped to organize the CEB, they encouraged landless peasants to struggle for land reform. At the end of the 1970s, more than 6,000 landless families gathered in an encampment on a por-tion of land located between three unproductive estates in Rio Grande do Sul. Priests were present and active at the encampment, but they delib-erately stayed away from leadership.[240] This occupation of several years turned out to be a confrontation with the government and symbolized the emergence of an autonomous peasant movement, leading to the for-mation of the Movimento dos Trabalhadores Rurais Sem-Terra (MST) in 1984. The rise of autonomous peasant initiatives also forced the unions to reposition themselves. In the 1979 CONTAG Congress, the delegates expressed their wish to favor the development of grassroots unionism,

---

[237] Branford, *The Last Frontier*, 134.

[238] Madeleine Cousineau Adriance, "The Brazilian Catholic Church and the Struggle for Land in the Amazon," *Journal for the Scientific Study of Religion* 34, no. 3 (1995), 378; Wright, *To Inherit the Earth*, 6–12.

[239] Adriance, "The Brazilian Catholic Church and the Struggle for Land in the Amazon."

[240] Wright, *To Inherit the Earth*, 59–60.

based on "the organization of an ever increasing number of groups such as union delegacies, union nuclei, community nuclei, educational teams." They demanded a greater inclusion of "part-time and seasonal workers" in the union's actions, as well as the creation of a common confederation uniting all Brazilian workers from the countryside and the city. Distancing itself from its role of mere administrative manager of the rural laborers, CONTAG also voted a proposition that harshly criticized Brazilian labor legislation, including the proper trade union structure, "established to protect the interests of the employer, the patron, more than the interests of the worker."[241] The Congress of 1979 marked the beginning of a new trend oriented toward more mass mobilization and basis militant actions. The year 1985 saw this trend accelerated with the fourth Congress of the organization held shortly after the fall of the dictatorship. Dozens of speakers declared themselves in favor of the democratization of trade unionism and the exclusion of corrupted union leaders.[242] Whereas MST had demanded in its January Congress the dispossession of all multinational landholders, the CONTAG Congress was marked by a decision in favor of the dissolution of all *latifundia*.

In the CVRC case, the conflict against VW emerged through this game of triple initiative: Church, trade unions, and autonomous peasant protest. In a report of 1976, the CPT already expressed its opposition against the VW project in Santana do Araguaia. The rural unions began to condemn the project in a document of 1977 and through various actions at the labor courts. Workers and ex-workers of the CVRC criticized the behavior of the company management at various moments, while in the 1980s, even the MST published a number of testimonies against Volkswagen.[243] These were the three movements that, together with the media and some European Third Worldists, turned the CVRC from a "development aid project" into a *latifundio*.

What did it mean to be a *latifundio* in the Amazon in the 1970s? The Land Statute defined an ideal, rational size of a property, which should cover between 2 and 120 hectares depending on the ecological conditions of the region and the type of activity practiced on the property.[244] This unity of measure was called the *modulo regional*. The *latifundio* was defined as a category of property of a size corresponding to 600 times or

---

[241] "Os trabalhadores rurais apóiam a criação da CGT," *A folha de São Paulo*, May 23, 1977, 18.

[242] Minc, *A reconquista da terra*, 78, 84.

[243] "A lei do gatilho," *Jornal dos trabalhadores sem terra*, September 1984.

[244] Minc, *A reconquista da terra*, 19.

more the *modulo regional*. To put it simply, the law defined the *latifundio* as much too big a property to correspond to an economically effective and socially useful use of land. During the 1970s, the *latifundio* became even more a symbol of social injustice, especially in the context of farming modernization.

The Brazilian land property regime had historically been "expropriating," in the sense that large masses of peasants, making up a majority of the land exploiters, were excluded from property. Traditionally these masses were absorbed as workforce in the biggest *fazendas*, where land was concentrated.[245] Land property was unevenly distributed, but this unequal system was more or less regulating the rural job market. This stability ended in the 1960s–1970s, when the rise of mechanized, modern *latifundia*, of which the CVRC was a model, broke the balance of the traditional Brazilian rural economy. Modern farms, in contrast to traditional *fazendas*, managed to sensibly increase the production rate by relying on heavy mechanization, chemical fertilizers, and a robotized management. The number of tractors used in Brazilian agriculture, for example, increased from 61,300 to 331,100 between 1960 and 1975, and the consumption of agrochemicals by farmers went up from 22,400 tons in 1965 to 78,500 tons in 1975.[246] This phenomenon is called "conservative modernization" because it saw technological modernization unfold within unchanged patterns of land concentration.[247] Modern *latifundia* involved big areas of land that sustained a very small number of people. Most of the employees of these *latifundia* were only needed for a couple of months. Not only were 1.5 million jobs lost in Brazilian agriculture between 1960 and 1970, while the country's population grew from 70 million to 93 million, so also did the share of permanent rural jobs compared to that of provisional contracts went down from 49 percent in 1960 to 30.5 percent in 1975.[248]

As a consequence, jobless or precariously employed peasants migrated either to the industrial south of Brazil, or to the "colonization frontiers" in the Amazon region, as they were massively encouraged by the Brazilian government since the mid-1960s. But at the same time, the government was undermining the bases of job production in the Amazon

[245] Martins, *Expropriação e violência*, 76–80.
[246] Minc, *A reconquista da terra*, 65; Ruy Moreira, "O plano nacional de reforma agrária em questão," *Revista terra livre* 1 (1986), 14.
[247] Marta Harnecker, *MST-Brésil: la construction d'un mouvement social* (Genève: Centre Europe-Tiers Monde, 2003), 24.
[248] Minc, *A reconquista da terra*, 66.

since it pushed for the "conservative modernization" to happen in that region as well. For Harnecker, the federal state encouraged migration to the Amazon because it was looking for a cheap workforce for its megalomaniac development projects in the region, especially in the mineral, timber, and hydraulic sectors.[249] We could add that this cheap workforce was also available for the private projects funded by SUDAM, which might explain VW's public endorsement of the Transamazonian highway, meant to become the main migration route (in)to the Amazon. The county of Conceição do Araguaia, which neighbored the VW ranch and was from the beginning of Operação Amazônia a privileged place for the opening of large-scale agro-industrial projects of private companies, quadrupled its population between 1960 and 1970.[250] During this same decade, 55 percent of the incoming migrants to the state of Pará came from the northeastern Brazilian states. This migration flow created a nomad reserve workforce, strategically suited for short-term work such as the establishment of a *fazenda*. In 1978, even the SBPC feared "that the projects of colonization, established along the highway axes, follow the goal of bringing to the Amazon big contingents of supplementary workforce, needed for the realization and maintaining of big projects and enterprises."[251]

The surplus of migrants implied that a job in a *fazenda* meant a lot for a worker but had little value for the landowner. Consequently, the modernization of Brazilian agriculture became a potential generator of frustration and violence. The unequal power balance between big landholders and rural workers made corporate abuses frequent. On the grounds of this tension, various actors of the land reform movement (Church, trade unions, autonomous peasants) used the concept *latifundio*, through which they constructed big property into a concept of the enemy. This construction appeared explicitly in certain activist writings, such as a report on violence in the countryside published in the early 1980s by CONTAG: "The attempts at eviction, the destruction of farming plots, the burning of houses, the appropriation of the products of the peasants' labor, the moral offenses, the threats to life, the battering, the torture, the captivity, the murder of workers have always accompanied

---

[249] Harnecker, *MST-Brésil*.
[250] José Alberto Magno de Carvalho, Morvan de Mello Moreira, and Maria do Carmo Fonseca do Vale, "Migrações internas na Amazônia: desenvolvimento e ocupação," ed. IPEA (Rio de Janeiro: IPEA/INPES, 1979), 211, 30.
[251] SBPC, *A SBPC e a Amazônia*, 4.

the latifundio."[252] More than a concept related to the surface area of land, the *latifundio* was a symbol of power, exerted with state complicity, taking very concrete manifestations such as the eviction of land squatters from the big *fazendas*. Many times, the army even intervened in order to leave the land free for a big company, as happened in the case of Liquifarm Suiá Missu, owned by an Italian company in the same county as the CVRC.[253] Taking advantage of the repressive climate of the dictatorship, the *latifundio* symbolized an illegitimate, undemocratically acquired power reflecting the servility of the Brazilian government toward big investors.

In fact, state power disappeared at the "local" level of big property as sociologist José de Souza Martins explains: "large landholdings have always been enclaves, governed by their own specific, although illegal, criteria of justice; places subject to the will of the landowner, who consequently became, and are still, the owner of the conscience of human beings."[254] The *latifundio* was, in sum, a small "autocracy," based on the use of violence, the ignorance of labor rules, and the quasi certainty of impunity for the landowner and his executives.[255] These sustainable characteristics secured the landowners' rule over their employees and collaborators, applied through a pyramidal structure of control and decision. The owner, mostly a rich entrepreneur based in São Paulo, did not directly put his hands in the business of his agricultural property. His main representative in the *latifundio* was the administrator, himself hierarchically superior to the security chief, who was at the head of a private police, making sure that the decisions coming from the top were applied. Landowners organized themselves, mostly through this private police, to protect their interest and land, often through the systematic use of violence. For the landowners, the growing number of job- and landless peasants who lived in the countryside was not only a cheap workforce reserve, but also a potential threat against the *fazendas'* stability.

As we see, and through the growing influence of the peasants' movement, *latifundio* came to be not only understood as a large surface of

[252] CONTAG, *A violência no campo pela mão armada do latifundio, 1981 a Junho 1984: torturas, prisões, espancamentos, assassinatos, impunidade e expulsão dos trabalhadores da terra* (Brasília: CONTAG, 1984), 2.

[253] Iara Ferraz, "Suià Missu," in *Brasile: responsabilità Italiane in Amazzonia*, ed. Osservatorio Impatto Ambientale (Roma: OIA, 1990).

[254] Martins, "The Reappearance of Slavery and the Reproduction of Capital on the Brazilian Frontier," 287.

[255] C. Daniel Dillman, "Land and Labor Patterns in Brazil during the 1960s," *American Journal of Economic Sociology* 35, no. 1 (1976).

land, but also as a network of oppression, exploitation, and monopoly.[256] This monopoly was a monopoly on land and resources, meaning that it concentrated power over humans as well as over nature. The concept of *latifundio* represents a problem for our case because it stands in dramatic opposition to what VW had attempted to build with the CVRC as a corporate image: that of a social and democratic company. Hence, it is necessary to explain the process through which the CVRC entered in the category *latifundio*.

Making the CVRC a Latifundio

In May 1977, an important regional newspaper, *Estado do Pará*, published an article condemning how big landowners were acting toward their employees.[257] It accused three *fazendas* of disregarding the legal employment procedures with the only aim of saving money. Of the three examples, one of the agricultural estates targeted in the newspaper's criticisms was the "Vale do Rio Cristalino." The critique was based on the testimony of Natal Viana Ribeiro. He was a northeastern migrant who offered his services to the CVRC from July 1974 to April 1975 at the head of six clearing workers. He complained he had not been paid by the company, which, according to him, had acted in complete disrespect of their contract. Even worse, Natal accused Mário Thomson (whom he wrongly identified as the owner of the CVRC) to have deliberately attempted to run him down and kill him with his *kombi* (the name given to the VW minivans). Natal said that after having finished his job, he was evicted from the *fazenda* while the ranch's staff addressed death threats to him. During the months and years following the article, it emerged that Natal's accusation against the CVRC management was only one among others.

Natal became intensively involved in the local rural union. He collected informal complaints from CVRC employees and ex-employees, encouraged them to undertake legal action, and promised to help find lawyers that would represent them in labor courts.[258] Shortly after the publication of Natal's accusations, FETAGRI of the state of Pará (member of CONTAG) sent a delegation to the county of Santana do Araguaia in order to find out more about the grievances of workers in the Cristalino

---

[256] Leonilde Servolo de Medeiros, "Le statut de la terre et les luttes des paysans Brésiliens," *Cahiers du Brésil contemporain* 27–8 (1995).

[257] "Trabalho na fazenda deixa três na miséria," *O estado do Pará*, May 20, 1977.

[258] CPT Belém, September 25, 1977, "Instrumento de nomeação de proposto"; GPTEC V6.2.1., Damasceno and Araújo to Nogueira, June 6, 1977.

fazenda. At the end of its inspection mission, the delegation reported that the CVRC had committed "innumerable abuses."[259] Some workers contracted by the *fazenda* had also begun to come spontaneously to FETAGRI. In the early 1980s, as the rural unions increased their links to progressive Church organizations, the CPT offices began to be filled with workers' charges against the VW ranch.[260] Many of the complaining workers were "core" employees of the *fazenda*, standing directly under the CVRC's administration: cowherds, electricians, basic farm personnel. What they blamed the CVRC for was similar to the classical accusations brought against many *latifundia*: work accidents without indemnity, unpaid overtime hours, abusive dismissals, generally accompanied by a physical eviction from the *fazenda* as well as death threats.[261]

One cowboy of Cristalino, for example, said that "after a labor accident he was immobilized for six days, and when he came back, he was dismissed, without being paid his salaries and other legal benefits."[262] Another cowboy argued that after having worked fourteen hours a day for eight months, "he was dismissed without delay and without having his benefits paid." An employee claimed that after a labor accident, the CVRC refused to provide him with the medical services stipulated in his labor contract. He had to get a doctor on his own, and, after his hospitalization, was dismissed without receiving indemnities. A worker from the northeastern state of Pernambuco said to the CPT that after two years as an employee of the CVRC he was personally humiliated by the ranch's managing staff, dismissed without any official document, and thus continued to have a valid employment contract without working and receiving any salary.[263] A farm helper and a woodworker made similar accusations.[264]

As guardians of this system, so the accusing workers asserted, gunmen were working for the *fazenda*, intimidating those who tried to claim their labor rights. A rural electrician said that after five months of work, he

---

[259] Ibid.

[260] "Neue Stellungnahmen zu den Beschuldigungen gegen die VW-Fazenda," *Brasilien Nachrichten* (84), 1984, 52–8.

[261] CPT Belém, September 25, 1977, Macelino. Hereinafter workers' testimonies found in the CPT archive will be cited according to the following model: CPT Belém, date, name of the deponent in short version.

[262] GPTEC V6.2.1., Damasceno and Araújo to Nogueira, June 6, 1977.

[263] CPT Belém, September 25, 1977, Macelino.

[264] Expedito Soares Batista, "Relatório: viagem à fazenda vale do Rio Cristalino da Volkswagen do Brasil, estado do Pará, Días 5, 6 e 7 de Julho de 83" (São Paulo: Deputado Expedito Soares, 1983). In Arquivo regional da CPT, Belém.

was "expelled from the *fazenda* by a professional gunman" working for the CVRC. An employee complained that CVRC gunmen forced him to sign a document containing false information and dismissing him without labor rights.[265] The CVRC had a private police force of nine armed men headed by the property's chief of security, Adão Ribeiro do Reis, whom many workers perceived as an authoritarian overseer. Cristalino's employees complained that Adão "oversees everything that the employees do. He forbids arms, criticisms, noise after 10 P.M., and alcohol."[266] A nineteen-year-old worker the CVRC had employed to remove toxic plants from the pastures said that he was constantly observed by the men of the security service. He was forced to pay a financial compensation from his own salary when he forgot to remove some plants.[267] This special CVRC police was similar to the security services existing in other *fazendas* of the region. It is probable that this police force also served as a means of dissuasion against a land invasion provoked by landless squatters.

If the workers' testimonies and the accusations of FETAGRI were true, it means that during the 1970s, the VW ranch developed a system of organization of power and repression corresponding to a *latifundio*'s "autocratic" structure: the administrator, Mário Thomson, was, thus, the incarnation of power in the *fazenda*.[268] He could even intervene in the private life of the employees. A famous episode in the farm was that of his behavior toward Zé Pedro, an employee known for the large size of his family.[269] Just after Zé Pedro's seventh child was born, "Dr. Mario" became furious that the farm had paid for all of the children's deliveries as provided in the CVRC's social guidelines. He convoked the worker and told him: "You'd better stop with these children if you do not want me to fire you." In 1978, Mário left the *fazenda* to launch his own farming project in the Amazon and was replaced as an executive director by Swiss agronomist Friedrich Georg Brügger.[270]

Adão's or Mário's "bad guy" image among the *fazenda*'s employees was obviously not only a consequence of the two men's personality, but also an illustration of the broader context of tensions resulting from the inequalities in Brazilian agriculture. The problem of the concentration of

---

[265] GPTEC V6.2.1., Damasceno and Araújo to Nogueira, June 6, 1977.
[266] "Aufbruch zur letzten Grenze," *Der Spiegel*, October 10, 1983.
[267] Buarque, "A capitania da Volkswagen."
[268] Dillman, "Land and Labor Patterns in Brazil during the 1960s."
[269] Buarque, "A capitania da Volkswagen."
[270] Coen, "Les multinationales rêvent aussi."

land had such a deep importance in rural cleavages that the simple fact of managing or possessing a property the size of the CVRC attracted the suspicion of violence. In fact, the ranch came into being with the original suspicion that it was built thanks to the expulsion of small peasants from the land on which they were squatting.[271] Formally, Volkswagen could easily prove the contrary. The CVRC's application file to the SUDAM subvention program, submitted in 1974, contained a certification by the municipal prefecture in Santana do Araguaia, officially guaranteeing that there were no peasants previously working or living in the project's area.[272]

However, given the dimensions of the Cristalino property, an unexpected encounter with previously established peasant families could not be completely excluded. A report by the National Conference of Brazilian Bishops (CNBB) dated in 1976 warned that although "formally, the [CVRC] project should not bring on problems with peasant squatters, practically it is difficult to really affirm it. In this regard, we can observe that in the county of Santana do Araguaia there are registrations of various cases of conflict with peasant squatters."[273] In addition, Brazilian and German journalists asserted that something troubling was discovered from an airplane, at the margins of the Cristalino property: "a minuscule plot with a log cabin and several heads of cattle."[274] They deduced that this could be a remaining trace, showing that there might have been small settlers occupying the ground before VW came, and that these settlers might somehow have been expelled by force. At any rate, the suspicions that emerged from this small affair, even if they might not be based on evidence, say a lot about the climate of tension that was already reigning in the southeastern Amazon region when VW arrived. The company might claim that its project was socially benevolent. In such a climate, it had no right to be mistaken, if it did not want to gain the image of an autocratic *latifundio* like any other.

In fact, as a consequence of the social discontentment it provoked, the CVRC would finally be represented as *latifundio* and integrated into the categories of land conflict. In 1978, the magazine *Movimento* ironically described Cristalino as VW's "*capitania.*"[275] Under the rule

[271] *Berliner extra Dienst*, March 11, 1975, 9–13.
[272] Arquivo do FINAM, SUDAM, Parecer n°037/74, November 29, 1974.
[273] CNBB, *Pastoral da terra – posse e conflitos – estudos da CNBB-CEP* (São Paulo: Paulinas), 180.
[274] "Wie dem Urwald eine Hazienda abgerungen wird."
[275] Buarque, "A capitania da Volkswagen."

of the Portuguese monarchy, the *capitanias* were immense territories attributed by the crown to Portuguese lords in charge of colonizing and administrating them. Brazil was first divided into twelve *capitanias* under the form of land strips of a width from 200 kilometers to 650 kilometers, held on a hereditary basis and, as such, a symbol of the arbitrariness of absolute power. As this comparison shows, the CVRC, due to its good relations with Brazilian development agencies like SUDAM or INCRA, became suspected of securing its monopoly on land thanks to arrangements with the authorities. In 1981, for example, in a report titled "Volkswagen's Latifundio Took Six Billion [Cruzeiros] from Our People," federal deputy Arnaldo Schmitt condemned the "privileges" INCRA awarded to VW. Although INCRA was an institution supposed to guarantee the equitable distribution of land, it exempted the CVRC various times from paying the property tax, as a reward for the *fazenda*'s alleged "productivity" and "efficiency."[276] The rural trade union in Santana do Araguaia also accused VW of not paying the so-called union tax with which the farming companies were supposed to contribute to finance the trade unions and the social security and health care programs.[277]

The conflict on the VW *fazenda* was also a dispute between agricultural models. The land movement's main argument was that the CVRC was structurally ineffective in creating jobs. Cristalino was a huge area of arable land managed by only a few directly contracted workers (between 180 and 350).[278] Since the beginning, the number of employees was planned to decrease drastically after the phase of setting up.[279] In 1980, fifty people were dismissed, about 20 percent of the total workforce contracted by the company at the time.[280] Usually a cowherd was not employed by the CVRC for more than one year. Contrary to what VW stated in some documents, personnel turnover was high, between 20 percent and almost 100 percent, depending on the year.[281] Criticizing the

---

[276] Arnaldo Schmitt, "Denúncia, 6 bilhões do povo para o latifúndio da Volkswagen" (Câmara dos Deputados, 1981). In the GPTEC archive.

[277] Batista, "Relatório."

[278] CPT Belém, Keith Hayward, March 25, 1985, "Relatório de uma visita ao interior dos estados de Goiás e do Maranhão."

[279] Sylva Ehlers, "Besuch auf der VW-fazenda 'Vale do Rio Cristalino,'" *Brasilien Nachrichten* (84), 1984.

[280] "VW-farm und Regionalentwicklung," *Brasilien Nachrichten* (93), 1986.

[281] CPT Belém, Keith Hayward, March 25, 1985, "Relatório de uma visita ao interior dos estados de Goiás e do Maranhão."

precarious character and the rarity of jobs at the CVRC, the advocates of land reform recommended a redistribution of the Cristalino property. In 1982, the coordinator of the CPT in the Araguaia-Tocantins said that "a project which concentrates land in one single hand has to be seen as dangerous. A ranch the size of that of Volkswagen could give a livelihood to at least 2,800 families working directly on the land, and even more if you count the teachers, commerce and service suppliers for this population."[282]

For Brügger and the VW officials in São Paulo and Wolfsburg, things had to be thought the other way around. Only the improvement in the technical capacities of production could lead to the general welfare, and only big companies, especially European ones, could achieve such a technical improvement. Asked by a journalist about the hypothesis of distributing land to landless peasants, Brügger expressed this position even more directly:

If you take, like, 200 hectares, then in Europe you will already have a couple of agronomists working in such a farm. Here you've got people who have just no idea, who have maybe lived in the north-east or the south, and then were transplanted [*sic*] into a new region, about which they have absolutely no experience of how certain crops just react. Then they crop the same way they have always done in the north-east and everything becomes ruined.[283]

Brügger thought that an agricultural property had to be put in the hands of those who "knew" how to handle it. A land reform, so he believed, would be counterproductive and could be realized only through "communism and expropriation." Interestingly, Brügger regularly used accusations of communism to answer criticisms – "Rezende is a communist!" he used to say to journalists about the local vicar, who was also a well-known opponent of the VW ranch.[284] The shadow of the Cold War seemed to hover over the discourse of Brügger, who, just before coming to Brazil, had worked as an agronomic adviser for the anticommunist Somoza regime in Nicaragua.[285] Supported by the United States and challenged by revolutionary movements, the authoritarian government of Somoza became a focus of the Cold War conflict in the late 1970s.

[282] "Interview mit Pater Ricardo Rezende Figueira am 1. Dez. 1982," *Brasilien Nachrichten* (78), 1983.
[283] "BN-Interview mit Herrn Brügger," *Brasilien Nachrichten* (93), 1986.
[284] "Aufbruch zur letzten Grenze."
[285] Arquivo do FINAM, SUDAM, April 27, 1981, "Curriculum vitae dos diretores da Cia. Vale do Rio Cristalino Agro-pecuária Comércio e Indústria."

From Land Inequalities to Urban Contention

The question of land inequalities permits a link to be traced between the issue of the distribution of natural resources and the problem of labor conditions in the countryside, which would later be at the core of the forced labor scandal hitting the Cristalino project in 1983. But to fully envisage the scope of actors intervening in this forced labor scandal, it is first necessary to reveal how the question of labor rights was experienced in Brazil's industrial core. Because VWB was not only an investor in the farming sector, but also in the first place an industrial company rooted in São Paulo's suburb of São Bernardo do Campo, we cannot ignore the upheavals that transformed the political position of the car workers in that region from the end of the 1970s. These upheavals had important consequences for Volkswagen's status in Brazilian society.

A short glimpse at the demographic evolutions characterizing Brazil during the military regime is enough to understand that land inequalities and territorial disequilibria have to be looked at within the same framework. Indeed, the drastic shrinking of stable employment in rural areas contributed to a previously unseen rural exodus. Between 1960 and 1980, 31 million Brazilians fled the countryside.[286] In the same period, 13 million people, mostly rural workers, left the northeastern states, while 16 million immigrated to the southeastern part of the country, around and within the industrial triangle formed by the three biggest Brazilian urban areas: São Paulo, Rio de Janeiro, and Belo Horizonte.[287] Instead of acting to limit this rural exodus, the federal government favored it through road building and conservative modernization in agriculture, so that an excess workforce would be available, on a cheap and flexible basis, for the country's industrialization.[288] In this regard, the situation of northeastern migrants coming to, for example, São Paulo, had one similarity with that of the northeasterners arriving on the Amazonian frontier: that of job scarcity and precariousness. In both cases, a majority of the migrants was spatially excluded. In the Amazon, they were excluded from land property and had to live at the periphery of the *latifundia*, squatting illegally when they were not selling themselves as seasonal workers from ranch

---

[286] Cliff Welch, "Globalization and the Transformation of Work in Rural Brazil: Agribusiness, Rural Labor Unions, and Peasant Mobilization," *International Labor and Working-Class History* 70, no. 1 (2006), 45.

[287] Doleschal, "Automobilproduktion in Brasilien und 'neue internationale Arbeitsteilung,'" 40.

[288] Ibid., 43.

to ranch. In the southeastern urban areas, they gathered in peripheral districts lacking basic infrastructure, widely known as *favelas*.

The automobile sector largely resorted to this available workforce. Between 1973 and 1980, the total number of workers coming from northeastern states increased by 70 percent among the employees of VW do Brasil.[289] During this same period, VWB's activities changed: the production of manufactured products for the Brazilian market lost its supremacy, while the production of car pieces for the VW factories in Europe dramatically increased. This phase of orientation to export, which primarily required unqualified tasks, was accompanied by the formation of an underprivileged category of poorly protected and underpaid working places, essentially occupied by northeasterners. In spite of having better conditions than these recently recruited categories of workers, the situation of VWB's regular workforce – in fact, the overall situation of automobile workers in Brazil – did not improve during the 1970s. The motor vehicle industry had benefited considerably from the military regime's policy, with an average rate of expansion of 15.6 percent since 1964, but the industry's high growth proceeded to the detriment of workers.[290] First, the "economic miracle" had perverse consequences for their working conditions. The generalization of extra hours, the intensification of working timetables and the authoritarian tendencies of the firms' management had been the price to pay for the productivity increase leading to economic growth. Second, although wages had increased regularly, they did not keep up with inflation.[291] While the Brazilian economy grew, the workers' buying power reduced.

Although these circumstances fueled a growing frustration, discontent remained contained over about a decade and a half by a state-controlled union structure similar to that functioning in rural Brazil. Here again, it was mainly the Church, which encouraged workers to defy the status quo, under the patronage of priests of working-class suburbs, who helped build an informal union movement from the basis of the existing union structures.[292] This grassroots trade unionism no longer focused its claims only on the regular, privileged workforce, but also included the interests

---

[289] Ibid., 168.

[290] John Humphrey, "Auto Workers and the Working Class in Brazil," *Latin American Perspectives* 6, no. 4 (1979), 73.

[291] Wolfe, *Autos and Progress*, 169.

[292] Margaret E. Keck, "El nuevo sindicalismo en la transición de Brasil," *Estudios sociológicos* 5, no. 13 (1987), 47–50.

of precarious workers in its concerns.[293] This new sense of collectiveness, together with the deterioration of working conditions and buying power in the automobile and steel sectors, composed the grounds for the renaissance of strike movements. In May 1978, a series of work stoppages occurred within the auto industry, launching a movement of massive strikes that, in spite of several ups and downs, proved contagious to many other employment sectors and remained lively until the early 1980s. These strikes were motored by one main claim: wage recovery to balance the inflation trend. Essentially started by the trade unions' grassroots – in spite of the initial hostility of a part of the unions' leadership, they attracted historic rates of participation and exceptional shows of strength such as the organization of several meetings in stadiums, which gathered hundreds of thousands of participants. The industries in the state of São Paulo, in which almost half of the jobs of the whole Brazilian secondary sector were concentrated, were the driving power of the strikes, especially the "ABC" São Paulo suburbs (Santo André, São Bernardo do Campo, and São Caetano do Sul), where most of the Brazilian automobile plants were located.[294]

Embodied by charismatic leaders such as the northeastern-born Luiz Inácio "Lula" da Silva, this new trade unionism claimed independence from state intervention of any kind. The strikes also carried political messages of wider significance, such as the political empowerment of workers. Supporting the transition to a civil rights society, Lula argued that the strikes proved the workers' will to participate in the struggle for democratic liberties, whereas until then they were not allowed to "participate in anything in this country except the process of production."[295] Besides, although the bigger strikes took place in foreign companies such as Ford, Volkswagen, Saab-Scania, or GM, the strikers' movement, which insisted on demonstrating its openness to dialog with foreign executives, stood in rupture with the traditional national populism of the Brazilian left. Lula even declared that "the only thing we want is the freedom to fight with capital, without making any distinction between national and multinational capital, because the national companies are in no way better than the multinationals."[296]

[293] Doleschal, "Automobilproduktion in Brasilien und 'neue internationale Arbeitsteilung,'" 260.

[294] Keck, "El nuevo sindicalismo en la transición de Brasil," 46–8.

[295] Luís Inácio da Silva, Mauri Garcia, and Timothy Harding, "Interview with Luis Inácio da Silva ("Lula"), President of the Sindicato dos Metalúrgicos de São Bernardo do Campo," *Latin American Perspectives* 6, no. 4 (1979), 99.

[296] Ibid., 93–4.

In fact, the ABC strikers' movement also relied on international solidarity as a means to pressure multinational firms. The emergence of foreign trade unionists as actors in the Brazilian workers' movement took place in 1977, when workers' representatives in Sweden intervened to enable the creation of a union committee in the Brazilian Saab-Scania plants.[297] During the strikes of the late 1970s and early 1980s, the German Union IG-Metall actively supported the workers of Volkswagen. IG-Metall not only put pressure on the VW senior management in Wolfsburg; it also organized and financed transnational exchanges between German and Brazilian workers' delegates, so as to share experiences, knowledge, and concerns.[298]

Foreign trade unionists were not the only "new actors" to make their appearance in the wave of the strikes. Concerned with gaining a reputation for expertise and credibility, the strikers favored the rise of the Departamento Intersindical de Estatística e Estudos Sócioeconômicos (DIEESE), an independent group of researchers providing data to the trade unions. Although it was created in 1953, DIEESE became a major actor in the workers' movement only in 1978.[299] That year it published statistical studies, used and confirmed by World Bank economists, proving that the official inflation numbers issued throughout the 1970s by the Brazilian government were false. Another actor that showed solidarity with the workers was the archdiocese of São Paulo, which organized successful collections of funds and essential goods to supply the strikers and their families. Neighborhood associations, student committees, and opposition politicians also participated in providing material support to the strikers.[300] Numerous strike leaders were willing to channel these new resources in terms of support, alliance, mobilization, and practices within a political structure. In 1979, they founded the Workers' Party (PT) on the left of the electoral spectrum. Its aim was to carry the unions' grievances into politics, and its base was overwhelmingly composed of working-class members. The PT's main mark of difference among the opposition parties to the military regime was its message that

---

[297] Humphrey, "Auto Workers and the Working Class in Brazil," 77.
[298] Mário dos Santos Barbosa, *Sindicalismo em tempos de crise: a experiência na Volkswagen do Brasil* (Santo André: Alpharrabio, 2003).
[299] Wolfe, *Autos and Progress*, 170.
[300] Maria Helena Moreira Alves, "Grassroots Organizations, Trade Unions, and the Church: A Challenge to the Controlled Abertura in Brazil," *Latin American Perspectives* 11, no. 1 (1984), 92.

democratization and civil rights should not be an end, but an instrument of social transformation.[301]

The ABC strikes not only transformed the workers' practices, they also transformed the automobile industry. Companies such as VW or Ford started to deliberately ignore Brazilian strike legislation to engage in direct bargaining instead. They had to accept the emergence of a workers' representation structure close to what they already knew in Europe and the United States. As far as VW was concerned, this move had nothing spontaneous. Sauer's first answer to the strike movement was to set up company factory commissions controlled by the VW management. It was only under the strikers' pressure that he agreed to participate in direct bargaining with independent workers' representatives.[302] In the end, the strike movement tarnished the reputation of VW in Brazil. Once considered a national model for social supplies and good salaries, VW was harshly called out for its dangerous working conditions, an opaque governing policy, pressure against the freedom of the press, and the brutal methods of VW security guards.[303] VW's reaction to the strikes did not help to improve this critical image. At the beginning of the work stoppages, it was the only company to call in the military police to repress the movement – both the Brazilian and the international press and trade unions spoke out against VW for this.[304] Besides, VW roughly sanctioned the workers having participated in work stoppages, by dismissing 1,300 of them in the early 1980s.[305]

Brazilian trade unions stated that out of all of the car companies, VW showed the most brutal reaction during the ABC strikes.[306] To make matters worse, scandals circulated showing that the company had lost the confidence of Brazilians. On April 16, 1979, eminent members of the Confederation of Jewish Congregations of São Paulo accused VWB

---

[301] Margaret E. Keck, *The Workers' Party and Democratization in Brazil* (New Haven, CT: Yale University Press, 1992), 40–60.

[302] Wolfe, *Autos and Progress*, 173.

[303] PA AA, Zwischenarchiv, Bd. 116.022, Deutsche Botschaft to Auswärtiges Amt, April 4, 1979.

[304] Mário dos Santos Barbosa, *Sindicalismo em tempos de crise*, 108–9.

[305] *Niedersächsischer Landtag. Stenographischer Bericht, 96. Sitzung. Hannover, den 12. Dezember 1985* (Hannover: Niedersächsischer Landtag, 1986), 1954. Investigations by the CNV recently proved that VW even transmitted a "black list" of strikers to the political police, as appears in the final report of the Fórum de Trabalhadores por Verdade, Justiça e Reparação (2015).

[306] PA AA, Zwischenarchiv, Bd. 116.022, Deutsche Botschaft to Auswärtiges Amt, April 4, 1979.

of hiding ex-Nazis among its German executives.[307] Even the German government began to have alarmed reactions to the growing disaffection of the Brazilians for VW. Chancellor Helmut Schmidt himself said that he was concerned to see VW becoming a negative symbol for the Third World.[308] Rolf Böhme, state secretary at the German Ministry of Finance, published a text in August 1980 in which he criticized VW's behavior and regretted that "German companies in Brazil are becoming synonymous with 'Multi,' with all the negative judgments contained in this expression."[309]

The hostility against the "Multis" in Brazil was becoming even stronger than Böhme feared because of the difficult economic context bringing Brazil to the mercy of its foreign lenders. As the new military president, João Figueiredo, took power in March 1979, he inherited the burdening economic consequences of Geisel and Netto's expansionist policies. Inflation had reached its highest level since 1964. The debt service (sum of the interest rates service together with the amortization of the foreign debt) had taken up two-thirds of the export earnings.[310] The high GDP growth rates of the 1970s had given place to stagnation. The second international oil shock of 1979 and the rising interest rates on foreign loans due to tight internal monetary policies in the United States caused this picture to worsen. Figueiredo replied by an adjustment program, which led to a decline in investment and brought Brazil into recession in 1980. The debt moratorium in Mexico, in 1982, by domino effect, annihilated any return to confidence, which Figueiredo's monetarist intentions were supposed to spark off on the financial market. In December 1982, Brazil had to turn to the International Monetary Fund, which imposed for the following two years a tough austerity program conditioning the reescalation of foreign loans.

The foreign-financed growth of the 1970s, made possible only by double-digit interest rates and legislative mechanisms protecting foreign lenders from inflation, had made of Brazil's debt the biggest in the world. Several former government executives held foreign banks and multinational firms as responsible for this disaster, accusing them of having pressured the Brazilian state to push forward big project policies and massive

---

[307] "Was ist los bei Volkswagen do Brasil," *Brasilien Nachrichten* (12), 1979.
[308] PA AA, Zwischenarchiv, Bd. 116.022, Deutsche Botschaft to Auswärtiges Amt, April 4, 1979.
[309] "Volkswagen und die 'Apertura.' Deutsche Unternehmen in Lateinamerika in der Kritik," *Vorwärts*, August 21, 1980.
[310] Baer, *The Brazilian Economy*, 83–86.

investments in public-private partnerships.[311] Multinational companies also fell into disgrace in the middle and popular classes, which were the most hit by the crisis, as they saw their real wages decrease from month to month due to the soaring inflation, while unemployment already affected one-fifth of the active population in 1983. The credit tightening and demand drop in manufactured goods particularly affected the automotive industry, which began to launch redundancy plans one after the other. Volkswagen dismissed 10,588 workers between September 1980 and March 1981, which did not help to improve the company's negative image.[312]

In the midst of the crisis, the spending of extravagant public and private funds in an Amazonian cattle ranch became increasingly complicated to justify. Walter Barelli, the director of DIEESE, designated the CVRC in April 1981 as evidence that VW had no financial difficulties and no need to fire workers in São Bernardo do Campo. "We all know," he said, "there is no crisis in the Volkswagen farming branch, which owns a big farm in the Rio Cristalino, conquered on the basis of fiscal incentives conceded by the Brazilian government."[313] Six months later at the national Congress, Deputy Arnaldo Schmitt placed the state subventions to the CVRC in perspective with the sacrifice asked of the Brazilian population in the frame of the governmental adjustment programs. He said it was a shame that VW had received so many subsidies in the Amazon, financially amounting to the earnings from the government plan to cut the pension of half a million Brazilian retirees by 10 percent.[314]

The gravity of the economic situation also provoked a dramatic increase in the hostility of Brazilians against VW's best political ally, the military regime, and fueled a previously unseen demand for democratization. In spite of a biased electoral system, the general polls of 1982 brought an astonishing progression to the opposition parties, which won the majority in the federal Congress. Brazil was on the eve of democratization and the political context becoming suitable for criticizing government-funded projects could jeopardize the future of Cristalino, as became clear in 1983, when the grave accusation of resorting to "slavery" in the Amazon was made against VW.

[311] "Ein Jahrzehnt in der Entwicklung verloren," *Der Spiegel*, November 14, 1983.

[312] Doleschal, "Automobilproduktion in Brasilien und 'neue internationale Arbeitsteilung,'" 125.

[313] "Montadora só quer lucros, diz economista," *O estado de São Paulo*, April 24, 1981.

[314] *Diário do Congresso Nacional. 19 de Setembro de 1978*, 10933.

4

Out-of-Date Modernity: Forced Labor
at Cristalino (1983–1986)

In July 1983, after they traveled to the Cristalino ranch as representatives of an inquiry commission about forced labor, members of the São Paulo state parliament made an unexpected encounter. On the last day of their visit, a cowman, Eliseu Batista de Oliveira, approached them as they were having lunch with a number of Volkswagen officials.[1] He was a disoriented, limping man with a flip-flop on one foot and a proper boot on the other. His eyes full of tears, he came closer to the men of the commission and explained that, after seven years of service, he had just been fired from the *fazenda* without being paid his unemployment compensation. He said, "I was fired because here there are rules which forbid using a 'pectoral' on the horses." One commission member asked him what a "pectoral" was, and Eliseu answered that it was a kind of metal star that he used to attach to the horse as an ornament. At this point, the chief manager of Cristalino, Brügger, who was watching the scene, intervened nervously: "we do not allow the use of accessories because this hurts the animal. Our rules were made to prevent 'them' from using this nonsense on the horses. The worker did not fulfill the rules, so I fired him." Indeed, the "pectoral" weighed 26 kg, and, according to the farm's veterinarian, it was a source of suffering that could jeopardize the life of the horse. In addition, the worker had been warned several times before being definitively discharged. It seemed that he had only himself and his stubbornness to blame.

---

[1] Batista, "Relatório"; José Aparecido Miguel, "Empresa nega denúncia de 'escravidão,' " *O estado de São Paulo*, July 17, 1983.

This little story crossed the Atlantic and was reported by journalists in Germany.[2] The curiosity was so intense that even VW in Wolfsburg had to provide explanations about this case, taking it as "a small example of the difficulties which can arise for an enterprise in the Amazon, while here in Europe there are some behaviors which are self-evidently required: the cowman refused persistently to comply and he received his dismissal because of animal torture."[3] Maybe Europeans found the story so interesting because at first sight it seemed to reproduce the cliché of a conflict between two radically different imaginaries: on one side, Western culture, so developed, sophisticated, and democratic that it could even afford the luxury of establishing rules about animal suffering; on the other side, the heavy weight of local, backward traditions of a Third World rural area marked by illiteracy. In this particular case, it seemed that the will to follow a tradition was so strong that the worker was even ready to jeopardize his job for it.

On the one hand, the case looked tremendously "self-evident" – to employ the expression of VW – and the way it was resolved seems to comply with the basic principles of civilization. A worker disrespected collective rules, so he deserved to be fired. On the other hand, there is something embarrassing in seeing VW advocating pro-animal concerns while it was responsible for massive forest fires and the destruction of a large area of wildlife. Similarly, it seems incoherent that the CVRC fired a worker because he "did not fulfill the rules" of not putting an ornament on his horse, while at the same time an inquiry commission was visiting the ranch because of the suspicion that VW "did not fulfill the rules" of Brazilian labor legislation. In fact, even if the commission members were not exactly insensitive to environmental problems, and did not understand any more than Brügger did what the point was in burdening one's horse with a 26 kg neckband, they clearly did not find the dismissal of Eliseu coherent. Ironically enough, they did not blame the worker for torturing his horse, but VW for following inconsistent policies toward its workers.

This chapter is precisely about that moment at which the modern discourse and the project of civilizing began to lose its consistency. What this anecdote about animal protection tells us is that at a certain point, certain practices taking place on the VW estate (slash-and-burn deforestation, tolerance of forced labor) began to move such a great distance away from

---

[2] *Brasilien Nachrichten* (81), 1983.
[3] Wetzel and Hertel to Wirth, September 9, 1983, in *Brasilien Nachrichten* (81), 1983.

VW's own modern discourse that the label of modernization legitimizing the CVRC project was no longer taken seriously. It became impossible for VW to seriously advocate that the respect of animals belonged to the ethic of a modern worker, while at the same time VW – as we will see – tolerated archaic practices of labor on its estate. This chapter shows how the CVRC project lost its legitimacy between 1983 and 1985, on the basis of a promised but not realized modernity. This loss of legitimacy was, in part, the result of protest action by a transnational network, starting with the initiative of certain individuals who had been invisible until then in the CVRC modernization project: the seasonal workers and their families. The actors supporting the rights of the seasonal workers selected an angle of attack that confronted VW and the Brazilian developmentalist institutions with their own rhetoric of modernity. To criticize the treatment of these workers, they resorted to the concept of *slavery*, which designates a primitive practice supposed to stand in opposition to the modernization project. The CVRC had been constructed as a model of modernity; criticisms about *slave* labor made it a symbol of archaism.

"Creating Politics Out of Violence": Brazil Discovers "Modern Slavery"

"From 1984 to 1986 Volkswagen had 700 to 800 laborers working on its estate in conditions of near slavery": such information is unverified. Not only is the timeframe debatable, neither is the number of presumed victims confirmed by any reliable source and even the use of the notion of slavery is arbitrary. Yet, it is a sentence from Sue Branford, a serious, thoroughly investigating British reporter, author of several brilliant books on the Amazon that follow the referencing patterns of academic research.[4] That hundreds of "slaves" worked on the VW ranch is presented today as an accepted and hence mostly unsourced fact in most literature on the Amazon that mentions that example. This is the consequence of a regime of forced labor that existed at Cristalino, starting very probably at the beginning of the clearing process in the mid-1970s and revealed to the public in 1983. This regime, although it widely adopted illegal features, did not differentiate itself much in this from others. Before VW was publicly accused of resorting to forced labor, various domestic firms had been implicated in similar affairs without raising public protest in the

---

[4] Sue Branford and Jan Rocha, *Cutting the Wire: The Story of the Landless Movement in Brazil* (London: Latin America Bureau, 2002), 132.

same proportions.[5] Therefore, that opponents of VW brought up – and managed to legitimize – the word "slavery" to describe forced labor at Cristalino tells more about how the scandal was represented in Brazilian society than about the facts at Cristalino themselves.

From April 1983 to 1986, seasonal workers reported having been held captive and being victims of violence at the CVRC. The reported facts occurred from 1980 to 1985. Most of the denunciations were not directed precisely against VW, but against smaller companies VW had contracted to clear the Cristalino estate. Workers complained explicitly about practices applied to them against their will: captivity, threats, violence, lies about working conditions. The reported facts pointed to a system of debt bondage, often also described as "peonage": a system under which an individual is indebted to an employer and forced, under pain of criminal punishment, to continue working for that employer.[6] However, I will not use the word "peonage" because it might create confusion with the Brazilian word *peão*, which designates all the workers contracted by subcontractors to clear forest at Cristalino. Although in many Latin American countries, the Spanish word *peon* always identifies a victim of coerced bondage, in Brazil, *peão* is a denomination widely used to describe seasonal laborers. It applies as well to categories of workers employed under perfectly legal conditions.[7]

Drawing from the testimonies left by the *peões* of Cristalino, it is possible to speak about cases of forced labor according to the official definition of the International Labor Organization, which states that forced labor includes "all work or service which is exacted from any person under the menace of any penalty."[8] Besides this general definition, the cases registered at Cristalino displayed other specific features often underlined in academic literature on forced labor. For example, the clearing workers at the CVRC, who left testimonies about their recruitment conditions, point out that they did not directly choose their employer. Some of them were contracted by a recruiter and then sold to an employer; others thought that they were contracted by VW while in reality they ended up working for a subcontractor; others were "sold"

---

[5] Figueira, *Pisando fora da própria sombra*, contains as an appendix a historical list of the *fazendas* accused of forced labor in the Amazon.

[6] Aziz Z. Huq, "Peonage and Contractual Liberty," *Columbia Law Review* 101, no. 2 (2001), 354.

[7] Martins, "The Reappearance of Slavery and the Reproduction of Capital on the Brazilian Frontier."

[8] ILO, "A Global Alliance against Forced Labour" (Geneva: ILO, 2005), 5.

by their subcontractor to another company, without being informed of this transaction. Lucassen considers "the freedom whether or not to choose one's own employer as decisive in distinguishing free from unfree labor because it consequently implies the freedom to choose one's labor conditions."[9] Brass puts this distinction in more general terms when he defines unfree labor as a regime that sees the "labor power of the subject as private property, and hence as an actual/potential commodity over which its owner has disposition" and this "regardless of whether this applies to employment that is either of time-specific duration ... or of an indefinite duration."[10] Such characteristics of forced labor were reported by CVRC clearing workers.

Nevertheless, it remains impossible to say in what proportion these cases existed and if this really affected all the clearing workers – most probably not. Every year, about 1,000 seasonal workers worked for clearing subcontractors at Cristalino.[11] During the CVRC's thirteen years of existence, VW concluded contracts with half a dozen clearing companies.[12] The heads of these companies were called *gatos* (cats), after the traditional Brazilian denomination, because they always "land[ed] on [their] feet."[13] Only three *gatos* were the subject of denunciations; no source that I know refers to cases of forced labor involving other *gatos*. Even Natal Viana Ribeiro, who was at the head of the rural trade union in Santana do Araguaia, was once the boss of a clearing company contracted by VW. In 1983–4, though, he collected denunciations from seasonal laborers against *gatos* and helped workers to defend their cases before the police and courts.

The documents reveal that a forced labor system existed that embraced the CVRC and other big ranches. Several sources evidence that the two *gatos* most often accused of forced labor, named "Chicô" and "Abilho," were VW's main subcontractors and controlled a majority of Cristalino's forest clearers.[14] For example, in the first half of 1983,

9 Jan Lucassen, "Free and Unfree Labor before the Twentieth Century: A Brief Overview," in *Free and Unfree Labour. The Debates Continue*, ed. Tom Brass and Marcel van der Linden (Bern: Peter Lang, 1997), 45–56, 47.

10 Tom Brass, "Some Observations on Unfree Labour, Capitalist Restructuring, and Deproletarianization," in Tom Brass and Marcel van der Linden, eds. *Free and Unfree Labour: The Debates Continue* (Bern: Peter Lang, 1997), 57–76, 58.

11 "Interview mit VW-Fazenda-Chef Friedrich Brügger."

12 Batista, "Relatório."

13 Le Breton, *Trapped*, 3.

14 CPT Belém, December 12, 1982, Companhia Vale do Rio Cristalino Agropecuária e Indústria / Andrade Desmatamento LTDA; Batista, "Relatório."

Abilho had a team of 403 workers under his orders on the VW ranch.[15] This does not mean that the hundreds of laborers Chicô and Abilho employed each year were all and permanently held captive and subject to violence. However, we can deduce from the content of the accusations brought against these two *gatos* that an absolute majority of Cristalino's seasonal laborers worked under the threat of becoming captive, if they were not directly captive. In many cases, the border between free and unfree labor regime is extremely difficult to identify, as sometimes the simple fact of hearing about some harm done to another worker could lead a worker to work under moral coercion, under the fear of becoming a victim himself.

It was, generally, the forest clearers themselves who undertook to describe what life looked like for them at Cristalino. They testified after having fled the ranch or being freed from captivity. The declarations of this hidden army of clearing workers spread in CPT's offices, newspapers, police stations, personal letters, process reports, and books.[16] Although the testifying *peões* often did not know each other, nor did they work in the same area of the ranch or over the same period, their declarations converge remarkably and give A coherent insight into the invisible *fazenda* of the *gatos* and *peões*. The results of a police inquiry issued in July 1983 confirmed the accusations the *peões* raised against their *gatos*.[17] The available testimonies constitute a limited sample, not covering all the clearing workers who served on the ranch. Therefore, what matters beyond the facts is the dimension of the public scandal these facts provoked, and the symbols activists and journalists used to construct this scandal. The word "slavery" became central in the process of denunciation against VW, although there is no self-evident category to deal with

---

[15] GPTEC V5.1.14./15, July 18, 1983, *gato*; Batista, "Relatório."

[16] I have worked with the testimonies of about fifty individuals, a majority of them being *peões*, the rest consisting of *peões*' relatives, or actors of the local life in the *peões*' cities of origin or recruitment. Since a couple of testimonies are anonymous or delivered under a nickname, I do not exclude the possibility that in a small number of cases, different testimonies were made by the same *peão*. Hence, I limit myself to giving an approximate number of the testimonies that I have used. Some testimonies were delivered to the CPT; others were registered by the local unions. They are visible in the archives of the CPT in Belém or of the GPTEC in Rio de Janeiro. The journalists of *Brasilien Nachrichten* also interviewed workers of the VW ranch. Labor law cases, police reports, and trial reports containing *peões*' declarations are also to be found at the CPT and GPTEC archives, while some of them were transcribed in *Brasilien Nachrichten*. Other testimonies are reported in the Brazilian press or in the specialized literature.

[17] CPT Belém, Delegacia SESP de Conceição do Araguaia – Pará, July 22, 1983, "Relatório."

the practices that took place in the CVRC, for they regard peripheral, seasonal, and provisional forms of production. This production engaged rural laborers who, at other times of the year, dedicated themselves to other activities, including independent labor.

Although historically contestable in this case, VW's critics brought up the concept of slavery to create a paradox. Talking about slavery enabled them to discursively associate VW with an age-old practice that modern capitalism was supposed to end. It symbolized the failure of farming modernization to reform labor conditions and enhance human dignity. In the specific case of the Amazon, where forced labor was held to have been a historically widespread practice, even after the 1888 official abolition of slavery, the Cristalino scandal pointed to a return to the past rather than a project for a better future.

The system of debt bondage had hit hundreds of thousands of rubber-tappers in the last quarter of the nineteenth century, when the Amazon world monopoly on rubber led to the expansion of the activity, boosted by the Industrial Revolution.[18] Mainly illiterate and uninformed about their own labor rights, Amerindians, Caboclos, and migrant workers from the Brazilian northeast engaged in deals with local rubber traders who acted fraudulently. The rubber-tappers received a ridiculous remuneration, often insufficient to cover the price of the transport, housing, food, and working tools, which the traders charged to them once they arrived at the rubber extraction site. As workers had to tap rubber restlessly, under the constant surveillance of armed supervisors, literature named this system forced labor or slavery.[19] Weakened by the collapse of the rubber economy around 1920, these forced labor networks were revived for a short duration through the U.S. demand during the Second World War. From the late 1960s, as the demand for a cheap workforce increased once again, with the establishment of big cattle ranches, timber estates, and mining complexes in the region, cases of forced labor involving a similar system of workers' indebtedness started to be reported. Pedro Casaldáliga, bishop of São Felix, a prelacy located in Pará, wrote an open letter in 1972 to denounce these acts of – according to him – "slavery," in which he described the clearing workers of big cattle ranches as "almost always misled regarding payment, place, working conditions, medical

---

[18] Barbara Weinstein, *The Amazon Rubber Boom, 1850–1920* (Stanford, CA: Stanford University Press, 1983).
[19] Le Breton, *Trapped*, 9.

attendance. Having to pay even for transportation in the framework of a system according to which they submit themselves to the frauds and abuse of the subcontractors. Once in the forest of the fazendas, without a possibility to leave. Enclosed in the 'green hell.' Controlled by gunmen and gatos."[20]

Data collected by the CPT showed that between 1970 and 1993, the recourse to forced labor affected at least 308 Amazonian *fazendas* and 85,000 workers.[21] Admittedly, research on the period between the second rubber boom and the start of cattle ranch colonization is lacking to date. But the probability is strong that, at least in part, the local networks of brokers who extorted the rubber tapped by workers so as to trade it overlapped with the networks, which stood available to organize the clearing of big farms from the late 1960s. This possibility led sociologist José de Souza Martins to speak about a "rebirth" of local networks of forced labor at that period, made possible by the demand created through the capitalist integration of the Amazon.[22]

Most of the forced labor cases registered since the 1970s have been attributable to Brazilian companies, including significant groups such as the Bradesco Bank, the Banco de Crédito Nacional, or the energy company Supergásbrás.[23] Violations of the labor law that occurred under the responsibility of these national groups did not raise emotion because forced labor was considered a practice to be expected in the Amazon. But the judgment was different for a multinational, which had promised modernity and been the advertising light of SUDAM. As Laak underlines, the failure of a big development project can be defined according to the project's own yardstick.[24] Because VW and the Brazilian development agencies constructed the CVRC into a spearhead model, every deviation from its mission of modernization became a reason to delegitimate it. Volkswagen, whose alleged benefits for the region had been largely publicized, was expected to help provoke a change in social standards. Instead, the company cooperated with traditional Amazonian networks of human exploitation, which could not but have negative consequences for the credibility of developmentalist ideology.

---

[20] Dom Pedro Casaldáliga, "Escravidão e feudalismo no norte do Mato Grosso," *Cadernos do CEAS* 20 (1972).
[21] Martins, "The Reappearance of Slavery and the Reproduction of Capital on the Brazilian Frontier."
[22] Ibid.
[23] Ibid., 20.
[24] Laak, *Weisse Elefanten*, 215.

The Forced Labor System at the VW Ranch

It was not VW directly that submitted its workers to forced labor, but local companies legally bound to VW by outsourcing contracts. On one side, this relationship blurred the degree of VW's responsibility in the affair of forced labor, but on the other side, it demonstrated that the presence of VW in the region willingly or unwillingly helped primitive labor networks to prosper. In this section, I will explain how these networks worked, as understanding these mechanisms is indispensable to discuss VW's responsibility in the matter.

Since the 1970s, recruiters had been advertising widely in pioneer cities to engage *peões* for the VW ranch. A well-known recruiter called Joaquim "Gringo" da Silva even offered jobs via southeastern Pará's local radio channels, saying that workers at Cristalino would receive the exceptional sum of 340,000 cruzeiros for clearing 2.5 hectares of pasture – the legal minimum salary in Brazil being about 30,000 cruzeiros per month at the time.[25] He used to claim that the VW ranch paid better than any other *fazenda* and that the company offered transport to the workers.[26] He announced this same advertisement over a loudspeaker while driving in the streets of the Amazonian cities he frequented to find workers.[27] The establishment of the German firm in southern Pará represented a great opportunity for him and his competitors. Throughout the whole area, these "brokers" sold the "fazenda da Wolksvagen," "fazenda da Volks," or "da Wolks Wagen" to jobseekers. They made use of the company's modern reputation, synonymous with good development, entrepreneurial success, and an abundance of jobs. The name "Volkswagen" was indefectibly linked to a symbol of social ascension: "getting a car," at a time in which millions of rural workers were looking at the supposed better living conditions in the southern metropolises of Brazil. Brokers used the magic VW acronym even if eventually they sometimes sent the workers to *fazendas* that had nothing to do with the CVRC.[28]

The mass effect created among potential workers at the evocation of Volkswagen fit the recruiters' techniques perfectly, as they did not go from town to town to pick up one or two workers, but rather tried to "catch many fishes in the same net."[29] They enrolled the workers in big groups and put them in small trucks that they drove to the place of

[25] GPTEC V7.10.2., May 21, 1984, *peão*.
[26] "*A lei do gatilho.*"
[27] GPTEC V7.28.1., August 17, 1984, *peões* (3).
[28] CPT Belém, November 1983, Carmo; GPTEC V9.54.3., Roziers to Pessek, May 6, 1987.
[29] CPT Belém, July 7, 1981, Silva, Gomes.

transaction. This technique of group catching was made possible by the habits of the workers themselves, who used to look for jobs in teams and give each other word when they learned about a work opportunity. The future forced laborers were often enrolled with friends, colleagues, or cousins accompanying them: the migrants' personal networks were the nets in which they ended up being caught.[30] Once "recruited," workers were sold to *gatos*. Volkswagen worked with six different *gatos* employing between 500 and 1,000 seasonal workers, depending on the season. Contracts were signed for only one season – usually from January to June – and renewed on a fluctuating basis. The best-known and most contested subcontracting company was the Andrade Desmatamento LTDA, run by Francisco Andrade Chagas, usually called by his nickname, Chicô.[31] Two other *gatos* of dubious reputation, working partially in collaboration with Chicô, offered their services to VW. Abilio Dias Araújo ("Abilio" or "Abilho"), a "big man" who liked to "wear checked t-shirts" and sported "a gold chain with a crucifix," had been working with the CVRC almost since the ranch was launched.[32] The third accused *gato* was called Hermínio, but he is mentioned only in a few testimonies or letters.[33]

The *gatos* offered their services to several big ranches in the region, which means that they could not be permanently present at Cristalino. As for the supervision of the workers, they would delegate their power to heavily armed *subgatos*. Each of the *subgatos* was responsible for a group of workers. The main *gatos* in southeastern Pará knew each other and collaborated, agreeing to "share" the available demand of big *fazendeiros* for a clearing workforce.[34] They could also buy or sell groups of *peões* to each other. *Gatos* were often bound through strong ties of family or friendship. Abilio's nephew was one of Chicô's gunmen.[35] Chicô used to work with his brothers, Batista and João, who both served as recruiters

---

[30] Ibid.
[31] CPT Belém, December 12, 1982, Companhia Vale do Rio Cristalino Agropecuária e Indústria / Andrade Desmatamento LTDA.
[32] GPTEC V5.1.14./15., July 18, 1983, *gato*; Le Breton, *Trapped*, 62. In the sources, this individual is designated as "Abilho," "Abilo," "Abilio," "Abilão," "Abilião," or "Abilhão." Since most of the sources for this chapter are transcriptions of oral testimonies, this problem of name spelling also shows up for other appellations (ex: "Chicô," "Chicó," and "Chico"/ "Rezende," "Resende" / or even town names: "São Felix" / "São Feliz").
[33] CPT Belém, Abreu to Gama, December 5, 1986; Batista, "Relatório"; GPTEC V5.1.14./15., July 18, 1983, *gato*.
[34] GPTEC V6.3., 1983, *peões* (2).
[35] GPTEC V5.1.21./22., July 18, 1983, *peão*.

of *peões*.[36] Chicô was also the stepbrother of another powerful *gato* of the area, Walter.[37] As for Abilio, he used to make "verbal contracts" with hotels offering rooms to laborers in search of a seasonal contract. These hotels, located in recruiting towns such as Nova Barreira, Campo Alegre, or Barreira-Velha, in Pará, served as a basis of recruitment.[38]

These links often extended to a whole local oligarchy, since the *gatos* enjoyed personal support within public authorities, as a guarantee for the prosperity of their business. Hermínio, for instance, was the stepbrother of Francisco Gomes Dantas, elected representative of Rio Maria, a key town in the recruitment of forced laborers.[39] Local policemen also knew the *gatos* well, and it was not rare that they would bring back a fugitive *peão* to his workplace and hand him back to his *gatos*.[40] The *gatos* were famous personalities in the pioneer front regions. With poor literacy and lacking the basic legal knowledge to correctly administer their enterprises, they built their entire reputation on violence. Everybody "knew" what they were capable of, and this lay at the core of their influence and impunity. In 1984, the CPT coordinator of Santana do Araguaia wrote about Chicô and Abilio that: "One just needs to go through the region to hear many people talking about them in panic and with a low voice."[41] The *gatos* themselves used this reputation to blackmail whoever would attempt to defy them. Chicô, for example, declared to the mother of a *peão* who had died in strange circumstances on the VW ranch: "they're saying around about that I am guilty for this, but they'd better not mess with me, 'cause I'm a rich man and I can give money to anyone I want, stab another one and then cross the Araguaia to the other side."[42] It was said that Chicô "used to kill *peões*" and this reputation spread among the local populations in the pioneer cities.[43]

Precisely because the people of the region normally knew the reputation of the *gatos* and heard about what they did to the workers, most

---

[36] Figueira, *A justiça do lobo*, 32–3; GPTEC V5.1.12., July 18, 1983, relative (*gato*).

[37] CPT Belém, July 6, 1983, Lima.

[38] GPTEC V5.1.14./15., July 18, 1983, *gato*; GPTEC V5.1.12., July 18, 1983, relative (*gato*).

[39] CPT Belém, November 1983, Carmo.

[40] Batista, "Relatório."

[41] *Brasilien Nachrichten* (84), 1984. Confirmed by GPTEC V.7.16.2., July 12, 1984, relative.

[42] GPTEC V6.50., September 5, 1983, relative. The Araguaia was the river separating Pará from the state of Goiás and bordering the main pioneer cities, about seventy kilometers east of the VW ranch.

[43] CPT Belém, June 26, 1983, Ribeiro; Figueira, *Pisando fora da própria sombra*, 202–11.

of the *peões* were migrant laborers coming from the northeast of the country, states neighboring Pará, or neighboring counties situated at 200 kilometers from the VW *fazenda*. The *peões* were usually between sixteen and forty years of age. They had been attracted to the pioneer regions by the rumor that in the now developing Amazonian forest, everyone could try his luck. They were landless peasants, sometimes with a family to support, and believed in the idea that this region contained land without men for men without land. Yet, since the state privileged the development of huge monoculture properties over a policy of distribution of small plots, their life often consisted of going from pioneer town to pioneer town to see if any *fazenda* of the area was in need of help to clear its terrains.[44] The fact that the victims were migrants meant that they had very little information about the functioning of forced labor networks in the regions – if they knew of the existence of forced labor at all. Thus, they could be trapped more easily than locals. It also implied that they had no dense social network – family, close friends – sufficiently close to the *fazenda* to assist them or to alert the police, the CPT, or the trade union in case of trouble. Thus, the prosperity of forced labor networks was directly linked to the waves of immigration drawn to the Amazon by the official colonization policy.

The *gatos* used to look for workers in the cities: Conceição do Araguaia, Redenção, Canabrava, Nova Barreira de Campos, Velha Barreira de Campos, Paraíso do Norte, or elsewhere.[45] These were points of recruitment, located at the edge of the Amazonian forest, where job seekers knew they could be taken on. These towns did not have to be situated in the direct neighborhood of Cristalino. Some of them were even located in other states, mostly in the north of Mato Grosso, the next southern state after Pará, or in Goiás, bordering the eastern part of Pará. After having been convinced to work for VW, the workers were usually brought to the town closest to the ranch, namely, Santana do Araguaia, a "platform" for workforce purchase that played a role for many *fazendas* in the county. In April 1984, Abilio "bought" forty-three people for the CVRC in Santana, for the price of 40,000 cruzeiros "per head," from Gringo, who was the main recruiter cited in the testimonies of *peões* who had worked in the VW *fazenda*.[46] Chicô's brother Batista was also a key

44 May 21, 1984, *peão*, in *Brasilien Nachrichten* (84), 1984.
45 Batista, "Relatório."
46 GPTEC V7.12.1., Delegacia de Policia de Paraíso do Norte to SESP, May 28, 1984; GPTEC V7.30.1., September 9, 1984, *peão*.

recruiter, as appears, for example, in the testimony of a veteran *peão* from the CVRC: "One day I overheard Batista boasting to Chicô about how he had bought us, like a herd of cattle. I was really scared when I heard that." The job of men such as Gringo and Batista was to "herd" workers and sell them to bosses like Chicô or Abilio.[47] The trafficking was based on solid relations, as Gringo himself told the police in 1984 when he said that Abilio was an "old fellow" who begged him to find rural laborers to work at the "Volkswagen *fazenda*."

Peões had no idea about the illegality of their recruitment.[48] They concluded an oral agreement with the broker that they considered a "contract" and claimed had been "signed verbally."[49] The "contract" included the quantity of work, the remuneration, and the working conditions, which were always considerably embellished. It also contained promises of advantages that sounded extraordinary for a seasonal contract, such as the provision of health care for the worker's family. Many of these contracts were false, as appears in this example of the *peões'* testimonies: "they told us that there everything would be for free, that nobody pays the hospital. Everything was false. Once you've crossed the Araguaia, everything begins to be crappy, and you keep on starving."[50] Brokers even lied about the nature of the work, as they did to workers Sabino and Adail in the mid-1980s. Adail, who was a mason, testified that although they made a contract with Joaquim Gringo da Silva to build two houses for "Mister Abilão," once arrived in Cristalino, they only did clearing work.[51]

It was also during the enrollment phase that the mechanism of debt captivity was launched. An "advance" of cash was distributed to the workers which, in reality, would serve as an initial debt on their arrival in the *fazenda*. Rapidly, this debt turned out to be the first reason to keep them clasped within the forest. The following example, related in a court audience report, is typical of how the mechanism of fraudulent indebtedness used to proceed:

The deponent was in the locality of Canabrava, Mato Grosso, as a gentleman known as Batista arrived and invited him to work in the fazenda of Wolksvagen

---

[47] "A lei do gatilho"; May 21, 1984, *peão*, in *Brasilien Nachrichten* (84), 1984.
[48] Figueira, "Por que o trabalho escravo?" 34.
[49] May 21, 1984, *peão*, in *Brasilien Nachrichten* (84), 1984; Batista, "Relatório."
[50] CPT Belém, July 1, 1981, Silva.
[51] "VW Farmarbeiter kommen zu Wort (Interview)," *Brasilien Nachrichten* (93), 1986. A similar example is reported in CPT Belém, Keith Hayward, March 25, 1985, "Relatório de uma visita ao interior dos estados de Goiás e do Maranhão."

[*sic*], under the following conditions: expenses for travelling, food and medicine, everything would be paid by Batista, and the work to be done in the fazenda would be the clearance of 20 alqueires [2.42 hectares] paid at 20,000 cruzeiros for each alqueire; ... the deponent, as he arrived in the fazenda, observed that everything was different from what had been agreed on, in fact even the travelling price, worth 42,000 cruzeiros, was deducted from the deponent's pay and Mr. Batista, who had made a contract with the deponent, transferred to his brother known as Chicô all the engagements made to the deponent; ... the deponent stresses that after they arrived at the work place he was forced to process the clearance of items that were not part of the oral contract ...: the deponent worked in the fazenda from January to April and never had any remuneration, for his remuneration was consumed by the exorbitant prices of the subsistence goods furnished on the farm, so that the deponent always found himself debtor to the gato.[52]

When he arrived at Cristalino, a *peão* who was a victim of this system already owed a cash advance to the *gato*, plus, often, the price the *gato* had paid for him to the broker. Then, the *peão* had to buy his work material and clothes and, from day to day, the food and basic goods he needed to survive at the *gato*'s "canteen" or "pharmacy."[53] Prices were high – about twice the regular prices charged in the official CVRC canteens, so that the amount the *peão* owed to the *gato* always exceeded the *peão*'s salary, and the debt of the *peão* was maintained or increased.[54] In the end, rather than being paid, the laborers were working to pay the price of their own captivity, as is made clear in the reported words of one worker in 1983: "he said that he was working only to pay debts, which could be summed up in: a pair of jeans, a pair of flip-flops and some food. He had been restlessly working for nine months, cutting wood, deforesting and he could not go out of there."[55]

This state of captivity was not only guaranteed by the feeling of debt in which the workers themselves were mentally stuck. It was also made possible by a strict control exercised by the *gatos'* corporation. At the doors of the CVRC, the new workers were meticulously inspected, and any object that could be used as a weapon was confiscated, even the personal knife that every Amazonian carries in his pocket.[56] They also had to submit to a blood test, in order to check if they had malaria. But as it

---

[52] CPT Belém, Juízo de direito da comarca de Conceição do Araguaia, December 12, 1985, "Termo de audiência."

[53] Batista, "Relatório."

[54] CPT Belém, July 1, 1981, Silva; GPTEC V7.28.1., August 17, 1984, *peões* (3).

[55] Batista, "Relatório."

[56] CPT Belém, July 1, 1981, Silva.

later appeared that catching malaria made no difference in the treatment received by and the amount of work demanded of a worker, it is obvious that the test was first and foremost a signal to the men: from the moment in which they entered the ranch, their bodies would be submitted to intensive control.[57] Administrative formalities were considered useless by the *gatos*; the *peões* did not even have to show their identification document or their *carta de trabalho*, although legally this should have been compulsory for seasonal recruitment.[58] The only important thing was that the body of the worker became captive and its physical force directed to the clearing operations, during which the *peões* were constantly watched by overseers pointing guns in their direction.[59]

If *peões* were victims of coercion, it was always on a seasonal basis. Rather than keeping them in his service when there was no demand from VW, at a certain point, the *gato* would decide to liberate them, mostly at the end of the clearing season. Most often, the *peões* would go away with empty pockets and walk hundreds of kilometers through the jungle before reaching the next town. Sometimes the *gato* demanded that the "debt" of captivity be paid until the last cent after liberation. In this case, the *gato* would go to the *peão*'s home, threaten his family, and steal valuables or furniture.[60] Sometimes – for example, if a *peão* had collaborated with the *subgatos* by assisting them in overseeing his "colleagues," but also in the case of particularly "satisfying" work, or even thanks to exterior help for paying the *peão*'s debt – a worker could be liberated on the order of the *gato*. The content of the following "letters of enfranchisement" (*cartas de alforria*), sent by a supervising gunman to his superiors, constitute one of the pieces of evidence that a system of unfree labor existed in Cristalino even after the year 1983 in which the scandal was made public:[61]

Wolks [N.B.: Volkswagen] July 12, 1984

Mr. Abilio

I write you these lines and it's just to inform you that this young man has been freed 'cause he's already fixed up all his debts here with us. Nothing else here everything's fine. Ass. Luis Felipe.

Luizão

---

[57] Figueira, *Pisando fora da própria sombra,* 341–2; "VW Farmarbeiter kommen zu Wort (Interview)."
[58] The *carta de trabalho* was a legal and obligatory labor document.
[59] CPT Belém, July 7, 1981, Silva, Gomes.
[60] May 21, 1984, *peão*, in *Brasilien Nachrichten* (84), 1984.
[61] Figueira, *Pisando fora da própria sombra*: joined reproductions.

Wolks July 12, 1984

Mr. Adão

Good afternoon
I ask you to free these 4 men for they've already liquidated all their debts
in the fazenda. Nothing else.

Grateful,
ass. Luis Felipe

From their recruitment to their possible liberation, the victims passed
through living conditions marked by isolation. On their first day, the
peões were taken to live in what they called the *gato*'s "canteen."[62] The
fazenda had an area of 1,400 square kilometers and the *gatos'* canteens
seasonally changed location according to the parts of the *fazenda* being
cleared. In 1984, Abilio's canteen was located eighty-seven kilometers
away from the *fazenda* entrance. The *peões* found themselves living in
thatch shelters or in huts of black tarpaulin, if not plastic, covered with
palm sheets, and sleeping in hammocks. Three dozen men would sleep in
the same barrack.[63] They almost never had contact with anybody other
than their colleagues, the *gato*, and his gunmen. It is important to stress
that many of the *peões* never saw any VW staff. The CVRC private security police did not have much idea of what was happening in the *gato*'s
business and canteen, so at least they said.[64] Only when a *peão* was close
to death would he sometimes be sent to the *fazenda* hospital, but this
happened very rarely, despite the frequency with which *peões* fell gravely
ill, as a result of their living conditions. The water they drank was, for
example, very dirty, "black with mosquitoes on the top."[65]

Mosquitoes were the daily plague of the *peão*. Of course, the jungle
was not a welcoming atmosphere and workers were exposed to a harsh
climate, the occasional threat of jaguars and snakes, and the constant
presence of wasps, but mosquitoes were the most dreaded since they carried malaria. *Peões* frequently caught malaria at Cristalino; some of them
died of it.[66] The hygiene and health promises made in the glittering VW
brochures did not exist in the *gatos'* enclaves. If a *peão* fell ill, he had to
pay for his medicine at the *gato*'s pharmacy, and this then became part of
his "debt" of captivity. If he still had the strength, he could drag himself

[62] GPTEC V7.17.1., July 13, 1984, *peão*.
[63] "VW Farmarbeiter kommen zu Wort (Interview)."
[64] "Der Sicherheitsbeauftragte der VW-Farm (Interview)," *Brasilien Nachrichten* (93),
1986.
[65] CPT Belém, July 1, 1981, Silva; July 6, 1983, Lima.
[66] GPTEC V.5.1.4., July 1, 1981, relative; V7.13.1., Nascimento to Alice, June 3, 1984.

some forty or fifty kilometers further to the VW hospital, as did José Camilho Da Silva, taken pity on by "Valder," the CVRC doctor: "Valder, the chief of the hospital told me that I should go home because [at Cristalino] there was no medicine to cure me. The remedy they had there was poisoning me, I couldn't take it anymore. He was sorry and did this act of charity. It is Valder who paid my travel back, who gave me 700 cruzeiros. I arrived in Goiás, almost dead, very swollen and spent six months in the hospital."[67] José was lucky to find this support, but his seventeen fellow team members were not. They were freed by the *gato* all at the same time, but they did not receive any money and had to leave all their valuable goods at the canteen. Their only way back home was by foot, hundreds of kilometers through the rain forest. José said he never heard anything about them again.

The *peãos*' work was to prepare the terrain for cattle raising, mainly by deforesting. They worked twelve to fourteen hours a day and seven days a week.[68] As one of them stated, they "were in prison from Monday to Monday, many times without eating."[69] Although mechanical equipment was promised during their recruitment, the *peões* were given only axes for the groundwork. Eventually, the job of felling big trees would be finished with chainsaws, but basically there was little technical investment, which stands in sharp contrast to the VW's high-tech cattle-raising methods.[70] The work was hard and exhausting. Physical violence was the central element holding the forced labor system together, because the fear of violence prevented the workers from fleeing. Two decades later, Ribamar, a former *peão*, pointed out that "After we had been there for a while we began hearing stories about people disappearing or getting beaten up.... We began to be afraid that we'd never get out of there. Maybe they'd shoot us in the back. Maybe they'd burn us to death and throw our bodies in the river."[71] It appears in the testimonies that not all the *peões* of the CVRC felt they had personally been victims of physical violence. However, all the testifying *peões* saw or heard about violence practiced on others.[72] According to Souza Martins, who made systematic

[67] CPT Belém, July 1, 1981, Silva.
[68] GPTEC V6.58.1., November 1983, *peão*; CPT Belém, Keith Hayward, March 25, 1985, "Relatório de uma visita ao interior dos estados de Goiás e do Maranhão."
[69] GPTEC V6.58.1., November 1983, *peão*; GPTEC V7.17.7., July 12, 1984, *peões* (2).
[70] CPT Belém, July 1, 1981, Silva.
[71] Le Breton, *Trapped*, 154.
[72] CPT Belém, June 26, 1983, Ribeiro. GPTEC V.5.1.15./16./17./18./19., July 18, 1984, *peões* (5).

studies on debt bondage including hundreds of Amazonian *fazendas* from the early 1970s to the early 1990s, the exposure of violence was a triggering moment in the captivity: "the awareness of unfreedom emerges when the gunmen at the farm show their weapons, or in front of others torture workers who have tried to escape without paying their debts.... It is by this kind of demonstration that other *peões* are terrorized and dissuaded from running away."[73]

Violence began with physical humiliation, such as a *gato* forcing a *peão* to chew the tip of his gun in front of the others, or a *peão* being tied naked to a tree.[74] It could then reach the stage of punch-up. One *peão* described how he had been "trampled on by Chicô's gangsters." Another saw the *gato* beating his companions, breaking their teeth, sending them to the VW hospital, and after a few days "putting them back in the wild forest" to work anew.[75] Four cases of murder were exposed in the media.[76] Relying on some testimonies, the CPT concluded that these deaths were probably the result of prolonged beating.[77]

As the first *peões* who fled from the *fazenda* began to speak freely about violence, testimonies flourished that described the VW ranch as a true hell. So many terrible stories were spread about the place that it is sometimes difficult to separate fact from fiction. In this regard, VW also bore the consequences of its international fame. Some dark anecdotes about the region's *fazendas* were projected onto Cristalino, even when the events described in these anecdotes might sometimes have happened in places other than the VW property. For example, the president of the rural trade union in the county of Santana do Araguaia stated that the *fazenda* personnel had left a small child to die without care, and that his parents, two *fazenda* employees, had to bury him under the bushes.[78] He would spread this story without furnishing any detail about when, how, and under whose responsibility this had happened. It was as if VW had to stand for all the negative consequences of the extension of the

---

[73] Martins, "The Reappearance of Slavery and the Reproduction of Capital on the Brazilian Frontier," 301.

[74] Batista, "Relatório"; "Escravidão e tortura na fazenda da Volks," *Tribuna metalúrgica*, June 5, 1983; GPTEC V.5.1.4., July 1, 1981, relative; CPT Belém, July 1983, Moscatele.

[75] CPT Belém, June 26, 1983, Ribeiro.

[76] "A lei do gatilho"; Miguel, "Empresa nega denúncia de 'escravidão'"; Batista, "Relatório."

[77] GPTEC V6.25., Ricardo Rezende Figueira, May 20, 1983, "Algumas questões sobre a fazenda Vale do Rio Cristalino." Since these cases have always been denied by VW personnel and never been judged, I chose not to mention them in detail in this report.

[78] Batista, "Relatório."

"ox frontier" in the Amazon. The CVRC, unlike the other big capitalist farms in Araguaia, had a name, a logo, an identity, because VW and SUDAM wanted to make a showcase of this ranch. Most of the other Amazon investors had made the choice of semi-anonymity: company bosses stayed in São Paulo and, unlike Sauer, never came to visit their ranch. They hid so as to decline responsibility in case of labor or land conflicts. Only a few people knew that the CODESPAR *fazenda* was a property of the National Credit Bank, that Bradesco owned 60,000 hectares in the south of Pará, or that Suiá Missu belonged to an Italian gas company. Volkswagen became the face of forced labor because it was the only visible logo around.

That there was latent violence on the ranch was, however, recognized by the *gatos* themselves. They claimed that the workers sometimes deserved correction for their undisciplined behavior. When the commission investigators from São Paulo asked Abilão if the *gatos* really practiced violence on the workers, he answered: "Of course we beat them!"[79] *Gatos* had rather vague ideas of the line between legality and illegality.[80] Chicô and Abilão were convinced that, as "creditors" of the workers' debts, they had the right to keep them captive. Hence the *gatos* often gave honest answers to the questions posed by investigators. It is striking to see how, in documents produced during the same period, VW continued to deny publicly what the *gatos* themselves confessed spontaneously: namely, that "debts" and violence served as means of pressure to make the *peões* work at Cristalino.[81] Brügger, who knew Chicô and Abilio "personally," even described, in an interview of 1984, the two men as the "best gatos in the region."[82] Only a few weeks after this interview with Brügger, Abilio was arrested by the police with his four gunmen during a rescue operation of 100 captive *peões* in a *fazenda* belonging to a Brazilian group.[83]

Given the criminal behavior of *gatos* such as Abilio, one might well ask what led *peões* to accept such dubious job offers. It was often because they had a family to feed. This also means that there were people worrying about them during their stay in the *fazenda*. As one *peão* said about his experience at the CVRC, "the family suffered a lot, all my children stopped going to school, they all lost one year and thought I was dead."[84]

---

[79] "Escravidão e tortura na fazenda da Volks."
[80] Figueira, *Pisando fora da própria sombra*, 341–2.
[81] Batista, "Relatório."
[82] *Brasilien Nachrichten* (82), 1984.
[83] *Brasilien Nachrichten* (84), 1984.
[84] May 21, 1984, *peão*, in *Brasilien Nachrichten* (84), 1984.

Journalist Binka Le Breton also interviewed a mother who, twenty-five years later, reported how frightened she was when her son spent some months on the VW *fazenda*, especially because she had heard so many unpleasant stories about that place.[85]

People would look actively for ways to contact their father, husband, or son living on the VW ranch. The luckiest families would receive letters from the workers. Sometimes these letters expressed the desperate situation of their authors.[86] Sometimes they hid the real conditions at Cristalino while indirectly suggesting them.[87] However, most of the families did not receive any news. One father was so desperate that in August 1980, he traveled from his home in Goiás to Cristalino in order to talk to his son.[88] But fear of the *gato*, who stood close to them with a weapon, impeded them from exchanging any words. Often the family would look in town for the recruiter or the *gato*. These men, in spite of their frightening reputation, were seen as the only connection between the jungle and the exterior world.[89] They would tell the families that the *peões* could leave the forest only after they finished paying their debts, or they would invent a lie to justify the prolonged absence of contact of the *peão* with his family. In one case, a *peão* had "verbally signed" a contract stipulating that the clearing company would provide money for his wife while he would be working at Cristalino.[90] The wife came several times to Chicô, asking for the money, but Chicô always answered that he did not know her husband. Once in the *fazenda*, he would swear to the *peão* that he had paid his wife as agreed. The worry that something might happen to their families, as well as the shame of returning home without money, were factors contributing to the *peões'* remaining at the CVRC. At the same time, the families' actions played a crucial role in revealing what was happening at Cristalino. Family members often went to the police, the STR, or the CPT, precisely because they did not receive information about the *peões*.[91] One spouse of a captive *peão* even traveled as far as Brasília to report to the Ministry of Labor about her husband's situation.[92]

---

[85] Le Breton, *Trapped*, 154–5.
[86] GPTEC V7.13.1., Nascimento to Alice, June 3, 1984; V7.13.3., Cirqueira to Cirqueira, June 3, 1984.
[87] CPT Belém, Silva to Silva, September 23, 1980.
[88] CPT Belém, July 7, 1981, Silva, Gomes.
[89] GPTEC V7.17.6., relative.
[90] GPTEC V6.58.1., November 1983, *peão*; and a similar case in Batista, "Relatório."
[91] CPT Belém, July 7, 1981, Silva, Gomes; November 1983, Carmo; May 28, 1984, relative, in *Brasilien Nachrichten* (84), 1984; GPTEC V7.17.5., July 12, 1984, relative.
[92] GPTEC V7.28.1., August 17, 1984, *peões* (3).

It would be wrong to envisage the *peões* as mere victims immobilized by fear. In spite of the high risk of physical punishment, there were attempts to escape from the work at the VW ranch.[93] In this respect, the rain forest with its thick vegetation was both a risk and an opportunity. In order to leave the *fazenda* and reach the next town it was necessary to walk hundreds of kilometers through the forest. One had to walk fast and move cleverly because the armed guards were usually right behind. Some fugitive *peões* were never heard of again. On the other hand, the forest offered possibilities to hide and shake the pursuers off; it made it impossible for the *gatos* to track the *peãos* once a certain distance from the cleared parts of the *fazenda* was reached.[94] Reaching this distance was the decisive step when fleeing, but it was a battle fought with unequal weapons: *gatos* and *subgatos* had jeeps and guns while *peões* were often not even wearing proper shoes.[95] For this reason, some *peões* would look for ways to leave the *fazenda* that did not necessitate direct conflict with the *gato*. The visit of an actor exterior to the *fazenda* could be an unexpected opportunity for this. As the investigation commission visited the farm, for example, one *peão* managed to approach the commission members and begged them to act for his salvation from captivity. Another *peão* recounted that he managed to escape from Cristalino with some other fellows by hitching a ride with a government agronomist: "Of course," the *peão* said, "he couldn't take us past the guard post, so we walked around it, through the forest."[96] Some *peões* might also invent tricks to fool their *gatos*. On one occasion, four underage *peões*, knowing that their *subgatos* were illiterate, handed them a sheet of paper containing written inscriptions.[97] They said it was a military draft, and that if they did not show up at the garrison house the army would come looking for them in the *fazenda*. Given their apparent age, it seemed credible to their guards that they were being called up for conscription. So the *subgato*, who was worried about getting into trouble with the authorities, let them go.

Peões who managed to escape would sometimes demonstrate solidarity with their fellow workers who had remained at the VW farm. When

---

[93] CPT Belém, July 7, 1981, Silva, Gomes.
[94] May 21, 1984, *peão*, in *Brasilien Nachrichten* (84), 1984.
[95] In fact, the very word *peão* in the colonial period designated "those who – being too poor to afford a horse – were forced to go on foot, and to walk without shoes": Martins, "The Reappearance of Slavery and the Reproduction of Capital on the Brazilian Frontier," 301.
[96] Le Breton, *Trapped*, 155.
[97] Batista, "Relatório."

Francisco Batista Lima fled in 1983, his companion José Mineiro was not able to escape with him, so after reaching home, he paid José's rent and fed José's wife and three children.[98] How escaped *peões* used their newly gained freedom was a crucial point, for these *peões* had the reputation of the *fazenda* in their hands and the possibility of making the forced labor system public. They were not, however, numerous enough to do so: of the forty-three laborers of a VW clearing team supervised by Abilio in 1984, eight managed to escape, and of these eight, only one of them, the same Francisco Batista Lima, registered a complaint with the police delegation in his hometown, Paraíso do Norte in Goiás.[99]

One might wonder why such a small number of the *peões* finally reached the point of testifying. The main impediment was fear of acting against influential *fazendeiros* or *gatos*. It is no wonder that the majority of the complaints were made in the workers' hometowns, in Goiás, Mato Grosso, or anywhere else as long as it was not too close to the *fazenda*. But even in these areas, a *gato* could still trace a fugitive, since the *gatos'* networks were organized to enable recruitment on a wide territorial basis. The simple fact of talking about what had happened on the VW ranch represented a potential danger of death, especially for an isolated individual. The priest in the town of Santa Terezinha, who had been approached by various *peões* coming back from the CVRC, explained that one of them "told me his situation, but did not want to be identified, out of fear and, he said, 'in order not to start anything with the justice,' because, according to him 'since I managed to leave free and alive it's better to forget what happened.'"[100] For this reason, the ex-*peões* usually came together in groups to the CPT in order to tell their story and denounce the system maintained by the *gatos*.

Protesting was even more difficult than denouncing. There were, however, some spontaneous initiatives directed against the *gatos*. Individual protest was too much of a risk, so it would come exclusively from *peões* who, shortly after their arrival in the *fazenda*, were not yet aware of the weakness of their position. Adail is a good example: he told his *gato* that he would never have come to the *fazenda* if he had known the true working conditions before "signing" the contract.[101] However, protest would in general come from groups, although the *gatos*, out of fear of

---

[98] May 21, 1984, *peão*, in *Brasilien Nachrichten* (84), 1984.
[99] "*A lei do gatilho.*"
[100] CPT Belém, Canuto to "Ministro da Justiça," July 4, 1983.
[101] "VW Farmarbeiter kommen zu Wort (interview)."

some insurrection, tried to keep the *peões* as isolated from each other as possible. For example, a group of eighteen *peões* decided to collectively face the *gatos* to protest for their right to leave the CVRC.[102] However, this protest was unsuccessful. The *gato* pretended to agree and let all the workers leave, but he then secretly followed them into the forest accompanied by his gunmen. After forty kilometers they began to shoot in the direction of the *peões*, forcing them to surrender and return to work. From that moment on they paid for their temerity with even more repressive supervision.

Protesting was easier outside the *fazenda*. The most significant group initiative occurred in 1980, after a *peão* died at his mother's home from the consequences of physical mistreatment received at the VW ranch. His cousin set up a petition supposed to show that the population stood together against these brutalities, so as to convince the authorities to act against them. In a few days, he gathered the signatures of ninety-two families of the town of Barreira do Campo.[103] Eventually, the city representative dismissed the petition as an "irresponsible act." This example shows that, given the political and legal context working against rural workers, grassroots initiatives had very little chance of working if they were not taken up by organized groups able to disseminate information beyond the local scale.

Workers' families were actually used to seeing a son disappear for months to a *fazenda* and possibly come back without money or even with corporal lesions. Many people were not ready to participate in acts denouncing forced labor because they perceived this practice as too strongly rooted in local custom to be curbed. Registers in the CPT offices showed that the labor system at Cristalino was a local reflection of a regionally widespread practice. Casaldáliga, in his paper denouncing "slavery" in 1972, stated that all *fazendas* in the southeastern Amazon resorted to forced labor.[104] An inquiry carried out by Rezende based on testimonies gathered since the early 1970s in southeastern Pará shows that most of the *fazendas* even contracted the same *gatos*.[105] It seems that these *gatos* were simply the most easily available way for *fazenda* owners to clear their estate rapidly, and that subcontractors respecting labor laws

[102] CPT Belém, July 1, 1981, Silva.
[103] GPTEC V6.50., September 5, 1983, relative. This example shows that some local inhabitants knew about exactions committed in the VW *fazenda* much before the press, or even the CPT, did.
[104] Casaldáliga, "Escravidão e feudalismo no norte do Mato Grosso."
[105] Figueira, *Pisando fora da própria sombra.*

hardly existed. Given this, could VW be held responsible for what the *gatos* did? Probably the whole developmentalist mentality was responsible, because it pushed ranchers to focus on the immediate enhancement of production rates and modern technology, making the improvement of labor conditions a secondary goal. Volkswagen's logic of production implied the exclusion of subaltern economic actors, seasonal workers in the first place.

This would also be the point of view of Souza Martins, for whom the development of capitalism necessarily goes through phases of primitive accumulation, in which the conditions for capitalist accumulation are built. This phase of "production of the mode of production" took shape in the Amazon through the forest clearance and building of farm infrastructure. Since investors did not consider this phase of preparation part of the process of capitalist accumulation, they sought to reduce the cost of clearing, creating pasture, and building infrastructure at the minimal possible rate. As a consequence, the most modern farm projects did not bother to ally with primitive, cheap forms of labor.[106] Sakamoto goes even further than Martins when he insists that "those who enslave in Brazil are no badly informed landowners hidden in backward *fazendas*. They are *latifundists*, many of them using high technology. The cattle receive a first-class treatment: balanced rations, vaccination with computerized control, birth control with artificial insemination, while the workers live in worse conditions than the animals."[107] For him, the use of an unfree workforce aimed at reducing the production costs of modern farms so as to guarantee the farms' competitiveness without jeopardizing the shareholders' margin of profit. Submitted to a globalized system in which their role was to produce commodities, modern Amazonian farms were forced to display ever increasing rates of productivity. In this context, they sought to balance, with a weak investment in peripheral activities such as clearing, installation of pastures, or building, the increasingly heavy investment necessary for the accelerated mechanization implied by international competition.

The case of Volkswagen exemplified this paradox of modern technology enmeshed with primitive labor practices. Cristalino was home to the most developed agro-technological project throughout all of Amazônia

---

[106] Martins, "The Reappearance of Slavery and the Reproduction of Capital on the Brazilian Frontier," 281.

[107] Leonardo Sakamoto, "A economia do trabalho escravo no Brasil contemporâneo," in *Trabalho escravo contemporâneo no Brasil. Contribuições críticas para sua análise e denúncia*, ed. Gelba Cavalcante de Cerqueira, et al. (Rio de Janeiro: UFRJ, 2008), 61–2.

Legal, and at the same time the biggest scandal of unfree labor under military rule. It is not in my scope of expertise to say whether VW was legally responsible for physical aggression, fraud, pressures, and robbery, which in the end were committed by its subcontractors and not by the company itself. But VW could not ignore the previous media reports about similar cases in the 1970s, the overall history of forced labor in the Amazon, and the dubious legal status of the subcontracting companies involved. It is clear that VW, at best, neglected the interest of the *peões* and the dimension of the perils to which the latter were exposed. The "model ranch" with its approximately 300 regular employees enjoying the social services idealized in company brochures did not include all these clearing workers, for the social and medical welfare of whom no investment was planned. It was, as such, a sort of Potemkin village of modernity, only there "for the English to see" (*"para inglês ver"*), as a Brazilian saying (dating back to the time when England was pressuring the country to abolish slavery) goes designating good resolutions, which in practice are rarely applied.

A Bridge between Grassroots Denunciation and Public Information: Pater Ricardo Rezende Figueira

The initiatives of the *peões* unveiled the existence of a forced labor system at Cristalino. But in order for their case to be heard, they needed wider support. On the local level, their first recourse was sometimes the rural trade union delegates, but most often the priests of the CPT. A priest in the county of Santana do Araguaia, Ricardo Rezende Figueira played a major role in revealing the debt labor scandal at Cristalino to the public.[108] A worker's son, Rezende, came from Juíz de Fora in the extreme south of Minas Gerais. A student in philosophy at the end of the Médici mandate, he remembered this time as marked by a suffocating local political context with "on one side, the Communist Party of Brazil," which supported rural guerrilla, and on the other side, the dictatorship of the "Brazilian army." As a young advocate of freedom and equality, he was looking for nonviolent alternatives to authoritarianism. Liberation theology, which he saw as a reinterpretation of faith grounded on the dialog with and the experience of disadvantaged social actors – "workers and jobseekers, peasants and landless, Indians and blacks, women, elderly people and

---

[108] The details on the path of Ricardo Rezende Figueira come from personal talks I had with him and notes he left at the CPT (conserved at the CPT archive in Belém and the GPTEC archive in Rio de Janeiro).

children" – corresponded to this "third way" he wished to take between leftist guerrilla and right-wing dictatorship.

He first looked for a region in which the Church was engaged in a "religious and social project inspired by liberation theology" and chose one of the most progressive of them: the prelacy at Conceição do Araguaia, covering the territory of Araguaia-Tocantins. In 1977, he moved to southeastern Pará to become a parish priest. No sooner had he arrived there than he was confronted with the archaic labor conditions that existed in the county, as he witnessed the capture of a young man who had tried to escape from a clearing subcontractor. Months after, he met Francisco de Assis, the first fugitive of a *fazenda* whom he had the chance to talk with.[109] Traumatized by his experience and devoured by malaria, Assis died in a delirious state shortly after. After him, Rezende met hundreds of seasonal workers fleeing forced labor regimes in the *fazendas*.

Rezende developed the local CPT and became the association's coordinator for the entire Araguaia-Tocantins area. From that position he observed the establishment of the big *fazendas*, particularly one that shook the county: the VW ranch, where Rezende did not go until 1983. Indeed, the priests of the Araguaia-Tocantins diocese shared one principle: they forbade themselves to do services within *latifundia*, because of restrictions on the freedom of religion that might be imposed by landholders. For the priests, it was also a way to show that they "did not agree with the practice of injustice and violence, which was a daily occurrence in such companies."[110]

Since 1974, the priests of the CPT had heard rumors and transcribed oral reports from ex-workers about violence committed at the VW ranch.[111] But they had no tangible proof and it would have been foolish to make dubious accusations against a powerful multinational company, whose ranch was praised by the authorities as a model for the whole country. The action by Cristalino's seasonal workers changed this fact. In April 1983, three *peões*, residents in the north of Mato Grosso, after being held captive during a clearing season and escaping from the VW ranch, turned to the CPT for help. On April 28, they gave a personal testimony in the city of São Felix do Araguaia, Mato Grosso, in presence of a notary and seven witnesses, including the city mayor, José Pontin.[112]

---

[109] Figueira, "Por que o trabalho escravo?" 31–2.
[110] Rezende to Klein, June 28, 1984, in "Neue Stellungnahmen zu den Beschuldigungen gegen die VW-Fazenda."
[111] Figueira, *Pisando fora da própria sombra*, 415–33.
[112] Figueira, *A justiça do lobo*, 32–3.

Rezende decided to address the political authorities. The newly elected governor of Pará, Jáder Fontenelle Barbalho, commonly called Jáder, was a figure of the opposition to the dictatorship. He had won the elections in 1982 on the basis of a progressive platform supporting human rights and denouncing land inequalities.[113] His victory by only about 40,000 votes over the federal government's candidate was a strong symbol, given the fact that the opposition parties traditionally had difficulties in attracting votes in rural states. Jáder's past as a student leader in Belém, an active opponent of the regime, and a member of the *autênticos*, the area of the MDB most radically engaged in favor of democratization, had helped him to build the image of a courageous politician who did not fear disregarding the oligarchies.[114] Rezende thought that Jáder might be the right person to solve the situation at the VW ranch, also because two years earlier the two men had taken part side by side in a religious mass in Belém against the arrest of priests close to the rural workers' movement.[115] After having informed Jáder of the accusations against VW, Rezende succeeded in booking an audience with him in the state capital, Belém, about 1,100 kilometers away from Conceição do Araguaia, at the beginning of May. Jáder, however, did not show up to the meeting and Rezende could only speak to the governor's staff, who explained that Jáder was in Brasília on political matters. The priest felt that the governor was just trying to avoid facing the problem, so he took with him one of the *peões* who had testified in São Felix and they traveled together to Brasília. But when they arrived, they were informed that Jáder had left for Rio de Janeiro. Rezende's reaction was to stay in Brasília and organize a press conference at the headquarters of the CNBB, at which the *peão* testified publicly.[116]

In front of Brazilian journalists and a reporter from the main French press agency AFP, Rezende unveiled in detail the mechanisms of the forced labor system maintained at Cristalino, based on *peões'* testimonies. He explicitly used the word "slavery" and warned that at the moment there might be 600 clearing workers employed as slaves in the Volkswagen *fazenda*. Although the press had not expressed any notable interest in the

---

[113] Edir Veiga, "A disputa para o executivo do Pará no pós ditadura militar de 1964" (UFPA, 2010).

[114] Edilza Oliveira Fontes, "A eleição de 1982 no Pará: memórias, imagens fotográficas e narrativas históricas," in *XI encontro nacional de história oral. memória, democracia e justiça*, ed. Associação Brasileira de História Oral (Rio de Janeiro, 2012); Marilia Ferreira Emmi and Roza Elizabeth Marin, "Crise e rearticulação das oligarquias no Pará," *Revista do Instituto de Estudos Brasileiros* 40–2 (1996), 51.

[115] Figueira, *A justiça do lobo*, 85.

[116] Le Breton, *Trapped*, 151–2.

problem of forced labor until then, the notoriety of Volkswagen brought the topic into the headlines. In a few days, various major Brazilian newspapers published accusatory articles, whose titles associated Volkswagen with the word "slavery," such as "The CPT Accuses: Volks has Slaves," "In Volks' Fazenda, there Are Slaves, a Priest Says," "The Church Denounces Slave Labor," "Volkswagen in Pará Uses Slave Workforce," or still "Slave Labor in Volks' Fazenda," while in Germany the *Frankfurter Rundschau* asked: "Slaveholding for the VW-Company?" and in London the *Times* announced that VW had "600 'Slaves on Plantation.'"[117]

An AFP international press release enabled the accusation to arrive in Germany also, where it might otherwise have remained unnoticed. In fact, most of the German media did not seem to find Rezende's accusations credible enough to be worth publishing. *Die Welt* even issued a very critical article against Rezende titled: "No Trace of Atrocities at the VW-farm."[118] Written by *Die Welt*'s correspondent in Rio de Janeiro, the article was based on phone interviews with executives of VW do Brasil and the German Embassy in Brasília. In the text, VWB contested all the charges raised by Rezende, insisting that the company was not responsible for facts imputed to the firms controlling the clearing workers at Cristalino. A representative of Bonn's embassy added that Rezende's denunciations were "largely exaggerated. The critique of certain groups towards multinational corporations is indeed nothing new." Even the German Episcopal Conference refused to condemn VW. Its representative Jürgen Aretz, responsible for the topics of development and human rights in Latin America, said that some Brazilian priests paid too much attention to "political things" and not enough to their pastoral duties. Aretz had been invited in the past to the VW ranch and did not hear anything of the complaints Rezende raised in the press conference.

Networking the Protest against Cristalino

The barely implicit attack of Aretz against Rezende shows how central the latter had become in the controversies about the VW ranch. He found himself in a bridge position, receiving information at the local level and

---

[117] "Em fazenda da Volks, há escravos, diz padre," *Correio Braziliense*, May 7, 1983; "CPT acusa: Volks tem escravos," *Diário da Manha*, May 7, 1983; "Igreja denuncia trabalho escravo," *O Globo*, May 7, 1983; "Volkswagen no Pará usa mão de obra escrava," *Jornal de Brasília*, May 7, 1983; "Sklavenhaltung für VW-Werk?" *Frankfurter Rundschau*, May 10, 1983; "600 'Slaves on Plantation,'" *Times*, May 10, 1983; "Trabalho escravo na fazenda da Volks," *O São Paulo*, June 3–9, 1983.

[118] "Von Greueltaten auf VW-farm fehlt jede Spur," *Die Welt*, May 13, 1983.

circulating information to media, trade union, political, and institutional areas. He and his collaborators had to learn "to conjugate internal and external pressures, dealing with national and international journalists. Normally the press was not interested in problems of slave labor. We learned to create politics out of violence and it became possible to establish a more intensive type of communication with journalists, and the news of human rights violations in the region began to occupy a larger space in social communication."[119] Rezende became the point of reference in the affair because of his grassroots involvement: the *peões*, seeing the Church as an organization that could understand their concerns, came to him. Moreover, his position as priest gave him access to Church networks: so also did the CNBB provide him with a platform to address the press in Brasília. Finally, his affiliation with the CPT, an organization enjoying wide sympathy among human rights activists, in the Brazilian left as well as abroad, helped make Rezende the most networked critic of VW's Amazonian project.

The network of denunciation of unfree labor at the CVRC started from the bottom. It was the *peões* or their family members who took the initiative of denouncing the *gatos*, seeking Rezende or, alternatively, their own parish priest, such as Pater António Canuto in Santa Terezinha or Pater Manoel Lujón in Canabrava, both located in the northern part of Mato Grosso.[120] Sometimes, the *peões*' families addressed the rural union offices: in this case, the complaints were passed to and gathered at a regional level by Natal Viana Ribeiro, leader of the rural union of the county of Santana to Araguaia.[121] Rezende, as the person responsible for CPT actions in the diocese of Araguaia-Tocantins, gathered and classified the testimonies registered by other priests, and also remained in contact with Natal and the local trade union. Rezende also encouraged the *peões* to deliver testimony to the police, often with the company of STR or CPT members, and he looked for lawyers to accompany *peões* in potential juridical confrontations with the *gatos* or VW.[122] Thus, *peões*, priests, and local trade unionists, with the support of certain local administrators such as the mayor of São Felix do Araguaia, José Pontin (PMDB, himself a priest and a friend of liberation theology), formed a small but dense grassroots network, whose internal contacts were regular and active. This

---

[119] www.ricardorezende.org/cpt.html, access date May 26, 2012.
[120] "Neue Stellungnahmen zu den Beschuldigungen gegen die VW-Fazenda."
[121] Batista, "Relatório."
[122] CPT Belém, Rezende to CPT members, July 18, 1983.

network constituted a social mattress for the *peões*, which gave them the moral support necessary to solicit the police and transformed individual initiatives into group actions of denunciation, thus giving coherence and credibility to the *peões'* testimonies.

Given the symbolic importance of the VW *latifundio* and the fact that dozens of *peões* testified at the STR or the CPT, the two organizations judged that it was worth seeking the intervention of the state. In May 1983, they started to circulate information through institutional channels. Their first step was to address, together with the *peões*, local police stations, which themselves transmitted the complaints to the secretary of public security in the government of Para, Arnaldo Moraes Filho.[123] A progressive PMDB politician, Moraes found the affair serious enough to urge his party colleague and governor of Pará, Jáder Barbalho to institute a number of security measures to protect the workers at the VW *fazenda*. As we know, Jáder had already been contacted by Rezende. The latter, noticing difficulties in having direct access to the state governor, called another politician of the left wing of the PMDB, Ademir Andrade, for assistance. Congressman for Pará in the federal parliament, Andrade was actually a notorious Marxist, who claimed to feel close to the rural workers' cause and acted to influence the PMDB's policies in Pará with leftist ideas.[124] He immediately accepted Rezende's request and started to pressure Jáder to intervene in the Cristalino case.[125]

While Rezende was seeking allies on the political scene in Pará state, the STR in Santana do Araguaia used the Brazilian structure of labor representation as another institutional channel to circulate the *peões'* claims. Paradoxically, the top-down structure of rural unionism, starting from the federal ministry of labor and going down to the local STR, facilitated this approach. Since this structure was elaborated to strictly control the unions' activities, the links between the different levels of decision were solid, and information could circulate rapidly between these different levels, even when it was moving from bottom to top. On the basis of the *peões'* testimonies, the STR of Santana do Araguaia contacted FETAGRI in Pará.[126] FETAGRI passed the notice to CONTAG, which informed the federal Ministry of Labor about the offenses committed at the CVRC.[127]

---

[123] GPTEC V5.1.32., Moraes to Jáder, August 16, 1983.
[124] "A praça muda de cor," *Veja*, October 17, 1984; Ricardo Rezende Figueira, *Rio Maria: canto da terra* (Petropolis: Civilização Brasileira, 2008), 68.
[125] CPT Belém, Andrade to Jáder, August 29, 1983.
[126] CPT Belém, Silva and Ferri to Macedo, June 1, 1983.
[127] CPT Belém, Silva and Ferri to Rezende, July 15, 1983.

The case was judged important enough by the two CONTAG national leaders to write in person to the minister of labor. Then, on the order of the ministry, the labor court of Pará launched an investigation into the VW ranch.

Another issue was to create a climate of public pressure on Volkswagen and the Brazilian government. In this operation, Rezende could count on the liberation theology networks, especially at the international level. The bishop of the diocese of Araguaia-Tocantins, Dom José Patrício Hanrahan, thought that he could convince the German church to pressure Volkswagen on European ground. On May 26, 1983, using the opportunity of being invited to an international bishops' seminar in Ireland, he made a detour via Cologne. In Cologne, at the headquarters of the German Episcopal Conference, he handed in a dossier stating in detail the facts of the denunciations made by the *peões* at Cristalino.[128] Prepared by Rezende, the dossier had been translated into German by another Amazonian priest, the Austrian bishop of Xingu, Erwin Kräuter. Hanrahan also wrote to his friends in the Flemish Lenten Campaign, who sent a letter of indignation to the branch of VW in Belgium, and to the Christian humanitarian NGO Misereor.[129] Various groups of West German activists, close to the Catholic left, made contact with Rezende and wrote messages of protest to the VW senior management in Wolfsburg. I will come back later to these actions of international solidarity and their effects.

Pressure from the Workers' Movement in São Paulo: Expedito Soares Batista

The liberation theology networks did not only spread across an international area. Since the strikes of the ABC in the late 1970s, there was also a growing proximity between the Church and the urban workers' movement, of which some actors also participated in denouncing the CVRC. One of them was Expedito Soares Batista, a deputy in the legislative assembly of the state of São Paulo. He was a former worker in the automobile plant in São Bernardo do Campo and became one of the leaders of the Volkswagen workers' strike in 1978. Consequent to his trade unionist involvement, he was fired without notice or compensation by VWB.[130] He led the steel trade union of São Bernardo do Campo

---

[128] "Bischof Hanrahan: 'Wir klagen Volkswagen des Mangels an Verantwortungsbewusstsein an' (Interview)," *Brasilien Nachrichten* (81), 1983.
[129] CPT Belém, Verheist to Hanrahan, January 9, 1984.
[130] CPT Belém, Rezende to CPT members, July 18, 1983.

and participated in the foundation of the PT. As a candidate in the state elections of 1982, he received the second highest number of votes for his party and entered the state parliament together with eight other PT representatives.[131] PT members maintained a high degree of relations with the trade unions. After being elected MP in his early thirties, Soares continued to view himself as the representative of his ex-colleagues from the Volkswagen plant.

The latter were watching the company's policy with attention, including its ranching activities in the Amazon. They immediately took note of Rezende's initiative of denouncing the forced labor cases at Cristalino and forwarded the notice to Soares. At the end of May 1983, the young parliament member gave three speeches on the topic in front of the state assembly, where he read some of the *peões'* declarations.[132] He used the platform as an opportunity to denounce the military regime's complicity with multinationals destroying biodiversity and exploiting the people in the tropical forest. He also made the link between VW's policy of subcontracting seasonal work in Araguaia and the company's growing trend of outsourcing the nonspecialized tasks in the urban area of São Paulo. "The philosophy" of VW, for Soares, was always the same, either in a farm or in a factory: for the nonspecialized part of the production, it relied on smaller companies offering very low loans and no social coverage. Soares thought that this policy, coupled with a complete absence of control by VW over the subcontractors' activities, favored the mistreatment of workers. Furthermore, it enabled VW to always deny its own responsibility for condemnable acts, even if these acts had happened on a VW property. Saying this, Soares was faithfully enunciating the discourse of the steel trade union of São Bernardo do Campo, which published a paper titled "Slavery and Torture in the Volks *Fazenda.*" Illustrated by offensive drawings that superposed the VW logo on scenes of extreme violence, the article started with a sentence depicting rural and urban workers as victims of the same oppressor: "In the city or in the countryside, patrons are all the same: they exploit the working class and use all violent means as an attempt to maintain the working class under submission."[133]

Although calling for unity between urban workers and small peasants was a classical Marxist posture, it was less classical to find political or

---

[131] *A folha de São Paulo*, November 25, 1982.
[132] GPTEC V6.26.1./2./3., Soares to Companheiros Trabalhadores da Volks, May 26, 1983.
[133] "Escravidão e tortura na fazenda da Volks."

FIGURE 4.1 Illustrations of the steel trade union in a paper on the CVRC. The international VW logo is visible on the hat of the two standing men on the left picture, and as a scar on the chest of a tied-up man on the right picture. This picture is referring to various converging *peões'* testimonies stating that a worker was tortured and tied naked to a tree by the *gatos*, while three others, according to the testimonies, were beaten, murdered, and thrown into the river.
Source: Image courtesy of Cleiton Cafeu. "Escravidão e tortura na fazenda da Volks," *Tribuna metalúrgica*, June 5, 1983.

union activists who really sought to put urban–rural solidarity into practice. This is especially the case as the steel protest movement of the ABC and its political avatar, the PT, were deeply urban movements. Most PT members lived in the "great São Paulo": they did not know much about the rural workers' daily life. Although the electoral system obliged political parties to be present in the whole country, the PT campaign in the elections of 1982 essentially focused on securing a popular basis in the state of São Paulo, where Lula was running for governor.[134] If the election proved a relative success for the PT in this urbanized region, the results were systematically disappointing in rural states. In Pará, the party's campaign for the control of state government hardly earned 1 percent of the votes. In the always more probable hypothesis of direct presidential elections, it was urgent to diversify its electoral basis. Making the link

[134] Keck, *The Workers' Party and Democratization in Brazil*, 123–66.

between urban and rural laborers could be the right starting point for a strategy of geographic expansion. Moreover, the PT had managed until then to differentiate its political practices from the authoritarian structure of communist parties, principally thanks to a message of "empowerment" concerning the workers.[135] The PT's project of giving to the invisible classes a chance to speak was well suited to rural laborers in the context of *latifundia* monopoly and trampling of democratic rights, which reigned in the countryside.

Finally, the PT's development as a party was strengthened in the early 1980s by the participation of small but active groups, both of the urban middle class (in São Paulo or Rio de Janeiro) and from rural backgrounds (principally in the Amazonian state of Acre thanks to rubber-tapper leaders joining the party), organized around emerging political messages such as political ecology, human rights, or native peoples' rights.[136] These topics were deeply linked with the Amazonian debate, and in spite of not lying at the center of the PT's program, they did influence the political discourse of the party. Soares, for example, understood that in the case of the CVRC, there was a factual link between the expansion of slash-and-burn deforestation and the prosperity of the forced labor economy. He considered that the exploitation of the poor and of nature were two sides of the same coin because they were both at the service of capitalist profit. In this regard, he concluded a text on the VW ranch with the following words: "the setting of these fires in our Amazon, which is considered the Earth's major ecological reserve, is extremely absurd. This reserve is being mangled, burnt, because of the greed for profit of those multinational, and even Brazilian companies, and also because of the irresponsibility of those who govern us."[137]

Only five minutes after the conclusion of Soares's first speech at the state Assembly, VWB issued a public reaction in which the company denied having anything to do with forced labor.[138] This reaction was so quick that Soares saw it as a sign that the multinational firm must have contacts with some members of the assembly, if not even parliament members discreetly working for the interests of VW. Nevertheless, after a few days, the company thought it appropriate to show its good will by inviting Soares to visit the ranch. And so he did.

---

[135] Ibid., 139.
[136] Ibid.
[137] Batista, "Relatório."
[138] GPTEC V6.26.1./2./3., Soares to Companheiros Trabalhadores da Volks, May 26, 1983.

Various Investigations and Mixed Political Outcomes in the Cristalino Affair

Soares set up a trans-partisan investigation commission to come with him, including three other deputies from the São Paulo assembly: Manoel Moreira and Tonico Ramos from the PMDB and Djalma Souza from the PT.[139] The head of the steel trade union in São Bernardo do Campo, Humberto Aparecido Domingues, also came along, as well as Cesar Concone, a DIEESE expert. They were accompanied by José Aparecido Miguel and Clovis Cranchi, journalist and photographer at the *Estado de São Paulo*, one of Brazil's major daily newspapers. On July 5, 1983, two airplanes belonging to Volkswagen headed north, in the direction of Araguaia. Besides the investigation team established by Soares, they transported three executives sent by VWB to participate in the commission's visit: Mauro Imperatori, chief of the VWB juridical department; Mauricio de Oliveira, manager of industrial relations; and Paulo Dutra, leader of the VWB delegation. Dutra, an assistant director of VWB, was the manager with responsibility for public relations and governmental contacts. His presence confirmed that the scandal of forced labor was above all a problem of image for the company because it threatened to ruin the prestige of the "model ranch."

In fact, during the first meeting of the commission, Dutra showed to the other commission members a pile of copies of newspaper articles.[140] He explained that the case had generated noise even in Japan and that during a meeting of VW shareholders in Germany, a woman stood up and protested against "slave labor" in the *fazenda*. He added: "the name of the company is being perverted throughout the world and this is causing enormous injury and defamation."[141] As he pronounced these words, the commission of investigation had been completed by local figures from Araguaia-Tocantins. Two rural workers' representatives were there: Natal Viana Ribeiro, the STR president in Barreira do Campo; and Altair, the STR delegate from Luciará, Mato Grosso, the hometown of the first three *peões* to have testified about their experience at Cristalino in April 1983. There was also Ricardo Rezende with another priest of the diocese, Benedito Rodrigues Costa.

[139] Batista, "Relatório."
[140] CPT Belém, Rezende to CPT members, July 18, 1983.
[141] "Escravidão e tortura na fazenda da Volks," *Alvorada – prelazia de São Felix do Araguaia*, July 1983.

Brügger acted as guide and decided about the path of the visit. Rezende remembers that "he was very anxious to impress us by showing us all the wonderful things they had done, the beautiful lawns, the nice buildings, the school and the club."[142] It was a habit at Cristalino to organize such visits. In principle, everyone (journalists, political decision makers, businessmen) was authorized to enter Cristalino, even those who criticized the project. But they were always given a guided tour and never left alone. The CVRC management used to show the visitors the beautiful side of the *fazenda*, the one that was visible in the Volkswagen advertisements. Indeed, all visitors' reports reproduce the impressive effect made by the solidity of VW's modern community in the forest, with all the unexpected services it offered to its members. A German Third World activist, after a guided tour given to her by Brügger, compared the *fazenda* to a comfortable "tropical country club."[143] A reporter from *Der Spiegel* had the feeling of being transplanted into a Marlboro advertisement.[144] Even Rezende confessed that Cristalino looked like "a paradise in the Amazonian immensity."[145]

Rezende and the other commission members, however, "didn't want to see the buildings"; they "wanted to see the *peões*," but, according to the priest, the management of Cristalino "made sure [the commission] never got anywhere near them."[146] However, an unexpected event occurred, which appeared to the commission members as a first indication that the *peões*' testimonies might be true. The commission members ran into a *peão* (a "black worker," Soares wrote later) only by chance.[147] According to Rezende::

he was looking terrible because he had malaria. You can imagine my surprise when he came up to me, seized me by the arm and said, "are you the padre?"

I nodded, and then he whispered into my ear, "you must save me!"

"Save you from what?" I said, in surprise.

"Get me out of here!" he said. "I've been working ten months and they won't let me leave because I owe them money. And now I've got malaria."[148]

At this point Rezende called the other members of the commission and asked the *peão* to repeat in front of them what he had just said. So the

---

[142] Le Breton, *Trapped*, 151.
[143] "Besuch auf der VW-Fazenda Vale do Rio Cristalino."
[144] "Aufbruch zur letzten Grenze."
[145] Figueira, *A justiça do lobo*, 33.
[146] Le Breton, *Trapped*, 151.
[147] Batista, "Relatório."
[148] Le Breton, *Trapped*, 151.

peão did. Furious, Brügger replied immediately to Rezende: "What sort of a priest do you think you are? I'm every bit as good a Catholic as you are, but you're completely and totally biased. You'll swallow whatever the *peões* tell you but you'll never listen to our side of the story."[149] After this short but meaningful episode, the team from VW behaved very cleverly, continuing to divert the conversation and, as Rezende later regretted, making the commission members end up "wasting time on stupid little things." Although the latter expressively asked, Brügger did not let them go by themselves to see the clearing areas in which the *peões* were working.

To learn more about the hidden world of the *gatos* and *peões*, the commission members decided to find out what the people of the region said about Cristalino. They went in the direction of two recruiting towns: Nova Barreira do Campo and Velha Barreira do Campo.[150] On their way, the commission members casually met the *gato* Abilio, transporting six or seven workers on the back of a Chevrolet C-14. The commission members asked him to stop and questioned him regarding the denunciations that had been made against his clearing company. Although he denied having behaved illegally, Abilio recognized somewhat naively that he and his assistants carried guns and sometimes had to hit recalcitrant workers. He confessed that one of the workers sitting in the C-14 was a fugitive *peão*, whom he had just captured to bring him back to the *fazenda*, because the *peão* still had to finish reimbursing his debt. Later in Nova and Velha Barreira do Campo, the commission attended two meetings organized by Rezende with the help of Natal. More than thirty workers participated to testify about their experience at Cristalino. These testimonies confirmed the accusations of debt bondage that had been raised until then against the *gatos*. Since many workers feared that their testimony might be followed by reprisals, the commission had to organize a taxi service in order not to let them go back home alone.

On the last evening of its trip, the commission had dinner with the CVRC management. The dinner finished amid an embarrassing atmosphere, because as Brügger began to distribute gifts to his visitors, Rezende insisted on discussing the topic of the *peões*. Brügger remained pained. He did not deny that some violence might exist in the *fazenda*. But for him, the exploitation of the *peões* by the *gatos* was inherent to the backwardness of the Amazonian economy. Volkswagen could not do much about it, he

---

[149] Ibid.
[150] Batista, "Relatório."

thought, since there was simply no alternative in the region to effectuate the clearing work than the half a dozen subcontractors available. As Rezende told Brügger how immoral he thought the system of casual labor was, the Swiss agronomist laughed: "Father, give me the name of one single *fazenda* in the South of Pará that doesn't work this way."[151]

Brügger considered that the *gatos*' and *peões*' stories were not Volkswagen's business; he would have preferred not to give any sign that could be interpreted as a plea of guilty from the company. Dutra, on the contrary, had been mandated to save the CVRC's reputation and judged it more appropriate that VW show some readiness to improve the situation of the clearing workers. At the end of the visit, an official compromise was agreed to between the CVRC management, Volkswagen, and the commission of investigation.[152] Under Dutra's pressure, Brügger had to sign a letter in which the CVRC committed itself to a more regular and effective control of the *gatos*' activity, as well as to suspend contracts with subcontractors using violence. Besides, the CVRC agreed to set up an independent commission overseeing subcontracted labor. The commission would be composed of one member each from the farm's management, the *fazenda* workers, and CONTAG. However, the text was first and foremost a declaration of good intentions, drawn to give a positive impression to the outside world, but not very likely to change daily practices within the *gatos*' area of influence.

The declaration was short, vague, and, in the end, not very engaging. It had no legal binding and left room for interpretation. In fact, in the absence of any juridical decision about Abilio and Chicô, the CVRC did not consider the dozens of converging *peões*' testimonies as valid evidence that its subcontractors used violence. Volkswagen continued for months to collaborate with the two *gatos*, until Abilio was arrested by the police in 1985. As for the commission that was supposed to oversee the clearing areas, it was not given any power to act and did not prove more effective than the VW security service. Three delegates could not oversee the ranch alone, as even Brügger recognized: "you actually cannot ask from us that we know everything which is happening over an area of 140,000 hectares. You've seen the territory's wide extension, you can imagine how it is to walk through a forest, where you almost cannot pass through, you can imagine how difficult it is to get anywhere here."[153]

---

[151] Le Breton, *Trapped*, 152.
[152] Batista, "Relatório."
[153] "BN-Interview mit Herrn Brügger."

Besides, the delegates led by Soares on one side and the management of VW on the other side did not draw the same conclusions about the commission's visit to Cristalino. Soares wrote a report in which he stated that the *peões'* accusation against the clearing subcontractors had been confirmed by the commission's findings: "What happens after the worker arrives in the forest is exactly what Padre Ricardo Figueira denounces in the documents of the Land Pastoral [the CPT]."[154] And to make clear that he saw not only the *gatos*, but also Volkswagen as blameworthy, he added that "Volkswagen closes its eyes before the subcontractors' disobedience to the law – and so, Volkswagen is jointly liable with them, for it takes advantage of the slave labor." In spite of these conclusions, VW spread the message that the commission presided over by Soares had cleared the company of all accusations. The department of public relations in Wolfsburg declared to the German press that "Pater Rezende, the rural trade-union delegate and the parliament members presented every allegation, which they had heard of. However, the executives of Volkswagen's cattle farm could irreproachably disprove every case, which had allegedly happened within their area of responsibility."[155] In Brazil, Dutra added that "If something happened, then it is the fault of the subcontractors, the middlemen." As I will later address, VW would adopt the same defense strategy in tribunals. As the accusations were difficult to negate, the company sought to escape their consequences by denying responsibility. Nevertheless, even this strategy was a problem, because it meant that VW was renouncing its ambition of modernizing the region and provoking, with its ranch, positive side effects for local labor relations.

In spite of VW's refusal to take responsibility, Rezende analyzed the experience of the commission as useful, because it had "built a bridge" between the clearing workers and the VW Company. At the same time, he regretted that he and the other commission members did not insist more: "[W]e weren't smart enough to get to the bottom of things," he later said about this episode. "I myself was young and ... not really equipped to discuss labor laws and criminal procedures, and those members of the commission who were better prepared weren't tough enough. We were extraordinarily naïve."[156] Soares, on the contrary, was satisfied with the accord passed with the CVRC and saw it as a historic step toward the transformation of labor relations within big Amazonian

---

[154] Batista, "Relatório."
[155] *Publik-Forum*, December 2, 1983.
[156] Le Breton, *Trapped*, 151–2.

farms.[157] Another Commission member, PMDB deputy Manoel Moreira, showed himself convinced by VW's argument that the company was not responsible for the faults committed by the *gatos*. He said: "what we have here is a system which reproduces the inhuman conditions that the *gatos* impose on the workers, when they dispose of people by putting a gun to their chest"; but at the same time, he insisted that: "to be honest, I certainly cannot say that Volkswagen management authorizes these machinations."[158] Although the commission's conclusions regarding the denunciation of the *gatos*' labor system unambiguously validated the *peões*' testimonies, the question of Volkswagen's responsibility remained unsolved.

A police inquiry that proceeded in the weeks following the commission's visit approached this question explicitly. The police headquarters in Conceição investigated in the *fazenda* as well as in the area of Santana do Araguaia, where they gathered testimonies from the *gatos* as well as ex-workers of the VW ranch. The final report of the police delegate José Maria Alves Pereira, dated July 22, 1983, drew conclusions close to the version put forward by VW.[159] The local police executive recognized that "The denunciations concerning battering and retention of workers made against the subcontractors are justified, principally regarding insolvent workers forced to work when they are ill"; but he also stated that the denunciations made against the "*fazenda* vale do Rio Cristalino, belonging to the Volkswagen group" were "not justified": according to him, not the CVRC, but the firms contracted to process the clearing services were "entirely responsible for the labor tasks contracted with the *peões*." That the police of Conceição do Araguaia, a rural county of 30,000 inhabitants in the Amazon, preferred not to level accusations against a big multinational, whose project was backed by an authoritarian government at the federal level, was hardly surprising.

Nonetheless, the Church and political and union actors did not agree with this position. They saw the recognition of Volkswagen's responsibility in tolerating the existence of a forced labor system on its own property as a necessity to save the victims' dignity as well as to impede the occurrence of new cases of – as they called it – "slavery." Several *peões* had themselves criticized Volkswagen's passive attitude regarding the *gatos*' actions. Sabino and Adail, for example, said about VW: "for

---

[157] Batista, "Relatório."
[158] *Publik-Forum*, December 2, 1983.
[159] CPT Belém, Delegacia SESP de Conceição do Araguaia – Pará, July 22, 1983, "Relatório."

sure, they are guilty as well, because they do not review anything. They can't just ignore what is happening there. What does it mean when you've got a land property, and you do not even know what's happening on its ground?"[160] Shortly after the police inquiry of Conceição, several figures of the Amazonian Church publicly condemned Volkswagen's attitude, as, for example, Bishop Dom José Patrício Hanrahan. In an interview, he "accused" Volkswagen "to have morally participated and to have lacked awareness of its responsibility. The firm treats its own employees well, but ignores the conditions of slavery of these *peões*."[161] As was to be expected, SUDAM officially claimed that VW was innocent. The state agency organized its own "investigation," consisting of a visit to Araguaia-Tocantins by twenty-two CONDEL members – including one state governor who came in person.[162] CONDEL visited the Cristalino *fazenda* and the Atlas Frigorífico slaughterhouse "for a whole day," and concluded in an official declaration signed by all council members – even Jáder – at the end of August 1983, that all the accusations made against VW were "unfair" and "unjustified."[163]

This report showed that the entrance of PMDB state governors into CONDEL after the elections of 1982 had not tempered SUDAM's infatuation with the VW development project. Jáder did not prove any different to the others. In July, he avoided accompanying CONDEL members to Cristalino, giving once again the impression that he was fleeing the question of forced labor. Furthermore, by signing the CONDEL report of August 1983, he participated in clearing Volkswagen of the accusations. Soon, it appeared that Jáder was handling both sides carefully in the conflict opposing Volkswagen to the actors of liberation theology and the workers' rights movement. Struck by the media appeal triggered by Rezende's and Soares's accusations against the CVRC, he began to show an at least apparent interest for the *peões*' concerns and opened up a dialog with the Church. On September 6, 1983, he received Rezende and Bishop Hanrahan in the governor's palace in Belém, where they discussed the results of the police inquiry of Conceição.[164] Jáder recognized that the police report left no doubt about the veracity of the *peões*' accusations

[160] "VW Farmarbeiter kommen zu Wort (Interview)."
[161] "Bischof Hanrahan: 'Wir klagen Volkswagen des Mangels an Verantwortungsbewusstsein an' (Interview)."
[162] "Neue Stellungnahmen zu den Beschuldigungen gegen die VW-Fazenda."
[163] Arquivo do FINAM, SUDAM, August 24, 1983, "Pauta da 185ª reunião ordinária."
[164] "Jáder recebe bispo e garante que vai tomar providências," *O Liberal*, September 7, 1983.

and promised that the document would be communicated to the attorney general of Pará.

However, while this meeting was probably supposed to serve Jáder's public image as a progressive opposition state governor willing to act against projects imposed by the military government, Jáder did not announce any political decision about the VW ranch. He could, for example, have used his seat within CONDEL to ask for a reconfiguration of the CVRC project. He could have voted against the renewal of the fiscal incentive funds attributed annually to the company.[165] He could even have sent a contingent of the military police to Cristalino in order to arrest Chicô and Abilio, as he did the same year to solve other cases of land conflict.[166] In the end, all that Jáder did was to assure the priests that the police inquiry made at Conceição would follow its legal path. After this, the governor invited Sauer and Dutra to Belém, probably to reassure himself about VW's good intentions.[167] The talk between Jáder and the VW management was not followed by any official engagement or common declaration, besides the fact that Jáder never gave a public word of criticism against the CVRC. Jáder's passivity illustrated the mixed results of the first wave of denunciation against forced labor at Cristalino. While public powers recognized that there was a forced labor problem at Cristalino and several inquiries explicitly inculpated the *gatos*, only some leftist deputies insisted on VW's responsibility. Besides, neither the government in Pará, nor the federal authorities, nor VW had put concrete measures into practice to put an end to Chicô and Abilio's business at Santana do Araguaia. The conflict over Cristalino was not yet over.

The Impact of the Transition to Democracy

As no measure was taken against Chicô, Abilio, or Hermínio, the three *gatos* continued their business as usual. At the end of the clearing season in 1984, Rezende received even more complaints from *peões* having fled the *fazenda*. Similar descriptions to those in the *peões'* testimonies of the previous year seemed to indicate that nothing had changed there. What, nevertheless, had changed in one year was the political climate in Brazil. The military regime and its policy had never known such low political

---

[165] After Rezende's denunciations were made public, CONDEL decided to renew the state subventions to the CVRC. Arquivo do FINAM, SUDAM, May 26, 1983, "Ata da 182ª reunião ordinária do conselho deliberativo."

[166] *O Liberal*, September 7, 1983.

[167] "Rio Cristalino leva Sauer ao governo," *A província do Pará*, September 20, 1983.

support as then. From January to April 1984, the Diretas Já campaign in favor of the introduction of direct presidential elections, giving rise to demonstrations of hundreds of thousands of Brazilians, displayed the extent of the defiance toward the government.[168] Not only was Diretas Já supported by all the opposition parties, but the campaign also received a very favorable echo within the media, including those with the widest audience, the television programs, which for the first time since 1964 took side with a movement defying the central government.[169]

At the end of the Diretas Já campaign, the PDS (Partido Democrático Social, the new name for the ARENA) majority in the senate, enabled the federal government to block a constitutional amendment for the instigation of direct presidential elections – thus fending off the opposition's slight majority in the Congress.[170] But it was too late. Diretas Já had already convinced the most moderate part of the ruling majority that the popular support for the "revolution" of 1964 had been lost. In July 1984, the vice president of the PDS formed a breakaway party and began to gather parliament members in order to look for an alliance with the PMDB.[171] The PMDB's candidate for president, Tancredo Neves, invested in August 1984, was consequently in position to win the indirect elections planned for January 1985. The end of the authoritarian regime was becoming a close and realistic perspective, alongside the project of a land reform, which was one of the opposition's main demands – although the extent of this land reform was more or less radical depending on the different opposition groups.

It was, in principle, a favorable moment for the *peões*, Rezende and their allies to widen their political support. Federal deputy Irma Passoni (PT) joined Soares and Andrade in their work of parliamentary lobbying in favor of the Cristalino *peões*.[172] A famous Catholic activist from the southern zone of São Paulo, she had been the leader of the Movimento do Custo da Vida (MCV) in 1978.[173] One of the most powerful popular movements during the military regime, the MCV was a collective of housewives that demonstrated against the rise in the cost of living.

---

[168] Daniel de Mendonça, "A vitória de Tancredo Neves no colégio eleitoral e a posição política dos semanários veja e isto é," *Revista alceu* 5, no. 10 (2005), 170.

[169] Jairo Sanguiné Júnior, "A imprensa e o processo de redemocratização do Brasil," *Sociedade em debate* 4, no. 3 (1998), 28.

[170] Skidmore, *The Politics of Military Rule in Brazil*, 242.

[171] Ibid., 250.

[172] CPT Belém, Gama to Moraes, July 20, 1984; Passoni to Rezende, August 3, 1984.

[173] Keck, *The Workers' Party and Democratization in Brazil*, 83, 95.

Passoni's involvement in the denunciation of forced labor at the CVRC was a sign of the symbolic dimension taken by this affair in the context of the political fall of the military regime.

At the grassroots level, the same mechanisms as in 1983 were put in place again. Actors from the CPT, the STR, and local representatives came together to register witness testimonies. This time, however, there was more geographical diversification and the Santana do Araguaia region was no longer the epicenter of the *peões*' complaints. A wave of testimonies was delivered by *peões* in their residence town of Paraíso do Norte (Goiás), where they had been recruited by Gringo in January 1984 with dozens of other workers, before being driven to Santana do Araguaia and sold to Abilio.[174] These testimonies gained visibility thanks to the initiative of Moisés Nogueiro Avelino, the mayor (PMDB) of Paraíso.[175] Alerted by the CPT about the return of *peões* having fled from Cristalino, he supported the *peões*' deposition at the local police station and contacted the judge at the tribunal in Conceicão do Araguaia, Enivaldo da Gama.[176] However, as a local judge, Enivaldo could do no more than write to state government executives and to the attorney general of Pará, in the hope of accelerating the judiciary investigations supposed to have already started in 1983.

The national climate leaning toward democratization also left room for initiatives of protest that could not have taken place one year before. Various city councilors of the town of Redenção (close to Conceição), including members of the PDS, together with CPT and STR members, signed a petition against the VW ranch, which they sent to Jáder.[177] In addition, the actors from the opposition to the military regime became more self-confident in the context of popular civil rights movements. In the previous year, for example, federal deputy Ademir Andrade had limited his action to a type of internal lobbying within the PMDB. In 1984, however, Andrade did not hesitate to send an offensive telex to Sauer: "Once again I am receiving denunciations about slave labor in the Company Vale do Rio Cristalino – It is lamentable that the management of this company permits this crime."[178]

---

[174] May 21, 1984, *peão*, in *Brasilien Nachrichten* (84), 1984.
[175] CPT Belém, Nogueiro to Gama, July 25, 1984.
[176] CPT Belém, Soares to Gama, July 17, 1984; Andrade to Gama, July 17, 1984; Gama to Moraes, July 20, 1984; Gama to Soares, July 20, 1984; Passoni to Rezende, August 3, 1984.
[177] GPTEC, V7.25.2., [Collective] to Jáder, August 15, 1984.
[178] CPT Belém, Andrade to Sauer, July 17, 1984.

The tone of the VW opponents had changed to become more aggressive, because the opposition to the military regime now felt legitimized by a majority of Brazilians. The "Cristalino affair" became a hot topic crystallizing the political conflict between advocates of the military regime and partisans of democracy and land reform. When, at the end of August 1984, the commission of investigation on land conflicts of the legislative assembly of Pará invited Rezende for a hearing, two assembly members delivered a tangible demonstration of this polarization.[179] As Rezende started to tackle the VW case, Paulo Fontelis, a PMDB deputy close to the clandestine Maoist PC do B Party, began to argue with a PDS deputy famous for being the descendant of a family of big landholders. The whole state assembly looked on shocked as the two men almost started to fight physically. It seems that contesting the VW project in that period meant questioning a whole system of land distribution, deeply associated with the declining Brazilian dictatorship.

The decline of this dictatorship, along with a political climate hostile to big landholdings, also encouraged the left to intensify pressure on the government of Pará. Jáder was receiving regular mail from judges and federal deputies asking him to finally take measures to solve the problems existing at Cristalino.[180] Even German activist Peter Klein, an executive of Amnesty International, in close contact with Rezende, started to directly address members of the Pará government. On October 15, 1984, Klein sent a letter to Jáder in order to express the irritation of the *peões'* supporters faced with the inaction of the authorities to reform labor relations in the VW *fazenda*.[181] Jáder remained silent, as usual. But Klein continued to lobby the state government of Pará by addressing other ministers. Months later, he managed to obtain an interview with Jáder's minister of justice, Itair Silva, and convinced him to express publicly his support for the Cristalino *peões*.[182] Itair Silva even described as "slavery" the system of labor existing at the ranch. He also said that the SUDAM report published in 1983 to clear Volkswagen of the forced labor accusations was wrong, and criticized SUDAM harshly for funding antisocial "development" projects in the Amazon.

---

[179] "Padre conta os mortos e fala de um sonho de paz," *A folha de São Paulo*, August 30, 1984.
[180] CPT Belém, Gama to Jáder, July 17, 1984; Passoni to Rezende, August 3, 1984.
[181] GPTEC V7.33.1, Klein to Jáder, October 15, 1984.
[182] "Interview mit dem Justizminister von Pará, Itair Silva," *Brasilien Nachrichten* (93), 1986.

Silva's declaration showed that the term "slavery" had become solidly associated with the image of the CVRC. Thanks to VW, the *peões'* defenders in Brazil had managed to make of the forced labor networks, which had been nothing but business as usual in the Amazon, a public affair. In 1975–6, environmental activists had taken up the case of the fire at Cristalino as an opportunity to make a political issue of the destruction of the tropical forest. This time, the rural workers and liberation theology movement used VW's notoriety to make of debt bondage in the Amazon a national problem. The engagement of Klein on the side of the *peões* showed that this communication against "slavery" had been efficient enough to reach the borders of Germany. Precisely, as Rezende said in an interview to a German newspaper, he and the CPT badly needed international solidarity to push forward their struggle against a multinational company.[183] The next section shows what form this solidarity took.

The Help of the German Solidarity Movement

The implication of a multinational firm in an affair of overexploitation of Third World laborers attracted the attention of the left alternative political scene in Germany because the latter had reached, by the early 1980s, a particularly advanced stage of familiarization with transnational topics. During the previous decade, there had been disappointments with domestic political developments, especially among those who had hoped that the 1968 student protests would foster a durable revolutionary wave. These disappointments had drawn the attention of German protest actors toward global inequalities. This option was reinforced by the emergence of successful ideological proposals with a transnational focus, such as liberation theology, which reinterpreted the universal message of the Christian faith or the green movement underlining the interconnectedness of the earth's ecosystems. The appeal of transnational, Third World–linked topics in German left politics favored the collaboration between German and Brazilian protest actors and the transcription into the German context of the controversy on "slavery" affecting VW. That way, what could have remained a local Amazonian affair became a topic with which even the senior management of global VW had to struggle.

---

[183] *Badische Zeitung*, October 25, 1985.

From Colonial Wars to Latin American Dictatorships: The Changing Focus of the German "Third World Movement"

The notion of a "movement of solidarity" sprang up in the 1950s, during the colonial war in Algeria, when intellectuals of the Federal Republic supported the Algerian liberation movement.[184] This marked the entrance of Third World countries as indirect actors into German protest politics. The fight for the self-determination of these countries imposed itself as one of the unifying topics of the extra-parliamentary protest that grew among German youth during the period of international effervescence of 1967–8. These movements attempted to break taboos of German society, on topics such as social hierarchies, sexual moral codes, state violence, or the Nazi past.[185] But many of the protesters, who were fascinated by the anticolonial movements, thought themselves as the mere West German declension of a worldwide uprising. They developed a radical critique of the war led by the U.S. Army in Vietnam, seen as a symbol of Western imperialism. The disillusionment following the protest wave of 1968 sprinkled among its former participants the idea that political change was hopeless within German society and, more generally, in all industrial countries. This pessimist view on national perspectives led thousands of activists to increasingly envisage the Third World as a space of possible revolutionary upheaval, and a political area from which to challenge domination.[186] In the early 1970s, hundreds of committees of support for Third World liberation movements blossomed in the cities of the Bundesrepublik.[187]

The German churches had "discovered" the Third World earlier than in 1968. Needless to say, they adopted a different perspective than revolutionary groups did. From the late 1950s to the late 1960s, many humanitarian associations were founded in the Protestant and Catholic parishes in reaction to the news of natural catastrophes, civil wars, or famines coming from Asian, African, or Latin American countries.[188]

---

[184] Claudia Olejniczak, *Die Dritte-Welt-Bewegung in Deutschland. Konzeptionelle und organisatorische Strukturmerkmale einer neuen sozialen Bewegung* (Wiesbaden: Deutscher Universitätsverlag, 1999), 86–92.

[185] Claudia Lepp, "Zwischen Konfrontation und Kooperation: Kirchen und soziale Bewegungen in der Bundesrepublik (1950–1983)," *Zeithistorische Forschungen / Studies in Contemporary History* (2010), 5.

[186] Olaf Kaltmeier, "Über die 'Dritte-Welt'-Bewegung in der BRD. Zwischen Unterschriften und Straßenkampf," *Friedens-Forum* (2001).

[187] Werner Balsen and Karl Rössel, *Hoch die internationale Solidarität: zur Geschichte der Dritte-Welt-Bewegung in der Bundesrepublik* (Köln: Kölner Volksblatt, 1986).

[188] Ibid., 282–5.

Most of these groups focused on actions of solidarity such as fundraising for food distribution or the creation of socio-medical services in damaged countries. The creation of the NGOs Misereor for the Catholic Church (1958) and Brot für die Welt (1959) for the Protestant Church illustrated this trend at the national level. For many young German Christians, these organizations were the first schools of international solidarity, but also the first confrontation with global injustices.[189] A part of these engaged Christians did not remain insensitive to the discourse of the student movements and their opening to Third World countries on behalf of the solidarity against oppression. Especially in Catholic parishes, a generation of young priests influenced by the uproars of 1967–8 took a growing influence in the organization of humanitarian groups.[190]

Attentive to initiatives coming from Catholic personalities in the Global South, these priests felt encouraged to radicalize their political critique by the conference of Medellin in 1968. Liberation theology not only represented a revolutionary platform for politically engaged believers, but also provided a response to the decline of the Christian faith in Germany, where the number of faithful was decreasing. Controversies concerning the collaboration of some parts of the Church with the Nazi regime as well as media-echoed philosophical debates on the "death of God" had undermined Catholic motivations. As Herzog states, liberation theology seduced progressive Catholics because in this pessimistic context, it proposed that the "focus of a lived faith should be on this world and not hereafter; that God suffered with human beings; that God was experienced when human beings were in solidarity with each other."[191] Therefore, "numerous theologians and laypeople found in left-wing activism and liberation theology precisely the kind of revitalized faith they had been searching for." In 1968, the German Catholic community experienced its own political breakup, with many parishes joining the protests, using a repertoire of actions in complete rupture with traditional Catholic performances. As Werner and Rössel explain, "everywhere in the Bundesrepublik, Church action groups organized Beat- and

---

[189] Lepp, "Zwischen Konfrontation und Kooperation," 9.
[190] Claudia Olejniczak, "Dritte-Welt-Bewegung," in *Die sozialen Bewegungen in Deutschland seit 1945: ein Handbuch*, ed. Roland Roth and Dieter Rucht (Frankfurt/Main: Campus, 2008), 325–6.
[191] Dagmar Herzog, "The Death of God in West Germany. Between Secularization, Postfascism, and the Rise of Liberation Theology," in *Die Gegenwart Gottes in der modernen Gesellschaft. Transzendenz und religiöse Vergemeinschaftung in Deutschland*, ed. Michael Geyer and Lucian Hölscher (Göttingen: Wallstein, 2006), 446–7.

Rock-masses, in which people were supposed to beckon against the war in Vietnam, hunger, misery and oppression in the Third World."[192]

Around 1970, an event crystallized the link between the critique of economic inequalities by liberation theology, solidarity with the Third World, and the responsibility of West Germany in global mechanisms of exploitation. This event, the so-called Cabora-Bassa affair, accelerated the move of humanitarian Catholic groups toward a radical critique of the dominant conception of "development" in Germany.[193] Cabora-Bassa was a controversial dam project planned in Mozambique, in the context of an independence war in which Germany supported the Portuguese colonizer. The dam was supposed to provide energy to a future settlement of 1 million European arrivals, with the benediction of the apartheid government of South Africa. The participation of five major German firms in the project made of Cabora-Bassa a breakpoint moment among Third World activists within West German Christian parishes. Many of them recognized that mere humanitarian help was no longer enough, given the frequent enmeshment of German financial interests in projects that threatened Third World populations.

The Catholic southwestern city of Freiburg, close to the French border, became the epicenter of this politicization process under the leadership of Freiburger Aktion Dritte Welt (Freiburger Third World Action, AK3W). This humanitarian group close to the Catholic Church was created in 1968, initially in order to encourage the transfer of German aid funds to countries in need, regardless of economic or political issues. In reaction to Cabora-Bassa, the group started protest actions against the Siemens firm involved in the dam project. In 1980, a declaration of the Freiburger group summed up its own ideological evolution: "Insofar as our group became aware of the connection between the capitalist economic structure in industrial countries, and the misery, exploitation and oppression of the Third World, our position towards the FRG's social system changed. We increasingly understood ourselves as a part of the left."[194]

From then on, politicized and fiercely critical of the German government and firms, the Third World movement started to focus its struggles on places where German interests were intertwined with movements of oppression and injustice. By 1973, the projector was put on Latin America.

---

[192] Balsen and Rössel, *Hoch die internationale Solidarität*, 282–5.
[193] Niels Seibert, *Vergessene Proteste. Internationalismus und Antirassismus 1964–1983* (Münster: Unrast-Verlag, 2008), 80–90.
[194] Balsen and Rössel, *Hoch die internationale Solidarität*, 292–7.

Pinochet's bloody military coup in Chile led to numerous manifestations of emotions in Europe and the blossoming of committees of "Chile solidarity" everywhere in West Germany. As in the mid-1970s, the hope that international pressure might defeat Pinochet disappeared, many of these committees changed names and extended their interest to the whole Latin American region. Another military coup, this time in Argentina, reanimated these committees in 1976. But it was the conflict in Nicaragua between the left-revolutionary, Sandinista movement and the hardliner conservative dictator Somoza in 1977–9, that affected the German Catholic Church the most; its members began again to create myriads of local solidarity groups.[195] The presence of many German companies in Nicaragua, working in solid collaboration with the dictatorship, triggered the indignation of German Catholics: BASF, Bayer, Siemens, VW, and AEG were there, besides Mercedes Benz, whose general executive in Nicaragua was Somoza himself.

Around 1980, El Salvador, again a Central American country governed by a military dictatorship, kept Latin America at the center of attention.[196] European Catholic milieus were especially affected as the archbishop of El Salvador, Oscar Romero, a figure of the opposition movement, was shot to death during a service at the cathedral in the capital city, and a massacre killing forty faithful was carried out by the army during his funeral. On September 26, 1980, dozens of theologians, priests, Church employees, and theology students organized, in solidarity with El Salvador, a spectacular occupation of the cathedral of Cologne.[197] The opposition against Latin American authoritarian regimes, the solidarity with the Latin American left, and the critique against German economic policy in the region had become unifying mottos within the Christian solidarity movement.

Two European Visions of Cristalino: The Confrontation between Brazilian Solidarity Groups and Volkswagen in Germany

There were dozens of local committees of solidarity with Brazil in West Germany in the early 1980s, many of them linked with Catholic parishes in the Bundesrepublik and having partnerships with Brazilian NGOs. Many of these groups reacted to the news of forced labor coming from the Cristalino farm. The Brasilieninitiative association in Freiburg took

---

[195] Ibid., 402–3.
[196] Ibid., 459–79.
[197] Ibid., 487.

the affair extremely seriously. Brasilieninitiative had started to exist in 1979, as during a visit of President Figueiredo to Germany, a number of Brazilians living in Germany, as well as Germans interested in Brazil, had the idea of setting up an information stand in the street in order to enlighten Freiburg's inhabitants about the Brazilian military regime.[198] *Brasilieninitiative* launched a journal, *Brasilien Nachrichten*, which became specialized in overseeing the social consequences of German investments in Brazil.

From 1979 to 1986, *Brasilien Nachrichten* (*BN*) dedicated dozens of articles to the VW ranch. From 1983, several Brasilieninitiative members led detailed investigations about the forced labor system at Cristalino, soliciting the point of view of the VW executives, staying in permanent mail contact with Rezende and Soares, and effectuating several trips to Araguaia. *BN*'s editor, Peter Klein, who was also the director of Brazilian coordination at Amnesty International Deutschland, became the pivot between Brazilian and German associations for all matters regarding the Volkswagen farm. Although Brasilieninitiative was not directly religious, the association did not hide its admiration for liberation theology, and plainly recognized itself as the local avatar of the German "solidarity movement."[199]

As Brasilieninitiative was founded, the mutation of this solidarity movement into a protest bloc had already taken place. Another association, which harshly criticized the CVRC, illustrates this evolution, with a curriculum similar to that of the Freiburger AK3W. In fact, it even bore almost the same name, Aktionskreis Dritte Welt (AK3W) – shared by many local solidarity committees in Germany – although it did not start in Freiburg, but in Recklinghausen, in the north of the Ruhr urban area. The action group was founded in the Catholic parish of St. Peter, in the old town of Recklinghausen, by fourteen engaged Catholics who, according to two of them (Thomas Hax and Peter Möller), were looking for "the good feeling of being able to do something for the less moneyed people in this world."[200] Initially, AK3W of St. Peters was entirely dedicated

---

[198] "1978–2008, 30 Jahre Brasilieninitiative Freiburg eV.," *Vauban actuel*, December 6, 2008.

[199] "Was ist es was VW so blind macht? Zur Auseinandersetzung um die VW-Fazenda," *Brasilien Nachrichten* (81), 1983.

[200] For this and all the following on AK3W St. Peter, see Thomas Hax-Schoppenhorst and Peter Möller, "Nestverweis für schräge Vögel. der AK 3. Welt St.Peter verläßt nach 27 Jahren die Gemeinde," in *Brücken und Gräben. Sozialpastorale Impulse und Initiativen im Spannungsfeld von Gemeinde und Politik*, ed. Norbert Mette, Ludger Weckel, and Andreas Wintels (Münster: LIT, 1999), 68–76.

to charity actions. Its members collected donations, which they sent to the Franciscan brothers of Piripiri, in the Brazilian northeastern state of Piauí. The principle was to "bore wells, build schools, erect chapels and manage garden plots with the money of the wealthy Germans." The local church leadership and the parish council looked sympathetically at the small NGO; some members of AK3W even joined these institutions.

Everything changed with the first study excursion to Brazil by ten people of the group in 1979. They traveled three months over the country while, as Hax and Möller remember,

It was the eventful time of the metal workers' strike in the South of Brazil, the time of bloody land conflicts, when rice crop growing was supposed to lose ground for the benefit of cattle-raising, focused on international commerce. [Liberation theologians] questioned with appealing theses the world economic order and designated worldwide poverty as a state of war, to which the rich acquiesced with terrifying passivity.

During their trip, in which they had many conversations with religious actors, the AK3Ws changed the way they had been looking toward Brazil: "It was over with the cliché of the somewhat tired Latinos who would prefer to doze in the sun. From then, the thoughts of the action group members were intensively bewildered by words which [we] had considered only half-heartedly and unknowingly: global economic order, indebtedness, capital transfer." As they came back to Germany, the AK3Ws were shaken, disillusioned, and politicized. Piripiri's human misery, they started to realize, should be seen as the local consequence of an overall context of systemic inequalities. It was no longer taboo to question the influence of West German living standards on poverty in the Third World. They criticized their own past charity action, which they summed up as the illusion of creating a small oasis of German donations in the middle of a starving world.

From that point on, AK3W actions became more radical and managed to attract an increasing audience – they called for better working rights at VWB and Mercedes do Brazil, protested against gigantic sugarcane plantations, lobbied for the protection of the tropical rain forest, denounced the incapacitation of Amerindian tribes, and argued in favor of land reform. Through postcard actions, street theater, information stands, school visits, collaboration with movies, and Third World solidarity reviews, AK3W made a name throughout the entire Bundesrepublik. Because of its solid establishment in Brazil, VW became AK3W's main target: the Third World solidarity supporters of St. Peters protested against high remittances from VWB to Wolfsburg compared to a weak investment in the Brazilian market.[201] They criticized the massive dismissals that took place at VWB in the period of the Brazilian economic crisis and, of course, showed massive indignation against the CVRC project. Beyond critiques, the action group sought to develop a dialog with the company. From 1981 to 1983, Thomas Hax regularly communicated with the director of VW's Brazil department in Wolfsburg, Otto Adams. With time, the two men developed a tense relationship: Adams blamed Hax for being too emotional and not ready for a rational dialog. Furthermore, he considered that Hax systematically tried to give a negative image of VWB to German public opinion. Hax sent some copies of the letters that he received from Adams to magazines with a wide audience such as *Der Spiegel, Stern*, or the *Frankfurter Rundschau*. He also irritated Adams by quoting passages of these letters in a Christian radio show on *Norddeutscher Rundfunk*.[202]

After the forced labor scandal, AK3W sent copies of its exchanges with Adams to several other solidarity associations, encouraging them to take public positions against the VW ranch as well. The "Brazil working group" of the Dritte Welt Haus ("Third World House") of the city of Bielefeld, for example, included these documents in a dossier of investigation about the presumed crimes committed at Cristalino.[203] It sent the dossier to the German media and to documentation centers throughout the country. About seventy-five kilometers northwest of Bielefeld, in Mettingen, another Third World solidarity group, the Institut für Brasilienkunde (Institute of Brazilian Civilization, IfB) participated in circulating critical texts against Cristalino.[204] The IfB, a Franciscan association, was founded in 1969 and, just like AK3W St. Peter, started with mere charity activities, gathering money to support the humanitarian works of Franciscan monks in the Brazilian northeast.[205] With the radicalization of the Third World movement in Germany, the IfB increasingly took political positions endorsing the theses of the Brazilian left. It started to publish German translations of texts written by liberation

[201] "Not in Brasilien schlägt Wellen im Revier"; *Brasilien Nachrichten* (81), 1983; Adams to Hax, 1981–3, in Arbeitsgruppe Brasilien, ed. *Die Farm am Amazonas*.
[202] Adams to Hax, 1981–3, in Arbeitsgruppe Brasilien, *Die Farm am Amazonas*, 32–5.
[203] Ibid.
[204] *Brasilien-Dialog* (2), 1983; *Brasilien-Dialog* (4), 1984 both contain several texts accusing the VW ranch.
[205] Institut für Brasilienkunde, www.brasilienkunde.de, access date May 26, 2012.

theologians, and, in its review, *Brasilien-Dialog*, critical reports on the unbalanced economic relation between Germany and Brazil.

Beyond "Brazilianist" associations such as the IfB, AK3W, or Brasilieninitiative, organizations dedicated to wider areas participated in publicizing the denunciation of forced labor at Cristalino in Germany. In Bonn, the Informationsstelle Lateinamerika (Point of Information on Latin America, ILA) began to intervene in 1983, as its director, Gernot Wirth, put pen to paper to address a letter of protest to VW senior management in Wolfsburg.[206] The ILA was an association of the alternative left, dedicated to providing information about German business in Latin American dictatorships, but not only. The ILA's aim was also to unveil in Germany the actions and messages of Latin American protest groups that were not known by the European media, such as trade unions, peasants' organizations, Church grassroots communities, feminists, and ecologists.[207] As most of the Third World solidarity organizations in Germany, the ILA disseminated its ideas through a review, titled after the name of the association.

Another publication, the Catholic magazine *Publik-Forum*, issued several articles and special reports on the suspicions of slavery at Cristalino, largely based on information provided by the CPT.[208] *Publik-Forum* – launched in 1962 – was an engaged paper enjoying a certain level of circulation (between 20,000 and 30,000 copies sold every month), which made of the magazine a sort of platform of the Christian left. *Publik-Forum* promoted a Church "from the bottom"; it regularly provoked controversy through its critical tone against the Catholic hierarchy, its liberal positions on topics such as homosexuality or priests' celibacy, and its acknowledged admiration for liberation theology.[209] *Publik-Forum* and all the associations cited previously were, in part, the fruit of the emergence of Third World solidarity in Germany during the 1960s and 1970s. Many of these groups worked together and shared information and contacts. The solidarity movement had created networks of pressure made up of local groups and militant publications, often paying attention to economic and political evolutions in specific geographic areas – for

---

[206] Wetzel and Hertel to Wirth, September 9, 1983, in *Brasilien Nachrichten* (81), 1983.

[207] Informationsstelle Lateinamerika, www.ila-web.de/verschiedenes/ila.htm, access date May 27, 2012.

[208] "Folter auf der VW-Farm? Ausbeutung und Zustände wie in einem Straflager," *Publik-Forum*, June 24, 1983; *Publik-Forum*, December 2, 1983; "VW do Brasil. Blutspur am Rio Araguaia," *Publik-Forum*, November 29, 1985.

[209] Publik-Forum, www.publik-forum.de, access date May 27, 2012.

example, Brazil. They were especially interested in the ethics of German firms in the Global South, and served as a mouthpiece for protest actors such as Rezende or Soares in the German territory.

What was the role of these German actors in the conflict that – indirectly – opposed the seasonal workers of Cristalino to VW? First, the German solidarity groups constituted a source of information about Cristalino other than VW's communication department. Brasilieninitiative carried out an impressive work in this respect. It published *peões'* testimonies, reports sent to Peter Klein by Soares and Rezende, documents from SUDAM or the police in Santana do Araguaia, propaganda documents issued by Volkswagen, and letters by VW representatives. Brasilieninitiative sent two of its members to the county of Santana do Araguaia: Sylva Ehlers in 1984, Peter Klein in 1985. They both visited the VW ranch and the region, where they interviewed many actors involved directly or indirectly in the so-called slavery affair: former seasonal workers, clergy members, medical personnel, VW security guards. Impressed by the results of Brasilieninitiative's research, Expedito Soares even used the material sent to him by Peter Klein to prepare his speeches on the VW ranch at the state parliament of São Paulo. He distributed Portuguese translations of articles from *Brasilien Nachrichten* to the state deputies, who received these texts, written by Germans about a Brazilian *fazenda*, with curiosity and enthusiasm.[210]

Brasilieninitiative also helped the outside world to know the *fazenda* and its actors better. The figure of Friedrich Brügger, for example, was "discovered" by the association. Klein and Ehlers met him several times for interviews in São Paulo and Cristalino. They regularly offered him the chance to react to criticisms and to give his opinion on the problem of forced labor, through texts that were published in *Brasilien Nachrichten*. Brügger did not master the communication skills of a Wolfgang Sauer, a Paulo Dutra or an Otto Adams. He had clear-cut ideas about agricultural politics, ecology, and Amazonian crop culture. He flung his convictions with a remarkable frankness, without adapting to the expectations of his interlocutors. When talking to members of Brasilieninitiative, he would express his incomprehension toward the accusations raised against the *gatos*, or the credit given in Europe to Rezende, whom he saw as an extremist. Neither did he understand the "ecological concern" that Europeans raised about the *fazenda*: for him, all this was based on scientific ignorance. As a "multi," he thought, VW was an easy target for all

[210] *Brasilien Nachrichten* (84), 1984.

sorts of critiques, as if the company had to pay for the whole capitalist system.[211] More surprisingly, Brügger did not hesitate to grumble about his own superiors in Wolfsburg, whom he blamed for not being offensive enough. He would have liked to sue Rezende, and felt betrayed by the refusal of VW to do so. But the most interesting part of Brügger's confidences to the writers of *Brasilien Nachrichten* was when he gave his opinions about the *peões*.

One of the arguments that Brügger used to disqualify the testimonies of the *peões* was their identification with the chronic "backwardness" of northern Brazil. According to him, they were "nomads," naturally lazy and reluctant to take on regular employment or work efficiently. They had no idea about how to rationally cultivate a plot of land. They fought with each other at every opportunity and were unwilling to build a family. For Brügger, developing "these people" was an almost impossible task, even for the "new civilization created" by VW in the Amazon. Underlining that the *peões* should be made responsible for their own problems, Brügger did not want to know about "debt slavery," which he saw as a pseudo-humanitarian concept invented to justify the workers' laziness. He considered that "if one works slowly, dilly dallies, it can happen to them that during the clearing days they spend more money in the *gato*'s shop than what they earned after the surface they have actually cleared has been counted. In Europe it is in principle not really different. Only that there a worker is precisely 'slave of the bank,' to which he owes his debts." Instead of earning money, Brügger said, the *peões* augmented their debts "because they live beyond their means" and "eat mountains of rice instead of working."

Such declarations were shocking for European activists, who claimed to defend the dignity of the poor on behalf of solidarity between human beings – a leftist Swiss journalist once confided to Rezende, after a meeting with Brügger, that "this guy ... is a case for Freud rather than for Marx."[212] With Brügger, the activists of Brasilieninitiative had flushed out the ideal polarizing figure, someone whose declarations were certain to shock a part of the German public. His vision of modernity corresponded exactly with the critiques against dependent development emitted by liberation theology in Brazil or Brazilian solidarity groups in Germany: it was

---

[211] For this and the following on Brügger, see ibid.; Brügger, "Volkswagen nimmt Stellung zu Anklagen"; *Brasilien Nachrichten* (82), 1984; BN-Interview mit Herrn Brügger (93), 1986; Ehlers, "Besuch auf der VW-Fazenda Vale do Rio Cristalino"; "Der Sicherheitsbeauftragte der VW-Farm (Interview)."

[212] GPTEC V9.11., Banderet to Figueira, July 27, 1986.

an elitist modernity, necessarily driven by the "know-how" of industrially superior countries, excluding the poor and prohibiting any kind of critique against technological progress. After 1983, the successive *Brasilien Nachrichten* releases only rarely omitted to publish one (if not two or even three) texts, interviews, or quotations by Brügger. Brügger himself, who knew that his texts would be published and felt misunderstood by European public opinion, saw *Brasilien Nachrichten* as a tribune from which he could address German society and deconstruct the unfair – he thought – accusation raised against the VW ranch. This game became pitiless: the more Brügger talked, the more he appeared as a caricature of the developmentalist mentality. Unwillingly, he became the best argument for the activists who demanded the end of the VW *fazenda*.

But the solidarity movement did not only construct negative figures such as Brügger, from which the readers of *Brasilien Nachrichten* were supposed to dissociate themselves. It also constructed personalities of the Brazilian left into models of activism. In particular *Brasilien Nachrichten*, *Publik-Forum*, *Brasilien-Dialog*, even *Der Spiegel* and other German magazines made Ricardo Rezende Figueira a star of the solidarity movement.[213] Rezende was idealized as a friend of the poor risking his life for workers' rights and the preservation of the forest, a "David" fighting alone against Volkswagen, the "Goliath" of global capitalism. Rezende readily played this game: he could not refuse the support of the international press, given his situation in the Amazon, where his conflicts with several big landowners in affairs of forced labor had left him in a fragile position. As *Publik-Forum* wrote, Rezende had so many enemies that he could only be happy about the support of new German friends; he was "denigrated as a notorious liar by the VW management. He is also seen as a nuisance by other big landholders in Brazil. In the end, his relative high level of notoriety in Europe might be the reason why the many death threats he has received until now have not become reality so far."[214]

The ideological support of Christian Third World solidarity groups enabled Rezende to resort to an effective network for communicating messages in Europe. He especially developed a friendly relationship with Peter Klein, who invited him for two weeks to Germany to talk about the problems of forced labor at the VW ranch. There, Rezende gave interviews in the local press and made a conference tour during which he

---

[213] *Publik-Forum*, June 24, 1983; "Interview mit Pater Ricardo Rezende Figueira am 1. Dez. 1982"; "Aufbruch zur letzten Grenze."
[214] *Publik-Forum*, November 29, 1985.

talked in front of hundreds of people about the *peões*, the *gatos* and how the VW *fazenda* contributed to social imbalances in the Amazon.[215] He was, for example, on October 22 at the adult education center in Freiburg for Brasilieninitiative.[216] On October 28, he talked in the main amphitheater of the prestigious university of Heidelberg for the charity association Food First.[217] On October 31, he talked in Cologne for Amnesty International, after which he made a visit to the headquarters of the Justitia et Pax commission, an organ affiliated with the German Episcopal Conference, specialized in development, human rights, and peace policy.[218] By handing to Justitia et Pax a report of more than 100 pages, full of data about the cases of forced labor at Cristalino from 1980 to 1985, Rezende hoped to sensitize the executive institutions of the German Church, which until then had been quite supportive of VW's initiatives in Brazil.

The cycle of conferences given by Rezende was part of the German Third World groups' strategy to circulate independent information about the VW *fazenda* to the widest audience possible, as an alternative to the advertisement campaigns carried out by Wolfsburg to praise the "model ranch." This strategy corresponded to the promise made by Peter Klein in a letter to Rezende: "we will publish an important part of your material here, to make public opinion in Germany aware of the problems."[219] Brasilieninitiative considered that its role was to inform, explain, and transmit concrete images of the daily life of the seasonal clearers. As she came back from her trip to Cristalino, Ehlers wrote, in reference to the *peões*, that "in Germany, ten thousand kilometers from there, in the middle of the reality of the Federal Republic, it is often difficult to imagine the life and the suffering of these people who have to live in a climate of violence, injustice and exploitation."[220]

AK3W St. Peter also took initiatives supposed to be heard by a wider public, for example, as Thomas Hax addressed German consumers, asking them to boycott VW products in order to protest against the exploitation of the seasonal workers at Cristalino.[221] It scarcely needs to be said that

---

[215] Gerhard M. Kirk, "Von verletztem Menschenrecht auf der VW-farm," *Badische Zeitung*, October 25, 1985.
[216] CPT Belem, October 1985 "Landkonflikte, Brasilieninitiative."
[217] CPT Belém, Food First Information and Action Network, October 29, 1985.
[218] GPTEC V8.20.1., Amnesty International, October 1985, "Landkonflikte in Brasilien."
[219] GPTEC V7.36., Klein to Rezende, November 14, 1984.
[220] Ehlers, "Besuch auf der VW-Fazenda 'Vale do Rio Cristalino.'"
[221] *Brasilien Nachrichten* (81), 1983.

this call was above all symbolic, given the reduced size of the association at St. Peters. Still, these kinds of initiatives had at least a chance to be heard in certain circles, which played a role in the cultural exchanges between Germany and Brazil. Besides its massive presence in the local press, AK3W St Peter had active contacts with more than 100 Brazil solidarity groups relaying its messages in all of Germany. In 1985, two members of the group accepted more than 180 invitations to speak in parishes and at political and trade unions' meetings.[222]

AK3W St Peter and the other solidarity groups involved in the denunciation of forced labor at Cristalino reproached VW for claiming abusively that it brought modernity and development to the Amazon. Ehlers, for example, concluded from her visit to Cristalino that VW confused profit maximization and export gains with development aid, "while development certainly means for VW something fully different than for a rural workers' family in Pará."[223] The scandal of forced labor became the pretext for a political battle between two radically opposed visions of Germany's role in developing the Third World. On one side, Brasilieninitiative, AK3W, the ILA, the Third World House, and other associations claimed to convey the voice of the millions of Brazilian poor. On the other side, VW defended the idea that only multinational companies could furnish to Brazil the investments necessary to modernize agriculture and increase food production.

Even before the emergence of the question of the seasonal workers, a debate had taken place between these two visions of development, during a podium discussion organized by AK3W in Recklinghausen in November 1982. Titled "Brazil – Progress for Whom?" the debate had, as guests, Peter Klein as well as two Catholic priests from the Recklinghausen region.[224] Otto Adams and Bernhard Henning, a VW reseller in Recklinghausen, had been invited by Thomas Hax as representatives of the business world. Harsh censure against the VW policy in Brazil came from the public and the religious participants: they accused multinational concerns of collaboration with the dictatorship, and designated the automobile firms as structurally co-responsible for the social imbalances that were the plague of Brazil. Peter Klein summed up that "VW is a bracket that blocks the socioeconomic progress in Brazil." Adams expressed an exactly contrary stance. The industrialization by automobile companies, he said, had

---

[222] Hax-Schoppenhorst and Möller, "Nestverweis für schräge Vögel."
[223] *Brasilien Nachrichten* (84), 1984.
[224] "Not in Brasilien schlägt Wellen im Revier."

enabled the enhancement of the workers' living standards, and, with its ranching project, VW would help respond to Brazilian food needs.

Adams was quite alone defending this business-friendly vision of development in the podium discussion at Recklinghausen. He remained angry at Hax for having placed him in a position of ideological isolation.[225] In July 1983, Hax received a letter from two other VW executives, accusing him of unfairness toward VW's contribution to Brazilian development.[226] After having recommended Hax put his "preconceived ideas" aside, they added: "Maybe then even you would be able to recognize the extent of cultured lifestyle and humanitarian progress that European firms have brought to Brazil," and finished the letter with a provocative question: "What is making you so blind?" Quite violent in contrast to the diplomatic style that VW had adopted until then, this letter illustrated the growing embarrassment of Wolfsburg with respect to Cristalino. Once again, Hax did not restrain himself from circulating the piece. The Third World House in Bielefeld published and commented on the whole exchange, while Peter Klein wrote an article in *Brasilien Nachrichten* out of the polemic, titled "What Is Making VW so Blind?" Morally condemning VW's "ignorance of the human misery and suffering," he asked: "What is trying to open our eyes?" and answered, referring to the priests of the CPT: "the initiative of courageous men from the Catholic Church."[227] Indeed, the conflict between Third World solidarity groups and VW in Germany also became a battle over Christian values.

Advocating the compatibility between "beneficial economy" and Christianity, VW increasingly answered the critiques by trying to occupy the terrain of moral values and demonstrating that benevolent businessmen were better Christians than was, for example, a Marxist priest such as Rezende. Rezende's "calumnious" accusations, the VW executives said, were an insult to Christian dignity. For Brügger, "Especially from the Church, one would expect that the truth be defended," and the Church should always stay "away from politics" anyway.[228] Two VW commentators, writing to a reader of *Publik-Forum* to persuade him that the accusations against the CVRC were pure gossip, also stressed that "All this is even more regrettable insofar as here it is apparently a representative of the Church [Rezende] who is working with inadmissible

[225] Adams to Hax, 1981–3, in Arbeitsgruppe Brasilien, *Die Farm am Amazonas*, 32–5.
[226] Hornig and Wetzel to Hax, July 12, 1983, Arbeitsgruppe Brasilien, *Die Farm am Amazonas*, 35.
[227] *Brasilien Nachrichten* (81), 1983.
[228] "Fazenda Vale do Rio Cristalino, Volkswagen nimmt Stellung zu Anklagen."

methods."[229] Similar attacks were addressed to Thomas Hax by the VW representatives, who wrote him: "Until now we have presumed that you were acting out of noble motivations. But today we unfortunately have to fear that you are turning out to be a bigot who in reality resembles the historic destroyers of Christian thought."[230]

To show that, by contrast, VW was faithful to Christian principles, the company management looked for allies within the Church hierarchy, against the partisans of liberation theology. The task was not very difficult, for leftist engaged, pacifist, and Third World–solidarity Christians had been irritating the German Catholic elite – especially the Central Committee of German Catholics – at least since 1967–8, when certain parishes expressed their sympathy for subversive student movements.[231] Tensions between conservative Church officials and progressive parochial associations had become frequent even locally, for example, in St. Peters, Recklinghausen. When AK3W became omnipresent in the local press, the parish representatives began to find the association too visible, especially in comparison with the parish itself.[232] The activists' conversion to political reflection and shock actions had also led them to criticize the parish hierarchy, its static conception of the liturgy, and its principle of avoiding political topics during the service. Volkswagen began to exploit these tensions within the Church to secure a Christian legitimacy for itself in the conflict over the CVRC.

Wolfgang Sauer himself engaged in this process, especially during a symposium organized by the Vatican in November 1985 in the papal university, Urbaniana, in Rome, in which the VW chief spoke out in favor of a business-friendly Church.[233] The "dialog" at Urbaniana – from which Catholic NGOs such as Misereor or Mission, but also liberation theologians, were excluded – was dedicated to the ethics of German companies in the Third World. The symposium guests were essentially bankers and company chiefs, but also representatives from the German conservative parties CDU/CSU, whose Konrad Adenauer foundation sponsored the meeting. More than a dialog, it turned out to be a rout of the

---

[229] Strömel and Hertel to Baber, November 12, 1985, in *Brasilien Nachrichten* (93), 1986, 38–9.

[230] Hornig and Wetzel to Hax, July 12, 1983, in Arbeitsgruppe Brasilien, ed. *Die Farm am Amazonas*, 35.

[231] Lepp, "Zwischen Konfrontation und Kooperation," 13.

[232] Hax-Schoppenhorst and Möller, "Nestverweis für schräge Vögel."

[233] For this and the following, see "Römisches Symposium über die Verantwortung für die Zukunft der Weltwirtschaft," *Orientierung*, December 15–31, 1985.

market-friendly area of the German Catholic Church. Indeed, during the meeting, a ceremony was organized in which Cardinal Höffner, chairman of the German Episcopal Conference, distributed papal decorations to a number of prestigious businessmen – the president and the vice president of the German businessmen confederation both received the Order of St. Gregory, the highest Catholic decoration.

Sauer and his Amazonian farms were the stars of the meeting. In a greatly applauded speech, he invited the VW critics to come to the ranch and see for themselves how Cristalino benefited Brazilian rural workers.[234] He attacked these "pretending believers" who pushed the Church to see in the concentration of economic power an instrument of exploitation of the weak. He insisted that the "economy" actually furnished daily food for billions of human beings, especially in Brazil, where foreign capital had created "hundreds of thousands of jobs."[235] He finished his speech with a vibrant call to the Brazilian Church, in the name of shared Christian values: "We cannot understand that a part of the Church in Brazil joined the side of the communists," and, to the address of the German Third World movement, he added that "We feel sad that even notoriously false affirmations are brought to public opinion in Europe, in order to arouse hostile behaviors." VW's defense strategy, in sum, had not changed. Even several years after the so-called slavery scandal, the company stuck to the same argument as during the 1970s; it continued to present the CVRC as a humanitarian project. The German political context, however, had changed, as we will see in the next section, with some voices calling into question the German development model.

Cristalino in Parliament: The Political Debate in Lower Saxony

Shortly before the forced labor scandal occurred, two major changes in German politics modified the context of reception of Third World topics. In September 1982, divisions between social democrats and liberals (FDP) over economic policy led to the dissolution of the center-left federal government and its replacement by a conservative-liberal coalition under the leadership of the Christian-democrat Helmut Kohl. Seen as close to business circles, the new government spawned hostility within the Third Worldist movement, not only because of its alignment

---

[234] *Niedersächsischer Landtag. Stenographischer Bericht, 96. Sitzung. Hannover, den 12. Dezember 1985,* 9154.

[235] "Römisches Symposium über die Verantwortung für die Zukunft der Weltwirtschaft."

with U.S. international policy, but also because of its German-centered conception of solidarity. According to this conception, only Third World countries involved in business with Germany deserved development aid.[236] The Kohl government's friendly relations with several Third World dictatorships, as well as its ideological aversion to leftist activism and extra-parliamentary protest, also exacerbated the polarization between state policy and social movement. Paradoxically, the coming to power of a government considered hostile to international solidarity had the effect of remobilization of the activists and triggered a growing engagement by the progressive Church and the trade unions together with the movement of Third World solidarity.[237]

The second political event impacting the solidarity movement was the emergence of the ecologist party Die Grünen (Greens), whose success in the elections of 1983 led to the formation of a green faction in the federal parliament, the Bundestag. The entry of the Greens into the political game ushered in a problematic politicization of German "Third Worldism."[238] Created in the late 1970s, the young party had partly come from the new social movements (particularly the feminist, peace and students" groups) of the 1960s, which themselves had largely constituted the ground for the emergence of a Third World concern in politics. Some green MPs such as Gabriele Gottwald had come into first contact with political activism within the committees of solidarity with Latin America during the 1970s. Green electoral programs in the early 1980s contained aggressive measures against the presence of multinational firms in Third World countries such as the "interdiction of overexploitation of foreign resources by German firms," the "step by step withdrawal of the 'Multis' from their interdependence with Third World countries," as well as a redefinition of Global North–Global South economic relations in which "the interests of poor countries should be taken into account before all things."[239] According to Werner and Rössel, although most of the Greens' propositions on the topic were vague and perceived as unrealistic, the parliamentary work of the party from 1983 gave a completely new angle to development policy debates in the Bundestag, whose tone became less technocratic and less Eurocentric.[240]

---

[236] Balsen and Rössel, *Hoch die internationale Solidarität*, 386–7.
[237] Olejniczak, "Dritte-Welt-Bewegung," 328–9.
[238] Balsen and Rössel, *Hoch die internationale Solidarität*, 510.
[239] Green electoral program for 1980: www.boell.de/downloads/stiftung/1980_Bundes programm.pdf, access date May 27, 2012.
[240] Balsen and Rössel: *Hoch die internationale Solidarität*, 510.

On the one hand, the Greens' contribution to political debate constituted an undreamed-of evolution for the solidarity movement. On the other hand, the relation between the Greens and extra-parliamentary solidarity groups was not necessarily based on trust. While some deputies of the party collaborated regularly with the grassroots solidarity movements, there was no systematic partnership between Third World groups and the Greens.[241] Many activists regretted the absence of a complete programmatic conception of the Greens in the domains of development and foreign policies. Others were, in general, skeptical about the fact that the participation in parliamentary politics might lead to any social change, especially in view of a possible future alliance of the Greens with the SPD, a party that many activists considered sympathetic to Third World exploitation. However, the political conditions introduced by the federal elections of 1983, which confirmed popular support of the Kohl government, favored a rapprochement between solidarity groups and the Greens. While in the 1970s, the tendency of Third World activism had been directly to lobby the social-liberal government in power to obtain changes in foreign and economic policies, this time the conservative-liberal majority was much less open to dialog with NGOs. In this context, the Green factions in the federal and state parliaments became a political receptacle of the associative world, which made them an object of both projection and frustration for the Third World solidarity movement.

In such a political configuration, it should come as no surprise that the first parliamentary debate about the controversial practices of VW in Brazil was brought up by the Green Party, at the end of 1985, in the parliament of Lower Saxony, a state holding 20 percent of VW's shares. It is useful to add here that the ecology party and VW were hostile to each other. The Greens had an execrable reputation in Wolfsburg, because they defended projects unfavorable to the growth of the automobile industry, such as a massive transfer of goods and people transportation from road to rail, the development of public transport, and a drastic reduction of speed limits on highways.[242] At the end of May 1983, VW management distributed within the company 4,000 copies of a document titled "The Greens – The Steady Way towards Catastrophe" (*"Die Grünen – der sichere Weg in die Katastrophe"*), which warned about the consequences of the Greens' growing political influence for the future of the automobile industry. The document, to which the state government of Lower Saxony publicly

---

[241] Ibid., 518–20.
[242] www.boell.de/downloads/stiftung/1980_Bundesprogramm.pdf

paid lip service, contained extravagant accusations.[243] For example, it said that the party had received a 400 million deutschmark fund from the East German state and predicted that the implementation of the Green political program would lead to collective suicides.

Probably both out of political conviction and in retaliation for VW's aggressive critiques, the Greens undertook several initiatives in the parliament of Lower Saxony, which aimed at questioning the company's practices in the Third World. On June 27, 1985, they addressed to the government of Lower Saxony, whose representatives sat on the VW board of supervision, a parliamentary question expressing concerns about the responsibility of VW in the disequilibrium of Brazil's balance of payment.[244] The Greens were not the only political actors worried about VW's deteriorating reputation in Brazil: the damning reports about the Cristalino ranch, published in national magazines such as *Der Spiegel*, *Stern*, or *Publik-Forum*, had spawned irritation within the ranks of the CDU and the SPD. Johann Bruns, president of the SPD in Lower Saxony, issued a parliamentary question in August 1984 to the state government accusing VW of "environmentally destructive attacks on the rain forest" – curiously, the text only tackled the topic of deforestation without talking about the exploitation of the *peões*.[245] The chief of the CDU state parliamentary faction, Werner Remmers, was much more direct when he learned about Rezende's accusations against Cristalino. He met his co-party member and minister of finance of Lower Saxony, Burkhard Ritz, and urged, "But you guys are in the supervising board [of VW]; do something about that! What's actually happening out there?"[246] Remmers also shared these concerns publicly. During the opening ceremony of a *Misereor* charity campaign, he insisted that "it is a shame when the foreign subsidiaries of German firms, such as VW do Brasil, behave under the local regime like they would never be allowed to behave here in this country."[247]

[243] Theo Romahn, "Die Grünen, der sichere Weg in die Katastrophe. Leitfaden für Mitglieder der automobilen Gesellschaft," ed. Initiative Automobile Gesellschaft (Düsseldorf: Drittes Jahrtausend, 1983); *Niedersächsischer Landtag. Stenographischer Bericht. 33. Sitzung. Hannover, den 14. Oktober 1983* (Hannover: Niedersächsischer Landtag, 1983), 2941.

[244] Niedersächsischer Landtag, 10. Wahlperiode, Drucksache 10/4522, Erich von Hofe, June 27, 1985, "Die wirtschaftlichen Regelungen mit Brasilien."

[245] Niedersächsischer Landtag, 10. Wahlperiode, Drucksache 10/3128, Johann Bruns, August 29, 1984, "140 000 ha Farm des VW-Konzerns in Brasilien."

[246] *Niedersächsischer Landtag. Stenographischer Bericht*, 96, 9154.

[247] "Sklavenarbeit und Folter auf der VW-Farm?" *Brasilien Nachrichten* (79), 1983. Though these were personal initiatives, it is of note that voices from conservative organizations

When, in November 1985, the Green faction of the state parliament posed a priority parliamentary question (*große Anfrage*) to the Lower Saxon government concerning VW do Brasil, which was followed by a parliamentary debate, Remmers – who, in the meantime, had become the state's minister of justice – remained silent. This was probably out of party discipline, since the Green question implicitly accused the CDU state government of conniving with VW's controversial practices.[248] The debate on the "Policies of the State of Lower Saxony toward the Volkswagen Subsidiary VW do Brasil" took place on December 12, 1985.[249] Under the keyword "responsibility," Green speaker Horst Schörhusen evoked the short-term agricultural vision of the VW ranch, insisting that the transformation of transitional rain forest into pastures had unpredictable ecological consequences. Making the link between deforestation and forced labor, he also denounced that "VW do Brasil is linked with subcontractors, which make quite dirty business with the contract workers who process the clearance," stressing that VW was "morally co-responsible" because "who profits from the workforce of the contract workers is also responsible for their living and working conditions."[250]

The question of "responsibility" posed by the Greens was also addressed to Germany as a whole and its responsibility in the Third World's social misery. Schörhusen argued that Germany was responsible for what its firms did in the Third World.[251] He added that Lower Saxony should watch out for the consequences of the investments of its companies on the living standards of southern populations. "We are not only interested in the profit made by VW do Brasil," he said, "but also in the question, for whom is this a profit?" The Lower Saxon Greens also presented the VW *fazenda* as a wrong model of development, based on land concentration, whereas the Cristalino estate could, with an alternative model, give labor and food to 3,000 families. They saw in Cristalino the model of a "particularly capital-intensive, ecosystem-consuming and

---

also took position against VW's policy in Brazil. A British member of the European Parliament from the Tory Party wrote a protest letter to VW in which he harshly attacked the system of forced labor at Cristalino: CPT Belém, Adams and Brandes to Simpson, February 13, 1985.

[248] Niedersächsischer Landtag, 10. Wahlperiode, Drucksache 10/5118, Jürgen Trittin, November 19, 1985, "Politik des Landes gegenüber der Volkswagentochter VW do Brasil."

[249] *Niedersächsischer Landtag. Stenographischer Bericht, 96. Sitzung,* 9152–4.

[250] *Die Grünen informieren,* December 11, 1985.

[251] For this and the following, see *Niedersächsischer Landtag. Stenographischer Bericht, 96. Sitzung,* 1952–4, 59–61.

unsocial form of economy." Besides, the Green's speeches paid tribute to Rezende and insisted on the credibility of the locally based priest. Their faction's chief, Jürgen Trittin, accused the state government of "trusting more the assertions of a VW manager than the declarations of a priest," in complete contradiction with the CDU's claim to be a "*Christian-democratic union*."

The reaction of the state parliament to the interventions of the Greens took on the tone of a sacred alliance for German industry, with the other party factions largely reproducing the advocacy discourse of VW. Just as VW had been saying for two and a half years, CDU Minister of Finance Burkhard Ritz recognized that "there have been problems between intermediary employers and workers," but considered that this was all "outside the area of influence of VW." Ritz not only repeated the words of the VW executives during his speech, he also had previously transmitted to the parliament members a written answer to the Greens' question, which he recognized had been directly written in Wolfsburg. Schörhusen claimed this was "a scandal" while a SPD speaker, shocked, argued that it was "the first time in this parliament that the government answers a parliamentary question with a position paper coming from the executive suite of a company." Indeed, this method demonstrated the strong imbrications between governmental institutions and the VW Company in Germany.

These imbrications partly explained why the conservatives and liberals at power at the federal level as well as in Lower Saxony never accepted as valid any critique against the VW ranch. Ritz, for example, did not want to call VW's probity into question. Referring to Sauer's intervention three weeks before at Urbaniana, he saw the farm as an operation of benevolence. He further argued: "For me, the declarations of a successful businessman who leads VW do Brasil carry much more weight than all the polemics that can arise anywhere in the world." VW represented the German economy in Brazil and by advocating the company, Ritz thought he was defending the reputation of Germany in the world: he was shocked that the Greens dared to humiliate "a German name, a melodious German name, namely VW." In fact, the parliament members of the CDU and the FDP, in reply to the Greens' critiques, praised the positive role of German companies in Brazil, saying, like the VW executives used to say, that these companies were a "motor of social progress." "Defaming Volkswagen," for the FDP faction in the state parliament, meant attacking a company dedicated to the interests of the German workers, and thus coming out to attack these workers. For the CDU, the accusations Rezende made about

Cristalino were a demonstration of the "intolerable way" in which the German companies were "discriminated against in the Second and Third World." Even the SPD refused to attack the VW ranch, for its speaker, Willi Arens, considered that he could not "express a judgment" from the position and the place wherein he was speaking. This careful position is comprehensible insofar as the VW ranch had been planned and opened in the mid-1970s with the support of an SPD-ruled government. Arens's speech, far from calling the model of the VW ranch into question, suggested that Cristalino could become a springboard for agrarian research in which the state of Lower Saxony could invest its knowledge.

With the debate in the Lower Saxon parliament, it was the first time that the forced labor affair at Cristalino was extensively discussed within German politics. Some Brazilian solidarity actors, especially members of Brasilieninitiative and AK3W-St Peter, had been associated with the preparation of the Greens' initiative. More generally, the Brazilian solidarity networks had been previously informed of it.[252] At the beginning, the anti-Cristalino activists were enthusiastic about the idea. The ILA published an article announcing that the association was "excited" about knowing the answer of the Lower Saxon government to the Greens' parliamentary question. In the end, things did not go exactly as the solidarity activists had hoped.

Schörhusen, the Greens' speaker, delivered a sometimes confused speech that betrayed an imprecise vision of the Amazon, probably based on images circulating in the mass media. For example he affirmed that on its ranch, VW treated hundreds of "Indians" in the Amazon "like slaves."[253] This example shows that the help of political actors who were not specialized in the topic was both an opportunity for the protest movement against Cristalino to gain visibility, and, at the same time, an obstacle to a clear explanation being provided to German decision makers and citizens. As Amazonian forced labor was not an easy topic, the Greens in the parliament of Lower Saxony made a big speech against Volkswagen do Brasil (VWB) in which forced labor at Cristalino was the central example, but not the only one. Basically, the Greens used the case as an opportunity to validate their party-founding theses that social inequalities, global disequilibrium, democratic deficit, and environmental destruction were all intertwined phenomena. They also took advantage

---

[252] GPTEC V8.30., "Alberto" to Rezende, December 12, 1985; "VW do Brasil – Anfrage," *ILA INFO* (89), 1985.
[253] *Die Grünen informieren*, December 11, 1985.

of being in possession of a "hot topic" thanks to their dialog with the associative world, in order to affirm their role as the agenda-setting, subversive force of the parliament.

The generalist approach the Greens took gave the members of Brasilieninitiative the impression that the party was not giving the problem of forced labor the attention it deserved, and that it appropriated the long-term, intensive, and difficult work of the association in a self-interested and amateurish way. In the end the Greens' action provoked both frustration and hope, as is clear in a letter written by an activist of Brasilieninitiative to Rezende about the preparation and the unfolding of the debate:

The Greens called me and I indicated Peter [Klein] and Sylvia [Ehlers] as witnesses and sources of documents. Besides, I wrote a long letter, correcting a series of inaccuracies in the text [prepared by the Greens] and giving them a couple of tips. Unfortunately they (the Greens)[254] did not properly prepare themselves (Peter Klein had sent them more than 100 pages of photocopies) and due to the arbitrariness of the president of the parliamentary session ... the Greens found themselves in a very weak position, without ammunition against the accusations of the government party. Their fault, they left everything for the last moment and almost did not read the documents. Sylvia and Peter were really angry. But in any case the question was raised, maybe it will have consequences.... In the end I think the result was positive.[255]

On the one hand, the Greens' simplifying approach was the price for the "Cristalino affair" to reach a large audience. On the other hand, the Brasilieninitiative activists were not necessarily seeing the gap between their expectations as associative actors and the reduced margin of power of a small opposition party. Because of the greatly reduced size of their faction in comparison to that of the CDU and the SPD, the Greens only had five minutes available to argue their point of view and five more minutes to comment on the government's response – the remaining speaking time of the forty-minute debate was distributed among the bigger factions.[256] Another problem was the lack of credibility of the Greens on the German political scene, where they were considered undisciplined and unreliable. This controversial image forbade the Lower Saxon SPD to support too expressively the Greens' parliamentary initiatives. If it were to express proximity with the Greens, the SPD might lose its most moderate voters. But the Greens' alleged irresponsibility was also a good excuse

---

[254] The parentheses are from the original text.
[255] GPTEC V8.30., "Alberto" to Rezende, December 12, 1985.
[256] *Niedersächsischer Landtag. Stenographischer Bericht*, 96. Sitzung, 9156.

for the SPD not to look into a tricky political subject. Because of its historical link with VW, and the unavoidable weight of automobile workers in the party's Lower Saxon electorate, it would have been a perilous game for the SPD to throw accusations against the company.

Thus, during the parliamentary debate of December 12, Arens regretted not to be in a position to express a judgment on forced labor at Cristalino "because the Greens, of course, present assertions, which cannot even be proved."[257] The Greens' status as the black sheep of German politics was confirmed at the end of the parliamentary debate, as the president of the assembly, a member of the CDU, decided to take a disciplinary sanction against Schörhusen on the ground of "verbal injury" against the state government.[258] Schörhusen was sanctioned (as Green MPs regularly used to be) because he had designated as "a complete lie" Ritz's assertion that the accusations against the VW ranch were based on gossip.

For the activists working against forced labor at Cristalino, letting the Greens represent their cause in a parliamentary debate was comparable to attempting to transmit information about Cristalino to the mass media. On the one hand, party initiatives and press articles enabled a larger public to be sensitized, and pressure to be put on political decision makers. On the other hand, it could also mean losing the complex topic of debt bondage in a broader, often cheap "cosmopolitanist" discourse, built on commonplaces such as the "Amazon as the lungs of the earth," the "persecuted indigenous tribes," or the "starving Third World," as Amazonian problems were often treated in the press and in the discourse of political parties or big NGOs. In any case, such a step was necessary to compete with the powerful communication machine of a multinational company.

Understanding the role of public opinion and globalized media networks in pushing forward a political cause was not a simple concession given to modernity by the Brazilian and German activists advocating the *peões* of Cristalino. The networks of denunciation and protest against forced labor at Cristalino, in fact, were also the result of processes that VW and SUDAM themselves had sought to appropriate in their discourse of modernization. These latter claimed to integrate the Amazon into global economic exchanges, import European know-how into Brazil, build a city in the middle of the jungle, bring an isolated and wild area under the control of the Brazilian central state, and optimize farming production with the help of the newest scientific findings. They claimed to do

[257] Ibid., 9152.
[258] Ibid., 9160–1.

all this in the name of development, as a path toward universal welfare. The activists against forced labor were not much different, as they used these very processes that the CVRC claimed to incarnate: they resorted to transnational exchange of knowledge and information, sought to link urban and rural problems in a integrative model of Brazil's social inequalities, sought alliances within some parts of the centralized state's institutions, and resorted to the newest findings of natural sciences in order to link environmental issues with labor exploitation. Just as VW and SUDAM, these activists claimed to act in the name of universal welfare, but they used the keyword of solidarity rather than development.

Whereas the CVRC was founded in the early 1970s on the grounds of a clear delimitation between modernity and archaism, the social conflicts on labor conditions at the CVRC led to a complete blurring of this delimitation. In fact, the actors protesting against Cristalino, from the Amazonian clearing workers to the German Third World solidarity groups, attacked what they saw as the incoherence of a dominant discourse of modernization, which produced the contrary of what it had announced it would do. By constructing a movement against "modern slavery," these actors tried to deconstruct the discourse of Amazonian modernization elaborated by the state and the big firms. The CVRC increasingly appeared as the incarnation of a (paradoxically) out-of-date modernity, working hand in hand with archaic practices. Rezende, a central actor in the denunciation of forced labor, summed up this strategy of deconstruction in a significant sentence:

The Volkswagen Company, which uses the computer, the 21st century, the furthest developed capitalism, lives with forms of work from the 18th century, and this, every day. It is impressive how this can live together: high technology, hyper-developed capitalism, with forms of slavery in a Fazenda.[259]

---

[259] Ricardo Rezende Figueira, "Volkswagen – von der Zusammenarbeit des 21. Jahrhunderts mit dem 18. Jahrhundert," *Brasilien Nachrichten* (1983), 62.

5

Cristalino's Unhappy Ending

> The farm as well as a neighboring slaughterhouse, in which we participated together with a series of renowned Brazilian firms, turned out to be a financial disaster.... Out of a tax-saving development model of the Brazilian state, we got a ruinous affair causing a loss of several hundred million.[1]
>
> *Carl H. Hahn, former executive of VW, 2005*

"Repudiated by the New Republic": VW Goes, Cristalino Stays

The Sale of the Ranch between Economic and Political Motives

In its February 1987 issue, the VW magazine, *Autogramm*, announced the end of the project to its readers. "Bush-farm and slaughterhouse," so the magazine stated, had "been sold off as a result of an agreement between VWB and Ford do Brasil."[2] In fact, the two Brazilian companies, leaders in the car industry with 40 percent and 25 percent, respectively, of the national market share, merged in 1987 into the biggest holding in Latin American history, named Autolatina.[3] The economic crisis of the early 1980s, besides diminishing the middle-class consumer market, had been followed by the adoption of governmental price controls in Brazil, confirmed in February 1986 by an anti-inflation plan including a general freeze on the final prices of goods.[4] This conjectural factor, together with the fragmentation of the market caused by the rise of

---

[1] Hahn, *Meine Jahre mit Volkswagen*, 57.
[2] "Buschfarm und Schlachthof verkauft," *Autogramm*, February 1987.
[3] Doretto, *Wolfgang Sauer*, 393.
[4] Baer, *The Brazilian Economy*, 111.

recently arrived brands such as Fiat, had led VW and Ford to abandon the perspective of returning to the levels of profit of the previous decade. The two firms actually complemented each other, because they were not directly competing in the same market segments. As such, the creation of Autolatina could be interpreted as a survival reflex at a complex economic conjuncture, where the parent companies in Germany and the United States were already thinking about withdrawing from Brazil. The joint venture, which was Sauer's idea, imposed itself as the only rational way of saving the two Brazilian branches, by mutualizing large parts of the operating and production costs.[5]

In this event, the unstable placements of both companies had to be cancelled in order to enable the necessary reinforcement of Autolatina's finance capacity. Cristalino and Atlas were directly concerned by this measure, as they had turned out to regularly need capital assistance. According to *Autogramm*, VW could no longer afford to sustain such projects, which would inevitably necessitate supplementary subsidies in the future.[6] Although, in exchange, Ford was already negotiating the sale of its domestic electrical firm Philco, invoking Autolatina as a reason for ending the CVRC project was hardly credible. This simple bookkeeping explanation contradicted the strong emotional investment of VWB's leaders in the farm project and its high political significance in the Brazilian context. As mentioned earlier, Sauer had been receiving admonitions from Wolfsburg recommending a drastic reduction of VWB's investments since the early 1980s. Therefore, if VWB's problems of liquidity and its need to concentrate financially on its core activities were nothing new, why should they suddenly become a pretext to sell the CVRC?

Autolatina was not the cause of Cristalino's sale, but rather an ideal opportunity to get rid of a project, which VW wanted – and needed – to stop for completely other reasons. The considerable media noise provoked by the alliance between VW and Ford enabled the end of the ranch to be turned into a discrete side event, for which VW did not have to justify itself very much. The true reasons for the sale of Cristalino were much less glorious than the Autolatina project. The CVRC bore the consequences of the political turmoil in which a section of Brazilians was rising against land concentration and, concurrently, in which the fight against modern forced labor was being institutionalized. But the most

---

[5] Doretto, *Wolfgang Sauer*, 393.
[6] "Buschfarm und Schlachthof verkauft."

decisive factor was that VW in Germany no longer wanted to support a project that jeopardized its corporate reputation. Therefore, when it became clear that the Amazonian projects would never be financially viable, there were no arguments left for VW to further invest money in them.

The fall of the military regime created a climate in which criticizing the political choices of the deposed government had become fashionable. Since the victory of the PMDB candidate, Tancredo Neves, in the indirect presidential election of January 1985, Brazil was governed by a civilian government, and a constituent assembly was elected in 1986. When, weakened by illness and at age seventy-five, Neves died before his inauguration day, his vice president, José Sarney, a late dropout from the former authoritarian majority, became president with the paradoxical task of having to assume a left-wing agenda, including a large land reform. Sarney even created a new ministry entirely dedicated to this reform, at the head of which he named an advocate from Pará indicated by the CNBB and reputed for his sympathy for the rural workers' movement.[7] In May 1985, at the Fourth CONTAG Congress, the president announced the National Plan of Land Reform (PNRA) in front of 4,000 rural workers; the Plan promised to settle 1,400,000 families in four years thanks to the expropriation of unproductive *latifundio* owners. The new political establishment thought of the land reform as a means of asserting its popular legitimacy in spite of an economic context marked by historically high inflation – 235 percent in 1985 – which penalized the purchase power of the people. Having himself favored land concentration as a governor of the northeastern state of Maranhão, Sarney was politically at the right of the new governing personnel and did not personally lean toward land reform. As it later turned out, he would do nothing concrete during his term to accelerate structural change in the land property system. When he left power in 1989, PNRA had settled fewer than 90,000 peasant families.[8]

Yet, Sarney had to answer an increasing demand for land reform, measurable through the constant presence of the topic in the media, within parliaments, and all over rural Brazil, where numerous demonstrations and invasions of properties by landless groups were taking place. Over the months following the PNRA announcement, 50,000 families participated

---

[7] Bernardo Mançano Fernandes, *A formação do MST no Brasil* (Petrópolis: Vozes, 2000), 195.

[8] Bastiaan Reydon, Ludwig Plata, and Héctor Escobar, "Intervención en el mercado de tierras Brasileño: análisis de la experiencia reciente," *Debate Agrario*, no. 31 (2000), 179.

in land occupations, often coordinated by the MST.[9] Because he was not willing to rapidly approve large governmental operations of expropriation, the president reacted by identifying certain scapegoats to feed the expectations of public opinion. In March 1985, he indicated his disposition to revise the situation concerning big projects in the Amazon, which had concentrated land with the help of fiscal incentives. He emphasized the examples of Volkswagen and of Daniel K. Ludwig's Jari project. A journalist from the daily *O estado de São Paulo* depicted this strategy as a perilous xenophobic move, characterizing the aversion for foreign business brought up, he thought, by the new democracy:

Similar to the 1950s, the land problem is starting once again to be handled emotionally and not according to wise economic and social criteria. Those who proceed that way are interested in knowing neither what useful things VW is realizing for Amazônia Legal, nor what it intends to do there in terms of grain and meat production as well as reforestation. It is as if the name Volkswagen were enough to be repudiated by the New Republic.[10]

VWB itself felt besieged by the surrounding hostility toward big agribusiness. In June 1985, after an audience with Governor Jáder in Belém, Sauer felt it was necessary to make the surprising announcement that he was favorable to the principle of a land reform, while he insisted that the correct way of doing it was "not to touch productive areas."[11] At the same time, he said, "unproductive areas bring no good to the country" and their owners deserved to be expropriated. To preserve Cristalino from popular anger, Sauer was thus joining up a foundational idea of the Brazilian left. The inefficient and undesirable form of farming in the Amazon was no longer that of small peasants, which the VW publications had been so far describing as unable to rationally manage a crop of land. Cristalino invented for itself an enemy, which it shared with the landless movement, namely the unproductive, traditional rural oligarchies and land speculators, against which VW could, after all, claim that its "modern ranch" still made sense. Unfortunately, this discourse stood in contradiction with previous VW positions, notably expressed through the voice of Brügger, and such contradiction made it particularly difficult to erase Cristalino's reputation as a symbol of land inequalities. Well aware of the danger, the firm's executives started to think in early 1986 about selling Cristalino in order to prevent the problems that might result

---

[9] Branford and Rocha, *Cutting the Wire*, 32.
[10] "Reforma da agricultura," *O estado de São Paulo*, March 26, 1985.
[11] "Presidente da Volkswagen apoia o plano," *A folha de São Paulo*, June 6, 1985.

from a future occupation of the estate by landless groups, who might benefit from popular or even governmental support.[12]

As a product of this context, an even more crushing motive to put an end to VW's ranching activities was the accusation of "slavery" sticking to the company, which made it impossible to restore the social-friendly image that Cristalino once had. Admittedly, VW had stopped resorting to the worst *gatos* in Araguaia, Abilio, Hermínio, and Chico – the arrest of the latter by the police actually helped make this decision.[13] Nevertheless, in 1986, a spokesperson from the Land Reform Ministry (MIRAD) in Brasília informed German reporters: "We are still receiving complaints about violation of the labor law at VW."[14] The same year, the CPT received new testimonies of *peões* asserting they had been victims of forced labor at Cristalino. MIRAD even published a list of farms explicitly accused of having practiced "slave labor," including the VW ranch.[15] At that point, even Brügger admitted in front of an English ranch visitor that "certain forms of slavery" might have existed on the ranch. He even tried to justify debt bondage: "it was necessary to have certain control over these lazy Brazilians. They stay two or three months in hotels, accumulating debts. Someone comes and pays the debts. A contract of two or three months is made and they can leave only after."[16] To be sure, things started to be truly embarrassing for VW as Brügger, transgressing the most elementary rules of corporate communication, pronounced similar words in an interview to *Der Spiegel*, one of Germany's leading press magazines: "the peões lounge around the villages, leave people to pay their debts and then try to clear off, hence it might happen that the Gatos get a bit vigorous. We're living here on the edges of society. It is a big mistake to evaluate the regrettable living conditions of Brazilian seasonal workers with European standards."[17]

That did not fit the images held by VW in Wolfsburg: the company had not proclaimed itself as a modernizer of the Amazon to accept a decade later the idea of flirting with the "edges of society." True

---

[12] "Medo de invasão," *Istoé*, March 5, 1986.

[13] "Der Sicherheitsbeauftragte der VW-Farm (Interview)," *Brasilien Nachrichten* (93), 1986.

[14] "Volkswagen. In einer Randgesellschaft," *Der Spiegel*, November 11, 1986.

[15] MIRAD, "Conflitos de terra: trabalho escravo" (Brasília: MIRAD, 1986).

[16] CPT Belém, Keith Hayward, March 25, 1985, "Algumas informações sobre a Cia. Vale do Rio Cristalino." *Gatos* often paid for a couple of hotel nights spent by the *peões* in recruiting towns, before demanding back the money and using this debt as a pretext to hold workers captive.

[17] "Volkswagen. In einer Randgesellschaft."

enough, Sauer's presentations about Cristalino at the German board of management meetings used not to arouse much reaction.[18] Until the mid-1980s Wolfsburg had simply chosen to leave him managing the project without intervening, probably because VW senior management was simply not interested in the topic, which made no particular sense in VW's global strategy. Meanwhile, things changed as the forced labor problems of the ranch threatened to ruin the image of the company in Brazil and even in Germany, where well-networked activists of the Third World solidarity movement were on the lookout for Brügger's next gaffe. Wolfsburg began to lose patience in 1983 as a call for the boycott of the company's products was launched by German activist Thomas Hax. Of course, this initiative was a drop in the ocean, as Hax was widely unknown to the millions of VW consumers. Still, it symbolically turned the ranch into a direct threat for VW's core industry – the automobile. The simple idea of it was enough to make the ranch a potential danger for the company: Sauer's eccentric Amazonian dreams could be tolerated only as long as they did not disturb VW's serious car business. With the call for boycott, the impermeability between the two things had been transgressed, and on the occasion of his next trip to Germany Sauer was convoked to Wolfsburg, where his superiors told him that it was time to think about getting rid of the Amazonian operation.[19]

While in the following years Sauer did his best to delay the decision of closing the ranch, Brügger, as always, made the matter even worse. As he understood that the Germans were not ready to continue backing the project, he progressively enclosed himself in an attitude of resentment. As a ranch visitor noted in 1986: "Brügger sees himself surrounded by a hostile world: in Brazil by the 'communist' church, in Germany by the Greens, by the matrix in Wolfsburg, which refuses new investments."[20] The growing gap between Brügger and Wolfsburg illustrated how the German company had morally abandoned the CVRC. Wolfsburg's declining support for the project was the main reason that pushed VWB to sell the ranch.

Finally, the fact that VW's Amazonian engagement was becoming a financial disaster also explained why VW dropped it. That in May 1986 VW applied to SUDAM for a new increase in the CVRC's incentive funds

[18] VW Unternehmensarchiv 373/239/1, December 7, 1981, "Protokoll Nr.42/1981 der Sitzung des Vorstands der Volkswagenwerk AG."
[19] Doretto, *Wolfgang Sauer*, 353.
[20] GPTEC V9.11., Banderet to Figueira, July 27, 1986.

for the eighth time in twelve years illustrated the poor financial health of the project.[21] In the degraded economic climate of the 1980s, commercial perspectives for Cristalino's "ox of the future" looked nothing like they did in the previous decade, when sustained GDP growth rates seemed to announce the rise of a large middle class adopting European patterns of consumption. The country's bleak social situation had even pushed the government to freeze national meat prices at a substantially lower level than the costs of production of fattened ox at Cristalino, which lay around $300.[22] There simply existed no market in Brazil for a cattle farm managed after the pattern of such expensive modern technology. This lack of profitability had already convinced VW between 1984 and 1986 to cede about one-fifth of the CVRC's capital shares to other companies, including Ericsson do Brasil and various Brazilian banks and insurance firms.[23] Even Atlas had to suspend its production in 1986 due to the fall in demand for beef among Brazilian consumers.

Volkswagen had already taken distance from the slaughterhouse in 1985, when it had sold most of its shares to remain with only 1.9 percent of the total, while the Bradesco bank recuperated 51.3 percent of them.[24] Even more than the ranch, the Atlas factory quickly revealed itself as a financially impracticable affair, at least in the frame of VW's requirements concerning quality and technical level. An internal SUDAM report, which listed the weaknesses of the project in October 1985, left little hope regarding future chances of success.[25] Atlas's failures seemed to demonstrate that VW had learned nothing from the misfortunes of the CVRC: SUDAM blamed the project's design for a lack of consideration of the region's structural problems, such as the absence of roads and bridges and the high malaria index. A botched preliminary prospecting operation had not enabled the parties to detect the existence of a phreatic table in the subsoil of the terrain chosen to build the factory. This made it necessary to build a technical basement with extremely elevated financial costs. As a result of the project's technical delays and cost increase, most of Atlas's providers mistrusted the company's capacity to meet payment deadlines, and VW and its partners encountered constant difficulty in

[21] Arquivo do FINAM, SUDAM, 659/86, May 1986, "Parecer DAC/DAI n° 126/86-AF."
[22] "Volkswagen. In einer Randgesellschaft."
[23] Arquivo do FINAM, SUDAM, Sauer and Prange to Kayath, December 1, 1986.
[24] Arquivo do FINAM, SUDAM, October 1985, "Processo SUDAM n°004235/85 – Parecer DAP/DAI n°051/85."
[25] Arquivo do FINAM, SUDAM, October 1985, "Atlas Fligorifico [*sic*] S/A – Projeto Técnico Economico-Financeiro."

buying factory equipment as well as contracting loans. Atlas had to solicit the help of foreign creditors. But the maxi-devaluation of the Cruzeiro consequent to the crisis of the early 1980s seriously affected Atlas's capacity to repay the loans contracted in U.S. dollars, not to mention the unmanageable interest rates of the inflation-indexed IFC loans, comprised between 13 percent and 17 percent a year.[26] Since VW had acted as guarantor for these loans, it had to take responsibility for their reimbursement years after its withdrawal from the Atlas project. As former German VW executive Carl H. Hahn remembers in his memoirs: "The contracts with the International Finance Corporation (IFC) left us at the top of the debts of South America's biggest slaughterhouse."[27]

As a consequence of all these reasons, VW put its shares in the *fazenda* and slaughterhouse up for sale in 1986. The offer comprised the whole Cristalino estate, its production tools, 43,136 formed hectares of pasture, and 46,712 head of cattle, for a price of $80 million besides $12 million of debt that VW intended to transmit to the new owner.[28] No one was interested in such a disproportionate deal for a nonprofitable business with a damaged reputation. Brazil's first media consortium, O Globo, offered $10 million, a price considered risible by Brügger, who personally would not have ceded the *fazenda* for less than $30 million.[29]

In the end VW concluded a contract with the Matsubaras, a Japanese migrant family of self-made businessmen specialized in cotton production, owners of various cattle ranches and a football team in the southern state of Paraná.[30] Although the Matsubaras offered only $20 million, their business profile matched the requirements of SUDAM, which preferred VW to pass the ranch to a group experienced and interested in farming production, so that the project did not end up in the hands of land speculators.[31] The sale contract was signed on December 1, 1986; three weeks later, VW also managed to sell its remaining shares of Atlas to Ricardo Manur, owner of the Leco e Vigor milk factories.[32] On June

[26] Arquivo do FINAM, SUDAM, October 28, 1982, "Investment Agreement between Atlas Frigorifico S.A. & International Finance Corporation."

[27] Hahn, *Meine Jahre mit Volkswagen*, 57.

[28] "Volks vende fazenda com 46 mil bois na Amazônia a grupo do PR," *O estado de São Paulo*, December 11, 1986; "Saír da pecuária, um projeto da Volks," *Istoé*, September 24, 1986.

[29] GPTEC V9.11., Banderet to Figueira, July 27, 1986.

[30] "Matsubara compra a fazenda da Volkswagen no norte do Pará," *O Globo*, December 11, 1986.

[31] Arquivo do FINAM, SUDAM, December 1, 1986, "Recibo de sinal e princípio de pagamento de venda e compra de ações e outras avenças."

[32] "Volks abandona a agropecuária," *Veja*, December 24, 1986.

11, 1987, SUDAM officially validated the transfer of the CVRC's stock control from VW to the Matsubaras.[33]

So finished VW's business with the Amazon, sold off to a regional group from the south for a disappointing sum, with a cattle herd and pasture complex quantitatively broad beyond expectations and a high indebtedness in spite of the many times capital support was increased by SUDAM. The Matsubaras did not offer to start any particular modernization or even maintenance of ranch equipment. As we will see, they would prove incapable of managing VW's legacy correctly and unable – or unwilling – to fulfil the escalated payment agreed to with the German company. The failed deal between VW and the Matsubaras contained no trace of the proud showcase of development and pioneer spirit of the CVRC's beginnings. The ranch had no particularly brilliant appraisal to show off, no social accomplishment for the region, not even the basic merit of having been the only one to respect the law in a lawless place. To make matters worse, the sale of the ranch did not mean that problems were behind VW, as the "slavery" affair continued for a couple of years to stick to the company's feet.

The Long Way to Justice and the "Resolution" of the VW Case
The protagonists of the VW ranch did not disappear after VW withdrew from the Amazon: they continued to argue in tribunals. Justice tribunals in the Brazilian countryside were traditionally favorable to big landowners, especially under the military regime, when public powers tended to exert pressure inhibiting judgments that might support the claims of landless workers and thus disturb social order.[34] Therefore, as in the frame of the "slavery" scandal, complaints were raised against the CVRC to the police and – more rarely – at tribunals, neither VW nor the *peões'* defenders expected that the complainants might win their case. An open letter from the CPT denouncing violence against rural workers in the southeastern Amazon (1984) addressed to Figueiredo, Jáder, the minister for land affairs, and the governor of Goiás, illustrated this lack of faith in the ability of the judiciary institutions to fight social inequalities: "We know that in the majority of these conflicts the judges' decisions, when they exist, are almost always of a flagrant partiality."[35] Yet, the return of

---

[33] Arquivo do FINAM, SUDAM, June 11, 1987, "Resolução n° 6413."
[34] Mauricio Godinho Delgado, *Democracia e justiça: sistema judicial e construção democrática no Brasil* (São Paulo: LTr, 1993), 48.
[35] "CPT klagt an," *Brasilien Nachrichten* (85), 1984.

democracy in Brazil rendered the outcome of the judiciary battle between VW and the *peões* a little more open.

This battle, however, opposed VW to only a handful of *peões* symbolically representing all the other presumed victims of the forced labor system. Only between four and six names regularly emerged in the justice reports, as most of the *peões* who had testified at the CPT, the STR, and police offices, did not carry their complaints forward in the form of judiciary action. There existed no tool such as class action in Brazilian legislation and most of the *peões*, who were socially and financially powerless individuals, did not feel capable of engaging in a David versus Goliath fight against a multinational firm. In the end, the process lasted almost fifteen years and would have engendered unbearable costs for the few remaining complainants without the constant support of lawyers provided by the CPT and the STR. Moreover, in spite of a final judgment, which gave rights to the *peões* and incriminated VW, it brought the workers only a symbolic amount of financial reparation. In these conditions, one understands why most of the *peões* preferred not to seek justice.

The legal action to which I am referring started on October 22, 1984. It was launched by four workers with the help of a lawyer working for the STR in Luciará (Mato Grosso), the *peões*' town of origin, as well as various law counselors from the CPT. By the early 1990s, French priest Frei Henri Burin des Roziers became the *peões*' lawyer, as well as appealing to the media on their behalf.[36] He had succeeded Ricardo Rezende Figueira as a coordinator of the CPT in Santana do Araguaia, after numerous death threats by *fazendeiros* had pushed the latter to leave the Amazon and become a sociologist specialized in forced labor in Rio de Janeiro.[37] The original – and risky – initiative by workers Pedro Vasconcelos, Francisco Rezende de Souza, José Desidério, and José Pereira de Souza consisted of attacking VW directly under labor law, and not only the *gatos*, who had employed them.[38] The four *peões* demanded an official recognition that they had been forced to work, and asked, as a compensation for the endured wrong, payment from the CVRC for the clearing of twenty *alqueires* and a salary covering three working months. They also demanded a corresponding compensation for diverse labor rights, which had been denied to them, such as holiday, weekend,

[36] Comissão Justiça e Paz (CJP) CNBB – Norte II, Trabalho escravo nas fazendas do Pará e Amapá 1980–1998, Belém-Pará, 1999.
[37] GPTEC V9.62., August 1997, "O Pote de Barro contra o Pote de Ferro."
[38] GPTEC V.10.1.50, Moraes, "Processo n°603/84," June 14, 1985.

and payment of the extra hours they had been forced to work. Finally, they demanded the CVRC produce proper labor documents and pay the unemployment rights, which they had been deprived of after leaving the *fazenda*.

These requirements were not particularly high, given the wrong of forced labor the workers claimed to have endured. The tendency of Brazilian justice to favor landowners obliged the workers to issue moderate claims. At the same time, these moderate claims showed that the workers' initiative was not a mere opportunistic one; the four complainants did not seek to profit from the international fame of VW to win millions of dollars in compensation. Yet, VW stayed on the line of defense it had adopted since 1983, namely, denying responsibility for what happened to workers contracted by the *gatos*. In a hearing on August 30, 1985 at the tribunal of Conceição do Araguaia, the Cristalino *fazenda* represented by Adão, chief of the farm's security service, refused any possibility of an agreement with the *peões*, alleging that such a step would "give a bad example to the other employees."[39]

In front of this deadlocked situation, the *peões* decided to confirm their lawsuit, in spite of a negative ruling issued two weeks later by court judge Eronides Sousa Primo. The latter considered that Volkswagen was not legally responsible for actions committed by subcontracting companies, and went so far as to sentence the *peões* to reimburse the costs of the law case and the firm's lawyer fees to the CVRC.[40] In view of the imbalance between the financial position of the complainants and the multinational firm that was acting behind the *fazenda*, the judge's decision can be described as a gesture reflecting the unfair power balance reigning in the rural Amazon. To be sure, Judge Eronides was particularly hostile to the cause of rural workers and the exponents of liberation theology. In September 1987, he falsely accused Ricardo Rezende Figueira in the national press of fomenting the creation of a terrorist group in the south of Pará with the support of Nicaragua's Sandinista government.[41]

It is uncertain whether what happened next was a consequence of the political climate of the New Republic or of the partial renewal of justice personnel due to regime change, but in March 1986, the complainants surprisingly won on appeal and the decision of Judge Eronides was

---

[39] CPT Belém, "Informação," Conceição do Araguaia, August 30, 1985.
[40] GPTEC V9.59.1., Gomes and Moraes, "Sentença contra a fazenda"; GPTEC V.10.1.57., "Processo 603/84: Conclusão," September 13, 1985.
[41] Figueira, *Rio Maria*, 128.

revoked.[42] Pedro T. Soprano, president of the regional tribunal of the Eighth Region (states of Pará and Amapá), judged that "the defendant as much as the Andrade Desmatamento firm are jointly responsible for the employees' rights," which resulted in the following sentence: "the judges of the regional labor tribunal of the Eighth Region agree unanimously to consider the employment relationship with the defendant Companhia Vale do Rio Cristalino, proved." However, the CVRC started a new proceeding demanding the transfer of all accusation charges over the Andrade Desmatamento enterprise belonging to the *gato* Chicô, which delayed the outcome of the lawsuit.[43] In sum, VW's strategy was not even to negate the facts, but to dissociate the cases of forced labor that happened at Cristalino from the image of the company. For the German firm, the whole affair related to traditional labor relations proper to the Amazon, not to VW's modern ranching program. From 1986 to 1989, the Cristalino lawsuit simply remained stuck in the office of the judge of Conceição do Araguaia, in spite of repeated calls by CPT lawyers to accelerate it.[44] The creation of a new district court for the area of Santana of Araguaia, which was supposed to take over the lawsuits concerning the county, was the cause of even worse administrative delays. After the case file was transferred from Conceição to Santana, it remained untreated again until 1992, when a judge confirmed the authenticity of the accusations raised by the *peões* and directed VW to fulfill all the financial and administrative demands of the workers.[45] The judge even ordered that the CVRC pay twice the value of the salary the *peões* should have received for clearing.

However, a sudden new development took place a few weeks later, when the court communicated that the lawsuit file had mysteriously disappeared: there was no written trace of the judgment and as such, no formal document obliging VW to pay.[46] Only because of the intensive lobbying of the CPT was the file finally "rediscovered" in 1994 as mysteriously as it had vanished. It came out that the lawsuit documents had simply been "forgotten" in a desk drawer belonging to the tribunal's official bookkeeper, to whom the file had been transmitted immediately after the ruling in order to calculate and actualize according to inflation the sum VW owed to the workers.[47] A new administrative transfer of

---

[42] CPT Belém, "Tribunal Regional do Trabalho da 8a regiao. Processo TRT RO 104/86," March 1986.
[43] CPT Belém, Abreu to Gama, December 5, 1986.
[44] GPTEC V9.62., August 23, 1997, "O Pote de Barro contra o Pote de Ferro."
[45] GPTEC V.70.1.102., "Sentença," June 19, 1992.
[46] GPTEC V9.62., August 23, 1997, "O Pote de Barro contra o Pote de Ferro."
[47] CNBB – Norte II, Trabalho escravo nas fazendas do Pará e Amapá, 1980–1998.

the file to the labor law tribunal of Conceição do Araguaia forced the complainants to wait one more year before the sentence of 1992 was finally confirmed. Only in 1997, when Cristalino was definitively auctioned off by VW, which had kept the mortgage on the ranch because of the Matsubaras' incapacity to pay its full value, did the payment finally take place. Volkswagen deposited 4,858 reais – meanwhile Brazil's new currency – at the tribunal for the complainants, a drop in the ocean representing 0.02 percent of the value of the auction earned by VW, but a symbolic victory for the workers.

This long judiciary struggle says a lot about the extreme difficulty of taking legal proceedings against big ranches in the Amazon, even after the fall of the military regime. All the mysterious obstacles, incomprehensible delays, transfers of the CVRC case from tribunal to tribunal, unless they constituted a simple coincidence or the symptoms of an ill-functioning institutional apparatus, seem to point at pressures to delay the definitive sentence. It also seems a little surrealistic that, although at a certain stage even the Brazilian government – through the voice of MIRAD – recognized the responsibility of VW in the forced labor affair, legal justice needed thirteen years to barely hint at it. This brought priest Henri des Roziers, who had largely played his part in this whole judiciary struggle, to the following conclusion: "to obtain their labor rights, small in value but great in dignity, from a billionaire company, the four workers had to fight fourteen years against the greed, lack of cooperation and bad faith of the powerful latifundio and the conniving justice of Pará."[48]

Cristalino after Volkswagen

The "*fazenda* Vale do Rio Cristalino" in Pará came back into the headlines in February 2013, when the regional press made an appraisal of the land conflicts that had taken place there since 2008.[49] The local CPT and workers' trade unions announced that these conflicts had provoked fourteen murders in only three years. The situation, in sum, was far from the dream of modernity driving the creation of the farm in 1973. Throughout the 1990s and 2000s, it became an even more disputed land estate, traversed by violent confrontations between interest groups, with hesitating interventions by the state and a latent problem of (lacking) environmental conservation. Cristalino became emblematic of the contemporary

---

[48] GPTEC V9.62., August 23, 1997, "O Pote de Barro contra o Pote de Ferro."
[49] Carlos Mendes, "Fazenda Rio Cristalino / Pará: 14 assassinatos e trinta marcados para morrer," *A folha do Pará*, February 17, 2013.

problems of the Amazon. The atmosphere there has come close to a civil war, with no certitude about who should take over the management of Cristalino. The natural production base and tools of the ranch have degraded and no conceptual or practical basis has emerged from which to improve the living conditions of local workers.

The Matsubaras did not do much for the farm, and, as they neither respected the payment steps agreed to with VW nor drew up a plan to commercialize beef, the car company finally sold the ranch to Brazilian businessmen Eufrásio Pereira Luiz and José Marcos Monteiro in 1997.[50] The Matsubaras had left soils to degrade and parasite weeds to invade the fields. This did not seem to much disturb the new owners who had no intention of practicing cattle breeding seriously, but rather wanted to profit from the land property legislation to make money. In fact, a law that was introduced in the frame of PNRA stipulated that unproductive land on which landless peasants squatted and that they claimed could be nationalized and redistributed according to a generous financial procedure of compensation for the owners. As if by chance, a group of landless peasants invaded Cristalino only a few weeks after Pereira and Monteiro acquired the CVRC. After a presidential decree of August 21, 1998 had declared the area of "social interest," INCRA initiated an expropriation proceeding accompanied by a promise of 40 million reais of compensation, twice the price for which the two businessmen had bought the ranch from VW.[51] Overall, as a rumor crossing the Araguaia region put it, it was very probable that the owners had discreetly opened the doors of their own ranch to landless peasants.

Confident that a large operation of redistribution with proper land titles would take place, 1,700 families from the region started to cultivate crops of land at Cristalino in February 1999. According to Ademir Andrade, meanwhile the senator of Pará, up to 3,000 families had settled on the ranch up to August.[52] INCRA, however, hesitated to process the promised expropriation procedure, due to pressure from the state company Nuclear Industries of Brazil (INB), which was simultaneously pushing through a program of uranium prospection in areas close to Cristalino. In November 1999, INB, which alleged that farming projects could disturb the mineral exploration of the region, discovered indicators of uranium in the subsoil of Cristalino, leading the government

---

[50] Le Breton, *Trapped*, 155–6.
[51] "Sem-terra e estatal disputam área no Pará," *O estado de São Paulo*, June 22, 1999.
[52] "Ademir Andrade pede imediata desapropriação de fazenda," *Agência senado*, August 5, 1999.

to suspend the process of expropriation.[53] As for the landless peasant families, drawn into Cristalino by the laxity of the two landowners and the encouragements of rural trade unions and INCRA, they were simply stuck. Andrade attempted to organize an agreement according to which the 3,000 peasant families could provide the necessary agrarian products and workforce to satisfy the needs of a future pole of mineral exploration, but his proposition remained unheard.[54]

This is when true chaos began to prosper. The families decided to stay, in order not to release the pressure on state authorities, and also because many of them had started to farm the land and had nowhere else to go.[55] Former employees of the CVRC, taking advantage of both their knowledge of the place and the confusion created by contradictory governmental announcements, continued to deforest the *fazenda* in search of valuable timber. Outsiders sought to take advantage of this disorder to get a piece of land. As Le Breton writes, "estate buildings were sacked and property stolen, bands of gunmen began to roam about freely, and the settlers were reduced to a state of fear and trembling. Rival groups of settlers moved in to get a slice of the action. Gold miners came swarming in and posted no fewer than 120 separate claims."[56] STR delegates started to express their surprise about the coming of hundreds of squatter families brought to the ranch under the banner of a small landless organization based in Brasília, which they had never heard about. To complicate matters further, it came out that areas in which families were living contained uranium on the land's surface, which led Ademir Andrade to make a speech in the senate warning about possible risks for human health.[57]

During the early 2000s, the peasant families of Cristalino managed to sustain relative media attention and political support within the federal parliament, thanks to the renewed success of the land reform issue, illustrated at a national scale by the growing popularity of the MST. The coming to power of the PT with the election of President Lula da Silva in 2002 also illustrated a revival of popularity for land reform. More particularly, the constant support of politicians of Pará such as Ademir Andrade, an old political companion of the Cristalino workers, helped the landless families of the former VW ranch not to fall into oblivion. Federal deputy

[53] "Sem-terra e estatal disputam área no Pará."
[54] "Ademir Andrade pede imediata desapropriação de fazenda."
[55] Le Breton, *Trapped*, 157.
[56] Ibid.
[57] "Ademir denúncia risco de contaminação por urânio em fazenda no Pará," *Agência senado*, September 3, 1999.

Paulo Rocha (PT), son of a poor and large rural workers' family of Pará also felt personally concerned by the fate of the Cristalino landless.[58] He repeatedly solicited the Ministry of Agrarian Development and the Ministry of Science and Technology, asking them to nullify the hypothesis that the area contained radioactivity and possibly uranium in its subsoil – a hypothesis that was blocking the expropriation proceedings.

The first Lula years promoted land redistribution as a program priority, although, reminiscent of Sarney, the PT president privileged media-friendly announcements of expropriation focused on single emblematic cases over structural reform. After the government pressured the National Department of Mineral Production, the latter discarded its remaining hopes regarding the existence of substantial quantities of uranium in Cristalino in April 2004. On May 19, 2004, Lula expropriated 87,000 hectares of the Rio Cristalino *fazenda* through a presidential decree.[59] In an email addressed to PT members, colleagues, and personalities involved in the Cristalino case such as Rezende, Rocha summed up the situation as follows:

> The struggle of these workers for a piece of soil, on which to live and produce, was arduous and long until the land was won. The first expropriation process, which lingered years in procedure, was finally suspended in 1998. A new procedure was opened in 2003 and, thanks to the interest and engagement of the Lula government, there was a more rapid administrative treatment.[60]

In spite of this decision, things are far from resolved in the *fazenda*. While about 80,000 hectares have painfully been distributed to the squatter families, many medium *fazendeiros* have begun to raise cattle illegally on the estate.[61] They have used threats to convince some families to leave the area, creating, according to Roziers, an authentic "climate of war" in the place.

Even more problematic are the 60,000 hectares officially still belonging to the CVRC, but which have been themselves invaded by 600 families who settled there in 2008, organized into a rival organization to the MST, called the National Federation of Workers of Family Agriculture (FETRAF).[62] As they started to occupy the place and demonstrate,

[58] GPTEC V9.67.1., Rocha to Lucena et al., May 20, 2004.
[59] Presidência da República: "Decreto de 19 de maio de 2004."
[60] GPTEC V9.67.1., Rocha to Lucena et al., May 20, 2004.
[61] www.mst.org.br/Clima-de-guerra-na-fazenda-Rio-Cristalino-no-Para, access date September 4, 2013.
[62] "Minha vida vale 20 mil reais no Pará," diz Frei Henry," www.mst.org.br/node/10251, access date September 4, 2013.

the general director of INCRA, Raimundo Oliveira, visited them with two delegates from the governmental party PT, federal congressman Raimundo Oliveira and state deputy Bernadete Ten Caten. They promised the FETRAF families that within ninety days the CVRC would be completely expropriated and transformed into a settlement project for the small peasantry.[63] The event provoked scenes of jubilation among the squatters. However, no concrete governmental act followed, and the incidents in situ worsened. Only in 2010, four workers were murdered as a consequence of the many conflicts traversing the place.[64] The situation became inextricable when rural trade unions also accused FETRAF members to be involved in a series of assassinations.[65] In February 2013, a director of property policy of the Santana do Araguaia STR, described the *fazenda*'s situation as one of the gravest in Brazil.[66] He predicted that the conflicts could end in a massacre if the federal and state governments did not act: "Many people have already died and others will yet if nothing is done." Faced with these complaints, INCRA has lately argued that generalized ecological degradation in the ranch has made it pointless to resume the process of expropriation.[67] The devastation of Cristalino's forests has left the *fazenda* with degenerated, unproductive soil, making it nearly impossible to sustain hundreds of families through farming activities.

The Cristalino case has thus become completely opaque: to say what is true in the declarations of state representatives, who pressures whom and who is in conflict with whom lies beyond the scope of academic research. NGOs such as the CPT still examine the case but without charging too closely in as they used to do in the 1980s, for the climate of violence has made it perilous for them to even enter the ranch. Thirteen years of controlled deforestation under the "reign" of VW and twenty-seven years of savage clearing processed by unidentified actors in a hurry to appropriate the land in order not to leave it to others have ravaged the soils.[68] The conquest of nature by humans did not create modernity or civilization, at least not as VW and SUDAM used to depict it in the early 1970s.

---

[63] Mendes, "Fazenda Rio Cristalino."
[64] Ibid.
[65] Verônica Iozzi, "Mais assassinatos no Pará geram indignação no MSTTR.," *Agência CONTAG de notícias*, December 17, 2010.
[66] "Clima de guerra na fazenda Rio Cristalino, no Pará."
[67] Ibid.
[68] Nelson Feitosa, "Ibama fiscaliza queimadas ilegais em assentamentos agrários de Santana do Araguaia, no Pará," *Ascom ibama*, October 10, 2012.

At the same time, alternatives to the model of dependent development once symbolized by the partnership between the two organizations did not emerge. The notions of Western know-how and high-tech ranching do not produce the social authority they once did. But the state apparatus hardly supports small peasants trying to create a possible alternative to top-down developmentalism in the form of cooperative agricultural projects. Even the different landless groups who occupy the ranch seem handicapped by internal rivalries. Although the certitudes and the optimism once guaranteed by the developmentalism discourse are gone, they have not been chased out by another political consensus. A common model of management and distribution of the resources in the rural spaces of the Amazon is yet to be found.

Conclusion: A Farewell to the "Pioneer" Mentality

The Companhia Vale do Rio Cristalino (CVRC), VW's cattle ranch in the Amazon from 1973 to 1986, was not the work of one individual. Many actors contributed to its birth, not only in the VW Company, but also in Brazilian administrative bodies such as the Superintendence for the Development of the Amazon (SUDAM). Yet, the project had one spokesperson with a special relationship to the media, the then CEO of VW do Brasil (VWB), Wolfgang Sauer. His life reflected the cultural plurality and cross-border nature of the ranching project, which mixed seemingly opposed objectives such as globalizing the Amazon (integrating the region into international economic exchanges) and nationalizing it (reinforcing both Brazilian identity and state in the region). After arriving in Brazil in 1961 and acquiring citizenship in 1982, he had continued to live in the country. Having started his career as a foreign executive, he died in 2012 as a Brazilian historical figure. His biography thus complicates the historiographical storyline about "missionaries" of development from Europe or the United States, who in the context of the Cold War used the "Third World" as an experimental field onto which they stubbornly imposed economic models elaborated in industrial countries.[69]

The standards that VW claimed to reach in terms of farming productivity and social welfare were those of the industrial world. But the roots

---

[69] Yves Dezalay and Bryant G. Garth, *The Internationalization of Palace Wars: Lawyers, Economists, and the Contest to Transform Latin American States* (London: University of Chicago Press, 2010), 87; Larry Grubbs, *Secular Missionaries: Americans and African Development in the 1960s* (Amherst: University of Massachusetts Press, 2009).

of the CVRC are also to be understood in the framework of a patriotic narrative of Brazilian history: a country of pioneers pushing the frontier of civilization from the coast to the west, with the Amazon as a horizon to follow, so as to tend toward the completion of a "great Brazil." Sauer's heroes were the *Bandeirantes*, early settlers who from the sixteenth century onward marched into the "wild" interior spaces and enslaved native groups on their way. His model for measuring the success of a development project was the capital, Brasília, built in only five years (1956–60) under supervision of the popular president, Kubitschek. The social imaginary to which Sauer constantly referred was the Brazilian nation, a Brazilian "we" in which he fully included himself. He fought several times for the survival of the Cristalino ranching program in the name of what he saw as the Brazilian interest, against the will of VW global management in Wolfsburg.

VWB's Amazonian investments were crucial elements of the company's strategy to build itself a truly Brazilian image. Celebrating the early activities of Atlas Frigorifico, a slaughterhouse launched in the Amazon by VW in partnership with SUDAM and different Brazilian companies in 1983, Sauer presented the project as the realization of a national dream: "the dream of occupying the 'Amazonian emptiness' is coming true. The future of the Amazon has effectively started and it is with great faith that a group of pioneers have erected Atlas Frigorífico, a new symbol of the country's integration, in the midst of the jungle."[70] Since 1977, VWB was also selling its cars with the advertising slogan: "a marca que conhece o nosso chão" ("the brand that knows our land").[71] It sounded like the self-confident assertion of a company that considered itself deeply rooted in the Brazilian territory, right up to the pioneer frontier of the rain forest.

In the context of the Cold War, the fact that VW was originally a German company also mattered. Most of the development historians have devoted their attention to a tête-à-tête between the United States and the Global South.[72] Therefore, they have studied development discourses on the basis of an industrial country, which had conceived foreign

[70] Vania Vaz, "A formação dos latifúndios no sul do estado do Pará: terra, pecuária e desflorestamento" (Universidade Nacional de Brasília, 2013), 121.

[71] "Trânsito livre," *Veja*, June 1, 1977.

[72] There are exceptions to this exclusive focus, such as Corinna R. Unger, *Entwicklungspfade in Indien: eine internationale Geschichte, 1947-1980* (Göttingen: Wallstein, 2015); Kiran K. Patel, *The New Deal: A Global History* (Princeton, NJ: Princeton University Press, 2016).

aid programs, in particular for Latin America, since the late 1930s.[73] The Cold War, which saw the United States competing with the Soviet Union for global influence, led to the integration by Washington of development aid into a consistent diplomatic policy.[74] That said, we still know little about other Western industrial countries that carried less legible visions of development.

As it became a major economic power after the Second World War, Germany was aware of the economic advantage it could gain from building partnerships with big countries of the Global South such as India or Brazil. But it was historically unprepared to assume social responsibilities in the "Third World." As Unger shows, the German government did not manage to agree on a strong institutional organ of decision in development policy in the 1960s, as political responsibilities in this field remained divided between three rival ministries.[75] In the following decades, German policy in the matter suffered several fundamental strategic changes resulting from the conflict between a "humanitarian" view and another view wedded to *realpolitik*, for which foreign aid should serve German economic interests.

In this regard, VW played an ambiguous role as a "German" institution promoting development in the world. The declarations of VW executives about the CVRC always swung between corporate language and humanitarian tones. Sometimes they simply presented the VW ranch as a model industry that would provide impulse to new economic practices and create a chain of demand. But on other occasions they described the ranch as a real development aid program, planned to nourish the poor with protein, educate the children of the Amazonian countryside, and provide the local population with decent housing. This flexible position reflected the absence of a strict developmentalist dogma coming from the home country, which gave Sauer and his local partners great freedom in conceiving the Cristalino ranch as a project situated in continuity with representations of Brazilian nationalism.

In the Brazilian context, development as a promise for positive change was intimately linked with the objective of exploiting the country's organic riches to the fullest. Perceived by the military regime's ideologues as a

---

[73] Eric Helleiner, "The Development Mandate of International Institutions: Where Did It Come from?" *Studies in Comparative International Development* 44, no. 3 (2009).

[74] Michael E. Latham, *The Right Kind of Revolution: Modernization, Development, and US Foreign Policy from the Cold War to the Present* (Ithaca, NY: Cornell University Press, 2011).

[75] Unger, "Export und Entwicklung," 79.

huge natural space, bursting with soil and subsoil resources, the Amazon was a symbol of this objective. Techno-scientific progress was presented as the central condition for Brazil to win the "war against nature" and disposed – so Sauer believed – the Cristalino project to "find answers to the most diverse natural phenomena in the midst of the forest."[76] The government put a range of fiscal incentives in place to facilitate the modernization of agronomic techniques so as to make the Amazon a global leader in beef export. In these conditions, a triumphant propaganda hid the fact that the amount of academic knowledge about the forest ecology was negligible. The institutions participating in the colonization of the Amazon did not discuss the risks implied by a massive use of clearing bulldozers or soil fertilizers. Such discussions were considered unnecessary as scientific knowledge would establish ways to handle the forest, technology would tame the wild and economic expertise would predict what the nation would receive from the forest's exploitation. This strict separation between politics on one side, and nature as a preserve of technical expertise on the other, formed the condition that allowed projects like Cristalino to come to light.[77] In this context, Cristalino's technological arsenal exempted VW from busying itself with the particularities of the local ecology and the possible environmental consequences of the project. As a result of this carelessness, the company kept coming across unexpected natural obstacles. The spreading of toxic weeds, soil degradation, and high cattle mortality all provoked considerable delays, cost increases, and major setbacks in the agronomic program. Such problems were not supposed to arise in the making of a big development project said to be able to take up any challenge posed by nature.

The CVRC project represented an Amazonian continuation of the Green Revolution, which had consisted of a multitude of initiatives of technology transfer to accelerate human access to soil resources in rural areas of the Third World. In the postwar decades, these programs received overwhelming support from governing institutions everywhere in the world. But in the late 1960s, the Green Revolution had begun facing challenges from the fringes of natural sciences by scientists underlining the environmental risks carried by technical progress and the limits of science in fixing potential damages to nature. Biologist Rachel Carson

---

[76] Doretto, *O homem Volkswagen*, 342.
[77] Timothy Mitchell, *Carbon Democracy: Political Power in the Age of Oil* (London: Verso, 2011); Bruno Latour, *Politiques de la nature: comment faire entrer les sciences en démocratie?* (Paris: La Découverte, 2004).

managed to turn her book *Silent Spring* (1962), which identified pesticides as a peril for the earth, into a global best-seller. Brazilian natural scientists adapted this message in the framework of local controversies during the mid-1970s. They attacked the government as well as big cattle-ranching companies on the grounds of scientific uncertainty, that is, the impossibility of predicting the effects of deforestation on soils, biodiversity, and climate. By surrendering the authority of science, these Brazilian scientists threatened the whole developmentalist logic, which cast them as possessors of material knowledge. At the same time, precisely because they were fundamental actors of this logic, they managed to disseminate the environmentalist warning even within the Brazilian administration. Deforestation became a matter of debate within various institutions of the military regime, including those such as SUDAM, which were in charge of developing the Amazon.

A victim of its own fame, VW's "model ranch" became one of the main targets of critical scientists who regarded forest clearing with alarm, when a NASA satellite photographed a fire of exceptional reach in the area of the Cristalino estate in 1976. Barely aware of the global environmental debate and culturally distant from the semantic codes of political ecology, the VW executives not only needed time to realize how the new image of the company as an "environmental villain" could endanger its reputation. They also showed themselves inept in justifying the making of giant fires from a technical point of view, as some scientists noted that the CVRC should have resorted to mechanical tree felling instead, while technocrats regretted the undifferentiated elimination of lucrative tree species. Some agronomists also raised their voices to say that these fires were irrational as they threatened the productivity of the ranch's soils over the mid- and long term.

The history of the CVRC thus testifies to a rising accountability for nature in human affairs and shows that natural things constitute unpredictable factors. They can lead to changing the outlines of a big project, lie at the basis of new political alliances, or contribute to interrogating dominant discourses. A look at colonization policies in the Amazon clearly brings to light how certain political representations of natural things provoked material changes in the environment. The idea of the Amazon as a declining forest, with limitless resources needing to be tapped, encouraged a massive scramble for clearing, pasturing, and fertilizing. But the political storm, which gathered criticisms against clearing at Cristalino, also shows how much environmental change modified the terms of political negotiation. This is why we need an integrated history of nature and politics rather than building up environmental history as a categorized field in which the material and the political are studied distinctly.[78]

At the time of the VW ranch, concerns with deforestation were not entirely new in Brazil. Since the emergence of a nationalist thought in the early nineteenth century, a section of the elites had cultivated a patriotic discourse in politics, literature, and the arts that glorified the specificity of tropical nature and its role in shaping Brazilian culture. On this basis, the rain forest had symbolized the richness, diversity, and "tropicality" of the nation. In fact, as it managed to cross the border of academic sciences, the wave of criticism against deforestation at Cristalino transformed into a discourse in which nationalism could merge with environmentalism. Parliamentary representatives, in particular, who argued that the ecological equilibrium of the forest was part of Brazil's territorial integrity, were enraged about this story of a foreign company squandering the national commons. Concerns over social equality joined this national-environmentalist platform criticizing the concentration of land in the hands of a capitalist firm. Leading opposition politicians also turned the struggle against Cristalino into a claim for democracy, as they blamed the military regime for supporting big private projects without concern for the wishes of the Brazilian people. By combining these different ideas, the criticisms against Cristalino managed to convince a broad range of actors, including grassroots environmentalist groups, scientists, politicians, journalists, administrators, and activists from the land reform movement. The following extract of a letter from a reader in Rio de Janeiro to the national daily *Jornal do Brasil* (1977) illustrates the new, at the same time environmentally sensitive and nationalist, mood stimulated by the fire at Cristalino:

> It is with great sadness that I address myself to the *Jornal do Brasil* to join my voice to thousands of others, so Brazilian as my concern is with respect to the national problems regarding the conservation of our patrimony.... I feel ill every time I hear those recommendations aiming to transform the Amazon into an enormous pasture. I feel ill knowing what Volkswagen is doing to the Amazon[79]

Not only actors concerned with the fate of the forest were looking at the Cristalino experiment with a skeptical eye, but so were activists

---

[78] It is thus necessary to revise the classification of different branches or levels of analysis in environmental history suggested by Donald Worster, "Transformations of the Earth: Toward an Agroecological Perspective in History," *The Journal of American History* 76, no. 4 (1990), 1090; and more recently by John McNeill, "Observations on the Nature and Culture of Environmental History," *History and Theory* 42, no. 4 (2003).

[79] Aloyso Fagerlande, "Ecologia," *Jornal do Brasil*, September 28, 1977.

interested in the life of landless rural laborers. Addressing both the scarcity of resources and the problem of monopolistic property that created unfair labor relations, the conflict over land emerged at the junction between nature and labor. By the late 1970s, trade unions, priests supporting liberation theology, and independent workers started to raise concerns over the way VW treated its Amazonian workforce. Activists described the CVRC as a *latifundio*, that is, a disproportionately big private property symbolizing violence, authoritarian management, and transgression of labor law in the countryside. This negative image provided the context for the forced labor scandal, which brought the VW ranch to the headlines again in 1983.

That year, a local network of Christian activists and trade union representatives helped seasonal clearing workers who had fled from Cristalino to publicly reveal a system of forced labor existing at the fringes of the ranch. Volkswagen had entrusted the management of the clearing workforce to Amazonian companies led by middle men called *gatos*. A heritage of the labor system that prevailed during the Amazonian rubber boom in the late nineteenth century, the practice of debt bondage had increased in the late 1960s, as the policies of forest colonization pushed forward the demand for a massive and cheap workforce. Volkswagen was in no way the only company to give up control over seasonal workers and outsource the clearing of its ranch to local firms that prospered at the fringes of legality. However, the CVRC case was the first to become the object of a public scandal that found a durable echo not only in the Brazilian, but also in the international press. What is more, the array of actors who tried to "help" the presumed forced laborers at Cristalino grew impressively diverse. Beyond persons who traditionally mobilized for labor rights and land equality, the battle against "modern slavery" – as many activists defined it – at the VW ranch also found support among members of the ruling, promilitary party of Brazil. Abroad, actors as politically different as the Flemish Lenten Campaign, the German Greens, and a parliamentary representative of the British Tory Party protested against forced labor at the VW ranch.

The study of forced labor in the Brazilian Amazon has been a booming field in the social sciences since the early 2000s, but the global dimension of the issue has been neglected so far. The present research underlines the international connections behind modern occurrences of forced labor, not only in terms of investment and production, but also through the transnational partnership of protest actors. Indeed, the divulging of documents revealing the existence of forced labor at the CVRC partly resulted from the formation of internationally open, new social movements in Germany after 1968. Actors of the environmentalist, Christian, Third World solidarity, and pacifist branches of the German left alternative scene created the pressure that finally led VW to abandon its Amazonian projects. Therefore, the Cristalino case confirms the existing research on how the internationalization of protest, notably in the Cold War context, could contribute to destabilizing powerful actors.[80] Yet, except for a few works exploring the transnational impacts of anticolonial or liberation theology movements, international protest history has so far privileged the analysis of exchanges within the industrialized world.[81] In particular, new social movements in Germany have often been analyzed against a background of exchanges with protest repertoires and actors in the Anglo-Saxon societies.[82] In proposing a dynamic geographical focus that follows protest networks spanning Brazil and Germany, I have shed light on some aspects of the multitude of human experiences that hid behind the hundreds of "committees of solidarity with the Third World" between 1968 and the fall of the Berlin Wall.

One notable characteristic of these committees was their strong penetration by environmentalist ideas, which this study illustrated with regard to the alliance between Third World solidarity activists and the Green Party that alerted German public opinion about forced labor on the VW ranch. In Germany, the problematization of both deforestation and social exploitation in the tropical forest was intertwined. The fact that the Amazon started to become a symbol of the environmental crisis in the late 1970s gave international visibility to the region. After having been concerned with tropical deforestation, European Third World supporters developed a greater attention for the Amazon. They started to report about the destruction of Amerindian villages, the murder of

---

[80] Carole Fink, Philipp Gassert, and Detlef Junker, eds., *1968: The World Transformed* (New York: Cambridge University Press, 1998); Jeremi Suri, *Power and Protest: Global Revolution and the Rise of Detente* (Cambridge, MA: Harvard University Press, 2003).

[81] Sean Scalmer, *Gandhi in the West* (New York: Cambridge University Press, 2011); Christoph Kalter, *Die Entdeckung der Dritten Welt: Dekolonisierung und neue radikale Linke in Frankreich* (Frankfurt: Campus Verlag, 2011); Massimo di Giuseppe, "Discovering the 'Other' America: The Latin American Encounters of Italian Peace Movements, 1955–1980," in *Peace Movements in Western Europe, Japan and the USA during the Cold War*, ed. Benjamin Ziemann (Essen: Klartext, 2008).

[82] Martin Klimke, *The Other Alliance: Student Protest in West Germany and the United States in the Global Sixties* (Princeton, NJ: Princeton University Press, 2009); Holger Nehring, "National Internationalists: British and West German Protests Against Nuclear Weapons, the Politics of Transnational Communications and the Social History of the Cold War, 1957–1964," *Contemporary European History* 14, no. 4 (2005).

rural workers and the resurgence of slavery-like practices. In sum, the progression of environmental concerns in Western Europe gave local activists in Brazil new opportunities for transcontinental alliances based on the denunciation of social injustice in the Amazon. Environmental apprehensions about endangered tropical forests lent support of international activists for the Cristalino workers, just as the growing demand for agricultural deforestation had fueled forced labor networks in the Amazon. The history of the VW ranch is an emblematic example of how the interests of socially disadvantaged workers could objectively merge with claims for the preservation of nature, in the frame of a larger critique of authoritarian policies of development.

To grasp this emblematic dimension is essential if we want to understand how the VW ranch could be constructed into a symbol of socioenvironmental injustice. Many Brazilian and foreign groups had invested in excessively large cattle ranches and participated in destroying the forest with armies of overexploited laborers. Contrary to the claim made by famous personalities such as landscape architect Roberto Burle Marx around 1976, there was no evidence that VW set the biggest forest fire in world history. But the social visibility of the project, its claim to be a "model ranch" illustrating development to perfection, and the fact that it was owned by a foreign company made of Cristalino an ideal catalyst of the emerging fears that the rain forest might be progressively destroyed. Similarly, VW was by no means the first or only ranch to rely on the services of *gatos*. Nevertheless, in a politico-economic climate marked by proliferating land conflicts, a wave of great strikes in the car industry, and a ravaging debt crisis, which stimulated the hostility against foreign economic actors, the VW ranch became an ideal target for the Brazilian left to attack. Because VW was a famous multinational company, this attack did not remain restricted within Brazilian borders, but also had repercussions abroad.

The Brazilian government and VW intended to work for globalization *in* the Amazon by bringing foreign investments. What they harvested turned out to be a globalization *of* the Amazon, through which the region became an object of global debates producing critiques of big development projects.[83] In effecting transnational advertising for the CVRC project and claiming to create a model of farming modernization, VW had contributed to attracting international attention toward the Amazon.

[83] I borrowed this distinction from Ans Kolk, *Forests in International Environmental Politics: International Organisations, NGOs and the Brazilian Amazon* (Utrecht: International Books, 1996), 61.

Transnational mobilization against abusive treatment of the workers and the environment in VW's modern ranch were the logical consequences of the global ambitions that accompanied the project.

The CVRC's loss of political legitimacy resulted from the emergence of multiple controversies. It was a partial, gradual, and splintered process, through which environmental indignation, land conflict, labor law scandal, and technical failure were pronounced at different moments by separate, albeit partly overlapping groups. To be sure, the present study does not claim that developmentalist ideas were suddenly rejected en bloc and banned forever just because of the mistakes of a ranching project. The rise and fall of Cristalino is rather a story about the accumulation of small defects, the discovery of signs of incoherence, and the proliferation of questions within the developmentalist framework. The failure of the CVRC did not foreshadow the end of development, but illustrated its passage from a consensual position into the realms of controversy, in which it has stayed ever since.

Cristalino acted as a catalyst for a multitude of frustrations generated by the socioenvironmental consequences of developmentalist policies. It symbolized how a big technical project could be fraught with disappointments and bad surprises. Therefore, the history of Cristalino matters because the various protests that degraded the image of the project also illustrated the step-by-step disintegration of the widespread belief that development was a straight route leading to the resolution of all problems. Although development remained a frequently quoted concept in the following decades of Brazilian politics, it grew imperfect, "fractured and lacked a clear rational set of approaches to guide its implementation."[84] The idea, which had driven governmental policies since the 1940s, of a consensual pact for the national economy mixing public and private interests to benefit both the rich and the poor did not survive the economic crisis of the early 1980s.[85] The plan of a green revolution for the countryside was buried in the late 1980s due to political divisions over the issue of land reform. An innovative section dedicated to environmental protection in the Constitution of 1988 confirmed that Brazil's completion as a nation did not necessarily lie in the fullest exploitation of its organic resources.[86] Hence, even if development did not fade away, the consensual ambitions that constituted its power of persuasion did.

---

[84] This is David Ekbladh's analysis concerning the perceived transformation of development in the 1970s: Ekbladh, *The Great American Mission*, 10.

[85] Velloso, *O último trem para Paris*.

[86] Hochstetler and Keck, *Greening Brazil*, 14.

At the same time, it should remain clear that the protest movements, which appeared in the history of Cristalino and continued to grow in the following decades, have not offered a consensual countermodel to replace developmentalism. Until recently, deforestation even continued to expand in the Amazon and although forced labor has decreased, it remains one of the region's greatest plagues. But infrastructural, farming, or mining projects in the Brazilian rain forest now regularly trigger demonstrations both in the country and abroad. Amerindians make the headlines by occupying the Brazilian Parliament when the state threatens to reduce their territory in the name of development. Social networks mobilize millions of people to petition against a dam in the Amazon or to pressure the Brazilian president to veto a reform aimed at increasing the flexibility of the forest code. The present study helps in understanding why such protests happen today, because it depicts a historical moment in which developmentalism started to lose ground faced with the emergence of novel alliances. The implication of nature in a critique of technocratic governance, the construction of the Amazon as an international political object, the rise of a globally idealized, autonomous worker at the center of Brazilian land conflict, the emergence of the – today institutionalized – campaigns against "modern slavery," and the utilization of transnational channels of communication by marginalized forest populations to challenge multinational companies: all these were new political constellations, which often cut their teeth struggling against big development projects and still contribute to shaping political relations today.

It has become a commonplace in reports about deforestation that the Amazon as a forest might disappear one day. That prediction might not be grounded scientifically, but the fact that it hangs over Amazonian politics like the sword of Damocles shows how economic perspectives have shifted, how our view on nature has changed, and how obsolete the idea of a pioneer frontier of development sounds by now. There could not be a greater contrast between the representations of the vanishing tropical woods in the early twenty-first century and the optimism of the early 1970s, according to which modern cattle ranches would revitalize the region and make it a symbol of the human capacity to tame the wild through the strength of an ever-progressing technology.

The CVRC was one of the last big projects born in the Amazon under the sign of that confident pioneer spirit that nowadays seems dated. On the one hand, Cristalino symbolized the advancement of the Brazilian nation-state into the wild, in historical continuity with the myth of a country realizing itself through a heroic march into its unknown interior territories. On the other hand, the project was depicted as a pioneer in the sense of embodying the avant-garde of development, creating the "ox of the future," and showing a path for the agricultural modernization of the tropics. In its initial phase, the VW ranch might thus have been one of the last development projects whose planners could ignore socioecological claims and feel unconcerned by political demands for democratic control. To be sure, the VW ranch was one of the last big projects that still conceptualized the Amazon as a frontier of civilization and a virgin and endless space rather than an arena of conflicts over ever-diminishing resources. In this sense, Cristalino's fathers were the Amazon's last pioneers.

References

Archival Sources

Archive of the Biblioteca Amilcar Cabral, Bologna
Arquivo da Superintendência do Desenvolvimento da Amazônia (SUDAM), Belém
Arquivo do Fundo de Investimento da Amazônia (FINAM), Belém
Arquivo regional da CPT, Belém
Câmara dos Deputados (online)
Grupo de Pesquisa Trabalho Escravo Contemporâneo (GPTEC), Rio de Janeiro
Senado Federal (online)
Bundesarchiv (BArch), Koblenz
Bundestagsarchiv, Berlin
Landtagsarchiv Niedersachsen (NLA-HstAH), Hannover
Niedersächsischer Landtag, Hannover
Politisches Archiv des Auswärtigen Amtes (PA AA), Berlin: Zwischenarchiv
VW Unternehmensarchiv, Wolfsburg

Audiovisual Material

Armstrong, Fanny. *Mclibel: Two Worlds Collide.* 53 minutes. United Kingdom, 1997.
Schott, Harald. *Die Fazenda am Cristalino.* 28 minutes. Germany, 1981.

Literature

Acker, Antoine, "The Brand that Knows Our Land: Volkswagen's 'Brazilianization' in the 'Economic Miracle,' 1968–1973." *Monde(s). Histoire, espaces, relations* 5, no. 6 (2015): 199–218.

Adriance, Madeleine Cousineau. "The Brazilian Catholic Church and the Struggle for Land in the Amazon." *Journal for the Scientific Study of Religion* 34, no. 3 (1995): 377–82.

Allegretti, Mary Helena. "A construção social de políticas ambientais: Chico Mendes e o movimento dos seringueiros." Universidade de Brasília, 2002.

Alves, Maria Helena Moreira. "Grassroots Organizations, Trade Unions, and the Church: A Challenge to the Controlled Abertura in Brazil." *Latin American Perspectives* 11, no. 1 (1984): 73–102.

Alves, Maria Helena Moreira. *Estado e oposição no Brasil: 1964–1984*. Bauru: Edusc, 2005.

Andrade, João Walter de. *A problematica amazônica e a atuação da SUDAM*. Belém: SUDAM (Ministério do Interior), 1968.

Apesteguy, Christine. "L'intervention fédérale en Amazonie: éléments pour une définition de l'état militaire au Brésil." EHESS, 1976.

Appadurai, Arjun. *Modernity at Large: Cultural Dimensions of Globalization*. Minneapolis: University of Minnesota Press, 1996.

Arbeitsgruppe Brasilien, Dritte-Welt-Haus e.V., ed. *Die Farm am Amazonas: Von Volkswagen lernen*. Bielefeld: Dritte-Welt-Haus, 1984.

Arndt, Heinz Wolfgang. *Economic Development: The History of an Idea*. Chicago: University of Chicago Press, 1987.

Baer, Werner. *The Brazilian Economy: Growth and Development*. Boulder, CO: Lynne Rienner Publishers, 2008.

Baer, Werner, Dan Bilder, and Curtis T. Mcdonald. "Austeridade sob diversos regimes políticos: o caso do Brasil." *Cadernos de estudos sociais* 3, no. 1 (1987): 5–28.

Balsen, Werner and Karl Rössel. *Hoch die internationale Solidarität: Zur Geschichte der Dritte Welt-Bewegung in der Bundesrepublik*. Köln: Kölner Volksblatt Verlag, 1986.

Bandeira, Luiz Alberto Moniz. *Das Deutsche Wirtschaftswunder und die Entwicklung Brasiliens: Die Beziehungen Deutschlands zu Brasilien und Lateinamerika*. Frankfurt am Main: Vervuert, 1995.

Barbira-Scazzocchio, Françoise, ed. *Land, People and Planning in Contemporary Amazonia*. Cambridge: Cambridge University, 1980.

Barbosa, Luiz C. *The Brazilian Amazon Rainforest: Global Ecopolitics, Development, and Democracy*. New York: University Press of America, 2000.

Barbosa, Mário dos Santos. *Sindicalismo em tempos de crise: a experiência na Volkswagen do Brasil*. Santo André: Alpharrabio, 2003.

Barth, Boris and Jürgen Osterhammel, eds. *Zivilisierungsmissionen: imperiale Weltverbesserung seit dem 18. Jahrhundert*. Konstanz: UVK, 2005.

BASA. *Nacionalização e aumento do capital do BASA: repercussões*. Belém: BASA, 1969.

Bastos, Pedro Paulo Zahluth. "A construção do nacional-desenvolvimentismo de Getúlio Vargas e a dinâmica de interação entre estado e mercado nos setores de base." *Revista economia* 7, no. 4 (2006): 239–75.

Bentes, Rosineide. "A intervenção do ambientalismo internacional na Amazônia." *Estudos avançados* 19, no. 54 (2005): 225–40.

Binswanger, Hans P. *Fiscal and Legal Incentives with Environmental Effects on the Brazilian Amazon*. Agricultural Research Unit discussion paper; no. ARU 69. Washington, D.C.:World Bank, 1987.

Bones, Elmar and Geraldo Hasse. *Pioneiros da ecologia: breve história do movimento ambientalista no Rio Grande do Sul*. Porto Alegre: Já, 2007.

Bonneuil, Christophe. "Development as Experiment: Science and State Building in Late Colonial and Postcolonial Africa, 1930–1970." *Osiris* 15 (2000): 258–81.

Borges, Durval Rosa. *Rio Araguaia, Corpo e Alma*. São Paulo: IBRASA, 1987.

Bouny, André. *L'Agent Orange: Apocalypse Viêt Nam*. Paris: Demi-Lune, 2010.

Branford, Sue. *The Last Frontier: Fighting over Land in the Amazon*. London: Zed Books, 1985.

Branford, Sue and Jan Rocha. *Cutting the Wire: The Story of the Landless Movement in Brazil*. London: Latin America Bureau, 2002.

Brass, Tom, ed. *Free and Unfree Labour: The Debates Continue*. Bern: Peter Lang, 1997.

Brocke, Madeleine. "Die Brasilianische Ökologie-Bewegung zwischen Utopie und Pragmatik: das Beispiel der AGAPAN in Porto Alegre/Brasilien." *Arbeitshefte des Lateinamerika-Zentrums, Münster* 15 (1993).

Brossart, Paulo. *O ballet proibido*. Porto Alegre: L&PM, 1976.

Brücher, Wolfgang. "Rinderhaltung im amazonischen Regenwald. Beiträge zur Geographie der Tropen und Subtropen." *Tübinger geographische Studien* 34 (1970): 215–27.

Bruno, Regina. "Le statut de la terre: entre réconciliation et confrontation." *Cahiers du Brésil contemporain*, no. 27–8 (1995): 33–62.

Buclet, Benjamin. "Entre tecnologia e escravidão: a aventura da Volkswagen na Amazônia." *Revista do programa de pós-graduação em serviço social da PUC* 13 (2005).

Bunker, Stephen G. *Underdeveloping the Amazon: Extraction, Unequal Exchange and the Failure of the Modern State*. Urbana: University of Illinois Press, 1985.

Calabre, Lia. "O Conselho Federal de Cultura, 1971–1974." *Estudos históricos* 37 (2006): 81–98.

Câmara dos Deputados. *Política florestal e concervacionista do Brasil. Conferência pronunciada pelo Dr. Paulo Azevedo Berutti, presidente do IBDF, na Comissão da Amazônia*. Brasília: Câmara dos Deputados, 1975.

Camarano, Ana Amélia. "Êxodo rural, envelhecimento e masculinização no Brasil: panorama dos últimos cinqüenta anos." *Revista brasileira de estudos de população* 15, no. 2 (1980): 45–66.

Campbell, Jeremy M. *Conjuring Property: Speculation and Environmental Futures in the Brazilian Amazon*. Seattle: University of Washington Press, 2015.

Cardoso, Fernando Henrique and Enzo Faletto. *Dependencia e desarollo en América Latina: ensayo de interpretación sociológica*. Santiago de Chile: Ed. Limitada para circulación interna, 1967.

Cardoso, Fernando Henrique and Geraldo Müller. *Amazônia: expansão do capitalismo*. São Paulo: Brasiliense, 1977.

Carrasco, Lorenzo, ed. *Máfia Verde: o ambientalismo a serviço do governo mundial*. Rio de Janeiro: Capax Dei, 2008.

Carreira, Evandro. *Recado Amazônico*. 4 vols., Brasília: Senado Federal, 1977.

Carson, Rachel. *Silent Spring*. Boston, MA: Houghton Mifflin, 1962.

Carvalho, José Alberto Magno de, Morvan de Mello Moreira, and Maria do Carmo Fonseca do Vale. "Migrações internas na Amazônia: desenvolvimento e ocupação," edited by IPEA. 193–243. Rio de Janeiro: IPEA/INPES, 1979.

Carvalho de Ostos, Natascha Stefania. "O Brasil e suas naturezas possíveis (1930–1945)." *Revista de Indias* 72, no. 255 (2012): 581–614.

Casaldáliga, Dom Pedro. "Escravidão e feudalismo no norte do Mato Grosso." *Cadernos do CEAS* 20 (1972): 60–68.

Castro Netto, David A. "Legitimação e ditadura: a propaganda comercial em foco." Paper presented at *ANPUH: XXV Simpósio Nacional de História, Fortaleza, 2009*.

Cavalcanti, Mário de Barros. da *SPVEA à SUDAM: (1964–1967)*. Belém: SUDAM, 1967.

Cehelsky, Marta. *Land Reform in Brazil: The Management of Social Change*. Boulder, CO: Westview Press, 1979.

Chaparro, Manuel Carlos. "Cem anos de assessoria de imprensa." In *Assessoria de imprensa e relacionamento com a mídia: teoria e técnica*, edited by Jorge Duarte. 33–51. São Paulo: Atlas, 2002.

Chirio, Maud. "La politique des militaires. Mobilisations et révoltes d'officiers sous la dictature Brésilienne (1961–1978)." Université Paris I – Panthéon Sorbonne, 2009.

Cleary, David. "Towards an Environmental History of the Amazon. From Prehistory to the Nineteenth Century." *Latin American Research Review* 36, no. 2 (2001): 65–96.

CNBB. *Pastoral da terra – posse e conflitos – estudos da CNBB-CEP*. São Paulo: Paulinas, 1980 (1976).

CNDDA. *A Amazônia em foco*, edited by CNDDA. Vol. 1, 1967.

CNV. *Relatório da CNV: Volume II. Textos temáticos*. Brasília: CNV, 2014.

Comissão Justiça e Paz (CJP) CNBB – Norte II, trabalho escravo nas fazendas do Pará e Amapá 1980–1998, Belém: CNBB, 1999.

CONTAG. *A violência no campo pela mão armada do latifundio, 1981 a Junho 1984: torturas, prisões, espancamentos, assassinatos, impunidade e expulsão dos trabalhadores da terra*. Brasília: CONTAG, 1984.

Cooper, Frederick. "Modernizing Bureaucrats, Backward Africans and the Development Concept." In *International Development and the Social Sciences: Essays on the History and Politics of Knowledge*, edited by Frederick Cooper and Randall M. Packard. 64–92. Berkeley: University of California Press, 1997.

"Writing the History of Development." *Journal of Modern European History* 8, no. 1 (2010): 5–23.

Cullather, Nick. *The Hungry World: America's Cold War Battle against Poverty in Asia.* Cambridge, MA: Harvard University Press, 2010.

Cysne, Rubens Penha. "A economia Brasileira no período militar." *Estudos econômicos* 23, no. 2 (1993): 185–226.

Dean, Warren. *With Broadax and Firebrand: The Destruction of the Brazilian Atlantic Forest.* Berkeley: University of California Press, 1995.

Delgado, Mauricio Godinho. *Democracia e justiça: sistema judicial e construção democrática no Brasil.* São Paulo: LTr, 1993.

Dezalay, Yves and Bryant G Garth. *The Internationalization of Palace Wars: Lawyers, Economists, and the Contest to Transform Latin American States.* Chicago: University of Chicago Press, 2010.

Dillman, C. Daniel. "Land and Labor Patterns in Brazil During the 1960s." *American Journal of Economic Sociology* 35, no. 1 (1976): 49–70.

Dockes, Pierre and Bernard Rosier. *L'histoire ambiguë: croissance et développement en question.* Paris: PUF, 1988.

Dockhorn, Gilvan Veiga. *Quando a ordem é segurança e o progresso é desenvolvimento.* Porto Alegre: EDIPUCRS, 2002.

Doleschal, Reinhard. "Automobilproduktion in Brasilien und 'neue internationale Arbeitsteilung': eine Fallstudie über Volkswagen do Brasil." Universität Hannover, 1986.

Doleschal, Reinhard, R. Dombois, E. Hildebrandt, R. Kasiske, and W. Wobbe-Ohlenburg, eds. *Wohin läuft VW?* Reinbek: Rowohlt, 1982.

Doretto, Maria Lúcia. *Wolfgang Sauer: o homem Volkswagen. 50 anos de Brasil.* São Paulo: Geração, 2012.

Dorsch, Sebastian and Michael Wagner. "Gezähmter Dschungel–industrialisierte Agrarwirtschaft–romantisierter Landloser. Die Mystifizierung des Ländlichen in der deagrarisierten Gesellschaft Brasiliens." *Geschichte und Gesellschaft* 33 (2007): 546–74.

Dreyer, Lilian. *Sinfonia inacabada: a vida de José Lutzenberger.* Porto Alegre: Vidicom Audiovisuais, 2004.

Droulers, Martine and François-Michel Le Tourneau. "Amazonie: la fin d'une frontière?" *Caravelle*, no. 75 (2000): 109–35.

Duarte, Jorge, ed. *Assessoria de imprensa e relacionamento com a mídia: teoria e técnica.* São Paulo: Atlas, 2002.

Duarte, Regina Horta. "Pássaros e cientistas no Brasil: em busca de proteção, 1894–1938." *Latin American Research Review* 41, no. 1 (2006): 3–26.

Dutra, Eurico Gaspar. "'O solo: a sua conservaçao,' discurso proferido pelo Presidente Eurico Gaspar Dutra em Itaperuna, em 19-9-1948." *Conjuntura econômica* 27, no. 12 (1973): 4–5.

Eardley-Pryor, Roger. "The Global Environmental Moment: Sovereignty and American Science on Spaceship Earth, 1945–1974." University of California, Santa Barbara, 2014.

Econorte. *Cia Vale do Rio Cristalino Agropecuária Indústria e Comércio. Processo de avaliação.* Belém: SUDAM, 1974.

Ekbladh, David. *The Great American Mission: Modernization and the Construction of an American World Order*. Princeton, NJ: Princeton University Press, 2011.

Emmi, Marilia Ferreira and Roza Elizabeth Marin. "Crise e rearticulação das oligarquias no Pará." *Revista do Instituto de Estudos Brasileiros* 40–2 (1996): 51–68.

Escobar, Arturo. *Encountering Development: The Making and Unmaking of the Third World*. Princeton, NJ: Princeton University Press, 1995.

Evans, Peter. *Dependent Development: The Alliance of Multinational, State, and Local Capital in Brazil*. Princeton, NJ: Princeton University Press, 1979.

Falesi, Ítalo Cláudio. *Ecossistemas de pastagem cultivada na Amazônia Brasileira*. Boletim Técnico do Centro de Pesquisa Agropecuária do Trópico Húmido, edited by CPATU Belém: CPATU, 1976.

FAO, *Estado de la informacion florestal en Brasil*. Santiago, Chile: FAO, 2003.

Faucher, Philippe. *Le Brésil des militaires*. Montréal: Presses de l'Université de Montréal 1981.

Fearnside, Philip M. "Cattle Yield Prediction for the Transamazonian Highway of Brazil." *Interciência* 4, no. 4 (1979): 220–6.

Fearnside, Philip M. "The Effects of Cattle Pasture on Soil Fertility in the Brazilian Amazon: Consequences for Beef Production Sustainability." *Tropical Ecology* 21, no. 1 (1980): 125–37.

Fernandes, Bernardo Mançano. *A formação do MST no Brasil*. Petrópolis: Vozes, 2000.

Ferraz, Iara. "Suià Missu." In *Brasile: responsabilità italiane in Amazzonia*, edited by Osservatorio Impatto Ambientale. 125–31. Roma: OIA, 1990.

Ferreira, Leila da Costa and Sergio B. F. Tavolaro. *Environmental Concerns in Contemporary Brazil: An Insight into some Theoretical and Societal Backgrounds (1970s–1990s)*. Working Paper. University of Campinas, 2008.

Fico, Carlos. "La classe média Brésilienne face au régime militaire. Du soutien à la désaffection (1964–1985)." *Vingtième siècle* 105, no. 1 (2010): 155–68.

"Versões e controvérsias sobre 1964 e a ditadura militar." *Revista Brasileira de história* 24, no. 47 (2004): 29–60.

Figueira, Ricardo Rezende. *A justiça do lobo: posseiros e padres do Araguaia*. Petrópolis: Vozes Ltda, 1986.

Pisando fora da própria sombra: a escravidão por dívida no Brasil. Rio de Janeiro: Civilização Brasileira, 2004.

"Por que o trabalho escravo?" *Estudos avançados* 14, no. 38 (2000).

Rio Maria: canto da terra. Petrópolis: Civilização Brasileira, 2008.

Filho, Daniel Aarão Reis. *Ditadura militar, esquerdas e sociedade*. Rio de Janeiro: Zahar, 2000.

Fink, Carole, Philipp Gassert, and Detlef Junker, eds. *1968: The World Transformed*. New York: Cambridge University Press, 1998.

Foland, Frances M. "A Profile of Amazonia: Its Possibilities for Development." *Journal of InterAmerican Studies and World Affairs* 13, no. 1 (1971): 62–77.

Fontes, Edilza Oliveira. "A eleição de 1982 no Pará: memórias, imagens fotográficas e narrativas históricas." In *XI encontro nacional de história oral*.

Memória, democracia e justiça, edited by Associação Brasileira de História Oral. Rio de Janeiro, 2012.

Foresta, Ronald A. *Amazon Conservation in the Age of Development: The Limits of Providence*. Gainesville: University of Florida Press, 1991.

Foweraker, Joe. *The Struggle for Land: A Political Economy of the Pioneer Frontier in Brazil from 1930 to the Present Day*. New York: Cambridge University Press, 1981.

Fowler, Cary and Patrick R. Mooney. *Shattering: Food, Politics, and the Loss of Genetic Diversity*. Tucson: University of Arizona Press, 1990.

Franco, José Luiz de Andrade and José Augusto Drummond. "O cuidado da natureza: a fundação Brasileira para a conservação da natureza e a experiência conservacionista no Brasil: 1958–1992." *Textos de história* 17, no. 1 (2009): 39–84.

"Wilderness and the Brazilian Mind (I): Nation and Nature in Brazil from the 1920s to the 1940s." *Environmental History*. 13, no. 4 (2008): 724–50.

"Wilderness and the Brazilian Mind (II): The First Brazilian Conference on Nature Protection." *Environmental History* 14, no. 1 (2009): 82–102.

Fraser, Valerie. "Cannibalizing Le Corbusier: The MES Gardens of Roberto Burle Marx." *Journal of the Society of Architectural Historians* 59, no. 2 (2000): 180–93.

Fregapani, Gélio. *A Amazônia no grande jogo geopolítico – um desafio mundial*. Brasília: Thesaurus, 2011.

Frey, Marc, Sönke Kunkel, and Corinna R. Unger, eds. *International Organizations and Development, 1945–1990*. Basingstoke: Palgrave Macmillan, 2014.

Freyre, Gilberto. *Casa-Grande & Senzala: formação da família brasileira sob o regime de economia patriarcal*. Lisboa: Livros do Brasil, 2001 (1933).

Nordeste: aspectos da influencia da canna sobre a vida e a paizagem do nordeste do Brasil. Rio de Janeiro: J. Olympio, 1937.

Ganem, Roseli Senna and Titan de Lima. "Código florestal: revisão sim, mais desmatamento não." In *Os 30 anos da política nacional do meio ambiente conquistas e perspectivas*, edited by Suzi Huff Theodoro. Rio de Janeiro: Garamond, 2011.

Garfield, Seth W., *A luta indígena no coração do Brasil: política indigenista, a marcha para o oeste e os Índios Xavante (1937–1988)*. Sao Paulo: UNESP, 2011.

In Search of the Amazon: Brazil, the United States, and the Nature of a Region. Durham, NC: Duke University Press, 2014.

Gheerbrant, Alain. *The Amazon: Past, Present, and Future*. New York: Harry N. Abrams, 1992.

Gilman, Nils. *Mandarins of the Future: Modernization Theory in Cold War America*. Baltimore, MD: Johns Hopkins University Press, 2003.

Giuseppe, Massimo de. "Discovering the 'Other' America: The Latin American Encounters of Italian Peace Movements, 1955–1980." In *Peace Movements in Western Europe, Japan and the USA During the Cold War*, edited by Benjamin Ziemann. 107–28. Essen: Klartext, 2008.

Goldemberg, José. "A Sociedade Brasileira para o Progresso da Ciência (SBPC). Seu contorno político." *Interciência* 6, no. 1 (1981).

Gomes, Angela de Castro and Jorge Ferreira. *Jango: as múltiplas faces*. Rio de Janeiro: FGV, 2007.

Grandin, Greg. *Fordlândia: The Rise and Fall of Henry Ford's Forgotten Jungle City*. New York: Metropolitan Books, 2009.

Green, James N. *We Cannot Remain Silent: Opposition to the Brazilian Military Dictatorship in the United States*. Durham, NC, and London: Duke University Press, 2010.

Gromow, Alexander. *Eu amo Fusca*. São Paulo: Ripress, 2003.

Gross, Anthony. "Amazonia in the Nineties: Sustainable Development or Another Decade of Destruction?" *Third World Quarterly* 12, no. 3–4 (1990): 1–24.

Grubbs, Larry. *Secular Missionaries: Americans and African Development in the 1960s*. Amherst: University of Massachusetts Press, 2009.

Haas, Peter M. "U.N. Conferences and Constructivist Governance of the Environment." *Global Governance* 8, no. 1 (2002): 73–91.

Hahn, Carl H. *Meine Jahre mit Volkswagen*. München: Signum, 2005.

Harnecker, Marta. *MST-Brésil: la construction d'un mouvement social*. Genève: Center Europe- Tiers Monde 2003.

Hax-Schoppenhorst, Thomas and Peter Möller. "Nestverweis für schräge Vögel. Der AK 3. Welt St.Peter verläβt nach 27 Jahren die Gemeinde." In *Brücken und Gräben. Sozialpastorale Impulse und Initiativen im Spannungsfeld von Gemeinde und Politik*, edited by Norbert Mette, Ludger Weckel, and Andreas Wintels. 68–76. Münster: LIT, 1999.

Hecht, Susanna B. *Cattle Ranching in the Eastern Amazon: Evaluation of a Development Policy*. Berkeley: University of California, Berkeley, 1982.

"Environment, Development and Politics: Capital Accumulation and the Livestock Sector in Eastern Amazonia." *World Development* 13, no. 6 (1985): 663–84.

Hecht, Susanna B. and Alexander Cockburn. *The Fate of the Forest: Developers, Destroyers and Defenders of the Amazon*. Chicago: University of Chicago Press, 1990.

Helleiner, Eric. "The Development Mandate of International Institutions: Where Did It Come From?" *Studies in Comparative International Development* 44, no. 3 (2009): 189–211.

Herzog, Dagmar. "The Death of God in West Germany. Between Secularization, Postfascism, and the Rise of Liberation Theology." In *Die Gegenwart Gottes in der modernen Gesellschaft. Transzendenz und religiöse Vergemeinschaftung in Deutschland*, edited by Michael Geyer and Lucian Hölscher. 431–66. Göttingen: Wallstein, 2006.

Hilton, Stanley E. "Vargas and Brazilian Economic Development, 1930–1945: A Reappraisal of His Attitude toward Industrialization and Planning." *Journal of Economic History* 35, no. 4 (1975): 754–78.

Hochstetler, Kathryn and Margaret E. Keck. *Greening Brazil, Environmental Activism in State and Society*. Durham, NC: Duke University Press, 2007.

Hoelle, Jeffrey. *Rainforest Cowboys: The Rise of Ranching and Cattle Culture in Western Amazonia*. Austin: University of Texas Press, 2015.

Holzmann, Urs. "Selektion auf erhöhtes Wachstum bei Nellore-Rindern." Eidgenössische Technische Hochschule Zürich, 1989.

Houtzager, Peter P. "State and Unions in the Transformation of the Brazilian Countryside." *Latin American Research Review* 33, no. 2 (1998): 103–42.

Humphrey, John. "Auto Workers and the Working Class in Brazil." *Latin American Perspectives* 6, no. 4 (1979): 71–89.

Hünemörder, Kai F. "Kassandra im modernen Gewand. Die umweltapokalyptischen Mahnrufe der frühen 1970er Jahre." In *Wird Kassandra heiser? Die Geschichte falscher Öko-Alarme*, edited by Frank Uekötter and Jens Hohensee. 78–97. Stuttgart: Steiner, 2004.

Huq, Aziz Z. "Peonage and Contractual Liberty." *Columbia Law Review* 101, no. 2 (2001): 351–91.

Ianni, Octavio. *Ditadura e agricultura. O desenvolvimento do capitalismo na Amazônia: 1964–1978*. Rio de Janeiro: Civilização Brasileira, 1979.

Illich, Ivan. *Celebration of Awareness: A Call for Institutional Revolution*. New York: Doubleday & Company, 1970.

ILO. "A Global Alliance against Forced Labour." Geneva: ILO, 2005.

Júnior, Jairo Sanguiné. "A imprensa e o processo de redemocratização do Brasil." *Sociedade em debate* 4, no. 3 (1998): 19–35.

Kalter, Christoph. *Die Entdeckung der Dritten Welt: Dekolonisierung und neue radikale Linke in Frankreich*. Vol. 9, Frankfurt: Campus Verlag, 2011.

Kaltmeier, Olaf. "Über die 'Dritte-Welt'-Bewegung in der BRD. Zwischen Unterschriften und Straßenkampf." In *Friedens – forum* (2001).

Katzman, Marvin. "Paradoxes of Amazonian Development in a 'Resource Starved' World." *Journal of Developing Areas* 10 (1976): 445–60.

Keck, Margaret E. "El nuevo sindicalismo en la transición de Brasil." *Estudios sociológicos* 5, no. 13 (1987): 33–86.

"Social Equity and Environmental Politics in Brazil: Lessons from the Rubber Tappers of Acre." *Comparative Politics* 27, no. 4 (1995): 409–24.

The Workers' Party and Democratization in Brazil. New Haven, CT: Yale University Press, 1992.

Keck, Margaret E. and Kathryn Sikkink. *Activists Beyond Borders. Advocacy Networks in International Politics*. Ithaca, NY: Cornell University Press, 1998.

Kiley, David. *Getting the Bugs Out: The Rise, Fall and Comeback of Volkswagen in America*. New York: John Wiley & Sons, 2002.

Kleinpenning, J. M. G Nijmegen. *The Integration and Colonisation of the Brazilian Portion of the Amazon Basin*. Nijmegen: Katholieke Universiteit, 1975.

Klimke, Martin. *The Other Alliance: Student Protest in West Germany and the United States in the Global Sixties*. Princeton, NJ: Princeton University Press, 2009.

Klingensmith, Daniel. *"One Valley and a Thousand": Dams, Nationalism, and Development*. New Delhi: Oxford University Press, 2007.

Kohlepp, Gerd. "Planung und heutige Situation staatlicher kleinbäuerlicher Kolonisationsprojekte an der Transamazônica." *Geographische Zeitschrift* 64, no. 3 (1976): 171–211.

Kolk, Ans. *Forests in International Environmental Politics: International Organisations, NGOs and the Brazilian Amazon.* Utrecht: International Books, 1996.

Laak, Dirk van. *Weisse Elefanten. Anspruch und Scheitern technischer Großprojekte im 20. Jahrhundert.* Stuttgart: Deutsche Verlags-Anstalt, 1999.

Lago, André Aranha Corrêa do. *Stockholm, Rio, Johannesburg: Brazil and the Three United Nations Conferences on the Environment.* Brasília: Instituto Rio Branco, 2009.

Lappe, Frances Moore, Joseph Collins, and Cary Fowler. *Food First: Beyond the Myth of Scarcity.* New York: Ballantine Books, 1979.

Latham, Michael E. *The Right Kind of Revolution: Modernization, Development, and US Foreign Policy from the Cold War to the Present.* Ithaca, NY: Cornell University Press, 2011.

Latour, Bruno. *Nous n'avons jamais eté modernes. Essai d'anthropologie symétrique.* Paris: la Découverte, 1991.

Politiques de la nature: comment faire entrer les sciences en démocratie? Paris: la Découverte, 2004.

Le Breton, Binka. *Trapped: Modern-Day Slavery in the Brazilian Amazon.* London: Kumarian Press, 2003.

Lepp, Claudia. "Zwischen Konfrontation und Kooperation: Kirchen und soziale Bewegungen in der Bundesrepublik (1950–1983)." In *Zeithistorische Forschungen / Studies in Contemporary History* (2010).

Lima, Saulo de Castro. "Da substituição de importações ao Brasil potência: concepções do desenvolvimento 1964–1979." *Aurora* V, no. 7 (2011): 34–44.

Lipschutz, Ronnie D. and Judith Mayer. *Global Civil Society & Global Environmental Governance. The Politics of Nature from Place to Planet.* New York: State University of New York Press, 1996.

Machado, Angelo B. "'Mentalidade conservacionista' – discurso proferido no 9 de Julho de 1975 na abertura da XXVII Reunião Annual da SBPC em Belo Horizonte." *Ciência e cultura* 27, no. 9 (1975): 935–7.

Marques, Deborah Caramel. "O progresso sob quatro rodas: propagandas do Fusca, aspirações da classe média, consumo e transformações políticas (Brasil 1964–1968)." In *História e- história* (2011): www.historiaehistoria .com.br/materia.cfm?tb=alunos&id=386.

Martins, Edilson. *Amazônia, a última fronteira.* Rio de Janeiro: CODECRI, 1981.

Martins, José de Souza. *Expropriação e violência: a questão política no campo.* São Paulo: Hucitec 1980.

Marx, Roberto Burle. "Conviver com a natureza." In *Arte e paisagem. A estética de Roberto Burle Marx,* edited by Lisbeth Rebollo Gonçalves. 59–70. São Paulo: USP/MAC, 1997.

"Depoimento no senado federal." In *Arte e paisagem. Conferências escolhidas,* edited by José Tabacow. 65–73. São Paulo: Nobel, 1987.

Maybury-Lewis, Biorn. *The Politics of the Possible: The Brazilian Rural Workers' Trade Union Movement, 1964–1985.* Philadelphia, PA: Temple University Press, 1994.

McNeill, John R. "Agriculture, Forests, and Ecological History: Brazil, 1500–1983." *Environmental Review* 10 (1986): 122–33.

"Observations on the Nature and Culture of Environmental History." *History and Theory* 42, no. 4 (2003): 5–43.

Meadows, Dennis, Donella Meadows, Erich Zahn, and Peter Milling. *The Limits to Growth: A Report for the Club of Rome's Project on the Predicament of Mankind.* New York: American Library, 1972.

Medeiros, Leonilde Servolo de. "Le statut de la terre et les luttes des paysans Brésiliens." *Cahiers du Brésil contemporain* 27–8 (1995): 63–78.

Meggers, Betty. *Amazonia: Man and Culture in a Counterfeit Paradise.* Washington, DC: Smithsonian Institution Press, 1996.

Mendonça, Daniel de. "A vitória de tancredo neves no colégio eleitoral e a posição política dos semanários Veja e Isto é." *Revista ALCEU* 5, no. 10 (2005): 164–85.

Merson, John. "Bio-prospecting and Bio-piracy: Intellectual Property Rights and Biodiversity in a Colonial and Postcolonial Context." *Osiris* 15 (2000): 282–96.

Mikesell, Raymond F. "Iron Ore in Brazil: The Experience of the Hannah Mining Company." In *Foreign Investment in the Petroleum and Mineral Industries: Case Studies of Investor–Host Country Relations*, edited by Raymond F. Mikesell and William H. Bartsch. 345–64. Baltimore, MD: Johns Hopkins University Press, 1971.

Millard, Candice. *The River of Doubt: Theodore Roosevelt's Darkest Journey.* New York: Broadway Books, 2005.

Miller, Shawn William. *An Environmental History of Latin America.* New York: Cambridge University Press, 2007.

Fruitless Trees: Portuguese Conservation and Brazil's Colonial Timber. Stanford, CA: Stanford University Press, 2000.

Minc, Carlos. *A reconquista da terra: estatuto da terra, lutas no campo e reforma agrária.* Rio de Janeiro: Zahar, 1985.

MIRAD. "Conflitos de terra: trabalho escravo." Brasília: MIRAD, 1986.

Mitchell, Timothy. *Carbon Democracy: Political Power in the Age of Oil.* London: Verso, 2011.

Mommsen, Hans and Manfred Grieger. *Das Volkswagenwerk und seine Arbeiter im Dritten Reich.* Düsseldorf: Econ, 1996.

Moran, Emilio F. "Deforestation and Land Use in the Brazilian Amazon." *Human Ecology* 21, no. 1 (1993): 1–21.

Moreira, Ruy. "O plano nacional de reforma agrária em questão." *Revista terra livre* 1 (1986): 6–19.

Nehring, Holger. "National Internationalists: British and West German Protests against Nuclear Weapons, the Politics of Transnational Communications and the Social History of the Cold War, 1957–1964." *Contemporary European History* 14, no. 4 (2005): 559–82.

Netto, José Paulo. "Em busca da contemporaneidade perdida: a esquerda Brasileira pós-64." In *Viagem incompleta. A experiência Brasileira (1500–2000). A grande transação*, edited by Carlos Guilherme Mota. 219–45. São Paulo: SENAC, 2000.

Noll, Izabel. "La construction du Varguisme. L'Ordre pour Principe, le Progrès comme Fin." EHESS, 2003.

Novaes, Regina R. "CONTAG e CUT: continuidades e rupturas da organizacão sindical no campo." In *o sindicalismo Brasileiro nos anos 80*, edited by Armando Boito Junior. 173–96. São Paulo: Paz e Terra, 1991.

Olejniczak, Claudia. *Die Dritte-Welt-Bewegung in Deutschland. Konzeptionelle und organisatorische Strukturmerkmale einer neuen sozialen Bewegung.* Wiesbaden: Deutscher UniversitätsVerlag, 1999.

"Dritte-Welt-Bewegung." In *Die sozialen Bewegungen in Deutschland seit 1945: Ein Handbuch*, edited by Roland Roth and Dieter Rucht. 319–46. Frankfurt/Main: Campus, 2008.

Onis, Juan de. *The Green Cathedral: Sustainable Development of Amazonia.* New York: Oxford University Press, 1992.

Pádua, José Augusto. "Biosphere, History and Conjuncture in the Analysis of the Amazon Problem." In *The International Handbook of Environmental Sociology*, edited by Michael Redclift and Graham Woodgate. 403–17. Cheltenham, Northampton: Edward Elgar, 2000.

"Um país e seis biomas: ferramenta conceitual para o desenvolvimento sustentável e a educação ambiental." In *Desenvolvimento, justiça e meio ambiente*, edited by José Augusto Pádua. 118–50. Belo Horizonte: UFMG, 2009.

Um sopro de destruição. Pensamento político e crítica ambiental no Brasil escravista (1786–1888). Rio de Janeiro: Zahar, 2002.

Palmeira, Moacir. "A diversidade da luta no campo." In *Igreja e questão agrária*, edited by Vanilda P. Paiva. 43–51. São Paulo: Loyola, 1985.

Patel, Kiran K. *The New Deal: A Global History.* Princeton, NJ: Princeton University Press, 2016.

Pereira, Elenita Malta. "A voz da primavera. As reivindicacões do movimento ambientalista gaúcho (1971–1980)." In www.revistahistoriar.com 1 (2008): 1–25.

Pinto, Lúcio Flávio. *Jari: toda a verdade sobre o projeto de Ludwig. As relações entre estado e multinacional na Amazônia.* São Paulo: Marco Zero, 1986.

"O garrancho Amazônico." Unpublished Manuscript (Undated).

Pompermayer, Malori José "The State and the Frontier in Brazil: A Case Study of the Amazon." Stanford University, 1979.

Prestre, Philippe Le. *The World Bank and the Environmental Challenge.* Toronto: Susquehanna University Press, 1989.

Rabelo, Genival. *Ocupação da Amazônia.* Rio de Janeiro: Gernasa, 1968.

Raffles, Hugh. *In Amazônia: A Natural History.* Princeton, NJ: Princeton University Press, 2002.

Reis, Arthur Cezar Ferreira. *A Amazônia e a cobiça internacional.* Rio de Janeiro Edinova, 1960.

Reydon, Bastiaan, Ludwig Plata, and Héctor Escobar. "Intervención en el mercado de tierras Brasileño: análisis de la experiencia reciente." *Debate agrario*, no. 31 (2000): 165–85.

Ribeiro, Berta Gleizer. *Amazônia urgente: cinco séculos de história e ecologia.* Belo Horizonte: Itatiaia, 1990.

Ribeiro, Maurício Andrés. "Origens mineiras do desenvolvimento sustentável no Brasil: ideias e práticas." In *Desenvolvimento, justiça e meio ambiente*, edited by José Augusto Pádua. 64–116. Belo Horizonte: UFMG, 2009.

Richter, Dieter. *Die Fazenda am Cristalino: eine Rinderfarm im Gebiet des feuchten Passatwaldes Brasiliens; ein Film der Volkswagenwerk AG; Lehrerbegleitheft.* Wolfsburg: Volkswagen A. G., 1980.

Rieger, Bernhard. *The People's Car: A Global History of the Volkswagen Beetle.* Cambridge, MA: Harvard University Press, 2013.

Rist, Gilbert. *Le développement: histoire d'une croyance occidentale.* Paris: Presses de Sciences po, 1996.

Rizzo, Giulio G. "Maiêutica de uma nova estética." In *Arte e paisagem: a estética de Roberto Burle Marx*, edited by Lisbeth Rebollo Gonçalves. 31–49. São Paulo: USP/MAC, 1997.

Rodríguez, Octavio. *La teoría del subdesarrollo de la CEPAL.* Madrid: Siglo XXI, 1988.

Rogers, Thomas D. *The Deepest Wounds: A Labor and Environmental History of Sugar in Northeast Brazil.* Chapel Hill: University of North Carolina Press, 2010.

Romahn, Theo. "Die Grünen, der sichere Weg in die Katastrophe. Leitfaden für Mitglieder der automobilen Gesellschaft," edited by Initiative Automobile Gesellschaft. Düsseldorf: Drittes Jahrtausend, 1983.

Sachs, Wolfgang, ed. *The Development Dictionary: A Guide to Knowledge as Power.* Johannesburg: Zed Books, 1992.

Sadlier, Darlene J. *Brazil Imagined: 1500 to the Present.* Austin: University of Texas Press, 2008.

Sakamoto, Leonardo. "A economia do trabalho escravo no Brasil contemporâneo." In *Trabalho escravo contemporâneo no Brasil. Contribuições críticas para sua análise e denúncia*, edited by Gelba Cavalcante de Cerqueira, Ricardo Rezende Figueira, Adonia Antunes Prado, and Célia Maria Leite Costa. 61–72. Rio de Janeiro: UFRJ, 2008.

Santos, Breno Augusto dos. *Amazônia: potencial mineral e perspectivas de desenvolvimento.* São Paulo: EdUSP, 1981.

SBPC. *27° Reunião Anual – Resumos.* São Paulo: SBPC, 1975.
  A SBPC e a Amazônia. São Paulo: SBPC, 1978.
  Ciêntistas do Brasil: Depoimentos; Edição Comemorativa dos 50 Anos da SBPC. São Paulo: SBPC, 1998.

Scalmer, Sean. *Gandhi in the West.* New York: Cambridge University Press, 2011.

Schmink, Marianne and Charles H. Wood. *Contested Frontiers in Amazonia.* New York: Columbia University Press, 1992.

Schneider, Christian. *Stadtgründung im Dritten Reich: Wolfsburg und Salzgitter: Ideologie, Ressortpolitik, Repräsentation.* München: Moos, 1978.

Schölermann, Günter. "Volkswagen do Brasil: Entwicklung und Wachstum unter den wirtschaftspolitischen Verhältnissen in Brasilien." Universität Oldenburg, 1982.

Schumacher, Ernst Friedrich. *Small Is Beautiful: A Study of Economics as if People Mattered.* London: Blond & Briggs, 1973.

Secreto, Maria Veronica. "A ocupação dos 'espaços vazios' no Governo Vargas: do 'discurso do Rio Amazonas' à saga dos Soldados da Borracha." *Estudos históricos*, no. 40 (2007): 115–35.

Seibert, Niels. *Vergessene Proteste. Internationalismus und Antirassismus 1964–1983*. Münster: Unrast-Verlag, 2008.

Shapiro, Helen. *Engines of Growth: The State and Transnational Auto Companies in Brazil*. New York: Cambridge University Press, 1994.

Shillings, Robert F. "Economic Development of the Brazilian Amazon." *The Geographical Journal* 151, no. 1 (1984): 48–54.

Sikkink, Kathryn. *Ideas and Institutions: Developmentalism in Brazil and Argentina*. Ithaca, NY: Cornell University Press, 1991.

Silva, Golbery do Couto e. *Geopolítica do Brasil*. Rio de Janeiro: José Olympio, 1966.

Silva, Luís Inácio da, Mauri Garcia, and Timothy Harding. "Interview with Luis Inácio da Silva ('Lula'), President of the Sindicato dos Metalúrgicos de São Bernardo do Campo." *Latin American Perspectives* 6, no. 4 (1979): 90–100.

Silva, Luisa Maria N. de Moura e. "'Segurança e desenvolvimento': A comunicação do Governo Medici." *Intercom* 9, no. 55 (1986): 35–54.

Simões, Solange de Deus. *Deus, pátria e família. As mulheres no golpe de 1964*. Petrópolis: Vozes, 1985.

Singer, Benjamin. *L'homme et les forêts tropicales: une relation durable*. Versailles: Quae, 2015.

Slater, Candace. *Entangled Edens: Visions of the Amazon*. Berkeley, CA: University of California Press, 2002.

Skidmore, Thomas E. *The Politics of Military Rule in Brazil. 1964–85*. ed. New York: Oxford University Press, 1989.

SPVEA. *Política de desenvolvimento da Amazônia. Superintendência do Plano de Valorização Económica da Amazônia 1954–1960*. Rio de Janeiro: SPVEA, 1961.

SUDAM. *Investimentos privilegiados na Amazônia*. Belém: SUDAM, 1966.

Operação Amazônia; discursos. Belém: SUDAM, 1968.

"Sudam 40 ano." Belém: SUDAM, 1970.

Amazônia Legal: manual do investidor. Belém: SUDAM, 1972.

Suri, Jeremi. *Power and Protest: Global Revolution and the Rise of Detente*. Cambridge, MA: Harvard University Press, 2003.

Tischler, Julia. *Light and Power for a Multiracial Nation: The Kariba Dam Scheme in the Central African Federation*. Basingstoke: Palgrave Macmillan, 2013.

Toledo, Caio Navarro de. "1964: o golpe contra as reformas e a democracia." In *Golpe militar e a ditadura. 40 anos depois (1964–2004)*, edited by Daniel Aarão Reis, Marcelo Ridenti, and Rodrigo Patto Sá Motta. 67–80. Bauru: Edusc, 2004.

Unger, Corinna R. *Entwicklungspfade in Indien: eine internationale Geschichte, 1947-1980*. Göttingen: Wallstein, 2015.

Unger, Corinna R. "Export und Entwicklung: westliche Wirtschaftsinteressen in Indien im Kontext der Dekolonisation und des Kalten Krieges." *Jahrbuch für Wirtschaftsgeschichte/Economic History Yearbook* 53, no. 1 (2012): 69–86.

"Histories of Development and Modernization: Findings, Reflections, Future Research," in: H-Soz-Kult, December 9, 2010, www.hsozkult.de/literature review/id/forschungsberichte-1130.

Vaitsman, Maurício. *Brasília e Amazônia: reportagens*. Rio de Janeiro: SPVEA, 1959.

Vaz, Vania. "A formação dos latifúndios no sul do estado do Pará: terra, pecuária e desflorestamento." Universidade Nacional de Brasília, 2013.

Veiga, Edir. "A disputa para o executivo do Pará no pós ditadura militar de 1964." UFPA, 2010.

Velloso, João Paulo dos Reis. *O último trem para Paris: de Getúlio a Sarney: "milagres," choques e crises do Brasil moderno*. Rio de Janeiro: Nova Fronteira, 1986.

Vidal, Laurent. *De Nova Lisboa à Brasilia. L'invention d'une capitale (19e–20e siècles)*. Paris: IHEAL, 2002.

Viola, Eduardo. "O movimento ecológico no Brasil (1974–1986): do ambientalismo à ecopolítica." In *Ecologia e política no Brasil*, edited by José Augusto Pádua. 63–110. Rio de Janeiro: Espaço e Tempo, 1987.

Volkswagenwerk A. G. *VW in Brasilien: mehr als Autos*. Wolfsburg: Volkswagen, 1973.

Volkswagenwerk A. G., Öffentlichkeitsarbeit. *Volkswagen – ein transnationales Unternehmen, Partner der Welt*. Wolfsburg: Volkswagenwerk A. G., 1980.

Volkswagen do Brasil, *Cristalino*. Volkswagen: São Bernardo do Campo, 1980.

Volkswagen do Brasil S. A. *Cristalino. Eine Rinderfarm im neuen Viehzuchtgebiet*. Volkswagen A. G.: Wolfsburg, 1983.

Weinstein, Barbara. *The Amazon Rubber Boom, 1850–1920*. Stanford, CA: Stanford University Press, 1983.

Welch, Cliff. "Globalization and the Transformation of Work in Rural Brazil: Agribusiness, Rural Labor Unions, and Peasant Mobilization." *International Labor and Working-Class History* 70, no. 1 (2006): 35–60.

Wellhöner, Volker. "*Wirtschaftswunder" – Weltmarkt – Westdeutscher Fordismus. Der Fall Volkswagen*. Münster: Westfälisches Dampfbot, 1996.

Westad, Odd Arne. *The Global Cold War: Third World Interventions and the Making of Our Times*. New York: Cambridge University Press, 2005.

Wilcox, Robert Wilton. "Cattle Ranching on the Brazilian Frontier: Tradition and Innovation in Mato Grosso, 1870–1940." New York University, 1992.

Wolfe, Joel. *Autos and Progress: The Brazilian Search for Modernity* Oxford: Oxford University Press, 2010.

Worster, Donald. "Transformations of the Earth: Toward an Agroecological Perspective in History." *The Journal of American History* 76, no. 4 (1990): 1087–106.

Wright, Angus and Wendy Wolford. *To Inherit the Earth: The Landless Movement and the Struggle for a New Brazil*. Oakland, CA: Food First, 2003.

Würtele, Werner, and Harald Lobgesang. *Volkswagen in Brasilien – Entwicklungshilfe im besten Sinne?* Tübingen: Arbeitsgemeinschaft Kath. Hochsch.- und Studentengemeinden, 1979.

Periodicals and Press Agencies

ABC (Spain)
A folha de São Paulo
A folha do Pará
Agência Amazônia de notícias
Agência CONTAG de notícias
Alvorada – prelazia de São Felix do Araguaia
Amazônia (publication of the AEA)
Amtsblatt der Europäischen Gemeinschaften
A província do Pará
Ascom Ibama
Autogramm
Automobilwoche
Badische Zeitung
Berliner Extra Dienst
Blätter der IZ 3. Welt
Blick durch die Wirtschaft
Brasilien-Dialog
Brasilien Nachrichten
Conjuntura econômica
Correio Braziliense
Correio da Manhã
Der Spiegel
Deutsch-Brasilianische Hefte
Deutsche Zeitung
Diário da Manhã
Diário do congresso nacional
Die Grünen informieren
Die Welt
Die Zeit
Frankfurter Allgemeine Zeitung
Frankfurter Rundschau
GEO (Germany)
Handelsblatt
ILA INFO
Institut für Brasilienkunde e.V. Informationen
ISTOÉ
Jornal de Brasília
Jornal do Brasil
Jornal dos trabalhadores sem terra
L'Hebdo (Switzerland)
Manchete
Movimento
Natur
Neue Rhein Zeitung/Neue Ruhr Zeitung
New York Times

O estado de Minas
O estado do Pará
O estado de São Paulo
O Globo
O Liberal
O São Paulo
Opinião
Orientierung
Público
Publik-forum
Quatro rodas
Recklinghäuserzeitung
Süddeutsche Zeitung
Stern
The Ecologist
The Economist
The Times
Tribuna metalúrgica
Vauban actuel
Veja
Vorwärts

Index